Math Expressions

Volume 1

Developed by
The Children's Math Worlds Research Project

PROJECT DIRECTOR AND AUTHOR
Dr. Karen C. Fuson

This material is based upon work supported by the
National Science Foundation
under Grant Numbers
ESI-9816320, REC-9806020, and RED-935373.

Any opinions, findings, and conclusions, or recommendations expressed in this material
are those of the author and do not necessarily reflect the views of the National Science Foundation.

HOUGHTON MIFFLIN HARCOURT

Teacher Reviewers

Kindergarten
Patricia Stroh Sugiyama
Wilmette, Illinois

Barbara Wahle
Evanston, Illinois

Grade 1
Sandra Budson
Newton, Massachusetts

Janet Pecci
Chicago, Illinois

Megan Rees
Chicago, Illinois

Grade 2
Molly Dunn
Danvers, Massachusetts

Agnes Lesnick
Hillside, Illinois

Rita Soto
Chicago, Illinois

Grade 3
Jane Curran
Honesdale, Pennsylvania

Sandra Tucker
Chicago, Illinois

Grade 4
Sara Stoneberg Llibre
Chicago, Illinois

Sheri Roedel
Chicago, Illinois

Grade 5
Todd Atler
Chicago, Illinois

Leah Barry
Norfolk, Massachusetts

Special Thanks

Special thanks to the many teachers, students, parents, principals, writers, researchers, and work-study students who participated in the Children's Math Worlds Research Project over the years.

Credits

Cover art: (t) © Arco Images GmbH/Alamy, (b) Eric Meola/Getty Images
Illustrative art: David Klug
Technical art: Morgan-Cain & Associates

VOLUME 1 CONTENTS

Unit 3 Addition and Subtraction of Whole Numbers and Decimals

* This lesson consists only of activities from the Teacher Edition.

Mini Unit 6 Volume, Capacity, and Weight

▶ Diagnostic Checkup for Basic Multiplication

1. $7 \times 5 = $ ___   2. $2 \times 3 = $ ___   3. $9 \times 9 = $ ___   4. $9 \times 6 = $ ___

5. $6 \times 2 = $ ___   6. $3 \times 0 = $ ___   7. $3 \times 4 = $ ___   8. $6 \times 8 = $ ___

9. $5 \times 9 = $ ___   10. $3 \times 3 = $ ___   11. $2 \times 9 = $ ___   12. $5 \times 7 = $ ___

13. $6 \times 10 = $ ___   14. $4 \times 1 = $ ___   15. $6 \times 4 = $ ___   16. $4 \times 8 = $ ___

17. $5 \times 2 = $ ___   18. $1 \times 3 = $ ___   19. $3 \times 9 = $ ___   20. $7 \times 6 = $ ___

21. $7 \times 2 = $ ___   22. $9 \times 0 = $ ___   23. $8 \times 9 = $ ___   24. $8 \times 7 = $ ___

25. $8 \times 10 = $ ___   26. $6 \times 3 = $ ___   27. $4 \times 4 = $ ___   28. $3 \times 8 = $ ___

29. $5 \times 5 = $ ___   30. $6 \times 0 = $ ___   31. $7 \times 9 = $ ___   32. $6 \times 6 = $ ___

33. $9 \times 2 = $ ___   34. $8 \times 3 = $ ___   35. $5 \times 4 = $ ___   36. $7 \times 7 = $ ___

37. $5 \times 10 = $ ___   38. $5 \times 1 = $ ___   39. $10 \times 9 = $ ___   40. $5 \times 6 = $ ___

41. $6 \times 5 = $ ___   42. $9 \times 3 = $ ___   43. $4 \times 2 = $ ___   44. $7 \times 8 = $ ___

45. $8 \times 2 = $ ___   46. $5 \times 0 = $ ___   47. $4 \times 9 = $ ___   48. $6 \times 7 = $ ___

49. $9 \times 5 = $ ___   50. $6 \times 1 = $ ___   51. $7 \times 4 = $ ___   52. $9 \times 8 = $ ___

53. $4 \times 10 = $ ___   54. $5 \times 3 = $ ___   55. $6 \times 9 = $ ___   56. $8 \times 6 = $ ___

57. $8 \times 5 = $ ___   58. $8 \times 0 = $ ___   59. $8 \times 4 = $ ___   60. $4 \times 7 = $ ___

61. $3 \times 5 = $ ___   62. $7 \times 3 = $ ___   63. $5 \times 9 = $ ___   64. $3 \times 6 = $ ___

65. $7 \times 10 = $ ___   66. $8 \times 1 = $ ___   67. $0 \times 4 = $ ___   68. $9 \times 7 = $ ___

69. $4 \times 5 = $ ___   70. $4 \times 3 = $ ___   71. $1 \times 9 = $ ___   72. $8 \times 8 = $ ___

Name _____ **Date** _____

Class Activity

▶ Diagnostic Checkup for Basic Division

1. $12 \div 2 =$ ___   2. $8 \div 1 =$ ___   3. $36 \div 9 =$ ___   4. $35 \div 7 =$ ___

5. $20 \div 5 =$ ___   6. $24 \div 3 =$ ___   7. $12 \div 4 =$ ___   8. $6 \div 6 =$ ___

9. $6 \div 2 =$ ___   10. $3 \div 3 =$ ___   11. $18 \div 9 =$ ___   12. $63 \div 7 =$ ___

13. $20 \div 10 =$ ___   14. $0 \div 1 =$ ___   15. $40 \div 4 =$ ___   16. $48 \div 8 =$ ___

17. $18 \div 2 =$ ___   18. $6 \div 3 =$ ___   19. $8 \div 4 =$ ___   20. $36 \div 6 =$ ___

21. $8 \div 2 =$ ___   22. $9 \div 1 =$ ___   23. $9 \div 9 =$ ___   24. $56 \div 7 =$ ___

25. $40 \div 5 =$ ___   26. $9 \div 3 =$ ___   27. $36 \div 4 =$ ___   28. $56 \div 8 =$ ___

29. $80 \div 10 =$ ___   30. $7 \div 1 =$ ___   31. $45 \div 9 =$ ___   32. $48 \div 6 =$ ___

33. $5 \div 5 =$ ___   34. $30 \div 3 =$ ___   35. $16 \div 4 =$ ___   36. $72 \div 8 =$ ___

37. $10 \div 2 =$ ___   38. $1 \div 1 =$ ___   39. $54 \div 9 =$ ___   40. $21 \div 7 =$ ___

41. $25 \div 5 =$ ___   42. $15 \div 3 =$ ___   43. $32 \div 4 =$ ___   44. $24 \div 8 =$ ___

45. $90 \div 10 =$ ___   46. $18 \div 3 =$ ___   47. $63 \div 9 =$ ___   48. $54 \div 6 =$ ___

49. $45 \div 5 =$ ___   50. $6 \div 1 =$ ___   51. $20 \div 4 =$ ___   52. $49 \div 7 =$ ___

53. $15 \div 5 =$ ___   54. $0 \div 3 =$ ___   55. $28 \div 4 =$ ___   56. $30 \div 6 =$ ___

57. $16 \div 2 =$ ___   58. $21 \div 3 =$ ___   59. $81 \div 9 =$ ___   60. $64 \div 8 =$ ___

61. $30 \div 5 =$ ___   62. $12 \div 3 =$ ___   63. $27 \div 9 =$ ___   64. $42 \div 7 =$ ___

65. $40 \div 10 =$ ___   66. $10 \div 1 =$ ___   67. $24 \div 4 =$ ___   68. $18 \div 6 =$ ___

69. $35 \div 5 =$ ___   70. $27 \div 3 =$ ___   71. $72 \div 9 =$ ___   72. $42 \div 6 =$ ___

Diagnostic Division Checkup

Vocabulary

equation

▶ Equal Groups

The students below do not remember how to find 4×8, but they know other multiplications. Help them find the answer by using what they already know.

8 8 $2 \times 8 = 16$ Marco knows that $2 \times 8 = 16$. How can he find 4×8?	8 8 8 8 8 $5 \times 8 = 40$ Hannah knows that $5 \times 8 = 40$. How can she find 4×8?
8 8 8 $3 \times 8 = 24$ Alison knows that $3 \times 8 = 24$. How can she find 4×8?	7 7 7 7 $4 \times 7 = 28$ Collin knows that $4 \times 7 = 28$. How can he find 4×8?

Tony and Anna do not remember how to find 24/4 ($24 \div 4$). Help them find the division answer by using what they know.

4 4 4 4 4 4 4 8 12 16 20 24 Tony knows how to count by fours. How can he find $24 \div 4$?	4 4 4 4 4 $5 \times 4 = 20$ Anna knows that there are 5 fours in 20. How can she find how many fours there are in 24?

Find the unknown number in each of the following equations .

1. $4 \times 3 = $ _____   2. $7 \times$ _____ $= 28$ 3. $27 / 9 = $ _____

4. $30 \div 5 = $ _____   5. $9 \cdot 3 = $ _____   6. $8 \times$ _____ $= 16$

7. $6 \times$ _____ $= 18$ 8. $21 \div 7 = $ _____   9. $35 / 7 = $ _____

Class Activity

▶ Solve and Discuss Word Problems

Write an equation for each word problem and solve the problem.

Show your work.

10. Tyler has 32 peaches. He wants to divide them equally among his 4 friends. How many peaches will each friend get?

_____

11. A guitar has 6 strings. If Trent has 4 complete packs of guitar strings, how many strings does he have in all?

_____

12. Ernesto's photograph album holds 6 pictures on each page. Ernesto has 48 pictures. How many pages will he fill?

_____

13. Rosa runs 3 miles every day. How many miles does she run in a week?

_____

14. Ali has a board 36 inches long. He wants to saw it into equal pieces 9 inches long. How many pieces will he get?

_____

15. Write and solve a multiplication and a division word problem of your own.

_____

_____

_____

Dear Family,

Your child has studied multiplication and division in past years but may not have reached total mastery. This part of *Math Expressions* guides students as they deepen and extend their knowledge. The main goals of this unit are

(1) to help students gain speed and accuracy in multiplying and dividing single-digit numbers;

(2) to help students see how multiplication and division relate to real-world situations;

(3) to introduce algebraic expressions and equations that feature these operations;

(4) to begin exploring proportions.

Target

Students discover patterns in the multiplication table that strengthen their understanding and also serve as memory aids. For example, knowing that the products of 9 form the pattern 10 – 1, 20 – 2, 30 – 3 (9, 18, 27) and so on is a memory aid, and knowing that the digits add up to 9 is a useful check. Students are given a variety of special materials that help them practice effectively. One tool that you will see coming home is the Target, which is used for individual practice. Ask your child to explain how it works, and encourage him or her to use it for a few minutes each day to practice those facts that still need to be mastered. Also have your child use the other practice materials that will come home.

Sincerely,
Your child's teacher

Carta a la familia

Estimada familia:

En años anteriores, su niño ha estudiado la multiplicación y la división, pero es posible que necesite practicar un poco más. Esta parte de *Math Expressions* guía a los estudiantes a medida que refuerzan y amplían sus conocimientos. Los objetivos principales de esta unidad son:
(1) ayudar a los estudiantes a adquirir rapidez y exactitud al multiplicar y dividir números de un dígito;
(2) ayudar a los estudiantes a ver de qué manera están relacionadas la multiplicación y la división con situaciones de la vida real;
(3) presentar expresiones algebraicas y ecuaciones que contienen estas operaciones;
(4) empezar a explorar las proporciones.

Objetivo

Se logra de varias maneras. Los estudiantes descubren, en la tabla de multiplicación, patrones que refuerzan sus conocimientos y que les ayudan a memorizar. Por ejemplo, saber que los productos de 9 forman el patrón 10 – 1, 20 – 2, 30 – 3 (9, 18, 27), y así sucesivamente, es una ayuda para memorizar. Además, saber que los dígitos suman 9 es una manera de comprobar. Los estudiantes reciben una variedad de materiales especiales que los ayudan a practicar de manera efectiva. Uno de los materiales que llevarán a casa es el *Objetivo*, el cual se usa para la práctica individual. Pida a su niño que explique cómo funciona, y anímelo a usarlo varios minutos cada día para practicar las operaciones que no domine. Pídale que use también los otros materiales de práctica que lleva a casa.

Atentamente,
El maestro de su niño

Multiplication as Equal Groups

Class Activity

Name _____

Date _____

Vocabulary

array   column
row   area

▶ Discuss Arrays and Area

An **array** is a rectangular shape. The objects in an array could have spaces between them, like muffins in a tin, or they could be touching, like the squares in a quilt. An array has **rows** going across and **columns** going down.

We can find the total number in an array by multiplying the number of rows by the number of columns.

1. How many muffins are on the tray?

_____

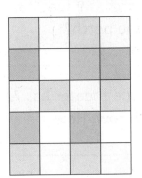

2. What equal groups do you see in the array of muffins?

_____

3. How many squares are in the quilt?

_____

4. What equal groups do you see in the quilt?

_____

Area is like an array. When we find the area of a rectangle, we find the number of square units that cover the rectangle. We don't usually see the square units.

The floor shown here is 6 yards long and 3 yards wide.

5. What is the area of this floor? _____

6. How should we label the answer? _____

6 yards

3 yards

Find the area of each rectangle.

7.

5 ft

4 ft

_____

8.

7 in

3 in

_____

9.

4 mi

6 mi

_____

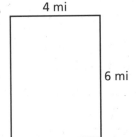

► Applications for Real-World Situations

Decide if each word problem is an array, area, or equal-groups situation. Then solve it.

10. A roller coaster with 7 identical cars can carry 42 people at the same time. How many people will each car carry?

Show your work.

_____

11. A package of stickers has 4 rows and 8 columns. How many stickers are in the package?

_____

12. A porch is 9 feet long and 5 feet wide. What is the area of the porch?

_____

13. A little theater has 72 seats in all. There are 8 seats in each row. How many rows are in the theater?

_____

14. A door is 7 feet tall. Its area is 21 square feet. How wide is the door?

_____

15. Lisa needs to buy 30 cans of apple juice for the class picnic. How many packages of 6 cans of apple juice should Lisa buy?

_____

16. A garden has an area of 36 square feet. It is 4 feet long. How wide is the garden?

_____

17. Mr. Brown bought a pack of 27 erasers. He can give his students 3 erasers each. How many students does he have?

_____

Vocabulary

length
width

► Use Letters for the Unknown Number

When you work with equations, you can use a letter to represent an unknown number.

We know the length and width of this rectangle but we do not know its area. When we write an equation, we can use the letter A to represent the unknown area.

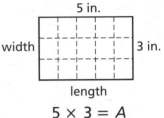

5 in.

width | 3 in.

length

$5 \times 3 = A$

For this rectangle the **width** is unknown. We can use the letter w to represent the width.

5 in.

$5 \times w = 15$ sq in.

w

Area = 15 sq in.

For this rectangle the **length** is unknown. We can use the letter l to represent the length.

l

$l \times 4 = 24$ sq in.

4 in.

Area = 24 sq in.

Write an equation for each rectangle below, using A, w, or l to represent the unknown number. Then find the unknown number.

18.
5 ft

8 ft

19.
7 yd

Area = 28 sq yd

20.

3 ft

Area = 27 sq ft

_____

_____

_____

The length and the width of each rectangle are whole numbers. How many different pairs of lengths and widths are there? List them.

21. $A = 21$

_____

22. $A = 24$

_____

23. $A = 16$

_____

24. $A = 13$

_____

25. **On the Back** Draw all the rectangles for exercise 23.

Arrays and Area

Class Activity

Vocabulary

Commutative Property
inverse operations

▶ Look for Patterns

Discuss the patterns in the
Multiplication Table. Then use your
Target with the Multiplication
Table. Place it as shown.

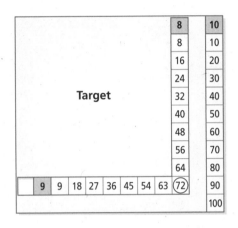

×	1	2	3	4	5	6	7	8	9	10
1	1	2	3	4	5	6	7	8	9	10
2	2	4	6	8	10	12	14	16	18	20
3	3	6	9	12	15	18	21	24	27	30
4	4	8	12	16	20	24	28	32	36	40
5	5	10	15	20	25	30	35	40	45	50
6	6	12	18	24	30	36	42	48	54	60
7	7	14	21	28	35	42	49	56	63	70
8	8	16	24	32	40	48	56	64	72	80
9	9	18	27	36	45	54	63	72	81	90
10	10	20	30	40	50	60	70	80	90	100

Think about the **Commutative Property** and **inverse operations**
as you solve each problem.

1. If $16 \times 5 = 80$, then what is
   5×16?

   _____

2. If $18 \times 7 = 126$, then what is
   $126 \div 7$?

   _____

3. If $192 \div 16 = 12$, then what is
   $192 \div 12$?

   _____

4. If $12 \times 8 = 96$ and $8 \times d = 96$,
   then what number is d?

   _____

5. If $432 \div 18 = 24$, then what is
   18×24?

   _____

6. If $a \times b = c$, then what is
   $c \div b$?

   _____

7. **Reasoning** Choose a problem above and explain how the
   Commutative Property helped you answer it. Choose another
   exercise and explain how inverse operations helped.

   _____

   _____

   _____

Vocabulary

factor
product

► Complete a Multiplication Table

8. Look at the **factors** to complete the Multiplication Table.
   Leave blanks for the **products** you do not know.

×	1	2	3	4	5	6	7	8	9	10
1										
2										
3										
4										
5										
6										
7										
8										
9										
10										

9. Write the multiplications you need to practice.

_____

_____

_____

_____

_____

_____

_____

_____

▶ Patterns With 10s, 5s, and 9s

These grids help us see some patterns. Look at the numbers across, down, and on a diagonal.

10s

1	11	21	31	41	51	61	71	81	91
2	12	22	32	42	52	62	72	82	92
3	13	23	33	43	53	63	73	83	93
4	14	24	34	44	54	64	74	84	94
5	15	25	35	45	55	65	75	85	95
6	16	26	36	46	56	66	76	86	96
7	17	27	37	47	57	67	77	87	97
8	18	28	38	48	58	68	78	88	98
9	19	29	39	49	59	69	79	89	99
⑩	⑳	㉚	㊵	㊿	60	70	80	90	100

5s

1	11	21	31	41
2	12	22	32	42
3	13	23	33	43
4	14	24	34	44
⑤	⑮	㉕	㉟	㊺
6	16	26	36	46
7	17	27	37	47
8	18	28	38	48
9	19	29	39	49
⑩	⑳	㉚	㊵	50

1. What pattern do you see in the 10s count-bys?

_____

2. Look at the 5s and the 10s together. What patterns do you see?

_____

3. Look at the 9s count-bys. How does each 9s count-by relate to the 10s count-by in the same column?

_____

How could this pattern help you remember the 9s count-bys?

_____

_____

9s

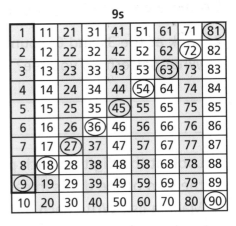

1	11	21	31	41	51	61	71	81
2	12	22	32	42	52	62	72	82
3	13	23	33	43	53	63	73	83
4	14	24	34	44	54	64	74	84
5	15	25	35	45	55	65	75	85
6	16	26	36	46	56	66	76	86
7	17	27	37	47	57	67	77	87
8	18	28	38	48	58	68	78	88
9	19	29	39	49	59	69	79	89
10	20	30	40	50	60	70	80	90

4. Look at the digits in each 9s product. What is the sum of the digits in each 9s product?

_____

How could you use this knowledge to check your answers when you multiply by 9?

_____

Class Activity

▶ The Puzzled Penguin

Help the Puzzled Penguin understand how Lucy did the mental math.

Dear Math Students,

Today my friend Lucy and I sold lemonade for 5 cents a glass. When we were done, my friend said, "There are 24 nickels here, so we made $1.20."

"How did you figure that out so fast?" I asked.

Lucy answered, "I started by multiplying 24 by 10, and then I . . ."

At that moment Lucy heard her mother calling and had to leave. I can't figure out what Lucy did. Why would anyone start by multiplying by 10 when a nickel is worth only 5 cents? Can you explain Lucy's thinking?

Thanks for your help.
Puzzled Penguin

Class Activity

▶ Add or Subtract From a Known Product

In each case, tell how you could find the unknown product.

1. You know $5 \times 6 = 30$, but don't know 6×6.

   _____

2. You know $5 \times 8 = 40$, but don't know 6×8.

   _____

3. You know $9 \times 10 = 90$, but don't know 9×9.

   _____

4. You know $7 \times 7 = 49$, but don't know 6×7.

   _____

5. You know $8 \times 10 = 80$, but don't know 8×11.

   _____

6. You know $6 \times 12 = 72$, but don't know 6×11.

   _____

Study the two tables.

5×6	30	5 sixes
6×6	30 + 6	5 sixes + 1 six
7×6	30 + 12	5 sixes + 2 sixes
8×6	30 + 18	5 sixes + 3 sixes
9×6	30 + 24	5 sixes + 4 sixes

5×8	40	5 eights
6×8	40 + 8	5 eights + 1 eight
7×8	40 + 16	5 eights + 2 eights
8×8	40 + 24	5 eights + 3 eights
9×8	40 + 32	5 eights + 4 eights

7. What strategy do the tables show for multiplying 6s and 8s?

   _____

   _____

Class Activity

▶ Make New Factors

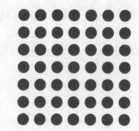

8. Look at the first array. Is 7 × 7 the same as
   5 sevens + 2 sevens? _____
   Mark the array to show that this is true.

9. How could you make new factors to solve 7 × 12?

   _____

10. Look at the second array. Is 4 × 6 the same as
    3 × 8? _____
    Mark the array to show that this is true.

11. How could you make new factors to solve 18 × 3 quickly?

    _____

Show how you could make new factors to solve the problems.

12. 5 × 18 _____   13. 16 × 4 _____

    _____   _____

14. 12 × 5 _____   15. 14 × 4 _____

    _____   _____

▶ Apply Various Strategies

Circle the name of the person who is right in each case. Explain why.

16. David says 9 × 6 is 54. Dana says it is 56. _____

17. David says 9 × 7 is 64. Dana says it is 63. _____

18. David says 8 × 7 is 56. Dana says it is 49. _____

19. David says 8 × 5 is 45. Dana says it is 40. _____

Rewrite each pattern to make it correct.

20. 3, 6, 10, 12, 15, 18, 21 _____

21. 8, 16, 24, 30, 32, 40, 45 _____

Going Further

▶ Addition and Multiplication Properties

Examples of addition and multiplication properties are shown below.

Property	Addition Example	Multiplication Example
Commutative	$13 + 6 = 6 + 13$	$12 \times 8 = 8 \times 12$
Identity	$4 + 0 = 4$	$25 \times 1 = 25$
Associative	$9 + (3 + 5) = (9 + 3) + 5$	$(7 \times 3) \times 2 = 7 \times (3 \times 2)$

Write the name of the property each equation represents.

1. $25 \times 1 = 25$ _____

2. $7 + 16 = 16 + 7$ _____

3. $6 \times (2 \times 4) = (6 \times 2) \times 4$ _____

4. $45 \times 5 = 5 \times 45$ _____

5. $(3 + 2) + 8 = 3 + (2 + 8)$ _____

6. $11 + 0 = 11$ _____

Write a number to complete each equation. Then write the name of the property you used.

7. $9 \times 8 = 8 \times \boxed{}$ _____

8. $34 = \boxed{} + 34$ _____

9. $8 + (\boxed{} + 9) = (8 + 2) + 9$ _____

10. $19 = 19 \times \boxed{}$ _____

11. $(3 \times 6) \times 4 = \boxed{} \times (6 \times 4)$ _____

12. $\boxed{} + 13 = 13 + 27$ _____

➡ 13. **On the Back** Describe each property in your own words.

_____

_____

_____

_____

_____

_____

_____

_____

_____

_____

_____

_____

_____

_____

_____

_____

_____

_____

_____

_____

_____

_____

_____

_____

_____

Multiplication Strategies

Class Activity

Name _____

Date _____

▶ The Factor Field

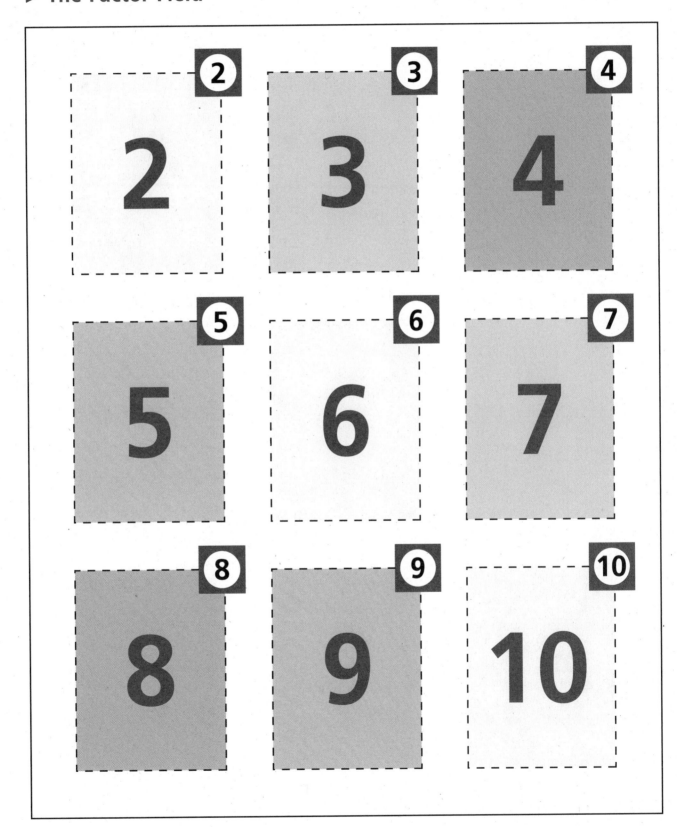

The Factor Field **20A**

Multiplication and Division Practice

$2\overline{)4}$	$2\overline{)6}$	$2\overline{)8}$	$2\overline{)10}$
2 × F = 4	2 * F = 6	2 · F = 8	2 × F = 10

$2\overline{)12}$	$2\overline{)14}$	$2\overline{)16}$	$2\overline{)18}$
2 * F = 12	2 · F = 14	2 × F = 16	2 * F = 18

$3\overline{)6}$	$3\overline{)9}$	$3\overline{)12}$	$3\overline{)15}$
3 · F = 6	3 × F = 9	3 * F = 12	3 · F = 15

$3\overline{)18}$	$3\overline{)21}$	$3\overline{)24}$	$3\overline{)27}$
3 × F = 18	3 * F = 21	3 · F = 24	3 × F = 27

$$2 \overline{)10} ^{5}$$

2 × 5 = 10

$$2 \overline{)8} ^{4}$$

2 · 4 = 8

$$2 \overline{)6} ^{3}$$

2 * 3 = 6

$$2 \overline{)4} ^{2}$$

2 × 2 = 4

$$2 \overline{)18} ^{9}$$

2 * 9 = 18

$$2 \overline{)16} ^{8}$$

2 × 8 = 16

$$2 \overline{)14} ^{7}$$

2 · 7 = 14

$$2 \overline{)12} ^{6}$$

2 * 6 = 12

$$3 \overline{)15} ^{5}$$

3 · 5 = 15

$$3 \overline{)12} ^{4}$$

3 * 4 = 12

$$3 \overline{)9} ^{3}$$

3 × 3 = 9

$$3 \overline{)6} ^{2}$$

3 · 2 = 6

$$3 \overline{)27} ^{9}$$

3 × 9 = 27

$$3 \overline{)24} ^{8}$$

3 · 8 = 24

$$3 \overline{)21} ^{7}$$

3 * 7 = 21

$$3 \overline{)18} ^{6}$$

3 × 6 = 18

Division Cards

$4\overline{)8}$	$4\overline{)12}$	$4\overline{)16}$	$4\overline{)20}$
4 × F = 8	4 * F = 12	4 · F = 16	4 × F = 20
$4\overline{)24}$	$4\overline{)28}$	$4\overline{)32}$	$4\overline{)36}$
4 * F = 24	4 · F = 28	4 × F = 32	4 * F = 36
$5\overline{)10}$	$5\overline{)15}$	$5\overline{)20}$	$5\overline{)25}$
5 · F = 10	5 × F = 15	5 * F = 20	5 · F = 25
$5\overline{)30}$	$5\overline{)35}$	$5\overline{)40}$	$5\overline{)45}$
5 × F = 30	5 * F = 35	5 · F = 40	5 × F = 45

$\frac{5}{4)20}$ $\frac{4}{4)16}$ $\frac{3}{4)12}$ $\frac{2}{4)8}$

4 × 5 = 20   4 · 4 = 16   4 * 3 = 12   4 × 2 = 8

$\frac{9}{4)36}$ $\frac{8}{4)32}$ $\frac{7}{4)28}$ $\frac{6}{4)24}$

4 * 9 = 36   4 × 8 = 32   4 · 7 = 28   4 * 6 = 24

$\frac{5}{5)25}$ $\frac{4}{5)20}$ $\frac{3}{5)15}$ $\frac{2}{5)10}$

5 · 5 = 25   5 * 4 = 20   5 × 3 = 15   5 · 2 = 10

$\frac{9}{5)45}$ $\frac{8}{5)40}$ $\frac{7}{5)35}$ $\frac{6}{5)30}$

5 × 9 = 45   5 · 8 = 40   5 * 7 = 35   5 × 6 = 30

Division Cards

$6\overline{)12}$	$6\overline{)18}$	$6\overline{)24}$	$6\overline{)30}$
6 × F = 12	6 * F = 18	6 · F = 24	6 × F = 30

$6\overline{)36}$	$6\overline{)42}$	$6\overline{)48}$	$6\overline{)54}$
6 * F = 36	6 · F = 42	6 × F = 48	6 * F = 54

$7\overline{)14}$	$7\overline{)21}$	$7\overline{)28}$	$7\overline{)35}$
7 · F = 14	7 × F = 21	7 * F = 28	7 · F = 35

$7\overline{)42}$	$7\overline{)49}$	$7\overline{)56}$	$7\overline{)63}$
7 × F = 42	7 * F = 49	7 · F = 56	7 × F = 63

$6\overset{5}{\overline{)30}}$	$6\overset{4}{\overline{)24}}$	$6\overset{3}{\overline{)18}}$	$6\overset{2}{\overline{)12}}$
$6 \times 5 = 30$	$6 \cdot 4 = 24$	$6 * 3 = 18$	$6 \times 2 = 12$
$6\overset{9}{\overline{)54}}$	$6\overset{8}{\overline{)48}}$	$6\overset{7}{\overline{)42}}$	$6\overset{6}{\overline{)36}}$
$6 * 9 = 54$	$6 \times 8 = 48$	$6 \cdot 7 = 42$	$6 * 6 = 36$
$7\overset{5}{\overline{)35}}$	$7\overset{4}{\overline{)28}}$	$7\overset{3}{\overline{)21}}$	$7\overset{2}{\overline{)14}}$
$7 \cdot 5 = 35$	$7 * 4 = 28$	$7 \times 3 = 21$	$7 \cdot 2 = 14$
$7\overset{9}{\overline{)63}}$	$7\overset{8}{\overline{)56}}$	$7\overset{7}{\overline{)49}}$	$7\overset{6}{\overline{)42}}$
$7 \times 9 = 63$	$7 \cdot 8 = 56$	$7 * 7 = 49$	$7 \times 6 = 42$

Division Cards

$8\overline{)16}$	$8\overline{)24}$	$8\overline{)32}$	$8\overline{)40}$
$8 \times F = 16$	$8 * F = 24$	$8 \cdot F = 32$	$8 \times F = 40$
$8\overline{)48}$	$8\overline{)56}$	$8\overline{)64}$	$8\overline{)72}$
$8 * F = 48$	$8 \cdot F = 56$	$8 \times F = 64$	$8 * F = 72$
$9\overline{)18}$	$9\overline{)27}$	$9\overline{)36}$	$9\overline{)45}$
$9 \cdot F = 18$	$9 \times F = 27$	$9 * F = 36$	$9 \cdot F = 45$
$9\overline{)54}$	$9\overline{)63}$	$9\overline{)72}$	$9\overline{)81}$
$9 \times F = 54$	$9 * F = 63$	$9 \cdot F = 72$	$9 \times F = 81$

$$8\overline{)40}^{\,5}$$

8 × 5 = 40

$$8\overline{)32}^{\,4}$$

8 · 4 = 32

$$8\overline{)24}^{\,3}$$

8 * 3 = 24

$$8\overline{)16}^{\,2}$$

8 × 2 = 16

$$8\overline{)72}^{\,9}$$

8 * 9 = 72

$$8\overline{)64}^{\,8}$$

8 × 8 = 64

$$8\overline{)56}^{\,7}$$

8 · 7 = 56

$$8\overline{)48}^{\,6}$$

8 * 6 = 48

$$9\overline{)45}^{\,5}$$

9 · 5 = 45

$$9\overline{)36}^{\,4}$$

9 * 4 = 36

$$9\overline{)27}^{\,3}$$

9 × 3 = 27

$$9\overline{)18}^{\,2}$$

9 · 2 = 18

$$9\overline{)81}^{\,9}$$

9 × 9 = 81

$$9\overline{)72}^{\,8}$$

9 · 8 = 72

$$9\overline{)63}^{\,7}$$

9 * 7 = 63

$$9\overline{)54}^{\,6}$$

9 × 6 = 54

Division Cards

$10\overline{)20}$

$10 \times F = 20$

$10\overline{)30}$

$10 * F = 30$

$10\overline{)40}$

$10 \cdot F = 40$

$10\overline{)50}$

$10 \times F = 50$

$10\overline{)60}$

$10 * F = 60$

$10\overline{)70}$

$10 \cdot F = 70$

$10\overline{)80}$

$10 \times F = 80$

$10\overline{)90}$

$10 * F = 90$

$\overline{)}$

$\cdot F =$

$\overline{)}$

$\times F =$

$\overline{)}$

$* F =$

$\overline{)}$

$\cdot F =$

$\overline{)}$

$\times F =$

$\overline{)}$

$* F =$

$\overline{)}$

$\cdot F =$

$\overline{)}$

$\times F =$

$$10\overline{)50}^{\,5}$$

10 × 5 = 50

$$10\overline{)40}^{\,4}$$

10 · 4 = 40

$$10\overline{)30}^{\,3}$$

10 * 3 = 30

$$10\overline{)20}^{\,2}$$

10 × 2 = 20

$$10\overline{)90}^{\,9}$$

10 * 9 = 90

$$10\overline{)80}^{\,8}$$

10 × 8 = 80

$$10\overline{)70}^{\,7}$$

10 · 7 = 70

$$10\overline{)60}^{\,6}$$

10 * 6 = 60

$$\overline{)}$$

· =

$$\overline{)}$$

* =

$$\overline{)}$$

× =

$$\overline{)}$$

· =

$$\overline{)}$$

× =

$$\overline{)}$$

· =

$$\overline{)}$$

* =

$$\overline{)}$$

× =

Division Cards

▶ Diagnostic Multiplication Quiz

1. 5 × 9 = ___   2. 3 × 3 = ___   3. 2 × 9 = ___   4. 5 × 7 = ___

5. 7 × 10 = ___   6. 8 × 1 = ___   7. 0 × 4 = ___   8. 9 × 7 = ___

9. 6 × 5 = ___   10. 9 × 3 = ___   11. 4 × 2 = ___   12. 7 × 8 = ___

13. 4 × 10 = ___   14. 5 × 3 = ___   15. 6 × 9 = ___   16. 8 × 6 = ___

17. 7 × 2 = ___   18. 9 × 0 = ___   19. 8 × 9 = ___   20. 8 × 7 = ___

21. 9 × 2 = ___   22. 8 × 3 = ___   23. 5 × 4 = ___   24. 7 × 7 = ___

25. 6 × 2 = ___   26. 3 × 0 = ___   27. 3 × 4 = ___   28. 6 × 8 = ___

29. 5 × 10 = ___   30. 5 × 1 = ___   31. 10 × 9 = ___   32. 5 × 6 = ___

33. 4 × 5 = ___   34. 4 × 3 = ___   35. 1 × 9 = ___   36. 8 × 8 = ___

37. 8 × 2 = ___   38. 5 × 0 = ___   39. 4 × 9 = ___   40. 6 × 7 = ___

41. 6 × 10 = ___   42. 4 × 1 = ___   43. 6 × 4 = ___   44. 4 × 8 = ___

45. 8 × 5 = ___   46. 8 × 0 = ___   47. 8 × 4 = ___   48. 4 × 7 = ___

49. 8 × 10 = ___   50. 6 × 3 = ___   51. 4 × 4 = ___   52. 3 × 8 = ___

53. 5 × 5 = ___   54. 6 × 0 = ___   55. 7 × 9 = ___   56. 6 × 6 = ___

57. 7 × 5 = ___   58. 2 × 3 = ___   59. 9 × 9 = ___   60. 9 × 6 = ___

61. 3 × 5 = ___   62. 7 × 3 = ___   63. 5 × 9 = ___   64. 3 × 6 = ___

65. 5 × 2 = ___   66. 1 × 3 = ___   67. 3 × 9 = ___   68. 7 × 6 = ___

69. 9 × 5 = ___   70. 6 × 1 = ___   71. 7 × 4 = ___   72. 9 × 8 = ___

Class Activity

Name _____

Date _____

▶ Diagnostic Division Quiz

1. 30 ÷ 5 = ___   2. 12 ÷ 3 = ___   3. 27 ÷ 9 = ___   4. 42 ÷ 7 = ___

5. 15 ÷ 5 = ___   6. 0 ÷ 3 = ___   7. 28 ÷ 4 = ___   8. 30 ÷ 6 = ___

9. 8 ÷ 2 = ___   10. 9 ÷ 1 = ___   11. 9 ÷ 9 = ___   12. 56 ÷ 7 = ___

13. 40 ÷ 10 = ___   14. 10 ÷ 1 = ___   15. 24 ÷ 4 = ___   16. 18 ÷ 6 = ___

17. 40 ÷ 5 = ___   18. 9 ÷ 3 = ___   19. 36 ÷ 4 = ___   20. 56 ÷ 8 = ___

21. 5 ÷ 5 = ___   22. 30 ÷ 3 = ___   23. 16 ÷ 4 = ___   24. 72 ÷ 8 = ___

25. 16 ÷ 2 = ___   26. 21 ÷ 3 = ___   27. 81 ÷ 9 = ___   28. 64 ÷ 8 = ___

29. 6 ÷ 2 = ___   30. 3 ÷ 3 = ___   31. 18 ÷ 9 = ___   32. 63 ÷ 7 = ___

33. 90 ÷ 10 = ___   34. 18 ÷ 3 = ___   35. 63 ÷ 9 = ___   36. 54 ÷ 6 = ___

37. 12 ÷ 2 = ___   38. 8 ÷ 1 = ___   39. 36 ÷ 9 = ___   40. 35 ÷ 7 = ___

41. 18 ÷ 2 = ___   42. 6 ÷ 3 = ___   43. 8 ÷ 4 = ___   44. 36 ÷ 6 = ___

45. 80 ÷ 10 = ___   46. 7 ÷ 1 = ___   47. 45 ÷ 9 = ___   48. 48 ÷ 6 = ___

49. 25 ÷ 5 = ___   50. 15 ÷ 3 = ___   51. 32 ÷ 4 = ___   52. 24 ÷ 8 = ___

53. 35 ÷ 5 = ___   54. 27 ÷ 3 = ___   55. 72 ÷ 9 = ___   56. 42 ÷ 6 = ___

57. 20 ÷ 5 = ___   58. 24 ÷ 3 = ___   59. 12 ÷ 4 = ___   60. 6 ÷ 6 = ___

61. 10 ÷ 2 = ___   62. 1 ÷ 1 = ___   63. 54 ÷ 9 = ___   64. 21 ÷ 7 = ___

65. 20 ÷ 10 = ___   66. 0 ÷ 1 = ___   67. 40 ÷ 4 = ___   68. 48 ÷ 8 = ___

69. 45 ÷ 5 = ___   70. 6 ÷ 1 = ___   71. 20 ÷ 4 = ___   72. 49 ÷ 7 = ___

Diagnostic Division Quiz

Vocabulary

combination

▶ Discuss Combinations

Joel is taking 3 shirts and 2 pairs of shorts to camp.

How many different outfits can he put together? _____

A chart helps us see all of the **combinations**.

1. Write an equation. _____

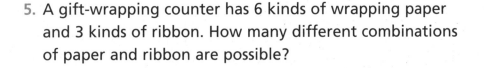

Suppose we know that Joel has 6 different outfits for camp. He has 2 pairs of shorts and an unknown number of shirts.

2. How many shirts does he have? _____

3. Write an equation. _____

4. Can you think of another way to write the equation?

_____

5. A gift-wrapping counter has 6 kinds of wrapping paper and 3 kinds of ribbon. How many different combinations of paper and ribbon are possible?

_____

6. A cafe offers 32 different bagel combinations. If there are 4 kinds of spread, how many different bagels are there?

_____

7. Roberto wants to buy a new bicycle. The bicycles in the shop come in small, medium, and large. For each size, there is a choice of blue, red, black, and green. How many different kinds of bicycles are there to choose from?

_____

Show your work.

Class Activity

Name _____   Date _____

▶ Make a Tree Diagram

Solve.

8. Sylvia has two pairs of shorts (white and gray) and three T-shirts (green, blue, and black). Complete the tree diagram below to show the number of different outfits Sylvia could wear.

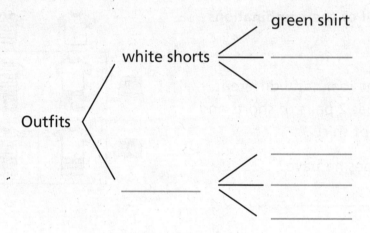

How many different outfits can Sylvia wear? _____

9. Each of Eduardo's textbooks must have a book cover. His choices for a math book cover include a solid color, a plaid pattern, a spiral pattern, or stripes. Make a tree diagram to show the number of different choices Eduardo has.

10. Jenni is packing socks (red, white, gray, or blue) and two pairs of sneakers (red sneakers and white sneakers) for a trip. Make a tree diagram to show the different choices Jenni has of combinations of socks and shoes.

Eduardo has _____ choices.

Altogether, Jenni has _____ combinations of socks and shoes.

Make Combinations

Vocabulary

product
factor

► Use Letters for the Unknown

Write an equation for each problem; then solve.

These equations have an unknown **product**.

11. What is p in these equations? _____
    Can you think of other ways to write the equations?

    _____

$$6 \times 3 = p$$
$$p = 6 \times 3$$

These equations have an unknown **factor**. Some are division and some are unknown multiplication.

12. What is f in these equations? _____
    Can you think of other ways to write the equations?

    _____

    _____

$$f = 18 \div 3$$
$$f = 18 / 3$$
$$3 \times f = 18$$
$$3 \cdot f = 18$$

Another way to write unknown multiplication is without the multiplication sign. This form is used in algebra.

$$3f = 18$$

Solve each equation.

13. $7 \times 7 = a$

    $a =$ _____

14. $b = 72 \div 8$

    $b =$ _____

15. $4 \cdot 8 = c$

    $c =$ _____

16. $63 \div 9 = d$

    $d =$ _____

17. $6e = 48$

    $e =$ _____

18. $30f = 60$

    $f =$ _____

19. $90 \div 3 = g$

    $g =$ _____

20. $2h = 50$

    $h =$ _____

Write an equation for each word problem and solve it.

21. Hester and her friends are making kites. They have 7 colors of paper and 3 kinds of ribbon for the tail. How many different kites can they make? Let k stand for the unknown number of kites.

    _____

22. Mr. Mason makes 4 sizes of toy trucks in several colors. Altogether there are 20 different trucks. How many colors are there? Let c stand for the unknown number of colors.

    _____

Name _____ **Date** _____

Going Further

▶ Guess and Check

The product of two numbers is 24. Their sum is 11. The table below shows how the Guess and Check strategy can be used to solve the problem.

First Guess: 6 and 4	Second Guess: _____ and _____	Third Guess: _____ and _____
Product: _____	Product: _____	Product: _____
Sum: _____	Sum: _____	Sum: _____
Check: Is the product 24? _____ Is the sum 11? _____	Check: Is the product 24? _____ Is the sum 11? _____	Check: Is the product 24? _____ Is the sum 11? _____

1. Work with a partner and complete the first column of the table for a guess of 6 and 4.

2. Make a new guess and use it to complete the second column. Complete the third column if you need to make another guess.

Use the Guess and Check strategy to solve each problem.

3. The sum of the ages in years of Karl and his sister Sabrina is 18. Sabrina is 4 years older that Karl. How old is Karl?

_____

4. The sum of three numbers is 10. The product of the numbers is 30. What are the numbers?

_____

5. In a pasture, there are goats and chickens. Eileen counted 10 heads and 28 legs. How many goats and how many chickens are in the pasture?

_____

Make Combinations

Name _____ Date _____

Vocabulary

comparison

▶ Comparisons With Unknown Numbers

You can use multiplication to solve **comparison** problems. All comparison problems involve a smaller amount and a larger amount.

1. There are 3 times as many deer as moose in the forest. If there are 5 moose, how many deer are there? *(The larger amount is unknown.)*

   _____

	3×m	
Deer (3m)		
Moose (m)	5	

2. There are $\frac{1}{3}$ as many moose as deer in the forest. If there are 15 deer, how many moose are there? *(The smaller amount is unknown.)*

   _____

Deer (d)	15
Moose ($\frac{1}{3}d$)	
	$\frac{1}{3} \times d$

3. There are 5 moose in the forest. There are 15 deer. How many times as many deer as moose are there? *(The multiplier is unknown.)*

   _____

	__×m
Deer (3m)	15
Moose (m)	5

4. Use the scoreboard to write 3 multiplication comparison word problems. Let each number be the unknown.

Red Team	Blue Team
6	24

   _____

   _____

   _____

   _____

   _____

   _____

   _____

   _____

   _____

▶ Solve Comparison Problems

Draw comparison bars, write an equation, and solve each problem.

Show your work.

5. Farmer Ruiz has 6 times as many cows as goats. He has 7 goats. How many cows does he have? Let c = the number of cows.

_____

6. Nadia hiked 20 miles this weekend. Her sister Maria hiked only $\frac{1}{4}$ as many miles. How many miles did Maria hike? Let m = the number of miles Maria hiked.

_____

7. A baker made 35 apple pies today. He also made 7 peach pies. How many times as many apple pies as peach pies did he make? Let t = how many times as many.

_____

8. Nate practiced the trumpet for 10 hours last week. This week he practiced only $\frac{1}{5}$ as long. How long did Nate practice this week? Let h = the number of hours Nate practiced this week.

_____

9. How many times as many dark crayons are there as light crayons? Let t = how many times as many.

_____

▶ Comparisons and Graphs

10. Brownville School and Highland School both bought new computers this year. Using multiplication, compare the number of computers the two schools bought. Express the comparison two ways.

Computers

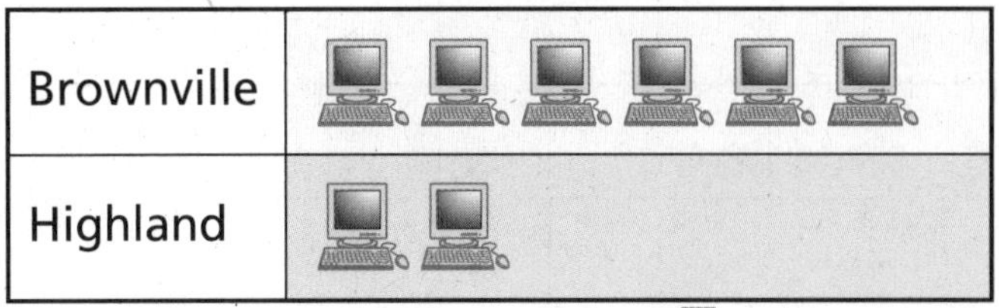

Brownville	🖥 🖥 🖥 🖥 🖥 🖥
Highland	🖥 🖥

Key: Each 🖥 = 1 computer

_____

_____

_____

_____

11. The bar graph shows the number of blocks that four students walk to school. Write two multiplication comparison word problems about this bar graph.

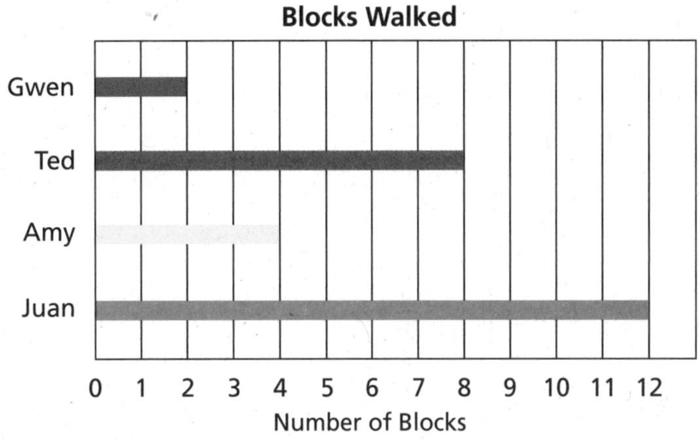

Blocks Walked

Gwen
Ted
Amy
Juan

0 1 2 3 4 5 6 7 8 9 10 11 12
Number of Blocks

_____

_____

_____

_____

_____

_____

_____

12. **On the Back** First, draw a vertical bar graph that shows the data in exercise 11. Then draw a pictograph for the same data. Let your icon equal 2 blocks.

Name Date

Dear Family,

Applying multiplication and division to real-world situations is accomplished mainly through word problems. These include area, arrays, equal groups, comparisons, and combinations. Multiplication and division are not separated, but are treated together from the start so that students can see how these operations relate to each other.

Some real-world situations are a little too complex to be solved without algebra. The third goal, using simple algebraic methods, is shown by a problem such as this:

A truck carried 6 chairs and a table weighing 40 pounds. Altogether the chairs and table weigh 100 pounds. How much does each chair weigh?

> *Equation:*
> $6 \cdot c + 40 = 100$

Factor Puzzles are introduced as a way to practice multiplications and divisions. A Factor Puzzle shows 3 of the 4 numbers found when 2 rows and 2 columns of the multiplication table intersect (see below). Students write outside the Factor Puzzle the rows and columns of the multiplication table, and so can find the unknown fourth number.

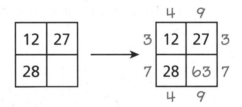

Students enjoy solving Factor Puzzles, and they can also create them. The Factor Puzzles show number pairs in proportional relationships. Students will work with these relationships again when they do equivalent fractions, ratios, and similarity.

If you have any questions or comments, please contact me.

Sincerely,
Your child's teacher

Estimada Familia:

Aplicar la multiplicación y la división a situaciones de la vida real se logra principalmente por medio de problemas verbales. Dichas situaciones incluyen área, matrices, grupos iguales, comparaciones y combinaciones. La multiplicación y la división se tratan de manera conjunta desde el principio, de modo que los estudiantes puedan ver cómo se relacionan entre sí.

Algunas situaciones de la vida real son demasiado complejas como para resolverlas sin recurrir al álgebra. El tercer objetivo, usar métodos algebraicos simples, se presenta por medio de problemas como éste:

Un camión transportó 6 sillas y una mesa que pesaba 40 libras. Juntas, las sillas y la mesa pesan 100 libras. ¿Cuánto pesa cada silla?

> *Ecuación:*
> $6C + 40 = 100$

Los rompecabezas de factores se presentan como una manera de practicar las multiplicaciones y las divisiones. Un rompecabezas de factores muestra 3 de los 4 números que se hallan cuando 2 filas y 2 columnas de la tabla de multiplicar se intersecan (ver abajo). Los estudiantes escriben, fuera del rompecabezas de factores, las filas y columnas de la tabla de multiplicar, y así pueden hallar el cuarto número desconocido.

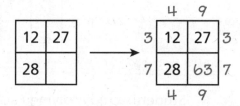

Los estudiantes se divierten resolviendo rompecabezas de factores y también pueden crearlos. Los rompecabezas de factores muestran pares de números en relaciones proporcionales. Los estudiantes volverán a trabajar con estas relaciones cuando estudien fracciones, razones y geometría de figuras semejantes.

Si tiene alguna duda o comentario, por favor comuníquese conmigo.

Atentamente,
El maestro de su niño

Understand Comparisons

Class Activity

Name _____ Date _____

Vocabulary

equal groups
array
area

▶ Write and Solve Situation Equations

You can multiply or divide to solve **equal groups** problems.

Write and solve an equation for each problem.

1. Amy has 5 cousins. She is making 2 puppets for each cousin. How many puppets will Amy need to make?

_____

2. Amy made 10 puppets to divide equally among her 5 cousins. How many puppets will each cousin get?

_____

3. Amy made 10 puppets for her cousins. Each cousin will get 2 puppets. How many cousins does Amy have?

_____

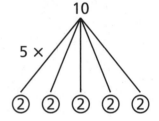

Things in an **array** are arranged in rows and columns.
The **area** of a figure is the number of square units that cover it.

4. A garden has 2 rows and 5 columns of bean plants. How many plants are there in all?

_____

5. The garden is 2 yards wide and 5 yards long. What is its area?

_____

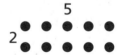

6. A garden has a total of 10 bean plants in 2 equal rows. How many columns does it have?

_____

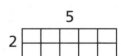

7. The area of the garden is 10 square yards. It is 2 yards wide. How long is it?

_____

8. A garden has a total of 10 bean plants in 5 equal columns. How many rows does it have?

_____

Practice With Multiplication Problems **33**

Class Activity

Vocabulary

comparison
combination

▶ Comparisons and Combinations

Write and solve an equation for each problem.

Comparison problems always involve a larger number and a smaller number.

9. Bill has 2 apples. Kim has 5 times as many apples as Bill. How many apples does Kim have?

Bill (B) [2]

$$B = \frac{1}{5} \times K$$

Kim (K) [2 | 2 | 2 | 2 | 2]

$$K = 5 \times B$$

_____

10. Kim has 10 apples. Bill has $\frac{1}{5}$ as many apples as Kim. How many apples does Bill have?

_____

11. Bill has 2 apples. Kim has 10 apples. How many times as many apples does Kim have as Bill?

_____

You will use all possible pairs of fillings and breads to solve these **combination** problems.

12. Paco is making sandwiches on white bread and rye bread. The fillings are cheese, tuna, ham, peanut butter, and egg salad. How many combinations can he make?

	C	T	H	P	E
W	WC	WT	WH	WP	WE
R	RC	RT	RH	RP	RE

_____

13. Paco made 10 different sandwiches. He used 5 kinds of fillings. How many kinds of bread did he use?

_____

14. Paco made 10 different sandwiches. He used 2 kinds of bread. How many kinds of fillings did he use?

_____

▶ Share Solutions

Write 4 multiplication or division word problems for the class to solve. Write one problem for each of the 4 types shown below.

Equal Groups

Array or Area

Comparison

Combination

Class Activity

Name Date

Vocabulary

factor
product

► Scrambled Multiplication Tables

The **factors** are at the side and top of each table.
The **products** are in the white boxes.

Complete each table.

A

×									
6	30	54	60	42	24	18	12	48	36
2	10	18	20	14	8	6	4	16	12
10	50	90	100	70	40	30	20	80	60
8	40	72	80	56	32	24	16	64	48
5	25	45	50	35	20	15	10	40	30
1	5	9	10	7	4	3	2	8	6
9	45	81	90	63	36	27	18	72	54
4	20	36	40	28	16	12	8	32	24
7	35	63	70	49	28	21	14	56	42
3	15	27	30	21	12	9	6	24	18

B

×										
	27	6	24	21	18	15	12	9	3	
	36	8	32	28	24		16	12	4	40
	9	2	8	7	6	5	4	3	1	10
	18	4	16	14		10	8	6	2	20
		14	56	49	42		28	21	7	
	72		64	56	48	40	32	24	8	80
	45	10	40		30	25	20	15	5	
	54	12	48	42	36	30	24	18	6	60
	90		80	70	60		40	30	10	100
	81	18	72		54	45	36	27	9	

C

×										
	100		20		70	50		90		10
	50	15		20	35		30		40	5
	10	3		4	7		6	9		1
		9		12	21	15		27	24	
		6	4	8			12	18	16	2
		12	8	16	28	20		36	32	
	90	27	18	36	63	45	54		72	
		18	12	24		30	36	54	48	6
		21		28	49		42		56	7
		24		32	56	40		72	64	8

D

×										
	48		42	12	36		18	6		30
	56	28		14		70	21		63	35
			70		60			10		50
		20	35		30		15	5	45	
	32			8		40			36	
	8	4		2			3	1		5
		8	14		12		6		18	10
	64		56		48	80	24	8		40
	72	36		18			27		81	
	24		21		18	30		3	27	

Write Word Problems

Name _____ **Date** _____

Vocabulary

function

▶ Input-Output Tables

A **function** is a rule that pairs each input with only one output. Functions can be shown in different ways. The table of input and output values at the right is one way to show a function.

The rule for the function table is *add 3* because every output is 3 more than its input. You can also write an equation as shown below the table. Write the output for the last row.

Rule: Add 3	
Input	Output
0	3
1	4
2	5
5	8
9	

$I + 3 = O$

Complete each table.

1.

Rule: Add 8	
Input	Output
1	9
2	
	11
4	
5	13

_____

2.

Rule: Multiply by 5	
Input	Output
0	
6	30
8	40
9	
	20

_____

For each table, write the rule and complete the table. Then write an equation.

3.

Rule:	
Input	Output
0	
2	8
3	12
4	16
	24

_____

4.

Rule:	
Input	Output
7	14
2	
15	22
	10
11	18

_____

Class Activity

Vocabulary
variable

▶ Functions and Equations

Functions can describe many situations in your everyday life. The table below shows late fees for an overdue library book.

A function table will often contain variables. A **variable** is a letter that is used to represent an unknown number.

We can represent the input (number of days late) by the variable d and the late fee by the variable f.

5. Write the rule in words and as an equation.

Rule in Words					
Equation					
Number of Days Late (d)	1	2	3	4	5
Late Fee (f)	10¢	20¢	30¢	40¢	50¢

For each function table, write the rule in words and as an equation. Then complete the table.

6.

Rule in Words					
Equation					
Bicycles (b)	1		3	4	5
Wheels (w)	2	4	6		10

7.

Rule in Words					
Equation					
Tricycles (t)	1	2		4	5
Wheels (w)	3	6	9		15

8.

Rule in Words					
Equation					
Tickets (t)	1	2	3	4	
Cost in dollars (d)	7	14		28	35

9.

Rule in Words					
Equation					
Inches of rain (r)	0	1		3	4
Inches of snow (s)	0	10	20	30	

Name _____   **Date** _____

Vocabulary

equation
parentheses

▶ Discuss Grouping Situations

How much did each student spend at the school store? Write the equation and solve.

Show your work.

1. Michael: I bought an eraser for 6 cents and 2 magnets for 9 cents each.

   Equation: _____

   Answer: _____

2. Emma: I bought 3 markers for 8 cents each and a notebook for 10 cents.

   Equation: _____

   Answer: _____

3. Alan: I bought 4 pencils for 3 cents each and 4 pens for 6 cents each.

   Equation: _____

   Answer: _____

4. Lucy: I bought 3 calendars for 30 cents each. One was bent, so it cost 5 cents less.

   Equation: _____

   Answer: _____

▶ Solve Equations With Parentheses

Solve each equation. Remember to do the operations in parentheses first.

5. $(4 \times 3) - 5 = n$ $n =$ _____

6. $6 + (10 - 2) = b$ $b =$ _____

7. $(9 - 2) \times 4 = c$ $c =$ _____

8. $12 + (5 \times 2) = q$ $q =$ _____

9. $(8 \times 7) - 6 = p$ $p =$ _____

10. $6 + (2 \times 3 \times 4) = f$ $f =$ _____

11. $(5 - 2) \times 9 = v$ $v =$ _____

12. $(10 \times 10 \times 10) - 10 = z$ $z =$ _____

Write an equation for each problem. Then solve.

13. A peach orchard has 8 rows of 9 trees. An apple orchard has 6 rows of 7 trees. How many trees are in both orchards?

    Equation: _____ **Answer:** _____

14. In all, 6 chairs and a table weigh 100 pounds. The table weighs 40 pounds. How much does each chair weigh?

    Equation: _____ **Answer:** _____

15. A parking lot has 10 rows with spaces for 9 cars in each row. There are now 70 cars in the parking lot. How many empty spaces are there?

    Equation: _____ **Answer:** _____

16. Lisa has 5 large bags with 8 oranges in each bag and some small bags with 3 oranges in each bag. Altogether, she has 58 oranges. How many small bags of oranges does she have?

    Equation: _____ **Answer:** _____

17. Rolando runs 5 miles every day. Stuart runs 2 miles every day. How much farther does Rolando run in a week than Stuart?

    Equation: _____ **Answer:** _____

18. Caroline had 25 flowers. She put some of them in a large vase. Then she put 3 flowers each in 6 small vases. How many flowers are in the large vase?

    Equation: _____ **Answer:** _____

19. Abdul and his brother can put 6 pictures on each page of their albums. Abdul's album has 8 pages, and his brother's has 5 pages. How many pictures will fit in both albums altogether?

    Equation: _____ **Answer:** _____

Equations With Parentheses

▶ Three-Way Combinations

A **combination** is a way of putting items together. You can find combinations in real-world situations.

1. Bert's Frozen Yogurt Shop serves 3 kinds of yogurt on 2 kinds of cones. How many different combinations are possible? Write the equation.

_____

2. Today Bert's Frozen Yogurt Shop started selling 4 different toppings to put on top of the yogurt. Now how many combinations are possible? Write the equation.

_____

3. Toby's Frozen Yogurt Shop serves 4 kinds of frozen yogurt on 2 kinds of cones. This shop offers 3 kinds of toppings. Draw tables showing how many combinations are possible. Then write the equation.

Show your work.

_____

4. Teresa is making dolls. She has 2 outfits, 4 colors of yarn, and 5 choices of shoes. How many different combinations are possible?

_____

5. Armando is packing for vacation. He has 6 shirts, 3 pairs of shorts, and 2 pairs of shoes. How many different outfits can he make?

_____

Vocabulary

comparison

► Comparison Problems

Solve each comparison problem.

Show your work.

6. Maria scored 6 points in the basketball game. Suzanne scored 4 times as many points as Maria. How many points did Suzanne score?

   _____

7. Ramon scored 10 points at the volleyball game. That was 5 times as many as David scored. How many points did David score? (Hint: Did David score more or fewer points than Ramon?)

   _____

8. Ana has $15 in the bank. Her sister Benita has $\frac{1}{3}$ as much money in the bank. How much money does Benita have in the bank?

   _____

9. Dana has 9 CDs. She has $\frac{1}{5}$ as many as Sonya. How many CDs does Sonya have?

   _____

10. Mr. Wagner has 32 horses on his farm. He has 4 times as many horses as Mr. Cruz. How many horses does Mr. Cruz have?

    _____

11. Chester has 49 CDs. Tony has $\frac{1}{7}$ as many as Chester. How many CDs does Tony have?

    _____

12. A pizza restaurant offers 9 kinds of toppings and 2 kinds of crust. A small cafe offers $\frac{1}{3}$ as many types of pizza. How many fewer types of pizza does the small cafe offer?

    _____

    _____

Name _____   Date _____

▶ Strategies for Finding Factors

Write the missing numbers.

1. Table 1

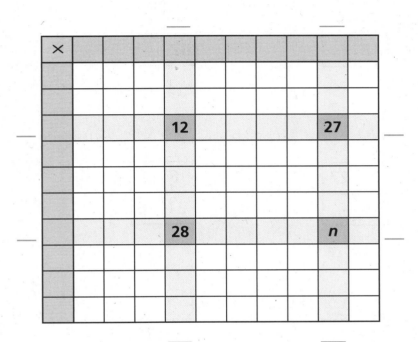

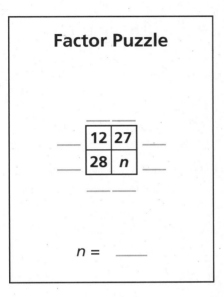

Factor Puzzle

12	27
28	n

n = _____

2. Table 2

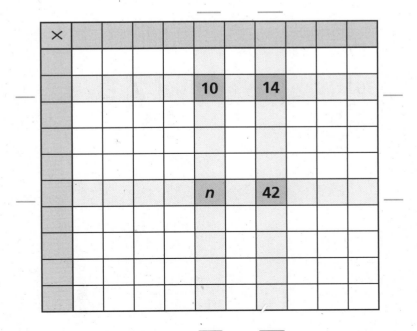

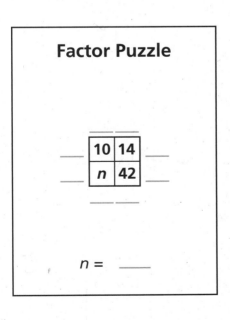

Factor Puzzle

10	14
n	42

n = _____

Class Activity

Name _____ Date _____

▶ Practice With Factors

Solve each Factor Puzzle.

3.

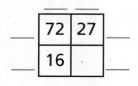

	14	35	
		45	

4.

	15	40	
	18		

5.

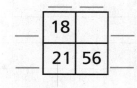

	14	6	
	42		

6.

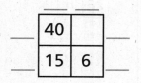

	40		
	15	6	

7.

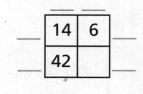

	72	27	
	16		

8.

	18		
	21	56	

9.

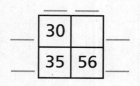

	30		
	35	56	

10.

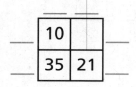

	10		
	35	21	

11.

		35	
	24	40	

12.

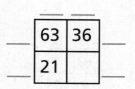

	63	36	
	21		

13.

	30		
	35	56	

14.

		27	
	10	45	

15.

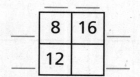

	8	16	
	12		

16.

	63	81	
	28		

17.

	5	10	
	25		

Practice With Factors

► Factor the Footprints (page 1)

Cut out pages 44A and 44C and tape them together to make a game board.

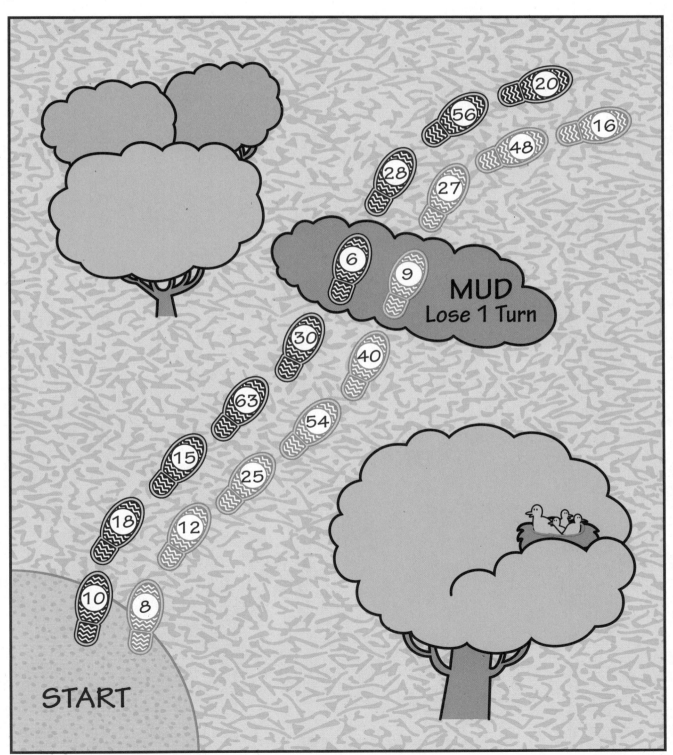

Practice With Factors

► Factor the Footprints (page 2)

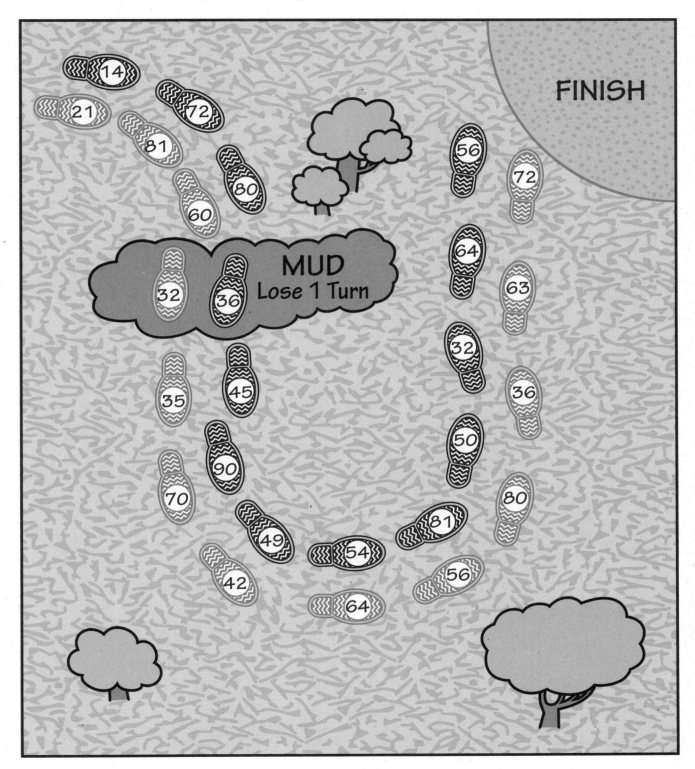

FINISH

MUD
Lose 1 Turn

► Write Equations

The information given in each problem makes a comparison chain.

Solve.

Show your work.

1. Molly's family stayed at the cabin for 4 days. Then Tonio's family moved in and stayed there 3 times as long as Molly's family. After that, Jenny's family moved in and stayed 4 times as long as Molly's family. How many days did these families spend at the cabin altogether?

   _____

   _____

2. Fallbrook School has 5 computers. Mapleville School has twice as many computers as Fallbrook School. Pinewood School has 6 times as many computers as Mapleville School. How many computers do these schools have in all?

   _____

   _____

3. Toby made 2 paper airplanes today. His friend Justin made 5 times as many paper airplanes as Toby, and his friend Leo made 4 times as many paper airplanes as Toby. How many paper airplanes did the three friends make today?

   _____

   _____

► Algebraic Chains

Find the unknown number in each equation. Write a 1 in front of an unknown that is alone if it will help you.

4. $a + 3a = 36$

   _____

5. $b + 4b + 2b = 28$

   _____

6. $5c + c + 2c = 16$

   _____

Class Activity

► Word Problems With Algebraic Chains

There are 3 times as many brown eggs as white eggs.
Altogether there are 24 eggs. How many eggs are
there of each kind?

Let w = the number of white eggs
Let $3w$ = the number of brown eggs

> You know there are 3 times as many brown eggs as white eggs. So you can show the white eggs as w and the brown eggs as $3w$.

$w + 3w = 24$
$4w = 24$
$w =$ _____ white eggs
$3w =$ _____ brown eggs

> Set up an equation. Remember w means $1w$.
> Then solve and check your answer.
> Do the numbers add up to 24?

Solve.

Show your work.

7. Joshua has 3 kinds of apples—red, green, and yellow.
   He has 4 times as many green apples as red and
   2 times as many yellow apples as red. He has 28 apples
   in all. How many of each kind does he have?

   _____

8. A rectangle has a perimeter of 24 m. Its length is
   3 times longer than its width. How long is each side?

   _____

9. A toy train has 20 cars—blue, purple, and orange. There
   are 4 times as many blue cars as purple cars. There are
   5 times as many orange cars as purple cars. How many
   cars of each color are there?

   _____

► Practice Algebraic Equations

Find the unknown number in each equation.

10. $5k + 2k = 42$

    $k =$ _____

11. $8(3 \times 2) = p$

    $p =$ _____

12. $z = (2 \times 9) + (3 \times 3)$

    $z =$ _____

13. $\frac{1}{8} c = 5$

    $c =$ _____

14. $20 \div r = 4$

    $r =$ _____

15. $\frac{1}{3} m = 7$

    $m =$ _____

Multistep Problems

Vocabulary

Commutative Property
Associative Property
expressions

▶ **The Commutative Property**

The arrays and equations at right show the **Commutative Property** of multiplication.

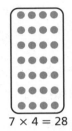

$4 \times 7 = 28$

$7 \times 4 = 28$

1. Explain the Commutative Property in your own words.

_____

_____

2. Is this property true of any two whole numbers that are multiplied together? How could you prove it?

_____

_____

Use the Commutative Property to find the unknown number *n* in these equations.

3. $57 \times 6 = 6 \times n$ 4. $n \times 5 = 5 \times 26$ 5. $48 \times n = 7 \times 48$

   $n =$ _____ $n =$ _____ $n =$ _____

▶ **The Associative Property**

The arrays and **expressions** at right show the **Associative Property** of multiplication.

6. Explain the Associative Property in your own words.

   $3 \times (5 \times 2) = (3 \times 5) \times 2$

_____

_____

$3 \times (5 \times 2)$

7. Do you think this property is true of any whole numbers that are multiplied together? Why or why not?

_____

_____

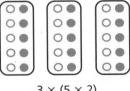

$(3 \times 5) \times 2$

Simplify each expression.

   $4 \times (2 \times 3)$ ____ $(4 \times 2) \times 3$ ____ $(4 \times 3) \times 2$ ____

8. Did you get the same answer each time? ____

Vocabulary
Distributive Property

▶ The Distributive Property

These arrays and equations show the **Distributive Property**.

9. How would you explain the word *distribute* as it
   relates to these equations?

   _____

4 threes + 4 twos = 4 fives
(4 × 3) + (4 × 2) = 4 × (3 + 2)

Multiplication can *distribute* over addition from the left or from
the right.

Left: 8 × (5 + 2) = (8 × 5) + (8 × 2)   **Right:** (5 + 2) × 8 = (5 × 8) + (2 × 8)

10. Are the two sides equal? _____

Write each problem with *one pair* of parentheses, then solve.

11. (6 × 3) + (6 × 4) = _____   12. (2 × 8) + (7 × 8) = _____

13. (9 × 5) + (9 × 2) = _____   14. (9 × 6) + (3 × 6) = _____

▶ Applications

**Write the property of multiplication that best describes each
situation.**

15. Roberto did not know the answer to
    13 × 5, so he found 10 fives and
    then added 3 more fives
    (10 × 5) + (3 × 5).

    _____

16. Ethan discovered that a rectangle
    with sides that are 6 inches by
    7 inches has the same area as a
    rectangle with sides that are 7 inches
    by 6 inches.

    _____

17. Matty wants to find out how many
    outfits she can make with 4 pairs of
    jeans, 5 sweaters, and 2 shirts. She
    discovers that she can group these
    numbers in any order and still get
    the same answer:
    (4 × 5) × 2 or 4 × (5 × 2)
    or (4 × 2) × 5.

    _____

Vocabulary
example
counterexample

► Examples and Counterexamples

Commutative Property: $a \times b = b \times a$

Write an example to support or a counterexample to disprove each statement.

18. Is addition commutative? Why or why not?

_____

19. Is subtraction commutative? Why or why not?

_____

20. Is division commutative? Why or why not?

_____

Associative Property: $(a \times b) \times c = a \times (b \times c)$

21. Is addition associative? Why or why not?

_____

22. Is subtraction associative? Why or why not?

_____

23. Is division associative? Why or why not?

_____

Distributive Property: $a \times (b + c) = (a \times b) + (a \times c)$

24. Is multiplication distributive over subtraction?
    Why or why not?

_____

25. Is multiplication distributive over division? Why or why not?

_____

26. **Explain** Tell how the Identity Property of Addition
    and the Identity Property of Multiplication are alike and
    how they are different. Give an example of each.

Going Further

▶ Algebra Code

The letters of the alphabet are shown below. Each letter has a value.

a = 1	b = 2	c = 3	d = 4	e = 5	f = 6
g = 7	h = 8	i = 9	j = 10	k = 11	l = 12
m = 13	n = 14	o = 15	p = 16	q = 17	r = 18
s = 19	t = 20	u = 21	v = 22	w = 23	x = 24
		y = 25	z = 26		

1. Find the sum of the letters in the word *math*.

     m   *a*   *t*   *h*

   ____ + ____ + ____ + ____ = ____

2. Find the sum of the letters in the word *mathematics*.

     m   *a*   *t*   *h*   *e*   *m*   *a*   *t*   *i*   *c*   *s*

   ____ + ____ + ____ + ____ + ____ + ____ + ____ + ____ + ____ + ____ + ____

   The sum of the letters in the word mathematics is _____.

3. What is the sum of the letters:

   a. in your first name? _____

   b. in your last name? _____

   c. in your whole name? _____

4. Compare your answer for exercise 3c with the answers of your classmates.

   a. Which student's name has the greatest sum? _____

   b. Which student's name has the least sum? _____

   c. Which student's names have the same sum, or nearly the same sum? _____

5. Find the greatest and least possible sums for a two letter word.

Properties of Multiplication

Class Activity

▶ Math and Science

Strong winds can form during thunderstorms. If the conditions are right, these winds can develop into a swirling column of air called a funnel cloud. When a funnel cloud touches the ground, it is called a tornado.

The Fujita scale (F-scale) classifies tornados by their wind speeds. Tornados in classes F0 and F1 cause light to moderate damage. F2 and F3 tornados can cause severe damage. Less than 2 out of every 100 tornados, or 2%, are strong enough to totally flatten buildings. These tornados are in the F4 or F5 category.

Tornados often occur along a line of thunderstorms. During a strong storm system, a meteorologist recorded these tornado wind speeds.

F-scale Classifications	
Category	Wind Speed (in miles per hour)
F0	40–72
F1	73–112
F2	113–157
F3	158–206
F4	207–260
F5	260–318

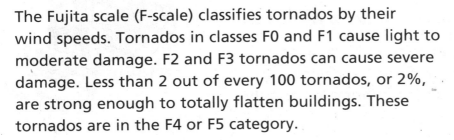

1. Organize this data in a table using the F-scale classifications.

_____

2. How many tornados were recorded in all? _____

3. How many tornados can be categorized as F0 or F1? Support your answer.

_____

_____

Suppose a large storm system generates 140 tornados. Assume that the ratio of F-scale classifications in this storm system is approximately the same as in the storm system on your chart.

4. How many of the tornados in this system would likely be classified as F2–F5? Explain your reasoning.

_____

► Rock Climbing Safety

Rock climbing is an exciting and dangerous sport. To protect climbers from falls, rock climbers usually work in pairs. A combination of camming devices, carabiners, and rope reduce how far a climber can fall if he or she slips. These devices limit a fall to about twice the distance a climber is from the last spot where a camming device was inserted.

Miguel and Cameron are preparing to climb to the top of a 75-foot peak. They will insert camming devices approximately every 20 feet. Use this information and the information above to solve these problems.

5. Will 3 camming devices be enough? How do you know?

_____

_____

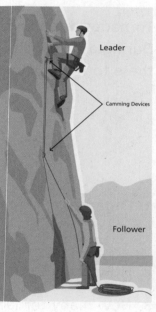

Leader

Camming Devices

Follower

6. They will need at least twice as much rope as the distance they will climb. Write and solve an equation to find the amount of rope they need.

_____

7. Cameron is the lead climber. She placed the second camming device and climbed about 10 more feet. Write and solve an equation to approximate the total distance Cameron has climbed so far.

_____

8. Suppose Cameron placed the third camming device, climbed about 5 feet, and then slipped. Write and solve an equation to show approximately how far she fell.

_____

9. When Cameron regains her footing after her fall, how much farther must she climb to reach the top of the peak? Use an expression to show how to solve the problem.

_____

Use Mathematical Processes

Name all the factor pairs for each number.

1. 10 _____   2. 15 _____

3. 21 _____   4. 16 _____

Complete each equation.

5. If $(5 \cdot 3) + (5 \cdot 4) = 35$, then $5(3 + 4) = $ _____.

6. If $A \times B = 132$, then $B \times A$ must $= $ _____.

Solve.

7. A roller coaster holds 28 people. There are 7 identical cars.
   How many people can ride in each car?

   _____

8. Dana made a rectangular quilt with 72 squares. There are 9 squares down.
   How many squares are there across?

   _____

9. A pancake shop serves 3 kinds of pancakes, 5 kinds of syrup,
   and 2 kinds of juice. How many different breakfast combinations
   are possible with one of each kind of item?

   _____

**For each function table, write the rule in words and as an equation.
Then complete the table.**

10.

Rule in Words							
Equation							
Input (*I*)	0	2	3	4		6
Output (*O*)	5	7	8		10	

11.

Rule in Words					
Equation					
Rides (*r*)	1	2		4	5
Tickets (*t*)	4	8	12		20

Name _____   **Date** _____

Solve each equation.

12. $3j = 24$

$j =$ _____

13. $90 = 10k$

$k =$ _____

14. $80 \cdot 0 = s$

$s =$ _____

15. $n = 24 - (7 \times 2)$

$n =$ _____

Use the Properties of Multiplication to solve for n.

16. $659 \times 1{,}357 = 1{,}357 \times n$

$n =$ _____

17. $(201 \times 340) \times 980 = n \times (340 \times 980)$

$n =$ _____

Solve.

Show your work.

18. Katie swam 3 lengths of the pool. Kurt swam twice as many lengths as Katie. Rosa swam 4 times as many lengths as Kurt. How many lengths did Rosa swim?

_____

19. Laura bought 3 yo-yos for 8 cents each and 4 whistles for 10 cents each. How much money did Laura spend?

_____

20. **Extended Response** Rolando wants to carpet the living room and dining room of his house. The living room is 10 yards by 6 yards. The dining room is 7 yards by 5 yards. How many square yards of carpet will Rolando need? Explain how you solved the problem. Write one equation that can be used to solve the problem.

_____

_____

_____

_____

_____

Class Activity

► Explore Metric Area

A rug is made of very small knots that each fill one **square millimeter**.

Vocabulary
square millimeter (sq mm)
square centimeter (sq cm)
square decimeter (sq dm)
square meter (sq m)

1. How many knots will the rug-makers have to tie to make one **square centimeter**?

_____

2. How many knots will the rug-makers have to tie to make one **square decimeter**?

_____

3. Last year the rug-makers made a square rug that was nine **square meters** in area. What was the length of each side?

_____

4. A year earlier the rug-makers made a rectangular rug that was 4 meters by 5 meters. What was the area of that rug?

_____

1 square millimeter

1 square centimeter

1 square decimeter

Class Activity

▶ Identify the Appropriate Unit

What metric unit is the most sensible unit for measuring each of the following?

5. the area of a postage stamp

_____

6. the length of a noodle

_____

7. the area of a tabletop

_____

8. the length of a ladybug

_____

9. the area of an envelope

_____

10. the length of a sidewalk

_____

Name an object you can measure using each of these units.

11. millimeter

_____

12. centimeter

_____

13. decimeter

_____

14. square millimeter

_____

15. square meter

_____

Family Letter

Dear Family,

Your child will be learning about geometry throughout the school year. This unit is about two kinds of measurement—perimeter and area. Perimeter is a measurement of length—the distance around a figure or an object. Area is a measurement of the amount of surface enclosed or covered by a figure or an object.

We measure area in square units, such as square inches or square centimeters.

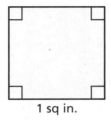

1 sq in.

1 sq cm

Your child will learn to calculate the area and perimeter of any rectangle, parallelogram, or triangle.

| **Rectangle** | **Parallelogram** | **Triangle** |
| 2 pairs of parallel sides right angles | 2 pairs of parallel sides no right angles | 3 sides |

Your child should continue to review and practice multiplications and divisions. Students will need to be very sure of these later in the year when they will learn more difficult concepts in multiplication and division.

If you have any questions or comments, please call or write to me.

Sincerely,
Your child's teacher

Calculating Perimeter and Area

Rectangle

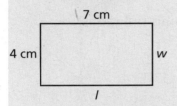

Perimeter = $2l + 2w$
Perimeter = $2 \times 7 + 2 \times 4$
Perimeter = $14 + 8 = 22$ cm

Area = $l \times w$
Area = 7×4
Area = 28 square centimeters or 28 cm^2

Parallelogram

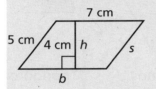

Perimeter = $2b + 2s$
Perimeter = $2 \times 7 + 2 \times 5$
Perimeter = $14 + 10 = 24$ cm

Area = $b \times h$
Area = 7×4
Area = 28 square centimeters or 28 cm^2

Triangle

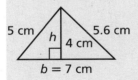

Perimeter = $s + s + s$
Perimeter = $5 + 7 + 5.6$
Perimeter = 17.6 cm

Area = $\frac{1}{2} b \times h$
Area = $\frac{1}{2} (7 \times 4)$
Area = 14 square centimeters or 14 cm^2

Square Units and Area **57**

Estimada familia:

Durante el año escolar, su niño aprenderá geometría. Esta unidad trata dos tipos de mediciones: perímetro y área. El perímetro es una medición de longitud: es la distancia que hay alrededor de una figura, o rodea a una figura o un objeto. El área es la medición de la superficie que cubre un objeto.

Medimos el área en unidades cuadradas, como pulgadas cuadradas o centímetros cuadrados.

1 pulgada cuadrada

1 centímetro cuadrado

Su niño aprenderá a calcular el área y el perímetro de cualquier rectángulo, paralelogramo o triángulo.

Rectángulo	**Paralelogramo**	**Triángulo**
2 pares de lados paralelos ángulos rectos	2 pares de lados paralelos no tiene ángulos rectos	3 lados

Su niño debe seguir repasando y practicando multiplicaciones y divisiones. Es importante que los estudiantes conozcan estas operaciones para que puedan aprender conceptos de multiplicación y división más difíciles en el transcurso del año.

Si tiene alguna pregunta o comentario, por favor comuníquese conmigo.

Atentamente,
El maestro de su niño

Calcular el perímetro y el área

Rectángulo

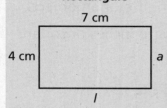

Perímetro = 2l + 2a
Perímetro = 2 × 7 + 2 × 4
Perímetro = 14 + 8 = 22 cm

Área = l × a
Área = 7 × 4
Área = 28 centímetros cuadrados ó 28 cm²

Parallelogram

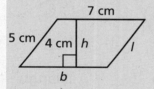

Perímetro = 2b + 2l
Perímetro = 2 × 7 + 2 × 5
Perímetro = 14 + 10 = 24 cm

Área = b × h
Área = 7 × 4
Área = 28 centímetros cuadrados ó 28 cm²

Triángulo

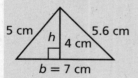

Perímetro = l + l + l
Perímetro = 5 + 7 + 5.6
Perímetro = 17.6 cm

Área = $\frac{1}{2}$ b × h
Área = $\frac{1}{2}$ (7 × 4)
Área = 14 centímetros cuadrados ó 14 cm²

Square Units and Area

Class Activity

Name _____   Date _____

▶ Formulas for Calculating Perimeter and Area

1. Look at the rectangles below.
   What does **perimeter** mean?
   What does **area** mean?

_____

_____

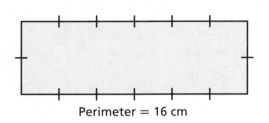

Perimeter = 16 cm

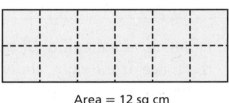

Area = 12 sq cm

On a separate sheet of paper, draw a rectangle for each
exercise 2-6. Mark each centimeter with a tick mark, and
write an equation that shows how to find the perimeter.
Then draw the **square centimeters** and write an equation
that shows how to find the area.

	Length	Width	Perimeter	Area
	6	2	6 + 6 + 2 + 2 = 16 cm	6 × 2 = 12 sq cm
2.	4	3		
3.	8	1		
4.	5	5		
5.	10	4		
6.	*l*	*w*		

The last row of the table should show your formulas for perimeter and area.

► Perimeter and Area of a Square

The figure at the right is a square. The length of one side of the square is given.

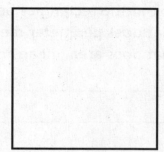

76 cm

7. Explain why you know the lengths of the other three sides of the square.

   _____

   _____

8. Perimeter is a measure of the distance around a figure. In the space at the right, show how addition can be used to find the perimeter of the square.

9. In the space at the right, show how multiplication can be used to find the perimeter.

10. **Discuss** To calculate the area of a rectangle, we find the product of two of its adjacent sides. Why can this formula also be used to find the area of a square?

11. In the space at the right, calculate the area of the square.

Solve.

12. How does doubling the each dimension of a rectangle that is not a square affect the perimeter and the area of that rectangle? Give an example to support your answer.

   _____

   _____

13. How does doubling the each dimension of a square affect the perimeter and the area of that square? Give an example to support your answer.

   _____

   _____

Class Activity

▶ Practice Finding Perimeter and Area

14. Write your perimeter formula and your area formula.

_____

Find the perimeter and the area of these rectangles.

15.

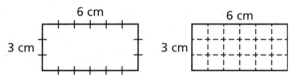

6 cm

3 cm

6 cm

3 cm

P = _____

A = _____

16.

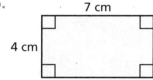

7 cm

4 cm

P = _____

A = _____

17.

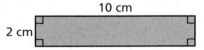

10 cm

2 cm

P = _____

A = _____

18.

8 cm

1 cm

P = _____

A = _____

19. Stephen drew a picture of his sister. It was 8 centimeters long and 5 centimeters wide. He wants to make a frame out of colored tape to put around the picture. How much tape will he need?

_____

20. Mu Lan wants new carpet for her bedroom. The room is 6 yards long and 5 yards wide. How many square yards of carpet will she need?

_____

21. The Webers want to build a patio that is 5 tiles long and 3 tiles wide. They want the patio to have an equal number of dark tiles and light tiles. Will their plan work? Why or why not?

_____

_____

Name _____   **Date** _____

▶ Add and Subtract Metric Units

22. Discuss A rectangle is measured in centimeters, and its perimeter is greater than 100 centimeters.

If the perimeter is written as a number of meters and centimeters, how many meters will be in the answer? Explain how you know.

Complete.

23. 1 m = _____ cm   **24.** 500 cm = _____ m   **25.** 3 m = _____ cm

Find the perimeter of each rectangle. Write each of your answers as a number of meters and centimeters.

26.

```
        2 m  80 cm
┌──────────────────────┐
│                      │ 90 cm
│                      │
└──────────────────────┘
```

P = _____ m _____ cm

27.

P = _____ m _____ cm

Solve.

28. In exercise 26, the sides of the rectangle are not the same length. How much longer is the longest side?

_____ m _____ cm

29. A garden in Trey's back yard is rectangular. The length of the garden is 2 m 60 cm greater than its width. The width of the garden is 3 m 75 cm.

What is the length of the garden? _____ m _____ cm

What is the perimeter of the garden? _____ m _____ cm

30. Discuss The same number is written to represent the perimeter and the area of a square. The only difference is that one number is labeled *units* and the other number is labeled *square units*.

What is the length of one side of the square?

_____

Perimeter and Area of Rectangles

► Estimate Area and Perimeter of an Irregular Figure

Estimate the area and perimeter of each figure.

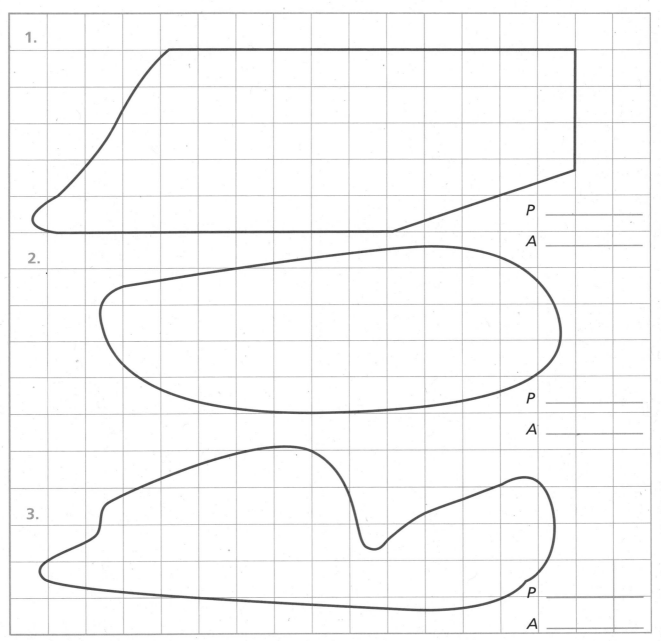

1.

P _____

A _____

2.

P _____

A _____

3.

P _____

A _____

On the Back Draw two rectangles with the same perimeter but different areas. Then draw two rectangles with the same area but different perimeters. Label your work.

Perimeter and Area of Rectangles

Class Activity

Name _____ **Date** _____

▶ Define Kinds of Angles and Triangles

Look at the angles. Describe a right angle, an acute angle, and an obtuse angle. _____

_____

_____

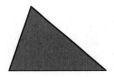

Acute angle   Right angle   Obtuse angle   Acute angle   Obtuse angle

We can name triangles for the size of their angles in three ways:

Acute triangle   Right triangle   Obtuse triangle

Answer the questions about the triangles above.

1. Can a triangle have more than one acute angle?

   _____

2. Can a triangle have more than one right angle?

   _____

3. Can a triangle have more than one obtuse angle?

   _____

4. If you put two identical right triangles together so that the longest sides touch, what figure do you form?

   _____

5. If you put two identical acute triangles or obtuse triangles together so that the longest sides touch, what figure do you form?

   _____

► Perimeter and Area of a Right Triangle

6. What is the area of the rectangle shown here?

_____

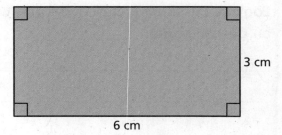
3 cm

6 cm

7. Draw a diagonal line and make two triangles.
   What is the area of each triangle?
   Why do you think so?

_____

_____

A triangle with a right angle (square corner) is called a
right triangle. Any right triangle is half of a rectangle.

What is the area of each right triangle shown below?

8.
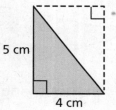
5 cm
4 cm

9.
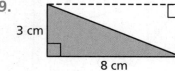
3 cm
8 cm

10.
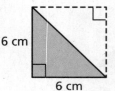
6 cm
6 cm

_____   _____   _____

**To show that a triangle is a right triangle, mark the right angle
with a small box. Find the area of each right triangle below.**

11.
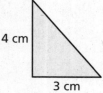
4 cm
3 cm

12.
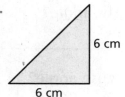
6 cm
6 cm

13.
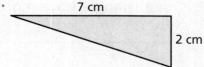
7 cm
2 cm

_____   _____   _____

14. This right triangle has sides of length a, b, and c.
    Write a formula for the area of any right triangle.

_____

15. Write a formula for the perimeter of any triangle.

_____

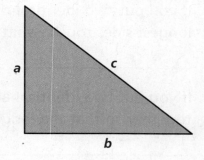
a
c
b

► Experiment with Parallelograms

The **height** of a **parallelogram** is a line segment that is **perpendicular** to the **base**.

Cut out each pair of parallelograms below and then cut along the dotted line that shows each height. Switch the pieces. Put the slanted ends together.

What figure do you form?

_____

Do you think it will always happen? Why or why not?

_____

16.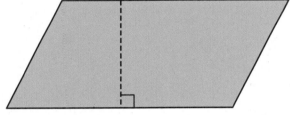

17.

18.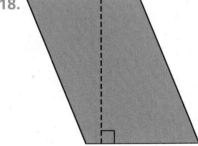

19.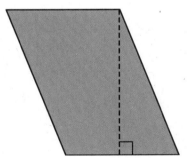

20.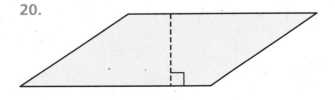

21.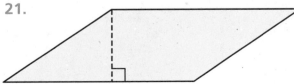

Area of Right Triangles and Parallelograms

Class Activity

▶ Find the Area of a Parallelogram

This parallelogram has height h. The measure of the base is b. The other side is s.

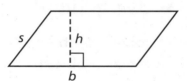

22. Write a formula for finding the area of the parallelogram.

_____

23. What measurement shown is not used for finding its area?

_____

24. Write a formula to find the perimeter of the parallelogram.

_____

25. What measurement shown is not used for finding its perimeter? _____

Find the area and perimeter of each parallelogram.

26.

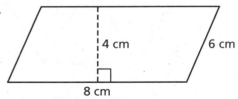

4 cm   6 cm
8 cm

$A =$ _____

$P =$ _____

27.

5 cm   6 cm
4 cm

$A =$ _____

$P =$ _____

28.

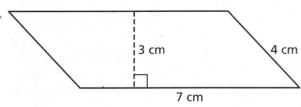

3 cm   4 cm
7 cm

$A =$ _____

$P =$ _____

29.

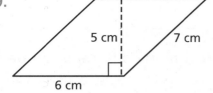

5 cm   7 cm
6 cm

$A =$ _____

$P =$ _____

30.

1 cm   2 cm
9 cm

$A =$ _____

$P =$ _____

31.

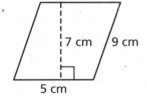

7 cm   9 cm
5 cm

$A =$ _____

$P =$ _____

Going Further

Name _____ **Date** _____

► Use a Simpler Problem

To solve a problem, sometimes you can think about a simpler problem.

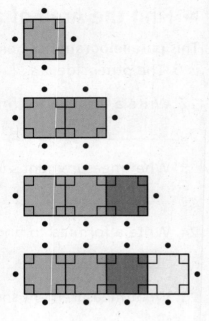

1. A restaurant has square tables that seat one person on each side. For large groups, they push tables together in a single row.

   How many tables will they need to seat a group of 36 people? _____
   Hint: Start with four people and one table and look for a pattern.

2. These three triangles are made from toothpicks. How many toothpicks do you need to make a row of 15 triangles?

   _____

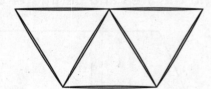

3. The inside of a bookshelf is 59 in. high. The five shelves in it are equally spaced and each shelf is 1 in. thick. What is the tallest book you can put on a shelf?

   _____

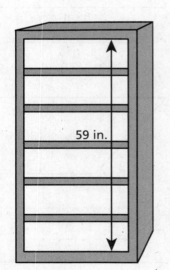

59 in.

4. How many different numbers can you make with the digits 1, 2, 3, and 4, using each digit only once?

   _____

Challenge

5. What is the greatest rectangular area you can completely enclose with 100 feet of fencing? Explain.

   _____

Area of Right Triangles and Parallelograms

Class Activity

Name	Date

▶ Experiment with Triangles

The acute triangles below are exactly the same. Cut them out and place sides *a* together. What shape do you form? Do the same with sides *b* and *c*.

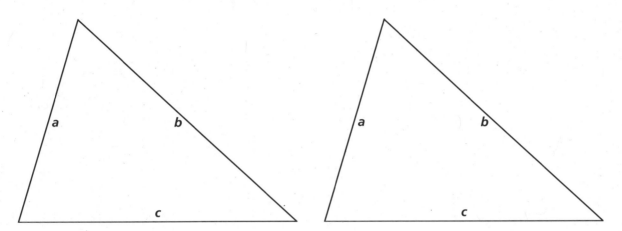

The obtuse triangles below are exactly the same. Cut them out and place sides *x* together. What shape do you form? Do the same with sides *y* and *z*.

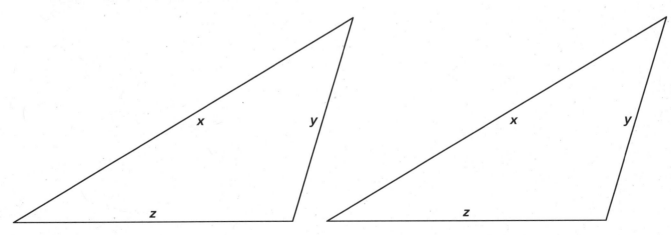

Name _____   Date _____

▶ Calculate the Area of a Triangle

Answer the following.

1. How does the **area** of the shaded triangle compare to the area of the parallelogram?

   _____

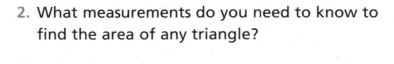

2. What measurements do you need to know to find the area of any triangle?

   _____

   _____

3. Write a formula for the area of any triangle.

   _____

The parallelogram and the shaded triangle shown here both have a **base** of 4 cm and a **height** of 3 cm.

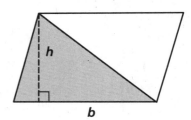

4. What is the area of the parallelogram?

   _____

5. What is the area of the triangle?

   _____

The height of a triangle is a line segment drawn from a vertex perpendicular to the base. Sometimes the base has to be extended.

Point *A* is a **vertex** of triangle *ADC*.

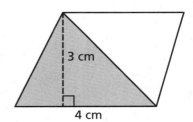

6. Which line segment shows the height of triangle *ADC*? _____

7. Which line segment shows the height of triangle *XYZ*?

   _____

8. How are the heights of acute, obtuse, and right triangles alike and different?

   _____

   _____

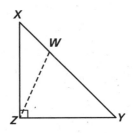

Class Activity

Find the area of each triangle below.
What kind of triangle is each?

9.

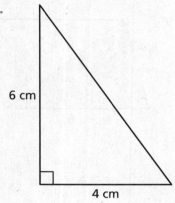

6 cm

4 cm

_____

10.

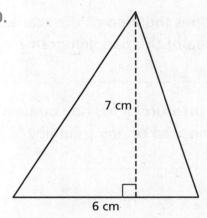

7 cm

6 cm

_____

11.

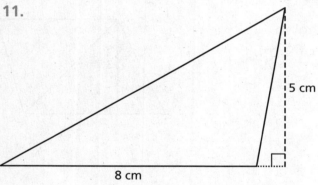

5 cm

8 cm

_____

12.

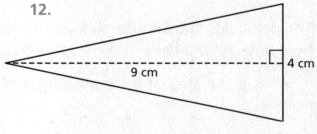

9 cm

4 cm

_____

13.

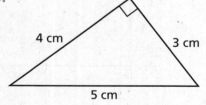

4 cm

3 cm

5 cm

_____

14.

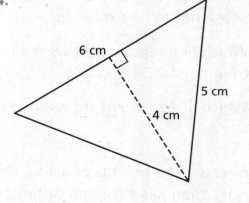

6 cm

5 cm

4 cm

_____

The Area of Any Triangle

Class Activity

▶ Draw Parallelograms and Triangles

Answer the following questions about triangle *ABC*.

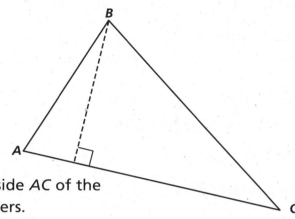

15. Measure and label side *AC* of the triangle in centimeters.

16. Measure and label the height.

17. What is the area of the triangle?

_____

18. Use your ruler to draw a line segment through *B* that looks parallel to *AC*.

19. Draw a line segment through *C* that looks parallel to *AB*. Label point *D* where the two new lines meet.

20. What is the area of parallelogram *ABDC*?

_____

21. Use the directions in exercises 15–20 for this obtuse triangle.

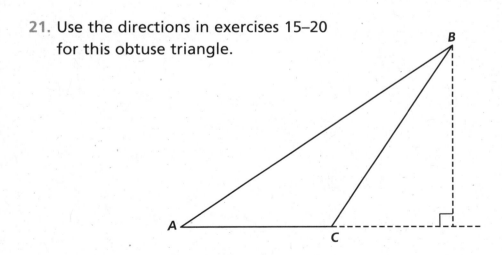

Complete.

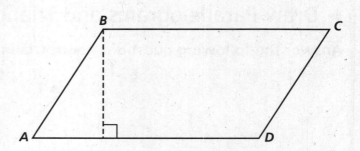

22. Measure and label side *AD*.

23. Measure and label the height.

24. What is the area of parallelogram *ABCD*?

_____

25. Join points *B* and *D*. Name the two triangles.

_____

26. What is the area of each triangle?

_____

27. What kind of triangles did you make in exercise 25?

_____

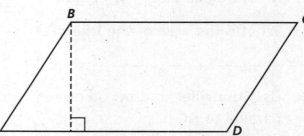

28. Divide parallelogram *ABCD* into two obtuse triangles.

29. What is the area of each obtuse triangle?

_____

30. Draw 2 different diagonals for parallelogram *EFGH*. Name the triangles. Measure, then find the area of each triangle.

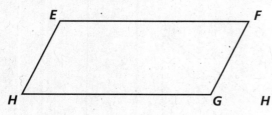 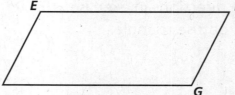

_____

_____

Vocabulary

dimensions

▶ Select Appropriate Measurements

Discuss the **dimensions** you need to find the perimeter of
a triangle.

Figure A

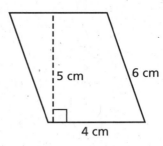

Figure B

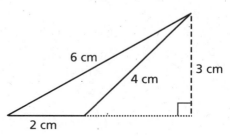

Figure C

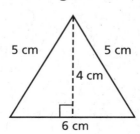

Find the perimeter of each triangle.

1. Figure A _____   2. Figure B _____   3. Figure C _____

Discuss the dimensions you need to find the area of a triangle.
Find the area of each triangle.

4. Figure A _____   5. Figure B _____   6. Figure C _____

Discuss the dimensions you need to find the perimeter and area of
a parallelogram.

Figure D

Figure E

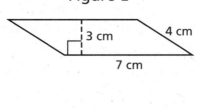

Figure F

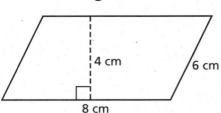

Find the perimeter of each parallelogram.

7. Figure D _____   8. Figure E _____   9. Figure F_____

Find the area of each parallelogram.

10. Figure D _____   11. Figure E _____   12. Figure F _____

Class Activity

▶ Practice Finding Perimeter and Area

Find the perimeter and the area of each figure.

13.

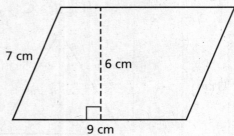

P = _____

A = _____

14.

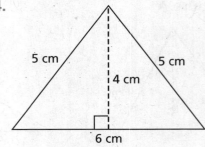

P = _____

A = _____

15.

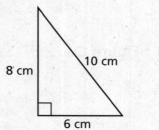

P = _____

A = _____

16.

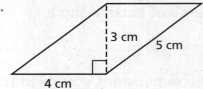

P = _____

A = _____

17.

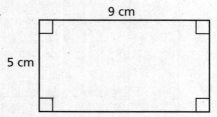

P = _____

A = _____

18.

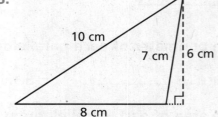

P = _____

A = _____

Consolidate Perimeter and Area

Vocabulary

complex figures
pentagon

▶ **Visualize Figures**

19. Find the area of the triangle.

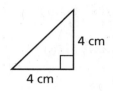

4 cm

4 cm

_____

20. Find the area of the rectangle.

_____

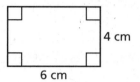

4 cm

6 cm

21. Find the area of the complex figure.

_____

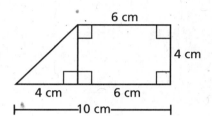

6 cm

4 cm

4 cm   6 cm

10 cm

▶ **Find Area and Perimeter of Complex Figures**

Find the area and perimeter of these complex figures .

22.

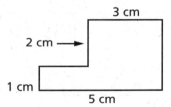

3 cm

2 cm →

1 cm

5 cm

P = _____

A = _____

23.

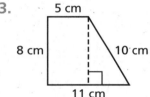

5 cm

8 cm   10 cm

11 cm

P = _____

A = _____

24.

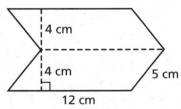

4 cm

4 cm   5 cm

12 cm

P = _____

A = _____

25.

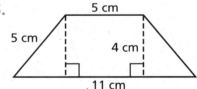

5 cm

5 cm   4 cm

11 cm

P = _____

A = _____

Challenge

26. Vadim needs to know the area of this **pentagon**, so he calls his friend Serena. Serena says she can figure out the area if Vadim will make just three measurements. Which three measurements does Vadim need to make?

_____

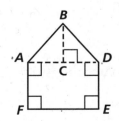

B

A   D

C

F   E

Vocabulary

hexagon
isosceles triangle

▶ Area of a Regular Pentagon

27. How many congruent isosceles triangles
are inside the regular pentagon?

_____

28. Measure the base and the height of the
isosceles triangle to the nearest centimeter.

_____

29. What is the area of the triangle?

_____

30. What is the area of the pentagon?

_____

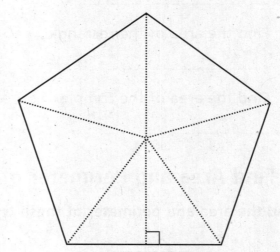

▶ Area of a Regular Hexagon

31. Estimate the area of the regular
hexagon by finding the area of the
isosceles triangle. Show your work.

_____

_____

_____

_____

_____

_____

_____

_____

32. What is the area of the hexagon *ABCDEF*?

_____

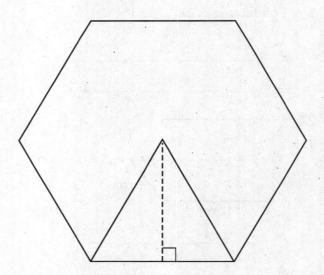

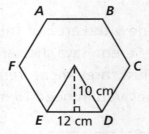

Consolidate Perimeter and Area

Class Activity

Vocabulary

inch (in.)
foot (ft)
yard (yd)
1 ft = 12 in.
1 yd = 3 ft
    = 36 in.

► Convert Units

The **inch** (in.), **foot** (ft), and **yard** (yd) are commonly used units of measure in the Customary System of Measurement.

Complete.

1. 24 in. = _____ ft

2. 24 ft = _____ yd

3. 12 ft = _____ in.

4. _____ in. = 5 ft

5. _____ ft = 6 yd

6. 12 yd = _____ ft

7. 72 in. = _____ yd

8. _____ in. = 3 yd

9. 10 yd = _____ in.

► Calculate Perimeter

Calculate the perimeter of each figure in feet.

10.

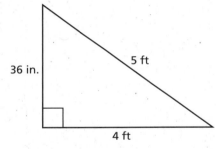

36 in.   5 ft   4 ft

11.

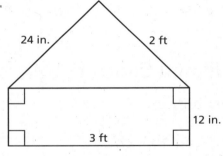

24 in.   2 ft   3 ft   12 in.

Calculate the perimeter of each figure in yards.

12.

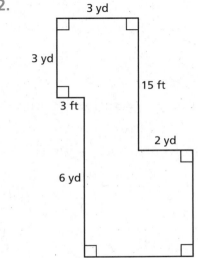

3 yd   3 yd   15 ft   3 ft   2 yd   6 yd

13.

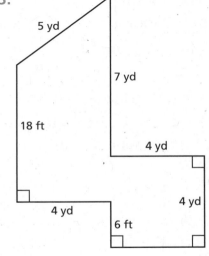

5 yd   7 yd   18 ft   4 yd   4 yd   4 yd   6 ft

Class Activity

Name _____ Date _____

► **Convert Compound Units**

A compound unit is a measurement that contains two different units. For example, if your height were measured in feet and inches, the measurement would be a compound unit.

Convert these units.

14. 1 yd = _____ ft

15. 1 ft = _____ in.

16. 1 yd = _____ in.

17. 2 ft 6 in. = _____ in.

18. 5 yd 2 ft = _____ ft

19. 3 yd 3 in. = _____ in.

20. 9 yd 1 ft = _____ ft

21. 4 yd 10 in. = _____ in.

22. 6 ft 5 in. = _____ in.

23. 12 in. = _____ ft

24. 3 ft = _____ yd

25. 36 in. = _____ yd

26. 19 ft = _____ yd _____ ft

27. 84 in. = _____ yd _____ ft

28. 54 in. = _____ ft _____ in.

29. 45 in. = _____ yd _____ in.

30. 99 in. = _____ ft _____ in.

31. 32 ft = _____ yd _____ in.

► **Add and Subtract Units of Length**

Add or subtract.

32.
  7 feet 10 inches
+ 3 feet 5 inches
———————————
  _____ feet _____ inches

33.
  9 yards 2 inches
− 5 yards 8 inches
———————————
  _____ yards _____ inches

34.
  2 yards 2 feet
+ 4 yards 6 feet
———————————
  _____ yards _____ feet

35.
  8 feet 3 inches
− 4 feet 9 inches
———————————
  _____ feet _____ inches

36.
  6 yards 10 inches
+ 2 yards 30 inches
———————————
  _____ yards _____ inches

37.
  10 yards 1 feet
− 3 yards 2 feet
———————————
  _____ yards _____ feet

38. Beth is 5 feet 3 inches tall. Her best friend is 4 feet 11 inches tall. How many inches taller is Beth?

_____

39. In a long jump competition, Ty jumped 13 feet 2 inches. How many inches farther than 4 yards did he jump?

_____

Customary Units of Length

Class Activity

Vocabulary

square foot
square yard

▶ **Calculate Area**

Calculate the area of each figure in **square feet**.

40.

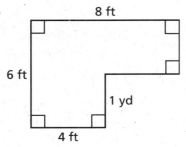

_____

41.

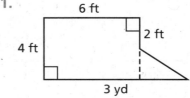

_____

Calculate the area of each figure in **square yards**.

42.

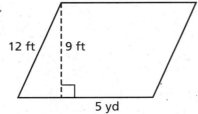

_____

43.

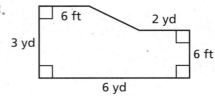

_____

Solve. Draw a picture if you need to.

44. A right triangle has sides of 4 ft, 5 ft, and 1 yd.
    What is its perimeter in feet?

    _____

    What is its area in square feet?

    _____

45. A parallelogram has a height of 2 ft and sides
    of 1 yd and 48 in.
    What is its perimeter in feet?

    _____

    What is its area in square feet?

    _____

▶ Use Paces to Estimate

46. Work with a partner to complete the first two rows of the table.
Use data collected by your classmates to complete the remaining rows.

Pair		Number of Paces	Length of a Pace	Estimate of Classroom
1	Width:			
	Length:			
2	Width:			
	Length:			
3	Width:			
	Length:			

▶ Measure Real-World Objects

47. Choose five different objects from your classroom. Complete the table below by estimating the length of each object to the nearest whole inch. Then measure to the nearest $\frac{1}{2}$, $\frac{1}{4}$, and $\frac{1}{8}$ inch.

Object	Estimate	Measure		
	to the nearest whole inch	to the nearest $\frac{1}{2}$ inch	to the nearest $\frac{1}{4}$ inch	to the nearest $\frac{1}{8}$ inch

Find the perimeter and area of each figure.

1.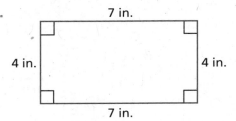

Perimeter _____

Area _____

2.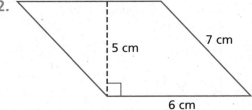

Perimeter _____

Area _____

3.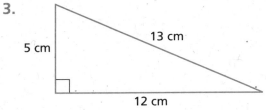

Perimeter _____

Area _____

4.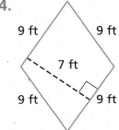

Perimeter _____

Area _____

Harry's room is 4 meters long by 3 meters wide. Solve the problems about his room.

Show your work.

5. Harry's mother wants to buy carpeting to cover the whole floor of his room. How many square meters of carpeting does she need?

_____

6. Harry wants to put a string of little lights all the way around his room near the ceiling. How many meters of lights does he need to have?

_____

Name _____   Date _____

Find the perimeter and area of each figure.

7.

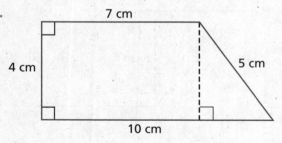

8.

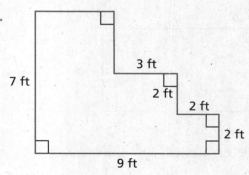

Perimeter _____

Area _____

Perimeter _____

Area _____

Show your work.

Solve.

9. A parallelogram has a height of 4 meters and sides of 5 meters and 7 meters. What is its area in square meters?

_____

10. **Extended Response** Gina is framing a picture that is 9 in. wide and 10 in. high. She has 3 ft of framing material. Does she have enough material to frame the picture? Explain your answer.
    (Remember: 1 ft = 12 in.)

_____

_____

_____

_____

_____

_____

Class Activity

► Discuss Fractions and Decimals

Fractions and decimals are special kinds of numbers. They tell the number of equal parts a whole is divided into, and the number of those parts that are being taken or described.

Fraction notation shows a whole divided into any number of equal parts.

1.   1 Whole [ ]

4 equal parts [| | |]

$\frac{1}{4} + \frac{1}{4} + \frac{1}{4} + \frac{1}{4}$

1 part [▨ | | |] $\frac{1}{4}$

1 of 4 equal parts

2.   1 Whole [ ]

5 equal parts [| | | |]

$\frac{1}{5} + \frac{1}{5} + \frac{1}{5} + \frac{1}{5} + \frac{1}{5}$

3 parts [▨ ▨ ▨ | |] $\frac{3}{5}$

3 of 5 equal parts

Decimal notation shows places to the right of the ones place. The tenths place shows 1 whole (such as a dollar) divided into 10 equal parts. The hundredths place shows each tenth divided into 10 equal parts.

3.

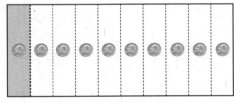

$\frac{1}{10}$ 1 of 10 equal parts

$ 0.10 one dime or one tenth of a dollar

0.1   1 in the tenths place

4.

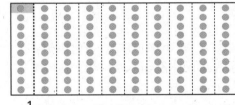

$\frac{1}{100}$ 1 of 100 equal parts

$0.01   one penny or one-hundredth of a dollar

0.01   1 in the hundredths place

The thousandths place shows each hundredth divided into 10 equal parts.

5.

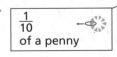

$\frac{1}{10}$ of a penny

$\frac{1}{1,000}$ 1 of 1,000 equal parts

$0.001 one-tenth of penny or one-thousandth of a dollar

0.001 1 in the thousandths place

► Decimals as Equal Parts of Sets

Decimal numbers are read as if they are fractions.

$\frac{37}{100}$ and 0.37 are both said as thirty-seven hundredths.

Write each fraction as a decimal number, and then say the number.

6. $\frac{7}{100}$ _____

7. $\frac{16}{100}$ _____

8. $\frac{4}{10}$ _____

9. $\frac{9}{10}$ _____

10. $\frac{5}{1,000}$ _____

11. $\frac{54}{1,000}$ _____

12. $\frac{81}{100}$ _____

13. $\frac{409}{1,000}$ _____

14. $\frac{2}{10}$ _____

15. $\frac{3}{100}$ _____

16. $\frac{16}{1,000}$ _____

17. $\frac{67}{100}$ _____

18. Discuss the patterns you can see in the exercises above. Then write how to say any decimal number.

_____

_____

Solve.

Show your work.

19. If you cut a lemon into 10 equal pieces, what decimal number would 3 pieces represent?

_____

20. A bag of pretzels contains 100 pretzels. What decimal number would 28 pretzels represent? What decimal number would 5 pretzels represent?

_____

21. A beehive is home to 1,000 bees. If 235 bees are out gathering pollen, what decimal number do those bees represent?

_____

22. What decimal number is represented by answering 92 of 100 test questions correctly?

_____

Decimals as Equal Divisions

► Visualize with Other Models

1. The bar below represents one whole or 1.

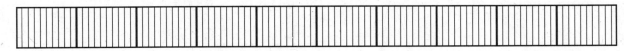

   a. Shade 6 tenths and then shade 2 hundredths.

   b. **Discuss** Why does the drawing show $0.6 + 0.02 = 0.60 + 0.02 = 0.62$?

2. The number line below is labeled by tenths from 0 to 1.

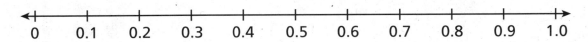

   a. Begin at 0 and circle a distance to show $0.28 = 0.2 + 0.08 = 0.20 + 0.08$.

   b. Circle a new distance to show $0.74 = 0.70 + 0.04 = 0.7 + 0.04$.

3. Shade the grids to show each amount.

   a. $0.4 = 0.40$ **b.** $0.36 = 0.3 + 0.06$ **c.** 0.001

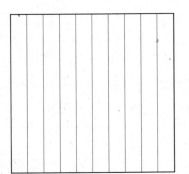 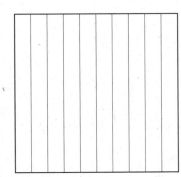 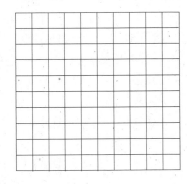

4. Use a sketch of money, a bar representing one whole,
   a number line, or one or more grids to prove that each
   statement below is true.

   a. $0.3 = 0.30$ **b.** $0.070 = 0.07$

5. **Discuss** Explain why writing zeros to the right of a decimal
   number does not change the value of the number.

Class Activity

► Practice Comparisons

We can use Secret-Code Cards to compare decimal numbers.
For example, these cards show that 0.4 > 0.09 and 0.09 > 0.007.

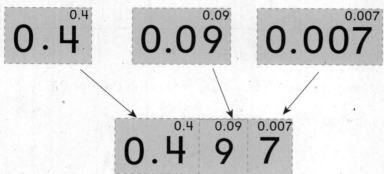

We can also use dimes to represent tenths and pennies
to represent hundredths to show that a dime is greater
than a penny and a penny is greater than a tenth of
a penny.

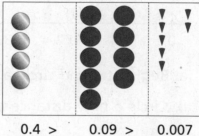

0.4 >   0.09 >   0.007

**Choose any method and use it to complete the following
comparisons. Write >, <, or =.**

6. 0.7 ◯ 0.700   7. 0.070 ◯ 0.07   8. 0.07 ◯ 0.7   9. 0.007 ◯ 0.7

10. 0.8 ◯ 0.62   11. 0.06 ◯ 0.3   12. 0.475 ◯ 0.62   13. 0.3 ◯ 0.29

14. 0.38 ◯ 0.038   15. 0.4 ◯ 0.38   16. 0.38 ◯ 0.380   17. 0.7 ◯ 0.71

18. 0.50 ◯ 0.5   19. 0.21 ◯ 0.2   20. 0.111 ◯ 0.11   21. 0.4 ◯ 0.404

22. Describe a method for comparing decimal numbers.

_____

_____

23. Describe something you must be careful about whenever you
compare decimal numbers.

_____

_____

► Decimal Secret Code Cards

0.1	0.01
0.1	0.0 1
0.2	0.02
0.2	0.0 2
0.3	0.03
0.3	0.0 3
0.4	0.04
0.4	0.0 4
0.5	0.05
0.5	0.0 5
0.6	0.06
0.6	0.0 6
0.7	0.07
0.7	0.0 7
0.8	0.08
0.8	0.0 8
0.9	0.09
0.9	0.0 9

.0 0
.0 0
.0 0
.0 0
> <

Class Activity

► **Decimal Secret Code Cards**

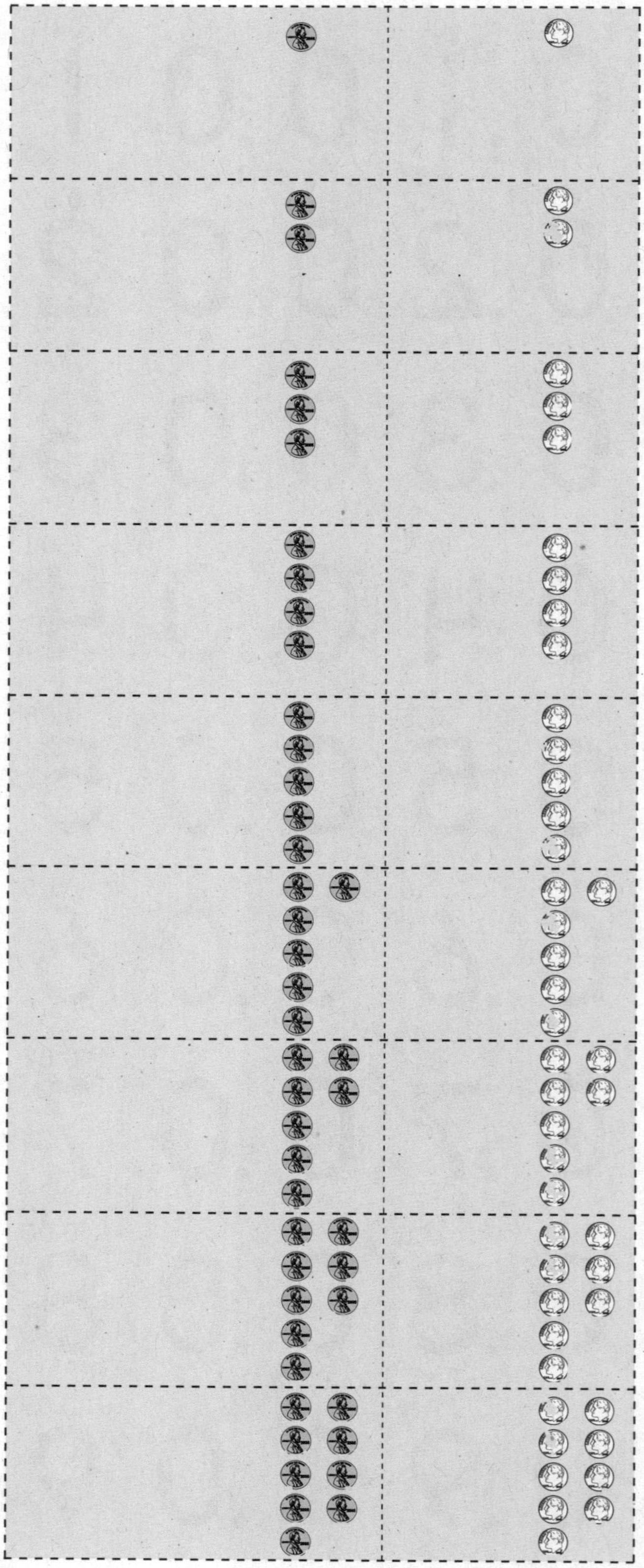

> <

Decimal Secret Code Cards

▶ Decimal Secret Code Cards

1,000				0.001
1,	0	0	0	0.001
2,000				0.002
2,	0	0	0	0.002
3,000				0.003
3,	0	0	0	0.003
4,000				0.004
4,	0	0	0	0.004
5,000				0.005
5,	0	0	0	0.005
6,000				0.006
6,	0	0	0	0.006
7,000				0.007
7,	0	0	0	0.007
8,000				0.008
8,	0	0	0	0.008
9,000				0.009
9,	0	0	0	0.009

0 0 0 0.
0 0 0.
0 0.
0.

Name _____ Date _____

► Decimal Secret Code Cards

	$1,000

	$1,000
	$1,000

	$1,000
	$1,000
	$1,000

	$1,000
	$1,000
	$1,000
	$1,000

	$1,000
	$1,000
	$1,000
	$1,000
	$1,000

	$1,000	$1,000
	$1,000	
	$1,000	
	$1,000	
	$1,000	

	$1,000	$1,000
	$1,000	$1,000
	$1,000	
	$1,000	
	$1,000	

	$1,000	$1,000
	$1,000	$1,000
	$1,000	$1,000
	$1,000	
	$1,000	

	$1,000	$1,000
	$1,000	$1,000
	$1,000	$1,000
	$1,000	$1,000
	$1,000	

Class Activity

Name _____ Date _____

► The Place Value Parade

Discuss the patterns you see in the Place Value Parade below.

← × 10 (Larger) **Place Value Parade** ÷ 10 (Smaller) →

Thousands	Hundreds	Tens	ONES	Tenths	Hundredths	Thousandths
1,000.	100.	10.	1.	0.1	0.01	0.001
$\frac{1,000}{1}$	$\frac{100}{1}$	$\frac{10}{1}$	$\frac{1}{1}$	$\frac{1}{10}$	$\frac{1}{100}$	$\frac{1}{1,000}$
$1,000.00	$100.00	$10.00	$1	$0.10	$0.01	$0.001

Use your Secret-Code Cards to make numbers on the frame.

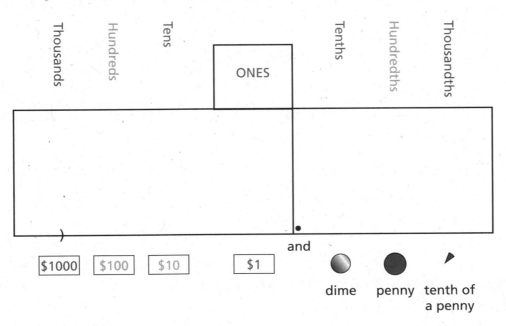

▶ Thousands to Thousandths

Write each mixed number as a decimal number, and then say it.

1. $7\frac{31}{100}$ _____

2. $4\frac{3}{100}$ _____

3. $435\frac{237}{1,000}$ _____

4. $78\frac{6}{10}$ _____

Write each decimal number as a mixed number, and then say it.

5. 6.04 _____

6. 39.7 _____

7. 92.038 _____

8. 717.46 _____

Write each as a whole or decimal number.

9. 4 tens _____

4 tenths _____

10. 67 hundredths _____

67 hundred _____

11. 7 thousand _____

7 thousandths _____

12. Explain a way to remember that tenths are larger than hundredths.

_____

_____

Compare. Write >, <, or =.

13. 82 ◯ 28

14. 103 ◯ 97

15. 749 ◯ 1,020

16. 478 ◯ 523

17. 6.3 ◯ 7

18. 21 ◯ 19.75

19. 38.4 ◯ 39

20. 5.3 ◯ 5.30

21. 7.04 ◯ 7.4

22. 64.20 ◯ 64.2

23. 15.07 ◯ 15.7

24. 0.04 ◯ 0.040

25. Write the numbers shown below in order from least to greatest.

0.007   1.5   0.03   1.09 _____

26. Write the numbers shown below in order from greatest to least.

4.026   4.133   4.2   4.101   4.1 _____

► **Secret Code Cards**

100	10	1
100	**10**	**1**
200	20	2
200	**20**	**2**
300	30	3
300	**30**	**3**
400	40	4
400	**40**	**4**
500	50	5
500	**50**	**5**
600	60	6
600	**60**	**6**
700	70	7
700	**70**	**7**
800	80	8
800	**80**	**8**
900	90	9
900	**90**	**9**

► Secret Code Cards

$1	$10	$100

$1	$10	$100
$1	$10	$100

$1	$10	$100
$1	$10	$100
$1	$10	$100

$1	$10	$100
$1	$10	$100
$1	$10	$100
$1	$10	$100

$1	$10	$100
$1	$10	$100
$1	$10	$100
$1	$10	$100
$1	$10	$100

$1	$1	$10	$10	$100	$100
$1		$10		$100	
$1		$10		$100	
$1		$10		$100	
$1		$10		$100	

$1	$1	$10	$10	$100	$100
$1	$1	$10	$10	$100	$100
$1		$10		$100	
$1		$10		$100	
$1		$10		$100	

$1	$1	$10	$10	$100	$100
$1	$1	$10	$10	$100	$100
$1	$1	$10	$10	$100	$100
$1		$10		$100	
$1		$10		$100	

$1	$1	$10	$10	$100	$100
$1	$1	$10	$10	$100	$100
$1	$1	$10	$10	$100	$100
$1	$1	$10	$10	$100	$100
$1		$10		$100	

Dear Family,

Your child has studied addition and subtraction with whole numbers and decimals in past years. Unit 3 of *Math Expressions* guides students as they study these topics in greater depth.

The main goals of this unit are

1. to help students extend their understanding of place value to include large numbers and decimals;
2. to help students add and subtract decimals and whole numbers;
3. to develop estimating and rounding skills as students engage in graphing activities;
4. to have students apply place-value concepts in a variety of real-world situations.

Students will extend and apply their knowledge of place value as they complete activities involving money and metric lengths. When the opportunity arises, ask your child questions about money amounts to help reinforce what is being taught in class.

To accomplish the second goal, students will use various methods of grouping. Students may use whatever method they prefer as long as they understand why it works and can explain it. To add and subtract accurately, students need to align the digits of whole numbers and decimals correctly. Observe your child as he or she adds and subtracts. Help align the digits when necessary.

The third goal is accomplished in several ways. Students will learn to use the scale on a graph to understand how to round a number. For example, they see that a number such as 3,879 is between 3,000 and 4,000, but closer to 4,000. So, 3,879 rounded to the nearest thousand is 4,000. Students will also be taught a method of *safe estimating* to prepare them for real-world situations. Ask your child to explain how this method works.

Finally, students will solve real-world problems that require adding and subtracting large numbers and decimals.

If you have any questions or comments, please call or write to me.

Sincerely,
Your child's teacher

Carta a la familia

Estimada familia:

Su niño ha estudiado la suma y resta de números enteros y decimales en años pasados. La Unidad 3 de *Math Expressions* guiará a los estudiantes a medida que estudien esos temas con más profundidad.

Los objetivos principales de esta unidad son

1. ayudar a los estudiantes a ampliar su comprensión del valor posicional para incluir los números grandes y los decimales;
2. ayudar a los estudiantes con la suma y la resta de decimales y números enteros;
3. desarrollar destrezas de estimación y redondeo al hacer actividades con gráficas;
4. hacer que los estudiantes apliquen el concepto de valor posicional a una variedad de situaciones de la vida diaria.

Los estudiantes ampliarán y aplicarán su conocimiento del valor posicional al realizar actividades con dinero y medidas métricas. Cuando se presente la ocasión, hágale preguntas a su niño sobre cantidades de dinero para reforzar lo que se enseña en la clase.

Los estudiantes lograrán el segundo objetivo utilizando varios métodos de agrupación. Los estudiantes pueden usar el método que prefieran, mientras comprendan por qué funciona y puedan explicarlo. Para sumar y restar con exactitud los estudiantes necesitan alinear correctamente los dígitos de los números enteros y los decimales. Observe a su niño mientras suma y resta. Ayúdele a alinear los dígitos cuando haga falta.

El tercer objetivo se puede cumplir de varias maneras. Los estudiantes aprenderán a usar la escala de una gráfica para comprender cómo se redondea un número. Por ejemplo, van a ver que un número como 3,879 está entre 3,000 y 4,000, pero está más cerca de 4,000. Por lo tanto, redondear 3,879 al millar más cercano da 4,000. También se les enseñará un método de *estimación segura* para prepararlos para situaciones de la vida diaria. Pídale a su niño que le explique cómo funciona este método.

Finalmente, los estudiantes resolverán problemas de la vida diaria que requieren la suma y resta de números grandes y decimales.

Si tiene alguna pregunta o comentario, por favor comuníquese conmigo.

Atentamente,
El maestro de su niño

Thousands to Thousandths

mm 10 20 30 40 50 60 70 80 90 100 110 120 130 140 150 160 170 180 190 200 210 220 230 240 250

cm 1   2   3   4   5   6   7   8   9   10 11 12 13 14 15 16 17 18 19 20 21 22 23 24 25

dm

1 dm   **2 dm**

meter

260 270 280 290 300 310 320 330 340 350 360 370 380 390 400 410 420 430 440 450 460 470 480 490 500

26 27 28 29 30 31 32 33 34 35 36 37 38 39 40 41 42 43 44 45 46 47 48 49 50

3 dm   **4 dm**   **5 dm**

510 520 530 540 550 560 570 580 590 600 610 620 630 640 650 660 670 680 690 700 710 720 730 740 750

51 52 53 54 55 56 57 58 59 60 61 62 63 64 65 66 67 68 69 70 71 72 73 74 75

6 dm   **7 dm**

760 770 780 790 800 810 820 830 840 850 860 870 880 890 900 910 920 930 940 950 960 970 980 990 1000 mm

76 77 78 79 80 81 82 83 84 85 86 87 88 89 90 91 92 93 94 95 96 97 98 99 100 cm

8 dm   **9 dm**   **10 dm**

1m

Class Activity

► Explore Metric Measures of Length

Use your paper ruler to answer each question.

Vocabulary
meter (m)
decimeter (dm)
centimeter (cm)
millimeter (mm)

1. How many decimeters equal one meter? _____

2. How many millimeters equal one centimeter? _____

3. How many millimeters equal one decimeter? _____

4. How many millimeters equal one meter? _____

5. How many centimeters equal one decimeter? _____

6. How many centimeters equal one meter? _____

The last row of the Place Value Parade shows metric measures of length. The most common units of measures are **meter** (m), **decimeter** (dm), **centimeter** (cm), and **millimeter** (mm).

7. Use your meter ruler to fill in the last four cells of the last row.

◄—— × 10 (Larger)   **Place Value Parade**   ÷ 10 (Smaller) ——►

Thousands	Hundreds	Tens	ONES	Tenths	Hundredths	Thousandths
1,000.	100.	10.	1.	0.1	0.01	0.001
$\frac{1,000}{1}$	$\frac{100}{1}$	$\frac{10}{1}$	$\frac{1}{1}$	$\frac{1}{10}$	$\frac{1}{100}$	$\frac{1}{1,000}$
$1,000.00	$100.00	$10.00	$1.00	$0.10	$0.01	$0.001
kilometer km	hectometer hm	dekameter dkm	meter m	decimeter dm	centimeter cm	millimeter mm

8. In Greek kilo means "thousand," hecto means "hundred," and deka means "ten." Write in the bottom row how many meters make a dekameter, a hectometer, and a kilometer.

▶ Measuring Real-World Objects

Read each measurement below. Say the number of meters, decimeters, centimeters, and millimeters.

For example, 7.284 m is 7 meters, 2 decimeters, 8 centimeters, and 4 millimeters.

9. 7.284 m   10. 45.132 m   11. 29.16 m   12. 304 m   13. 16.02 m

14. Measure two objects in your classroom using a metric ruler.

   _____

   _____

15. Add the lengths of the two objects you measured.

   _____

Write your own problems.

16. Write an addition word problem using the measurements in exercises 9 and 11.

   _____

   _____

   _____

   _____

   _____

17. Write a subtraction word problem using the measurements in exercises 10 and 12.

   _____

   _____

   _____

   _____

   _____

▲ Reading Large Numbers

To read large numbers, start at the ones place and make groups of three moving to the left. Each group of three has a special name. Read each group of three as if they were in the ones, tens, hundreds places and then add the special name for that group. (Do not add the name for the ones group.)

235,   467,   941,   582   two hundred thirty five billion

billion million thousand   four hundred sixty seven million

nine hundred forty one thousand

five hundred eighty two

Use your whole number secret-code cards to make the groups of three digits as shown below. Put them on the frame below to read them.

987,654,321,000   123,456,700,809   450,726,038,109

12,349,805,760   6,502,148,379   789,321,460,005

H T O   H T O   H T O   H T O

0 0 0 , 0 0 0 , 0 0 0 , 0 0 0

Billion   *Million*   *Thousand*   (Ones)

Place (whole)	Value	Place (decimal)	Decimal	Fraction
ONES	1	billionths	0.000000001	$\frac{1}{1,000,000,000}$
tens	10	hundred millionths	0.00000001	$\frac{1}{100,000,000}$
hundreds	100	ten millionths	0.0000001	$\frac{1}{10,000,000}$
thousands	1,000	millionths	0.000001	$\frac{1}{1,000,000}$
ten thousands	10,000	hundred thousandths	0.00001	$\frac{1}{100,000}$
hundred thousands	100,000	ten thousandths	0.0001	$\frac{1}{10,000}$
millions	1,000,000	thousandths	0.001	$\frac{1}{1,000}$
ten millions	10,000,000	hundredths	0.01	$\frac{1}{100}$
hundred millions	100,000,000	tenths	0.1	$\frac{1}{10}$
billions	1,000,000,000	ONES	1	

Cut out the two parts and tape them together.

▶ Symmetry Around the Ones Place

Write the numbers in the correct columns.

										1										
								1	0											
									0	1										

one

ten

1 tenth

1 hundred

1 hundredth

1 thousand

1 thousandth

1 ten thousand

1 ten thousandth

1 hundred thousand

1 hundred thousandths

1 million

1 millionth

1 ten million

1 ten millionth

1 hundred million

1 hundred millionth

1 billion

1 billionth

Class Activity

▶ Compare and Order Large Numbers

In 2001, the Census Bureau reported these populations for five counties.

County and State	Population
Saint Louis, MO	1,015,417
Fairfax, VA	985,161
Hennepin, MN	1,114,977
Allegheny, PA	1,270,612
Oakland, MI	1,198,593

1. Write the names of the counties in order from least population to greatest population.

   _____

2. Which counties have a population greater than 1 billion?

   _____

3. Which county's population is closest to 1 million?

   _____

A manufacturing company produces four different styles of shoes. The number of pairs of each style that was produced is shown in the table at the right.

Annual Production (pairs)	
Style A	245,360
Style B	181,405
Style C	196,730
Style D	268,220

4. Order the production numbers from greatest to least.

   _____

5. The company's goal was to produce a quarter million pairs of Style A shoes. Did the company achieve its goal? Why or why not?

   _____

6. Is nine hundred thousand pairs a reasonable estimate of the total production of all four styles? Why or why not?

   _____

   _____

Class Activity

Name _____ Date _____

▶ Represent Numbers Different Ways

In our place value system, numbers can be expressed different ways. For example, four different ways to represent the number 3,526 are shown below.

standard form	3,526
word form	three thousand, five hundred twenty-six
short word form	3 thousand, 526
expanded form	3,000 + 500 + 20 + 6

Write each number in three different ways.

7. 12,402

   word form _____

   short word form _____

   expanded form _____

8. eight thousand, three hundred ten

   short word form _____

   standard form _____

   expanded form _____

9. 700,000 + 60,000 + 9

   standard form _____

   short word form _____

   word form _____

Solve.

10. One way to write 500 using addition is 400 + 100. One way to write 500 using subtraction is 510 − 10. Show three other ways to write 500 using addition and three other ways using subtraction.

    _____

Going Further

▶ Different Systems of Numeration

There are many systems for writing numbers.
The numbers 1 to 10 are shown below using five different systems.

Tally System

Mayan Numerals

Grouped Tally System

Chinese Rod Numerals

Roman Numerals

I II III IV V VI VII VIII IX X

1. List some similarities you see in the number systems.

_____

_____

_____

2. List some differences you see in the number systems.

_____

_____

_____

3. How might the symbol for 5 in the Roman system have come from a picture of a hand?

_____

_____

4. What might the Roman symbol for 10 come from?

_____

_____

5. **Math Journal** Write an addition or subtraction equation using one set of symbols.

_____

Vocabulary

digit
increase
decrease

▶ Mental Math with Place Value

You can use your understanding of place value to change numbers.

Start with the number in the box for each problem.

4,374.56

1. **Increase** the number by 2,000.

   _____

2. **Decrease** the number by 0.03.

   _____

3. Make 2 more in the tens place.

   _____

46,795.8

4. Increase the number by 10,000.

   _____

5. Decrease the number by 0.7.

   _____

6. Make 4 more in the thousands place.

   _____

915,042.723

7. Increase the number by 0.005.

   _____

8. Decrease the number by 100,000.

   _____

9. Make 7 more in the hundreds place.

   _____

7,218,396,405

10. Increase the number by 2 billion.

    _____

11. Decrease the number by 1 million.

    _____

12. Make 4 more in the tenths place.

    _____

Answer each question.

13. What is the largest 3-digit whole number you can make with the **digits** 4, 9, and 1?

    _____

14. What is the smallest 3-digit whole number you can make with these same digits?

15. What is the largest 9-digit whole number that uses all the digits 1 through 9?

    _____

16. What is the smallest 9-digit whole number that uses all the digits 1 through 9?

Class Activity

▶ Visualize Numbers

This dot array helps you to visualize large numbers.

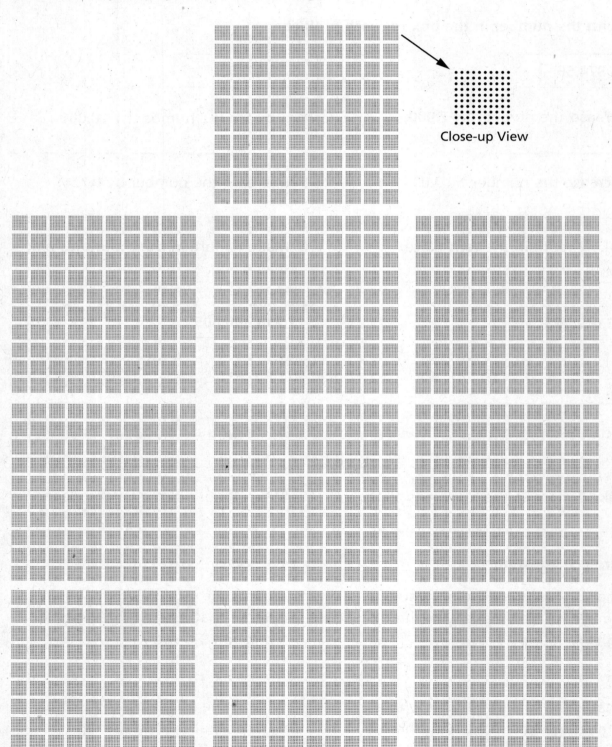

Close-up View

Use Place Value

▶ **Addition Problems**

When adding, remember to align the place values of the numbers.

Dear Math Students,

I am ordering a CD from a catalog. The price of the CD is $15 and the tax is $0.15. Altogether, then, I will have to pay $30 for this CD. The tax makes the cost twice as much! Doesn't this seem unreasonable to you? Or have I made some kind of a mistake?

Thank you.

Puzzled Penguin

1. Write a response to the Puzzled Penguin.

_____

_____

_____

_____

_____

_____

Add. Try to solve mentally.

2. $28 + 32¢ = _____

3. $42.05 + 63¢ = _____

4. 56¢ + $8.27 = _____

5. 43 + 0.26 = _____

6. 57.3 + 0.89 = _____

7. 92.17 + 1.6 = _____

8. 4 m + 0.03 m = _____

9. 2.5 m + 0.08 m = _____

10. 6 m + 0.007 m = _____

11. Explain how to add two decimal numbers. Give an example.

_____

_____

 12. **On the Back** Write a problem about adding measurements or adding decimals. Then solve the problem.

Add Whole Numbers and Decimals

► Compare Different Methods

There are many ways to add numbers. These methods each show the new groups in a different way. Each method has its own advantages and disadvantages.

New Groups Below

Step 1	Step 2	Step 3	Step 4	Step 5	Step 6
787.608	787.608	787.608	787.608	787.608	787.608
+561.739	+561.739	+561.739	+561.739	+561.739	+561.739
1	1	1 1	1 1	1 1 1	1 1 1
7	47	347	9.347	49.347	1,349.347

New Groups Above

Step 1	Step 2	Step 3	Step 4	Step 5	Step 6
1	1	1 1	1 1	1 1 1	1 1 1
787.608	787.608	787.608	787.608	787.608	787.608
+561.739	+561.739	+561.739	+561.739	+561.739	+561.739
7	47	347	9.347	49.347	1,349.347

Subtotal Method

Step 1	Step 2	Step 3	Step 4	Steps 5 & 6	Step 7
787.608	787.608	787.608	787.608	787.608	787.608
+561.739	+561.739	+561.739	+561.739	+561.739	+561.739
1,200.000	1,200.000	1,200.000	1,200.000	1,200.000	1,200.000
	140.000	140.000	140.000	140.000	140.000
		8.000	8.000	8.000	8.000
			1.300	1.300	1.300
				0.030	0.030
				0.017	+0.017
					1,349.347

▶ Discuss a Preferred Method

Each exercise can be completed by using the New Groups Above,
New Groups Below, or Subtotal Method.

Use any method to add.

1. 7,473,265 + 2,873,498

_____

2. 0.385 + 476.9

_____

3. 275.382 + 79.8365

_____

4. 43,675.329 + 4,693.94

_____

5. 375.038 + 2,473.69

_____

6. 8,092,375.62 + 78,396.705

_____

▶ Two Ways to Ungroup in Subtraction

Ungrouping allows you to subtract larger numbers from smaller numbers. You can ungroup in either direction.

Left to Right

```
      0 13          12              12 14
     1 3 5 3      0 1 3 15        0 1 3 15 13
     1,3 5 3      1,3 5 3          1,3 5 3
     - 7 6 9      - 7 6 9          - 7 6 9
```

Right to Left

```
        4 13         14             12 14
     1,3 5 3      2 4 13         0 2 4 13
     1,3 5 3      1,3 5 3         1,3 5 3
     - 7 6 9      - 7 6 9          - 7 6 9
```

> You can draw a magnifying glass around the top number to see inside it to ungroup.
>
>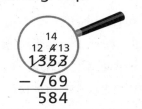
>
> ```
>        14
>     12 4 13
>     1,3 5 3
>     - 7 6 9
>       5 8 4
> ```

Answer each question.

1. How do we know we are not changing the value of the top number when we ungroup?

   _____

   _____

   _____

2. When the ungrouping is finished, in which direction do we subtract?

   _____

   _____

3. How can we check the answer?

   _____

   _____

   _____

```
        1,353
        /    \
     769      584
```

▶ Real-World Problems

Solve each problem.

4. One year the Sahara Desert received 0.791 inches of rain. That same year the rain forest in Brazil received 324 inches. How much more rain fell in the rain forest that year than in the desert?

_____

5. A newborn kangaroo measures about 0.02 meters in height. An adult kangaroo can measure up to 2.7 meters in height. How much shorter is the baby kangaroo than the tallest adult?

_____

6. Jack and Lelia have each been saving money. Jack has $136.83, and Lelia has nineteen dollars. How much less money does Lelia have than Jack?

_____

7. Colleen owns a tree nursery. Her tallest maple tree measures 2.32 meters, and her shortest measures 0.4 meters. What is the difference in their heights?

_____

Subtract Whole and Decimal Numbers

▶ Place Value Problems

When solving word problems, you need to pay close attention to place values. Remember to only add and subtract like place values.

Large Creatures   *Show your work.*

Dr. Magnuson is a scientist who studies whales and sharks. She and many other scientists think that sharks appeared on Earth about 395 million years ago, and whales appeared about 70 million years ago. They think that human beings appeared about 1,750,000 years ago.

1. About how much longer have sharks been on Earth than human beings?

   _____

2. About how much longer have whales been on Earth than human beings?

   _____

3. A baby blue whale weighs about 4,000 pounds. An adult blue whale weighs about 400,000 pounds. About how much weight does a blue whale gain as it grows up?

   _____

4. The largest living shark is the whale shark. It is about 1,200 cm long. The smallest living shark is the pigmy shark. It is about 25 cm long. How much longer is the whale shark than the pigmy shark?

   _____

5. Whales and dolphins are mammals from the same family. The average adult blue whale is about 2,620 cm long. The smallest dolphin, named Hector's dolphin, is about 125 cm long. How much longer is the blue whale than Hector's dolphin?

   _____

Small Creatures

Show your work.

6. Dr. Parvo is a scientist who studies butterflies and moths. He has learned that there are 15,000 kinds of butterflies and 100,000 kinds of moths. How many kinds of moths and butterflies are there altogether?

_____

7. The largest butterfly is the Queen Alexandra butterfly, which is 28 cm across. One of the smallest is the pygmy blue butterfly, which is 0.95 cm across. How much larger is the Queen Alexandra butterfly than the pygmy blue butterfly?

_____

8. When a monarch butterfly hatches, it is a tiny caterpillar 0.35 cm long. When the caterpillar is grown, it is about 5.1 cm long. How many centimeters does the monarch caterpillar grow?

_____

9. The egg of the elfin butterfly is 0.008 cm across. The egg of the zebra butterfly is 0.12 cm across. Which egg is smaller? How much smaller?

_____

▶ **Write Word Problems**

Make up an imaginary animal that is very large or very small. Give it a name. Decide on a length or height and a weight.

10. **On the Next Page** Write an addition and subtraction word problem about this animal and the measurement you decided on. Share your problems with the rest of the class.

Place Value Word Problems

▶ Is an Exact or Estimated Answer Needed?

Some problems ask for an exact answer, but other problems only need an estimate to answer the question. To decide which kind of answer you need to find, study the question carefully. Look for certain key words, such as *about, approximately, almost, nearly,* and *enough*. Those words usually mean you can estimate.

Example: Tim has a $10-bill. He wants to buy 29 red apples that cost $3.68 and 13 green apples that cost a total of $2.11. Both prices include sales tax.

Need Exact Answers	Need Estimated Answers
Q: How many apples does Tim want to buy?	Q: About how many apples does Tim want to buy?
A: Tim wants to buy 42 apples.	A: Tim wants to buy about 40 apples
Q: How much change should Tim receive?	Q: Does Tim have enough money to buy all the apples?
A: Tim should get back $4.21.	A: Yes, Tim has enough money.

Tell whether each problem needs an *exact* answer or an *estimated* answer. Then solve the problem. Write your answer in a complete sentence.

Show your work.

1. Kelly rode her bike on two trails this weekend. She rode 4.73 km on the Oak Trail and 3.42 km on the Pine Trail. Did she ride more than 8 km?

   _____

2. Ramiro and Suzy made 216 cookies for the bake sale. They had 37 cookies left over at the end of the sale. How many cookies did they sell?

   _____

3. Jamal wants to buy a book that costs $7.99 and a magazine that costs $3.75. He has two $10-bills. Does Jamal have enough money to buy both items?

   _____

Place Value Word Problems

Class Activity

▶ Practice With Regrouping and Reordering

The **Commutative Property** and **Associative Property** can help you add.

Properties	
Commutative Property of Addition	$a + b = b + a$
Associative Property of Addition	$(a + b) + c = a + (b + c)$

You can sometimes group or reorder numbers to help you use mental math more quickly. Explain how you could use the Commutative and Associative Properties to help you add mentally.

1.   30,000
     20,000 _____
     80,000 _____
     49,000
   + 70,000 _____

     _____

2.   90,000
     25,000 _____
     75,000 _____
     67,000
   + 10,000 _____

     _____

3.   5.75
     5.4   _____
     5.25 _____
     5.17
   + 5.6   _____

     _____

4.   1.500
     1.200 _____
     1.300 _____
   + 1.678

     _____

     _____

5. 8 million + 39 million + 2 million

   _____

   _____

6. 40 billion + 856 billion + 60 billion

   _____

   _____

7. $476.00 + $50.00 + $50.00

   _____

   _____

The **Distributive Property** can also help you compute mentally.

Distributive Property	$a \times (b + c) = (a \times b) + (a \times c)$

Discuss how you could use the Distributive Property to say each problem with only two factors. Then solve the problems mentally.

8. $(7 \times 25) + (7 \times 75) =$ _____

9. $(800 \times 9) + (200 \times 9) =$ _____

10. Use the Commutative Property to solve for n.
$968.73 + 532.15 = 532.15 + n$

_____

Find each answer by using the Associative Property.

11. $(749 + 600) + 400 =$ _____

12. $3.20 + (2.80 + 1.37) =$ _____

13. Use the Distributive Property to help you find the combined area of these rectangles.

```
            199 cm                          101 cm
       ┌──────────────────┐            ┌──────────────┐
10 cm  │                  │     10 cm  │              │
       └──────────────────┘            └──────────────┘
```

_____

_____

▶ Properties and Real-World Situations

Which property best describes each situation below: Commutative, Associative, or Distributive?

14. Miranda cannot add ($56,703 + $8,000) + $2,000 very easily. So, she regroups the problem as $56,703 + ($8,000 + $2,000).

_____

15. Brady did not know the answer to 2×403. So, he multiplied twice and then added the two answers together: $(2 \times 400) + (2 \times 3)$.

_____

Properties and Strategies

▶ Use a Pictograph

A pictograph uses symbols or pictures to show a certain number of items. The key to a pictograph tells you how many items each symbol or picture represents.

Use the pictographs to answer each question.

The graph shows the number of each color of button made at a factory this month.

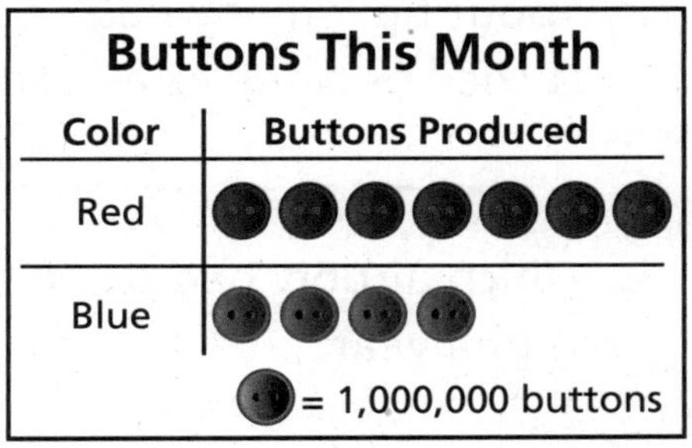

1. How many red buttons were made this month? How many blue buttons were made?

   _____

2. How many more red buttons were made than blue buttons?

   _____

3. Buttons are packaged in boxes of 100. How many boxes of buttons were produced?

   _____

Buttons This Month

Color	Buttons Produced
Red	●●●●●●●
Blue	●●●●

● = 1,000,000 buttons

The graph shows the number of vehicles that traveled on Highway 25 in one week.

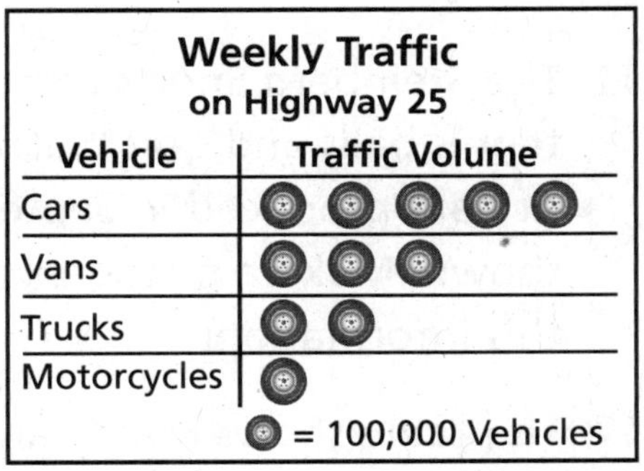

4. How many vans traveled on the highway that week?

   _____

5. How many fewer motorcycles traveled on Highway 25 than cars in one week?

   _____

6. Predict the number of trucks that might travel on Highway 25 in one month.

   _____

7. Each truck driver pays $10 a week in tolls. How much toll money is collected from truck drivers in one week?

   _____

Weekly Traffic
on Highway 25

Vehicle	Traffic Volume
Cars	◎ ◎ ◎ ◎ ◎
Vans	◎ ◎ ◎
Trucks	◎ ◎
Motorcycles	◎

◎ = 100,000 Vehicles

Use the pictograph to answer each question.

This graph has no key. The actual number of passengers at the Atlanta airport in one year was 80,171,035.

8. How many passengers does each person on the graph stand for?

_____

9. About how many passengers were there at the Los Angeles airport in one year?

_____

10. Which airport had 61,607,185 passengers in one year?

_____

The World's Busiest Airports

Airport	Traffic Volume
Atlanta	
Chicago	
Los Angeles	
London	

▶ Make a Pictograph

On a separate sheet of paper, draw a pictograph to show the information in each table. Each pictograph should have a title and a key.

11. The Steinberg Sports Factory makes tennis balls and golf balls. The number of balls produced in September is shown. Make a pictograph showing this information.

Number of Balls Produced in September

Ball	Number
Tennis balls	3,000
Golf balls	6,500

12. The table shows how many people speak the five most common languages spoken worldwide in the year 2000. Make a pictograph to show this information.

Number of Speakers of the Five Most Common Languages

Language	Number of Speakers
Bengali	200,000,000
Chinese	900,000,000
English	300,000,000
Spanish	350,000,000
Hindi (India)	350,000,000

Class Activity

Vocabulary

scale

▶ Introduce Scales as a Visual Aid to Rounding

The kingdom of Plutonia has 9 cities. Every year the king counts the population in each city and rounds the number. Below are **scales** that show the rounding units he uses for each one. A scale has numbers arranged on a line with fixed distances between each number.

Write the rounded population of each city.

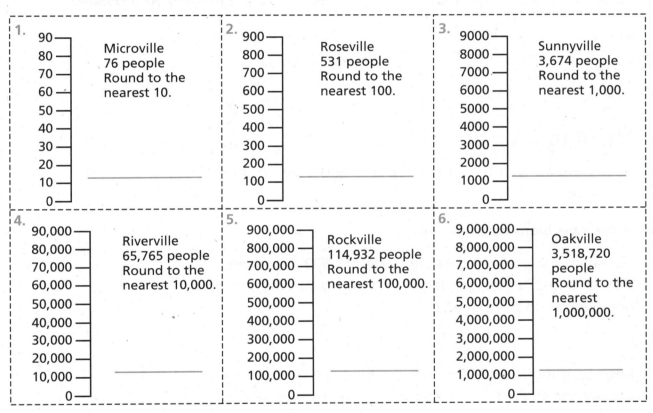

1.
90
80 Microville
70 76 people
60 Round to the
50 nearest 10.
40
30
20
10
0 _____

2.
900
800 Roseville
700 531 people
600 Round to the
500 nearest 100.
400
300
200
100 _____
0

3.
9000
8000 Sunnyville
7000 3,674 people
6000 Round to the
5000 nearest 1,000.
4000
3000
2000
1000 _____
0

4.
90,000
80,000 Riverville
70,000 65,765 people
60,000 Round to the
50,000 nearest 10,000.
40,000
30,000
20,000
10,000 _____
0

5.
900,000
800,000 Rockville
700,000 114,932 people
600,000 Round to the
500,000 nearest 100,000.
400,000
300,000
200,000
100,000 _____
0

6.
9,000,000
8,000,000 Oakville
7,000,000 3,518,720
6,000,000 people
5,000,000 Round to the
4,000,000 nearest
3,000,000 1,000,000.
2,000,000
1,000,000 _____
0

Write the rounded numbers that belong on the lines above and below each number. Then circle the correct answer.

7. _____

7,581

_____

Rounded to
the nearest
1,000.

8. _____

12,327

_____

Rounded to
the nearest
10,000.

9. _____

293

_____

Rounded to
the nearest
100.

10. _____

8,965,002

_____

Rounded to
the nearest
1,000,000.

▶ Practice With Rounding

Round to the nearest ten.

11. 23 _____

12. 75 _____

13. 156 _____

Round to the nearest hundred.

14. 291 _____

15. 1,610 _____

16. 834 _____

Round to the nearest thousand.

17. 2,315 _____

18. 10,987 _____

19. 15,204 _____

Round to the nearest 10 thousand.

20. 30,986 _____

21. 65,713 _____

22. 9,506 _____

▶ Round to Estimate

When you **estimate** you find a number that is close to the exact number.

Solve each problem by rounding.

Show your work.

23. Herminio has a stamp collection. He has 689 American stamps and 226 foreign stamps. About how many stamps does Herminio have in all?

_____

24. Karinne bought a glass of lemonade for 59 cents and a pretzel for 39 cents. Is $1 enough to pay for both items?

_____

25. The Brown Owl Bookstore has 1,897 novels and 1,405 comic books. About how many more novels does the store have than comic books?

_____

26. Mebrahtom drove 47 miles before noon. He drove 52 miles after noon. He said he drove nearly 100 miles altogether. Is he right?

_____

Jenna has $85. She wants to buy a sleeping bag for $53 and a backpack for $34. She rounds these numbers to the nearest ten and gets $50 and $30.

Added together, the numbers total $80. She decides that she has enough money to buy both things. Is she right? Discuss why or why not.

_____

_____

_____

Decide whether a *safe* estimate or an *ordinary* estimate is needed. Then estimate to find each answer.

Show your work.

27. Mrs. Jackson is catching a plane to Chicago. The last time she traveled, it took her 32 minutes to drive to the airport and another 21 minutes to park and get to the gate for check-in. How much total time should Mrs. Jackson allow herself to get from home to the check-in gate?

_____

28. This summer Kurt read one book with 278 pages, another with 312 pages, and another with 104 pages. About how many pages did Kurt read in all?

_____

29. Mr. Richfield plans to buy 2 cars for his business this year. He has $30,000 in the bank. One car that he likes costs $14,935. The other one costs $13,295. About how much do the two cars cost altogether? Does he have enough money in the bank?

_____

30. Jarod drove 379 miles on Monday and 422 miles on Tuesday. About how far did he drive altogether on these two days?

_____

Going Further

▶ Different Ways to Estimate

Complete.

1. Estimate a range for 2,526 + 8,490 by rounding to the thousands place.

   a. 2,526 rounds down to _____ and 8,490 rounds down to _____.

   b. The minimum value for the range is _____ + _____ or _____.

   c. 2,526 rounds up to _____ and 8,490 rounds up to _____.

   d. The maximum value for the range is _____ + _____ or _____.

   e. What is a reasonable estimate of a range for the exact sum?

   _____

2. Describe a method that can be used to make a better estimate of the *range* for the exact sum?

   _____

   _____

   Another way to estimate is to write the leftmost digit in each number and write all of the other digits as zeros. This method is called **front-end estimation**.

   For example, to estimate 4,588 − 2,616 using front-end estimation, change 4,588 to 4,000 and change 2,616 to 2,000. Then subtract. This method produces an estimate of 4,000 − 2,000 or 2,000 (which is close to the exact answer of 1,972).

3. Will front-end estimation *always* produce a reasonable estimate of an exact sum or difference? Give an example to support your answer.

   _____

   _____

4. **Discuss** Describe a method that can *always* be used to produce a reasonable estimate of a sum or difference.

Round Numbers to Estimate

Vocabulary
bar graph
double bar graph

▶ **Bar Graphs With Large Numbers**

A **bar graph** uses vertical or horizontal bars to show data.

Use the graphs to answer each question.

1. The bar graph shows 4 movies that have made a lot of money. About how much money did *Star Fleet* make?

_____

2. The actual amount of money that one of these movies made was $399,804,539. Which movie was that?

_____

3. John said *Super Heroes* brought in about $265 more than *Voyage to Venus.* Is he right? Explain.

_____

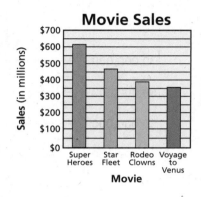

A **double bar graph** uses vertical or horizontal bars to compare related data.

4. Every year a city has a carnival with an afternoon picnic and an evening concert. The graph shows the number of people who attended each event during the past 3 years. Look at the attendance numbers. Do you see a pattern?

_____

5. This year (Year 4) about 45,000 people attended the picnic. The mayor wants to know how many chairs are needed for the concert. What will you tell him? Explain your answer.

_____

_____

_____

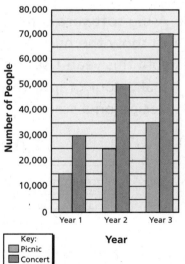

6. Think about next year's carnival (Year 5). If the pattern continues, how many people can be expected to attend the picnic that year? How many people can be expected to attend the concert?

_____

Name **Date**

▶ Make a Bar Graph

7. This table shows the area in square miles of each ocean. Use this information to make a bar graph.

The Oceans of the World

Pacific	64,200,000 sq mi
Atlantic	33,400,000 sq mi
Indian	28,400,000 sq mi
Arctic	5,100,000 sq mi

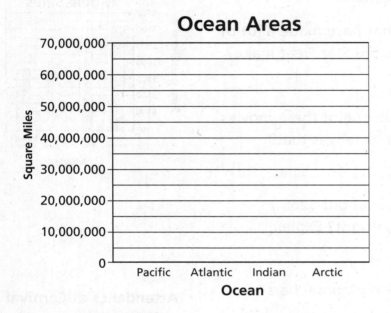

8. A big software company wants to use a bar graph to show the number of computer games that were sold this year. Use the information in the table to make your graph. This time you will need to decide on a scale.

Computer Games Sold This Year

Brave Bats	453,000
Power Zone	741,000
Flying Birds	318,000
The Empire	608,000
Men on Mars	97,000

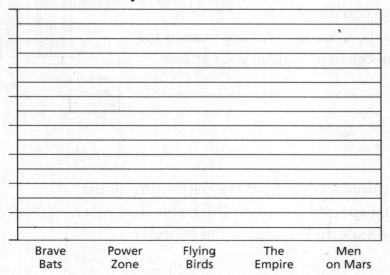

Bar Graphs and Rounding

Class Activity

► Round Decimal Numbers

Solve.

1. A number changed to 12.6 after it was rounded. To what place was the number rounded? Explain how you know.

   _____

   _____

2. A number changed to 3.25 after it was rounded. To what place was the number rounded? Explain how you know.

   _____

   _____

3. A number changed to 193 after it was rounded. To what place was the number rounded? Explain how you know.

   _____

   _____

4. Round to the nearest whole number.

   a. 31.75 _____

   b. 6.49 _____

   c. 11.5 _____

   d. 0.97 _____

   e. 319.1 _____

5. Round to the nearest hundredth.

   a. 4.051 _____

   b. 16.686 _____

   c. 0.994 _____

   d. 51.202 _____

   e. 775.115 _____

6. Round to the nearest tenth.

   a. 51.16 _____

   b. 8.55 _____

   c. 147.67 _____

   d. 0.84 _____

   e. 29.20 _____

7. Round to the nearest thousandth.

   a. 0.8109 _____

   b. 60.4554 _____

   c. 1.0007 _____

   d. 226.0965 _____

   e. 7.0528 _____

► Estimate Sums and Differences

8. Estimate each sum or difference.

a.
$$\begin{array}{r} \$17.25 \\ - \$11.79 \\ \hline \end{array}$$

b.
$$\begin{array}{r} 8.9 \\ + 5.8 \\ \hline \end{array}$$

c.
$$\begin{array}{r} \$3.52 \\ - \$1.54 \\ \hline \end{array}$$

d.
$$\begin{array}{r} \$6.36 \\ + \$6.81 \\ \hline \end{array}$$

e.
$$\begin{array}{r} 0.716 \\ - 0.698 \\ \hline \end{array}$$

f.
$$\begin{array}{r} 10.239 \\ + 9.062 \\ \hline \end{array}$$

Solve.

9. Rick thinks the total cost of a $89.95 soccer goal and a $9.99 soccer ball is $90.94. Write your estimate of the total cost; then write the exact cost.

Estimate _____   Exact Cost _____

Was Rick's answer reasonable? Explain why or why not.

_____

10. Marti subtracted 9.28 from 20.15 and found the difference to be 10.87.

Write an estimate of the difference. _____

Was Marti's answer reasonable? Explain why or why not.

_____

11. In a video racing game, Lee completed one lap in 47.312 seconds. Donna completed one lap in 45.401 seconds.

Which lap was faster? _____

How many seconds faster was the lap?

Estimate _____   Exact Answer _____

Is your exact answer reasonable? Explain why or why not.

_____

Class Activity

Vocabulary
discrete data
continuous data

▶ Analyze Data in Tables

Data can be discrete or continuous.

Discrete data usually involve counting. For example, the number of seeds in a watermelon is an exact, countable number. It is not related to the number of seeds in a different watermelon.

Continuous data usually involve measuring and time. For example, your height on your tenth birthday was related to your height on your ninth birthday. The data for your height was not always the same during that period of time, but it was continuous, or not interrupted.

Tables can be used to display data.

Afternoon Temperatures (°F)	
Time	**Temperature**
1 P.M.	76
2 P.M.	78
3 P.M.	81
4 P.M.	81
5 P.M.	80

The Heights of Five Trees (ft)	
Tree	**Height**
Bluewood	20
Sparkleberry	25
Weeping Willow	35
Nannyberry	20
Soapberry	30

1. Which table shows discrete data? Explain.

   _____

   _____

2. Which table shows continuous data? Explain.

   _____

   _____

3. **Discuss** Write another example of discrete data. Give a reason to support your example.

4. **Discuss** Write another example of continuous data. Give a reason to support your example.

Class Activity

▶ Analyze Data in Graphs

Compare these graphs.

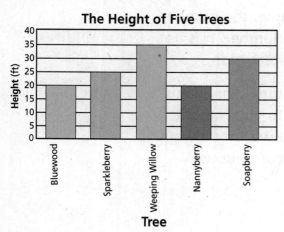

The Height of Five Trees

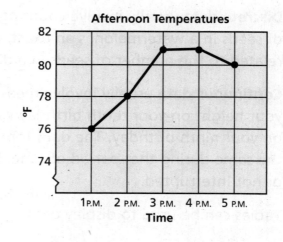

Afternoon Temperatures

5. Which graph shows discrete data? Why are the data discrete?

_____

_____

6. Which graph shows continuous data? Why are the data continuous?

_____

_____

7. Predict Suppose that the height of a sixth tree was added to the bar graph. Would it be difficult to predict what the height of that tree might be? Give a reason to support your answer.

_____

_____

8. Predict Suppose that the 6 P.M. temperature was added to the line graph. Would it be difficult to predict what the temperature might be? Give a reason to support your answer.

_____

_____

9. Predict Write a question that involves a prediction for one of the graphs. Discuss with your classmates possible answers for your question.

Discrete and Continuous Data

▶ Choose the Appropriate Graph

Write *bar graph* or *line graph* for each situation.

10. A graph showing the height of each student in a class.

_____

11. A graph showing the height of a seedling each day for a month.

_____

12. A graph showing your heart rate from the beginning of recess until the end of recess.

_____

13. A graph showing the number of people who attended each performance of a school play.

_____

14. A graph showing temperature of water that is being brought to a boil in a kettle.

_____

15. A graph showing the quiz scores for each student in a class.

_____

16. Describe a situation or a group of data for which a bar graph would be an appropriate display.

_____

_____

_____

17. Describe a situation or a group of data for which a line graph would be an appropriate display.

_____

_____

_____

▶ Double Line Graphs

The towns of Nudo and Cooper were established in 1890. The line graph shows how their populations have changed over time. Each point indicates the population at the end of the year shown on the scale.

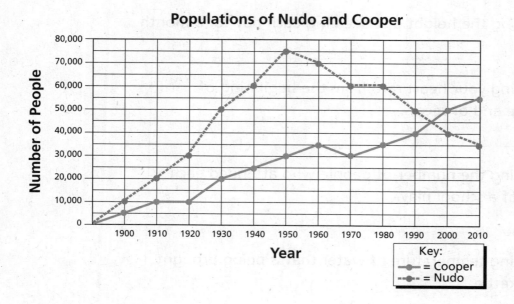

Populations of Nudo and Cooper

Key:
—●— = Cooper
--●-- = Nudo

18. How many people lived in Cooper in 1960?

_____

19. How many people lived in Nudo in 1940?

_____

20. The population of Cooper was greater than the population of Nudo for approximately how many years?

_____

21. Which town's population had an upward trend for the greatest number of years?

_____

22. During which year was the population of Nudo 25,000 more than Cooper?

_____

23. During which year was the population of Nudo 20,000 less than Cooper?

_____

24. During which decade did the population increase the most?

_____

25. When was the population of Nudo twice that of Cooper?

_____

Discrete and Continuous Data

▶ Triple Line Graphs (Optional)

During a recess period, the heart rates of three students were recorded each minute for five minutes. The line graph below shows three sets of data that were collected.

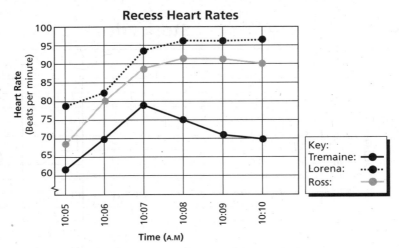

Recess Heart Rates

Key:
Tremaine: ●——●
Lorena: ●···●
Ross: ●——●

26. Whose heart rate was greatest at 10:07 A.M.? _____

27. Whose heart rate increased the most during the recess period? _____

28. **Predict** Suppose that two of the three students played the same game during recess. Is it possible to know for certain the names of those students? Explain why or why not.

_____

29. **Predict** Suppose that all three students played the same game during recess. At 10:07 A.M., one of the three students dropped out of the game. Which student most likely stopped playing? Give a reason to support your answer.

_____

30. Does the graph display discrete data or continuous data? Give a reason to support your answer.

_____

_____

► Make a Line Graph

31. Line graphs are often used to display the value over time of investments called stocks. Use the information below to make a line graph.

Stock Price (by month)	
January	$25
February	$30
March	$45
April	$50
May	$40
June	$55

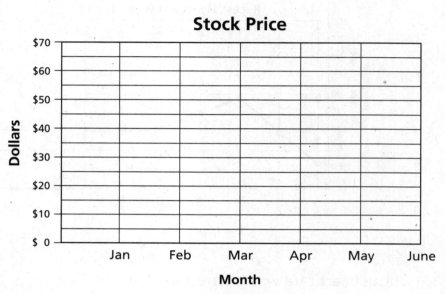

32. The population of the town of Bear Creek has increased during every decade since 1960. Use the information below to make a line graph. Include a scale and labels.

Population of Bear Creek (by decade)	
1960	996 people
1970	2,009 people
1980	3,521 people
1990	6,145 people
2000	7,613 people

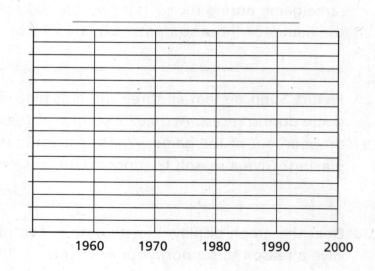

33. Math Journal Write a word problem about each graph. Challenge classmates to solve the problems you wrote.

Discrete and Continuous Data

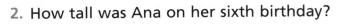

Class Activity

► Graphs With Decimal Numbers

Every year on her birthday, Ana's parents measure her height with a meter stick. The line graph shows her height at 4 different ages.

1. How much did Ana grow between her third birthday and her fourth birthday?

   _____

2. How tall was Ana on her sixth birthday?

   _____

3. A growth spurt is a period of very fast growth. Between which two birthdays did Ana have a growth spurt?

   _____

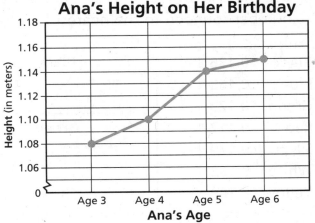

Ana's Height on Her Birthday

This bar graph shows the length of some common beetles.

4. What is the length of a bark beetle?

   _____

5. About how many bark beetles would have to line up end-to-end to be about as long as a tumblebug?

   _____

6. Estimate the length of a tumblebug in hundredths of a centimeter.

   _____

7. The actual length of one beetle shown is 0.150 centimeters. Which beetle is that?

   _____

8. A June bug is about 2.5 centimeters in length. About how many times as tall as the firefly bar would the June bug bar be?

   _____

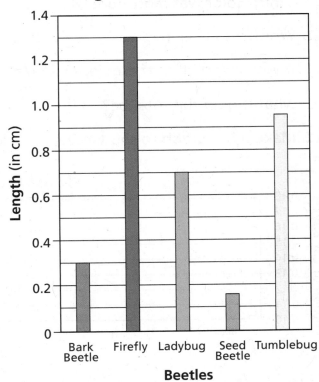

Length of Common Beetles

▶ Make a Bar Graph With Decimal Numbers

Last year, a car dealer kept track of the portion of car buyers who bought each color of car. The box on the left shows the information.

9. Use the box on the right to make a list that shows each number rounded to the nearest hundredth.

Black	0.136
Blue	0.168
Green	0.129
Red	0.117
Silver	0.179
White	0.162
Yellow	0.109

Black	
Blue	
Green	
Red	
Silver	
White	
Yellow	

10. Which color was most popular? _____

11. Which was least popular? _____

12. If you added all of these decimal numbers together,

    what should the total be? _____

13. Make a bar graph to show these rounded numbers.

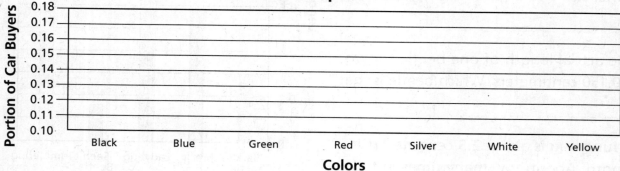

14. **On the Next Page** Draw a graph with decimal numbers. Write a problem about your graph.

Going Further

Vocabulary

histogram

► Read a Histogram

Discuss how this graph is like and different from a bar graph.

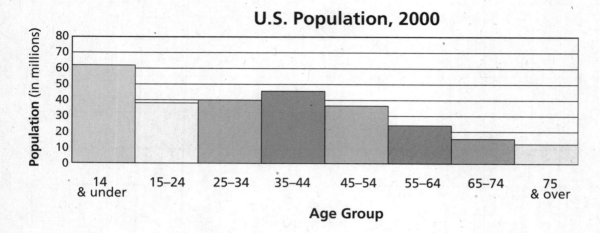

U.S. Population, 2000

A **histogram** is used when we need to group data. The groups are called ranges or intervals. The groups are often the same size. The bars touch because together they cover all of the numbers.

Use the histogram above to answer each question.

1. Which age group has the most people? _____

2. Which age group has the fewest people? _____

3. Which age groups have nearly the same number of people?

   _____

4. Which age group has about 45 million people? _____

5. About how many people are between the ages of 55 and 64?

   _____

6. About how many people are 65 years old or older?

   _____

7. About how many people are younger than 25? _____

▶ Situations in Word Problems

Change situations can be change plus situations or change minus situations.

Write a situation equation using an unknown.

```
                        ┌─────────────────────┐
                        │  Change Situations  │
                        └─────────────────────┘
```

| **Change Plus** | 9 + 4 = 13 | **Change Minus** | 13 − 4 = 9 |

Change Plus

Unknown Result

1. Dan had 9 cherries. Then he picked 4 more. How many does he have now?

_____

Unknown Change

2. Dan had 9 cherries. Then he picked some more. Now he has 13 cherries. How many did he pick?

_____

Unknown Start

3. Dan had some cherries. Then he picked 4 more. Now he has 13 cherries. How many did he start with?

_____

Change Minus

Unknown Result

4. Dan had 13 cherries. Then he ate 4 of them. How many does he have now?

_____

Unknown Change

5. Dan had 13 cherries. Then he ate some of them. Now he has 9 cherries. How many did he eat?

_____

Unknown Start

6. Dan had some cherries. Then he ate 4 of them. Now he has 9 cherries. How many did he start with?

_____

7. Choose a problem type. Write your own problem. Then write a situation equation and solve the problem.

_____

_____

_____

Class Activity

Collection situations can have an unknown total or an unknown partner.

Make a Break-Apart drawing and write a situation equation.
Use a variable for the unknown.

┌─────────────────────────────────┐
│   **Collection Situations**   │
│   │
│   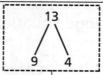   │
│   │
└─────────────────────────────────┘

Unknown Total

Put Together

8. Ana put 9 dimes and 4 nickels in her pocket. How many coins did she put in her pocket?

_____

Take Apart

9. Ana put 9 coins in her purse and 4 coins in her bank. How many coins did she have in the beginning?

_____

No Action

10. Ana has 9 dimes and 4 nickels. How many coins does she have in all?

_____

Unknown Partner

Put Together

11. Ana put 13 coins in her pocket. Nine are dimes and the rest are nickels. How many nickels are in her pocket?

_____

Take Apart

12. Ana had 13 coins. She had 9 dimes and the rest were nickels. She put all 9 dimes in her purse and all the nickels in her bank. How many nickels did she put in her bank?

_____

No Action

13. Ana has 13 coins. She has 9 dimes and the rest are nickels. How many are nickels?

_____

14. Choose a problem type. Write your own problem. Then write an equation and solve the problem.

_____

_____

Classify Word Problems

Class Activity

Additive comparison situations ask how many more or how many fewer. They can have an unknown quantity or an unknown difference.

Make a Break-Apart drawing and write an equation for each situation.

Comparison Situations

13
9	4

Unknown Difference

How Many More?

15. Ali has 9 balloons. Lisa has 13 balloons. How many more balloons does Lisa have than Ali?

_____

How Many Fewer?

16. Ali has 9 balloons. Lisa has 13 balloons. How many fewer balloons does Ali have than Lisa?

_____

Unknown Quantity

Leading Language

17. Ali has 9 balloons. Lisa has 4 more than Ali. How many balloons does Lisa have?

_____

Misleading Language

18. Ali has 9 balloons. He has 4 fewer than Lisa. How many balloons does Lisa have?

_____

19. Write a comparison problem with an unknown difference. Draw comparison bars, write an equation, and solve.

_____

_____

_____

20. Write a comparison problem with an unknown quantity. Draw comparison bars, write an equation, and solve.

_____

_____

Class Activity

► Additive and Multiplicative Comparison

You can use comparison bars to represent quantities in additive and multiplicative comparison situations.

Show your work.

Solve.

21. Two speedboats entered the harbor. One was 9 feet long, and the other was 3 feet longer. What was the length of the longer boat?

9	
9	3

_____

22. Later, two sailboats entered the harbor. One was 9 feet long. The other was 3 times as long. What was the length of the longer boat?

9		
9	9	9

_____

23. Ramona spent $72 at the theme park last week. Alicia spent $8 less than Ramona. How much money did Alicia spend?

_____

24. Jamie spent $72 during the soccer trip. Troy spent $\frac{1}{8}$ as much as Jamie spent. How much money did Troy spend?

_____

25. The length of a field is 123 meters. That is 17.2 meters more than the width. What is the width of the field?

_____

26. Alex and Martin played video games last night. Alex scored 8,000 points and Martin scored 2,845 points. How many fewer points did Martin score?

_____

Classify Word Problems

▶ Situation Equations

A situation equation shows the relationship between known quantities and an unknown quantity in the situation.

Show your work.

Write a situation equation for each problem. Then solve the equation.

1. There were 6 horses in the barn. More horses came into the barn. Now there are 10 horses. How many horses came into the barn?

   _____

2. There were 9 horses in the barn. Then some of them went out to the pasture. Now there are 4 horses left in the barn. How many are out in the pasture?

   _____

3. There were some horses in the barn. Then 3 more came in. Now there are 8. How many horses were in the barn to start with?

   _____

4. There were some horses in the barn. Then 7 of them went out. Now there are 3 left in the barn. How many horses were in the barn at the beginning?

   _____

▶ From Situation to Solution Equations

In a solution equation, the unknown quantity is by itself on one side of the equals sign.

Write a situation equation for each problem. Then write a solution equation and solve the equation.

5. There were 642 horses in the barn. More horses came in. Now there are 839 horses. How many horses came in?

   Situation equation: _____

   Solution equation and solution: _____

6. There were 935 horses in the barn. Then some of them went out to the pasture. Now there are 428 horses left in the barn. How many are out in the pasture?

Show your work.

Situation equation: _____

Solution equation and solution: _____

7. There were some horses in the barn. Then 347 more came in. Now there are 736. How many horses were in the barn to start with?

Situation equation: _____

Solution equation and solution: _____

8. There were some horses in the barn. Then 196 of them went out. Now there are 510 left in the barn. How many horses were in the barn at the beginning?

Situation equation: _____

Solution equation and solution: _____

► Word Problem Applications

Workers at the Burlington Balloon Factory make a chart each day to keep track of the number of balloons. Today someone spilled juice on the chart. Some of the numbers cannot be read.

9. Write an equation you can solve to find each unknown number. Then solve the equation.

The Burlington Balloon Factory

Color of Balloon	Number at Beginning	Number made today	Number at end of day	Equation	Solution
Yellow	2,498	3,261			
Red	1,945		4,147		
Blue		5,172	8,365		
Pink	498		1,498		
White	3,456	500			

Situation and Solution Equations

Name _____   Date _____

Write the situation equation. If needed, write the solution equation. Then solve the problem.

Show your work.

10. Vance's desk drawer had 1,427 pictures in it. Today Vance got some more pictures from his grandmother. Now he has 2,198 pictures. How many pictures did Vance get from his grandmother?

_____

_____

11. Emma has a big sticker collection. Today she gave 100 stickers to her friend Kyra. Now Emma has 6,100 stickers. How many did Emma have at the start?

_____

_____

12. There were some people at the theater early last night, and then 2,197 more people arrived. Then there were 3,256 people in the theater. How many arrived early?

_____

_____

13. Luisa took $10,000 out of her bank account. Now she has $15,000 left in the account. How much money was in her account to begin with?

_____

_____

14. Mr. Daniels has a collection of 2,146 stamps. He bought some more stamps. Now he has 3,125. How many stamps did he buy?

_____

_____

15. **On The Back** Write a change word problem that has large numbers. Then, write the situation and solution equations and solve the problem.

Situation and Solution Equations

Name _____ **Date** _____

▶ The Jump Rope Contest

Comparison problems can ask you to find an unknown difference
or an unknown quantity. Draw comparison bars when needed.

Solve.   *Show your work.*

1. Julia jumped rope 1,200 times. Samantha jumped
   1,100 times. How many more jumps did Julia do?

   _____

2. Ahanu jumped 1,050 times. Rolando jumped 1,080 times.
   How many fewer jumps did Ahanu do than Rolando?

   _____

3. Altogether the Blue Team jumped 11,485 times. The Red
   Team did 827 more jumps than the Blue Team. How many
   jumps did the Red Team do?

   _____

4. Altogether the Green Team jumped 10,264 times. The
   Yellow Team did 759 fewer jumps than the Green Team.
   How many jumps did the Yellow Team do?

   _____

5. Ted jumped 1,300 times. He did 100 more jumps than
   Mario. How many jumps did Mario do?

   _____

6. Isaac jumped 987 times. Carlos needs to do 195 more
   jumps to tie with Isaac. How many jumps has Carlos
   done so far?

   _____

7. Altogether the fourth graders jumped 345,127 times. If the
   fifth graders had done 2,905 fewer jumps, there would
   have been a tie. How many jumps did the fifth graders do?

   _____

Name _____ **Date** _____

Class Activity

► **Solve Mixed Word Problems**

Show your work.

8. Last night 45,239 people attended the soccer game. This is 5,856 more people than were at the baseball game. How many people attended the baseball game?

_____

9. Eva earned $1,268 over the summer. That was $145.60 less than Daria earned. How much did Daria earn?

_____

10. A chef has 935 plates for a banquet with 1,086 guests. How many more plates does he need?

_____

11. Ramon worked 1,910 hours this year. His sister worked 45.5 fewer hours than Ramon did. How many hours did Ramon's sister work?

_____

► **Solve With Mental Math**

Say and write the answer.

12. $7,000 + 10 =$ _____

13. $7,000 - 10 =$ _____

14. $20,000 + 5,000 =$ _____

15. $20,000 - 5,000 =$ _____

16. 500 thousand $+ 1,000 =$ _____

17. 500 thousand $+ 10 =$ _____

18. 40 million $+ 1 =$ _____

19. 40 million $- 1 =$ _____

► **Challenging Comparison Problems**

20. The hottest temperature recorded on Earth is 132°F. The temperature on the sun is 720,000,000°F. How much hotter is the sun than the hottest place on Earth?

21. An inch is 2.54 centimeters. That is about 27.46 centimeters less than a foot. About how many centimeters are in a foot?

_____

Comparison Problems

Name _____   **Date** _____ **143**

▶ Two-Step Word Problems

Solve.

1. Yesterday a factory made 256,000 cotton balls. The cotton balls were packed in bags of 1,000 each. A drugstore bought 180 bags. How many bags of cotton balls were left?

   _____

   _____

2. Langston can usually swim 100 meters in 51.34 seconds. Today he swam 0.09 second faster than his usual time. He learned that the world record is 47.79 seconds. What is the difference between Langston's time today and the world record?

   _____

   _____

3. A cactus was 38.2 centimeters tall in January. By June it had grown 0.45 centimeters. By December it had grown another 0.51 centimeters. How tall was the cactus in December?

   _____

   _____

4. A coin collector bought 10 rare coins for $5,450 each and sold them later for $6,125 each. How much money did the coin collector make on these 10 coins altogether?

   _____

   _____

5. The map below shows several towns and the distances in miles between them. Use the map to help you write word problems with two steps for the class to solve. Write your problems on a separate sheet of paper.

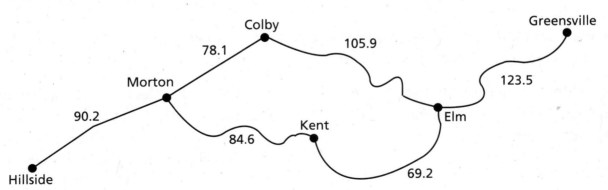

► Too Much Information

Read the following problem and then answer the question.

Kira is putting a wallpaper border around the top of the walls of her room. The dimensions of the room are 9 feet by 7 feet. The border material costs $8.00 per foot. How many feet of border material is needed?

1. Identify any extra information. Why isn't this information needed?

   _____

Solve the problem. Identify any information that is not needed.

2. Kyle read 34 pages on Monday and 28 pages on Tuesday. His book has 96 pages. How many pages has he read in all?

   _____

► Too Little Information

Read the following problem and then answer the question.

Mr. Hoon's class visits a museum. Each museum tour guide takes a group of 10 students. How many tour groups will there be?

3. Do you have enough information to solve this problem? What additional information do you need?

   _____

Solve each problem if possible. If a problem cannot be solved, tell what needed information is missing.

4. Ben earns $10 an hour babysitting. How much money did he earn babysitting on Saturday?

   _____

   _____

5. Jan made 8 booklets and used 6 sheets of paper in each. She bought special paper in packs of 5 sheets each. How many packs of paper did she buy?

   _____

   _____

▶ Problems With Multiple Solutions

Read the following problem and then answer the question.

The price list from a catalog is shown. If Dia spent between $15 and $20, what items did she buy?

Price List	
Candle	$3 each
Journal	$4 each
Artist Set	$9 each
Pillow	$11 each

6. Is it possible to have more than one solution? If so, explain how you know.

_____

_____

Solve the problem below. If possible, find two solutions.

7. Bethany filled 12 gift bags with 2 different prizes in each gift bag. She chose the prizes from the following packages at the store. She did not spend more than $15 in total on the prizes. Which packages did she buy?

Price Per Package		
Model Cars	(6 per pack)	$4 each
Clay Sets	(4 per pack)	$2 each
Paints	(3 per pack)	$1 each

_____

_____

▶ Problems With No Solution

Read the following problem and then answer the question.

Name two even whole numbers whose product is 19.

8. Can you find two even whole numbers whose product is 19? Why or why not?

_____

Determine if the problem can be solved. If it cannot be solved, explain why. If it can be solved, solve it.

9. Tom has 24 pictures to place on 8 pages. Each page must have the same number of pictures. How can he arrange the pictures?

10. Draw a square with a perimeter of 18. The length of each side of the square must be a whole number.

_____

_____

► Make a Double Bar Graph

The table below shows the number of watches sold at a jewelry store during the month of February.

February Watch Sales		
Week	Men's Watches	Ladies' Watches
1	8	6
2	24	28
3	4	2
4	10	8

1. Study the data in the table. If the data were to be displayed in a double bar graph, what numbers would you choose for the axis of the graph that shows the number of watches sold? Give a reason to support your answer.

   _____

   _____

   _____

2. On a separate sheet of paper or grid paper, draw a double bar graph to display the data. Make sure your graph contains a title and labels for the axes.

3. Write and solve a two-step word problem using the data in your graph.

   _____

   _____

   _____

   _____

   _____

3–22

Class Activity

Name _____

Date _____

Vocabulary

hypothesis

▶ Math and Social Studies

A **hypothesis** is a statement used as the basis for an investigation. One way to get more information about a hypothesis is to take a survey and analyze the data. The data supports or does not support the hypothesis.

1. **Make a Hypothesis** Make a hypothesis about something in your neighborhood.

   > *Examples*
   > *Half the students know the name of a town park.*
   > *Every student visits a town park at least once a week.*

   My hypothesis is: _____

2. **Write a Survey Question** Write a survey question you can ask to gain the data you need to test your hypothesis.

   > *Examples*
   > *What is the name of a park in our town?*
   > *How many times a week do you visit a town park?*

   My survey question is: _____

3. **Collect Data** Choose a group of people to answer your survey question.

4. **Organize Data** After you have collected the data, organize your data in a table. Explain how you chose to organize the data.

   _____

   _____

5. **Draw Conclusions** Compare your data to your hypothesis. Does the data support your hypothesis? How do you know?

   _____

   _____

6. **Make Predictions** Suppose you could survey 100 students in your school with your survey question. Do you think the data would be similar? Why or why not?

   _____

   _____

Vocabulary

categorical data
numerical data

▶ Displaying Categorical and Numerical Data

Data can be classified different ways.

Categorical data consists of words such as names or categories.

- The names of town parks
- The type of pet families have

Numerical data consists of numbers.

- The number of times a family visits a town park
- The number of people in a family.

7. **Categorical or Numerical Data** Look at the examples of categorical and numerical data that are shown. Decide if the data you collected is categorical or numerical data. Explain your choice.

_____

_____

8. **Classify Data** Some survey questions are listed below. Give an example of an answer to the survey question. Then decide if the data collected will be categorical or numerical data. Explain each choice.

   a. How do you travel to the your local park?

   _____

   b. How many hours a week do you spend at a town park?

   _____

9. **Display Your Data** Make a graph for your survey data. Explain your choice.

   _____

   Can you make a prediction based on your data? Why or why not?

   _____

   _____

Write each number.

1. twenty-three thousand, four hundred six _____

2. seven million, five hundred thirty thousand, nine hundred eighty-one _____

3. four tenths _____

4. three hundred sixty-two thousandths _____

Compare. Write > (greater than) or < (less than).

5. 564,899 ◯ 546,988

6. 2,539,750 ◯ 2,593,750

7. 0.813 ◯ 0.831

8. 0.6 ◯ 0.09

Add or subtract each pair of numbers. Then show how to estimate to check your answer.

9. 109,552 + 286,001 = _____

10. 0.42 + 1.675 = _____

11. 867,412 − 528,106 = _____

12. 5.481 − 1.51 = _____

Use the pictograph to answer each question.

13. How many students are in the fifth grade?

_____

14. How many more girls than boys are there in the fifth grade?

_____

Students in Fifth Grade

| Boys | • • • • • |
| Girls | • • • • • • • |

Key: • = 10 students

Use the bar graph to answer each question.

15. The graph shows the number of people at each school play last year. How many people saw a school play last year?

_____

16. How many more people saw "Wonderful Year" than saw "Alistair's Family"?

_____

Attendance at School Plays

Number of People: 0, 50, 100, 150, 200, 250, 300, 350, 400, 450

Summertime — 350
Tales of Friendship — 200
Wonderful Year — 400
Alistair's Family — 150

Play Title

Fish Population in Potter's Pond

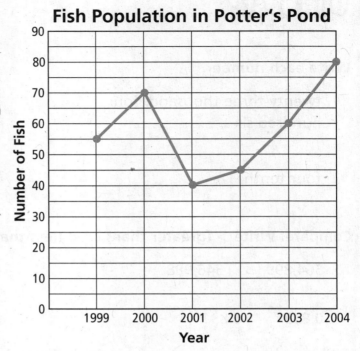

Use the line graph to answer each question.

17. The graph shows the fish population at the end of each year. What was the fish population at the end of 2002?

    _____

18. How much greater was the fish population in 2004 than it was in 1999?

    _____

Solve.

Show your work.

19. This week Roberto ran 5.83 miles on Monday and 6.6 miles on Tuesday. Last week he ran a total of 12.09 miles on Monday and Tuesday. Did he run more or less last week? How much more or less?

    _____

20. **Extended Response** The distance between Chicago and Los Angeles is 1,742 miles. The distance between Chicago and Philadelphia is 665 miles. The distance between Chicago and Detroit is 427 miles less than the distance between Chicago and Philadelphia. Explain how to find how much greater the distance between Chicago and Los Angeles is than the distance between Chicago and Detroit.

    _____

    _____

    _____

    _____

    _____

▶ Identify Lines

Use the words ray, angle, line, perpendicular, parallel, or oblique to name each figure.

Vocabulary

ray
angle
line
perpendicular
parallel
oblique

1.

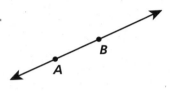

$\overleftrightarrow{AB}$

2.

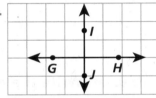

$\overrightarrow{CD}$

3.

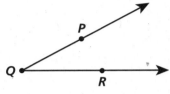

$\angle PQR$

4.

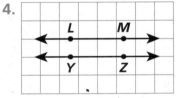

$\overleftrightarrow{LM}$ and $\overleftrightarrow{YZ}$

5.

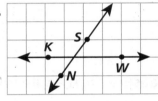

$\overleftrightarrow{GH}$ and $\overleftrightarrow{IJ}$

6.

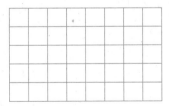

$\overleftrightarrow{KW}$ and $\overleftrightarrow{NS}$

Draw each figure. Use your ruler.

7. ray *QC*

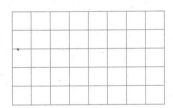

8. angle *DXV*

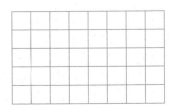

9. line *EU*

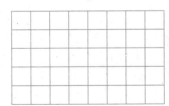

10. perpendicular lines
   ST and *JK*

11. oblique lines
   FT and *UO*

12. parallel lines
   CR and *NM*

Class Activity

Name _____ **Date** _____

► Use a Protractor

This is a **protractor**. We use it to measure **angles**. We measure angles in **degrees**. This angle measures 66°.

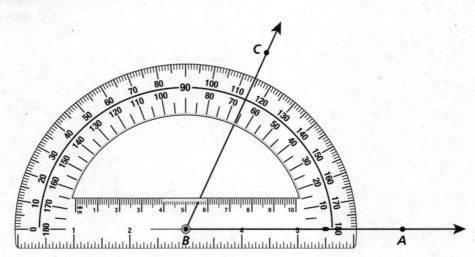

Measure each angle with your protractor. Write the measure.

13.

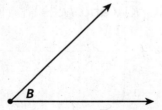

∠B = _____

14.

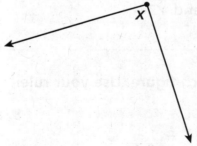

∠X = _____

15.

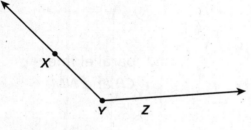

∠XYZ = _____

16.

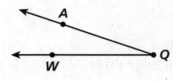

∠AQW = _____

Lines and Angles

▶ Vertical Angles

When two lines **intersect**, the angles formed are
opposite angles. ∠ABD is opposite ∠CBE.

Name another pair of opposite angles.

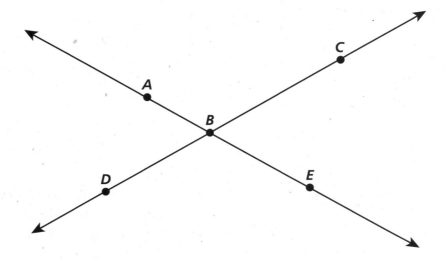

Pairs of opposite angles formed by intersecting lines are called **vertical angles**. Vertical angles have the same measure.

17. Name the vertical angles in the drawing above.

_____   _____

Use your protractor to measure each angle. Write the measure.

18. ∠ABC = _____   **19.** ∠DBE = _____

20. ∠ABD = _____   **21.** ∠CBE = _____

Compare the measures of these angles. Write >, <, or =.

22. ∠DBE ◯ ∠EBC   **23.** ∠ABC ◯ ∠DBE   **24.** ∠ABD ◯ ∠EBC

Class Activity

► **Complementary and Supplementary Angles**

Vocabulary

complementary
supplementary

Read these definitions and answer the questions below.

Two angles are **complementary** if the sum of their measures is 90°.	Two angles are **supplementary** if the sum of their measures is 180°.

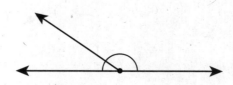

When put together, supplementary angles make a straight line.

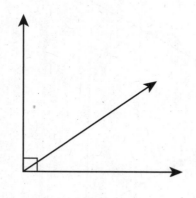

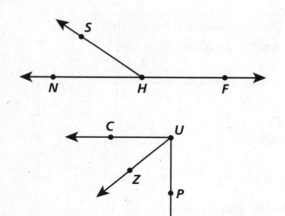

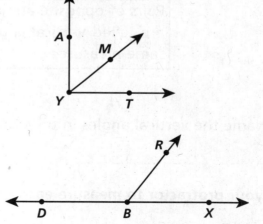

25. Name two straight angles. _____

26. Name two pairs of complementary angles.

_____   _____

27. Name two pairs of supplementary angles.

_____   _____

Dear Family,

This year's second geometry unit is about angles and how they are measured. Your child will learn how to measure angles in degrees and come to understand that a whole circle contains 360 degrees, or 360°.

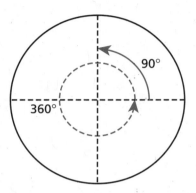

Your child will discover that the angles in a triangle always total 180° and the angles in a quadrilateral always total 360°. These discoveries will enable your child to solve many geometry problems.

Your child will use knowledge of angles to rotate geometric figures, investigate symmetry, and use circle graphs to display information about their world.

Favorite Kind of Book

If you have any questions or comments, please call or write to me.

Sincerely,
Your child's teacher

Estimada familia:

La segunda unidad de geometría del año trata los ángulos y cómo se miden. Su niño aprenderá a medir ángulos en grados y empezará a comprender que un círculo tiene 360 grados, ó 360°.

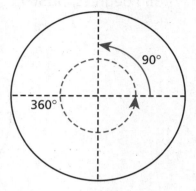

Su niño descubrirá que los ángulos de un triángulo siempre suman 180° y que los ángulos de un cuadrilátero siempre suman 360°. Estos descubrimientos le permitirán a su niño resolver muchos problemas de geometría.

Su niño usará el conocimiento de ángulos para girar figuras geométricas, investigar la simetría y usar gráficas circulares para mostrar información sobre su mundo.

Tipo favorito de libro

Si tiene alguna pregunta o comentario, por favor comuníquese conmigo.

Atentamente,
El maestro de su niño

Lines and Angles

Vocabulary

angle

▶ Measure Interior Angles of a Triangle

1. On a separate piece of paper, draw any type of triangle.

   Close to a vertex, label the angles A, B, C. Cut off each **angle**.
   Draw a straight line and arrange the angles on the line so that the vertices A, B, and C touch and the sides do not overlap.

   What do you notice about the total of the measures of the angles?
   ∠A + ∠B + ∠C = _____°

Find and record the unknown angle measure.

2.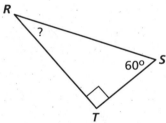

   ∠R = _____

3.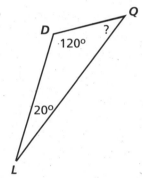

   ∠Q = _____

4.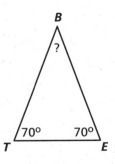

   ∠B = _____

5.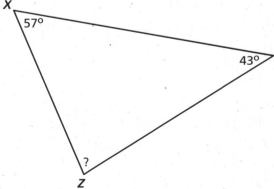

   ∠Z = _____

6. Draw a triangle on the grid by connecting any three points.

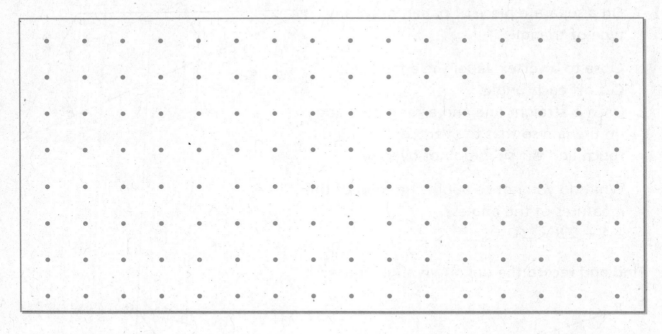

7. Use a protractor to measure two angles of your triangle.

_____

8. Predict the measure of the third angle.

_____

9. Measure the third angle to check your prediction.

_____

10. Two of the angles in this isosceles triangle have the same measure. What is that measure?

_____

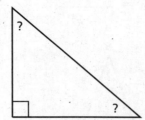

11. Each angle of the equilateral triangle has the same measure. What is that measure?

_____

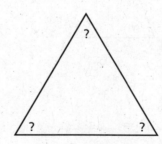

Name _____ Date _____

► Measure Interior Angles of a Quadrilateral

12. Look at these figures. Use what you know about squares and rectangles to find the total angle measures of figure A and of figure B.

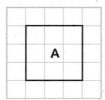
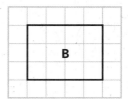

_____   _____

13. Use your protractor to find the total angle measures of these figures.

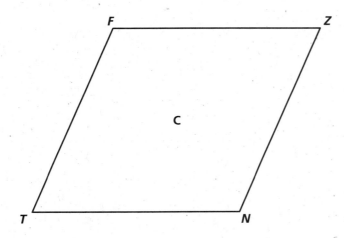
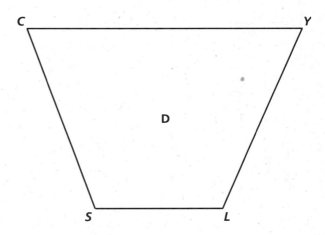

_____   _____

14. Write a general statement about the total angle measures of quadrilaterals.

_____

_____

_____

Class Activity

Without using your protractor, find the measure of the unknown angles.
Write the measure in each figure.

15.

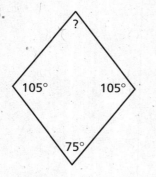

16.

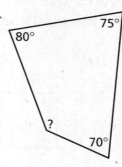

17.

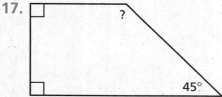

18.

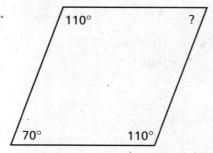

19.

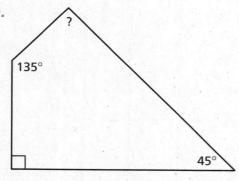

20.

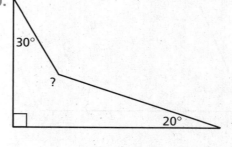

21. On a separate piece of paper, draw any type
of quadrilateral.

Close to a vertex, label the angles *A*, *B*, *C*, and *D*.
Cut off each angle. Arrange the angles around a
point so that they do not overlap.
What do you notice?
How many degrees are around the center of a circle?

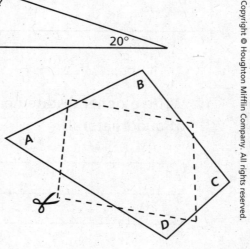

_____

_____

Polygons and Angles

Name _____   **Date** _____

Class Activity

Vocabulary

congruent
polygon

▶ Identify Congruent Figures

Congruent figures are the same size and shape.

Figure A and figure B are congruent.
They are the same size and shape.

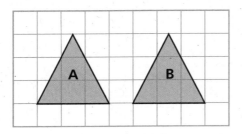

Figure C and figure D are congruent.
Although one figure has been turned,
both figures are the same size and shape.

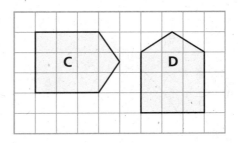

Figure E and figure F are not congruent.
They are not the same size.

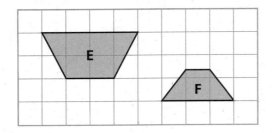

Figure G and figure H are not congruent.
They are not the same shape.

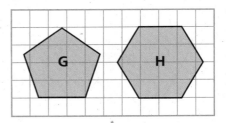

In each row, circle all of the polygons that look congruent.

1.
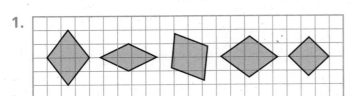

2.

3.
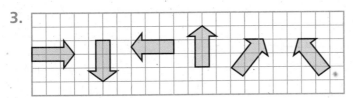

Compare and Contrast Polygons **161**

Name _____ Date _____

► Sort and Classify Polygons

Cut out the polygons. Choose a sorting rule. Use the Venn diagram to sort the figures.

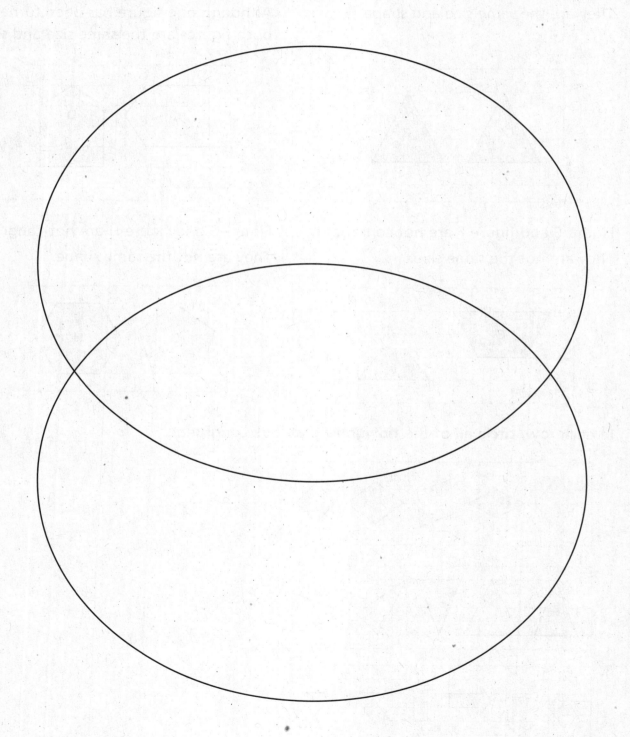

Compare and Contrast Polygons

Name _____ Date _____

► Identify Polygons

Cut out the strips. Then cut out the squares. Do not cut out each shape.

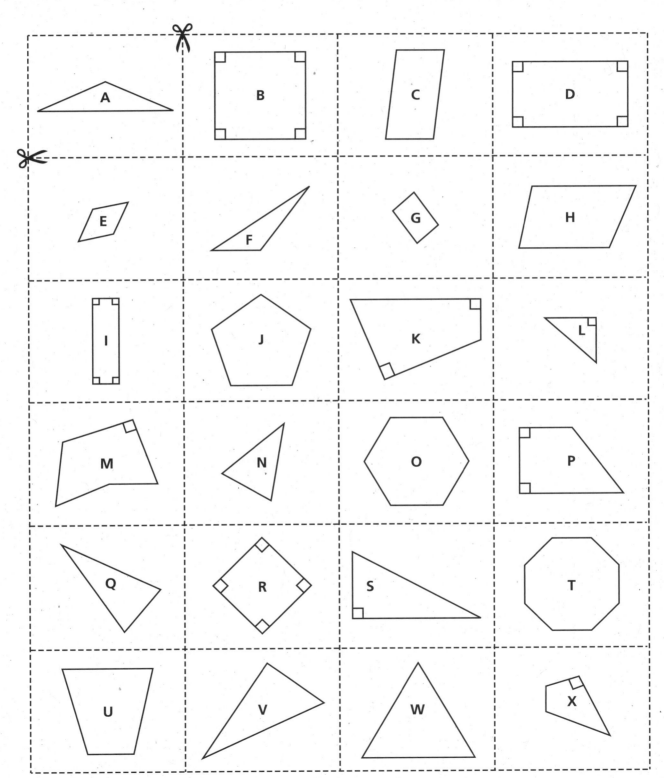

Compare and Contrast Polygons

Class Activity

▶ Draw a Figure Using Clues

**Using a straightedge, sketch the polygon that fits the given clues.
Be sure to label each angle measure.**

1. This figure is created by two joined complementary angles.

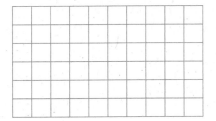

2. This polygon is congruent to a rectangle with an area of 20 square units and a perimeter of 18 units.

3. This is an isosceles polygon with one right angle and angles that total 180°.

4. This figure is created using two rays. It has a supplement that measures 45°.

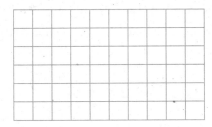

5. This polygon has the characteristics of a rectangle and a rhombus. It has a perimeter of 16 units and an area of 16 square units.

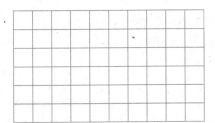

6. This isosceles polygon has one pair of opposite sides parallel and fewer sides than a pentagon. It has two congruent angles with a sum measure of 270°.

► Draw Multiple Figures Using Clues

Using a straightedge, sketch the polygons that fit the given clues.

7. a polygon with no pairs of opposite sides parallel, at most 2 acute angles, and a total angle measure of < 200°

8. a polygon with less than 5 sides and all sides with equal lengths

9. a polygon with at most 5 sides, at least one pair of opposite sides parallel, and at least 2 right angles

10. a polygon with at most 2 pairs of opposite sides parallel and at most 2 acute angles

11. a quadrilateral with 2 pairs of opposite sides parallel and at least one pair of congruent opposite angles that have a total angle measure of 180°

12. a polygon with at most 5 sides, at least 1 acute and 1 obtuse angle, at least one pair of opposite sides congruent, and one pair of opposite sides parallel

Compare and Contrast Polygons

Class Activity

Vocabulary

circle
straight angle
reflex angle

▶ Measure Angles in a Circle

You can show all the different types of angles in a 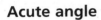 **circle** .

Acute angle

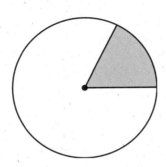

Greater than 0° and less than 90°

Right angle

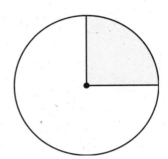

90°

Obtuse angle

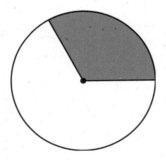

Greater than 90° and less than 180°

Straight angle

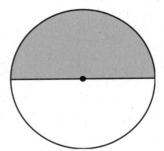

180°

Reflex angle

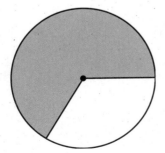

Greater than 180° and less than 360°

Circle

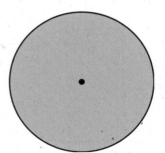

360°

Class Activity

► Draw Angles in a Circle.

**Use a straightedge and protractor to draw and shade
an angle of each type. Measure and label each angle.**

1. Obtuse

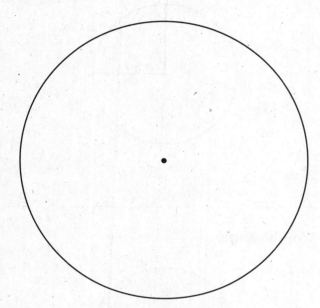

2. Straight

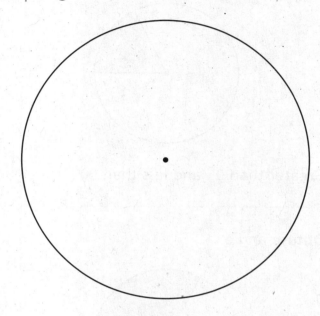

3. Acute

4. 3 Angles That Equal 360°

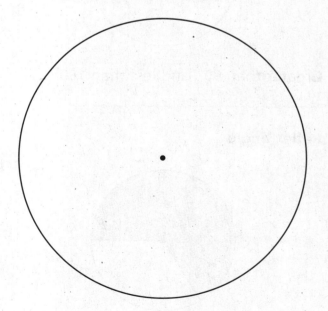

5. On a separate piece of paper, use a protractor to draw
angles with measures of 25°, 75°, 155°, and 180°.

Circles and Angles

Class Activity

Vocabulary

turn

▶ Turns of a Circle

The number of degrees (°) in a full circle is 360. You can turn an object around the center of a circle and use degrees to describe the **turn**.

A turn is described from the start position, which is marked 0°.

Each turn is measured from 0°.

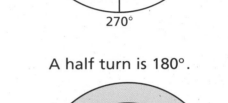

A quarter turn is 90°.

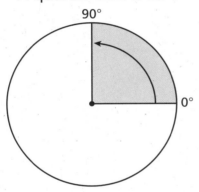

A half turn is 180°.

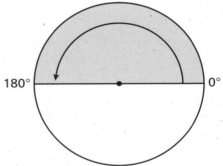

A three-quarter turn is 270°.

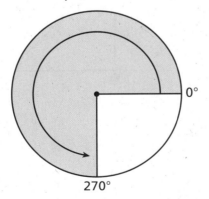

A full turn is 360°.

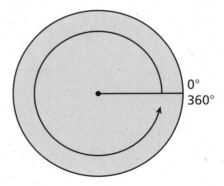

Class Activity

Name _____

Date _____

5. Draw the figure after a turn of 270° clockwise.

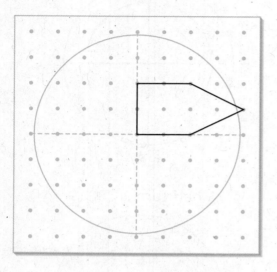

6. Draw the figure after a turn of 180° clockwise.

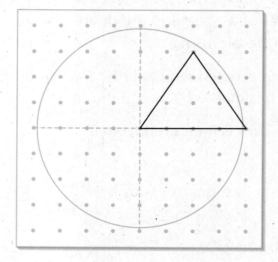

7. Draw the figure after a turn of 90° clockwise.

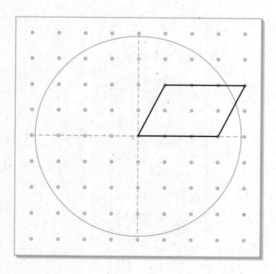

8. Draw the figure after a turn of 90° counter-clockwise.

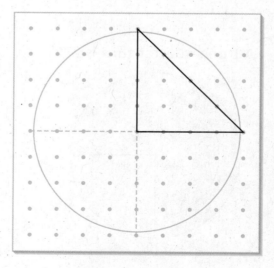

Circles and Angles

Class Activity

Name _____

Date _____

Vocabulary
line symmetry
line of symmetry

▶ Identify Line Symmetry

A figure has **line symmetry** if it can be folded in half so that the two parts match exactly. The fold line is a **line of symmetry**.

This figure has four lines of symmetry.

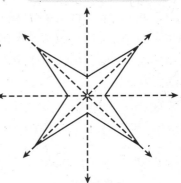

Each figure below has at least one line of symmetry.
Use your ruler and draw all of the lines of symmetry.

1.

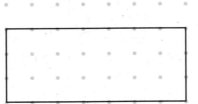

2.

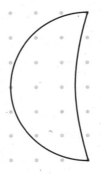

3.

4.

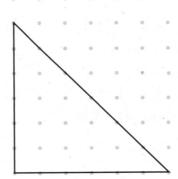

5.

6.

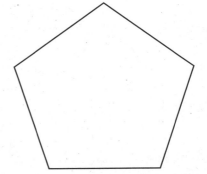

Class Activity

Name _____   **Date** _____

Vocabulary
rotational symmetry
quarter turn
half turn
three-quarter turn

► Explore Rotational Symmetry

A figure has **rotational symmetry** if it can be turned less than a full turn (360°) around a point and still be in the same horizontal and vertical orientation as it was before. Draw the figures in each quadrant after a counterclockwise rotation of 90°, 180°, and 270°. Fill in what kinds of rotational symmentry each figure has.

7. This figure looks the same after a **quarter turn**.

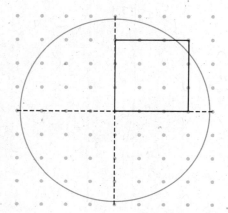

This figure has _____ rotational symmetry.

8. This figure looks the same after a **half turn**.

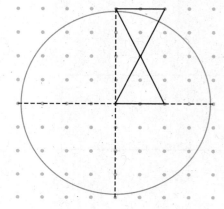

This figure has _____ rotational symmetry.

9. This figure looks the same after a **three-quarter turn**

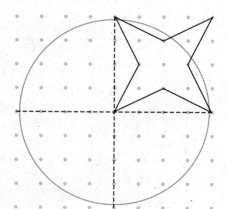

This figure has _____ rotational symmetry.

10. This figure will not look the same until it is returned to its original position.

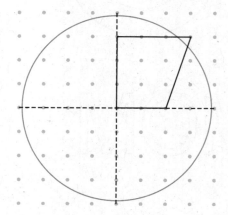

This figure has _____ rotational symmetry.

Symmetry

Describe the rotational symmetry for each figure.

11.

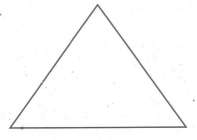

_____

12.

_____

13.

_____

14.

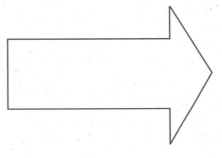

_____

15.

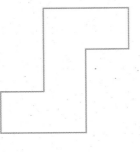

_____

16.

_____

17. Which figures above have line symmetry?

_____

18. Which figures above have both line symmetry and rotational symmetry?

_____

19. **On the Back** In the top right quarter of the grid, make a figure that has 90° rotational symmetry. Draw rotations of that figure in the other parts of the grid.

Symmetry

▶ Interpret Parts of a Circle Graph

This circle graph represents a survey of students. The
students were asked to name their favorite kind of book.

Favorite Books

Use the graph to answer the questions.

1. What kind of book was named twice as often as
   a humor book?

   _____

2. What kind of book was named half as often as
   an adventure book?

   _____

3. Is the number of students who chose either mystery or
   humor books more or less than the number of students
   who chose adventure books? Explain how you know.

   _____

   _____

   _____

   _____

4. For this survey, 125 students named fiction books as their
   favorite kind of book. How many students named mystery
   books as their favorite kind of book?

   _____

5. How many students were surveyed? Explain how you know.

   _____

   _____

   _____

▶ Plan and Make a Circle Graph

1. Discuss what a circle graph shows easily. Discuss what you can see easily in a circle graph, bar graph, and pictograph.

2. Use the table of information to create a circle graph.

Our Pets	
Kind of Pet	**Number**
Cat	120
Dog	60
Guinea Pig	20
No Pet	40

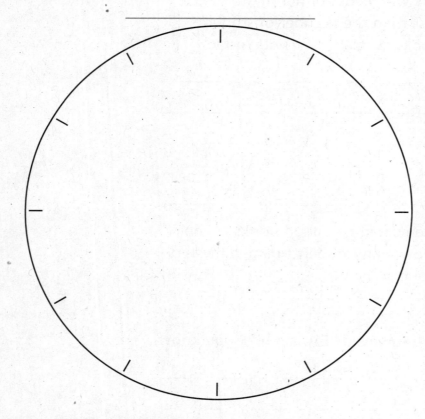

3. Write a problem that someone can solve using your circle graph.

_____

_____

_____

Circle Graphs

Name _____ **Date** _____

▶ Experiment with Circumference

1. Record the type of can, its **diameter**, and its **circumference** in the table.

Type of Can	Diameter		Circumference	
	mm	nearest cm	mm	nearest cm

2. Compare the diameter and circumference in centimeters for each can. What pattern does each pair of numbers have?

_____

_____

3. Write a rule that describes how to estimate the circumference of a circle when you know its diameter.

_____

_____

4. Write a rule that describes how to estimate the diameter of a circle when you know its circumference.

_____

_____

Vocabulary

radius

▶ Estimate Circumference Using Pi (π)

5. Write a formula that uses diameter to find the circumference of a circle.

_____

6. Write a formula that uses **radius** to find the circumference of a circle.

_____

Use the given measures to estimate the circumference of each circle. Use 3 for π.

7.

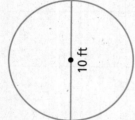

10 ft

_____

8.

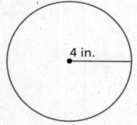

4 in.

_____

9. The fence that goes around a circular flower garden is 27 feet long. About how wide is the widest part of the garden?

_____

Use these angles to answer questions 1 and 2.

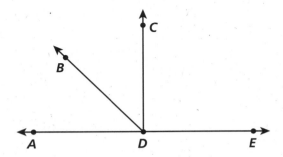

1. Name one straight angle.

   _____

2. Name one pair of complementary angles.

   _____

Write the measure of the unknown angle.

3.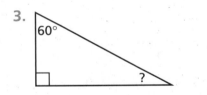

   _____

4.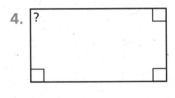

   _____

5. Circle all the polygons that look congruent to each other.

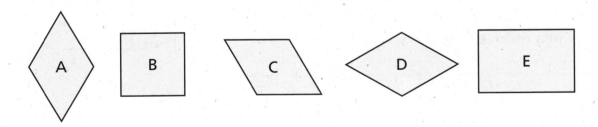

6. Draw the figure after a clockwise turn of 180°.

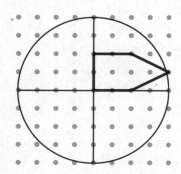

7. Draw all of the lines of symmetry for the equilateral triangle.

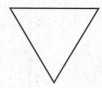

Use the circle graph to answer questions 8–10.

8. Who received the most votes?

_____

9. Who received the least number of votes?

_____

10. **Extended Response** Esai received 298 votes. Nathan received 87 votes. How many votes did Lavinia receive? Explain your answer.

_____

_____

_____

_____

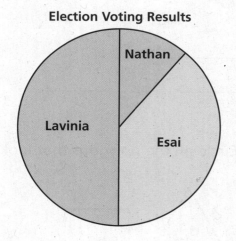

Election Voting Results

▶ Parts and Wholes

1. The head is what fraction of the whole worm?

_____

2. Draw a worm whose head is $\frac{1}{7}$ of the whole.

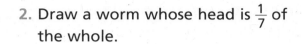

3. Divide this circle into fourths. Shade $\frac{1}{4}$.

4. This triangle is $\frac{1}{2}$. Make the whole.

5. This donut is $\frac{1}{6}$ of the group. Draw the rest of the group of donuts.

6. This is 1 whole group. Circle $\frac{2}{5}$ of the group.

7. What fraction of all your fingers are your 2 thumbs?

_____

8. What fraction of the apples was eaten?

   _____

9. What fraction of the fish did Alta catch?   _____

Dave	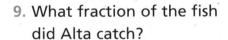
Alta	
Brent	
Stacy	

10. What fraction of the corn did Yuet eat?   _____

Yuet	
Mike	
Vasco	
Gracia	

11. Tim ate $\frac{2}{5}$ of the grapes, and Kate ate $\frac{1}{5}$. What fraction of the grapes did they eat altogether?

_____

12. Camila made 5 paper chain links and Mito made 4. What fraction of a 20-link chain have they made so far?

_____

Class Activity

Vocabulary
unit fraction
non-unit fraction

▶ Practice with Fractions

A **unit fraction** is one equal part of a whole. A **non-unit fraction** is built from two or more unit fractions.

What unit fraction does each shaded area show?

13.   14.   15.   16.

_____   _____   _____   _____

17. Write the non-unit fractions.

| $\frac{1}{6}$ | $\frac{2}{7}$ | $\frac{1}{9}$ | $\frac{3}{10}$ | $\frac{5}{6}$ | $\frac{1}{12}$ | $\frac{1}{8}$ |

Write enough unit fractions to make the non-unit fraction:

18. Make $\frac{2}{7}$. $\frac{1}{7} + \frac{1}{7} + \frac{1}{7} + \frac{1}{7} + \frac{1}{7} + \frac{1}{7} + \frac{1}{7} = \frac{7}{7}$

19. Make $\frac{4}{5}$. $\frac{1}{5} + \frac{1}{5} + \frac{1}{5} + \frac{1}{5} + \frac{1}{5} = \frac{5}{5}$

To add fractions, you put together fractions that are made of the same unit fraction.

$\frac{2}{6} + \frac{3}{6} = \frac{5}{6}$

2 sixths + 3 sixths = 5 sixths

2 ones + 3 ones = 5 ones

20. How is adding fractions like adding whole numbers?

_____

_____

How is it different?

_____

_____

Build Unit Fractions

Dear Family:

Your child is learning about fraction concepts. Using fraction bars, students learn about unit fractions, or fractions that are just one part of the whole, such as $\frac{1}{2}$ or $\frac{1}{4}$.

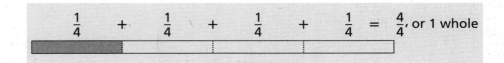

$$\frac{1}{4} \quad + \quad \frac{1}{4} \quad + \quad \frac{1}{4} \quad + \quad \frac{1}{4} \quad = \quad \frac{4}{4}, \text{ or 1 whole}$$

Non-unit fractions are sums of unit fractions.

Unit fractions are used to convert mixed numbers, which have a whole-number part and a fractional part, to improper fractions, where the top number (numerator) is larger than the bottom number (denominator).

$$\frac{3}{4} = \frac{1}{4} + \frac{1}{4} + \frac{1}{4}$$

$$2\frac{1}{4} = \frac{4}{4} + \frac{4}{4} + \frac{1}{4} = \frac{9}{4}$$

Fraction bars help students understand how to compare, add, and subtract fractions with like denominators.

$$\frac{a}{d} + \frac{b}{d} = \frac{a+b}{d}$$

$$\frac{1}{4} + \frac{2}{4} = \frac{3}{4}$$

$$\frac{a}{d} - \frac{b}{d} = \frac{a-b}{d}$$

$$\frac{3}{4} - \frac{1}{4} = \frac{2}{4}$$

If $a > b$, then

$$\frac{1}{a} < \frac{1}{b} \text{ and } \frac{a}{d} > \frac{b}{d}$$

$$\frac{1}{3} < \frac{1}{2} \text{ and } \frac{3}{7} > \frac{2}{7}$$

These skills extend to fractions with unlike denominators. We rewrite each fraction with a common denominator, using multiplication to make an equivalent fraction.

$$\frac{1}{3} \overset{\times 5}{\underset{\times 5}{=}} \frac{5}{15}$$

We add and subtract mixed numbers by treating the whole-number part and the fractional part separately, ungrouping 1 whole, if needed.

$$\begin{array}{r} 4\frac{1}{3} \\ - 2\frac{7}{15} \end{array} = \begin{array}{r} 3\frac{20}{15} \\ 4\frac{5}{15} \\ 2\frac{7}{15} \\ \hline 1\frac{13}{15} \end{array}$$

Sincerely,
Your child's teacher

Estimada familia:

Su niño está aprendiendo conceptos de fracciones. Al usar barras de fracciones, los estudiantes aprenden acerca de fracciones cuyo numerador es uno es decir, fracciones que son una parte del entero, como $\frac{1}{2}$ ó $\frac{1}{4}$.

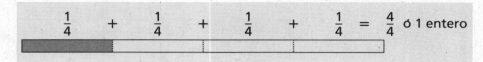

$$\frac{1}{4} \quad + \quad \frac{1}{4} \quad + \quad \frac{1}{4} \quad + \quad \frac{1}{4} \quad = \quad \frac{4}{4} \text{ ó 1 entero}$$

Las fracciones cuyo numerador es diferente de uno son sumas de fracciones cuyo numerador es uno.

$$\frac{3}{4} = \frac{1}{4} + \frac{1}{4} + \frac{1}{4}$$

Las fracciones cuyo numerador es uno se usan para convertir números mixtos, los cuales tienen una parte formada por un número entero y una parte fraccionaria, a fracciones impropias, donde el número de arriba (numerador) es mayor que el número de abajo (denominador).

$$2\frac{1}{4} = \frac{4}{4} + \frac{4}{4} + \frac{1}{4} = \frac{9}{4}$$

Las barras de fracciones ayudan a los estudiantes a comprender cómo se comparan, se suman y se restan las fracciones con denominadores iguales:

$$\frac{a}{d} + \frac{b}{d} = \frac{a+b}{d}$$

$$\frac{1}{4} + \frac{2}{4} = \frac{3}{4}$$

$$\frac{a}{d} - \frac{b}{d} = \frac{a-b}{d}$$

$$\frac{3}{4} - \frac{1}{4} = \frac{2}{4}$$

$a > b$ así que

$$\frac{1}{a} < \frac{1}{b} \text{ y } \frac{a}{d} > \frac{b}{d}$$

$$\frac{1}{3} < \frac{1}{2} \text{ y } \frac{3}{4} > \frac{2}{4}$$

Estas destrezas se aplican también a fracciones con denominadores distintos. Volvemos a escribir cada fracción con un denominador común, usando la multiplicación para hacer una fracción equivalente.

$$\times 5$$
$$\frac{1}{3} = \frac{5}{15}$$
$$\times 5$$

Sumamos y restamos números mixtos tratando la parte del número entero y la parte fraccionaria por separado, desagrupando 1 entero si es necesario.

$$4\frac{1}{3} = \overset{3\frac{20}{15}}{4\frac{\cancel{5}}{15}}$$
$$- 2\frac{7}{15} = 2\frac{7}{15}$$
$$\overline{ 1\frac{13}{15}}$$

Atentamente,
El maestro de su niño

Class Activity

▶ Compare With Fraction Bars

The fraction bars show the same whole divided into different unit fractions.

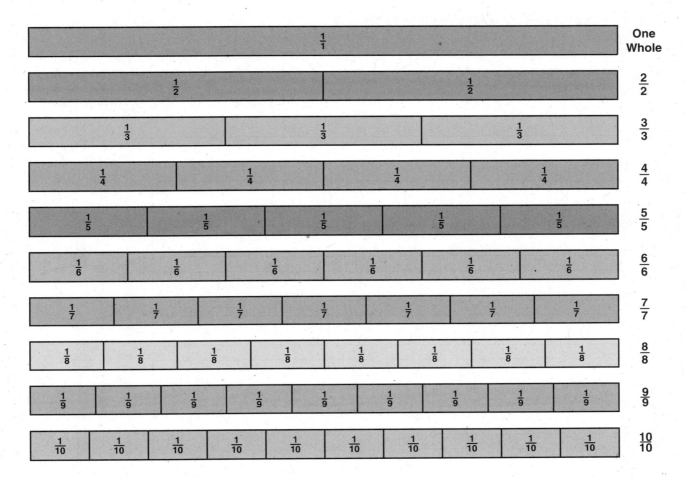

Which is greater? Explain how you know.

1. $\frac{1}{4}$ or $\frac{1}{5}$ _____ _____

_____

2. $\frac{9}{10}$ or $\frac{10}{10}$ _____ _____

_____

3. $\frac{2}{9}$ or $\frac{3}{9}$ _____ _____

_____

Write the greater fraction.

4. $\frac{1}{50}$ $\frac{1}{60}$ 5. $\frac{40}{45}$ $\frac{45}{45}$ 6. $\frac{2}{25}$ $\frac{4}{25}$ 7. $\frac{1}{99}$ $\frac{1}{100}$

Class Activity

▶ Compare Unequal Fractions

Compare each set of fractions as you follow the trail. Then write the correct sign (< or >) between the fractions.

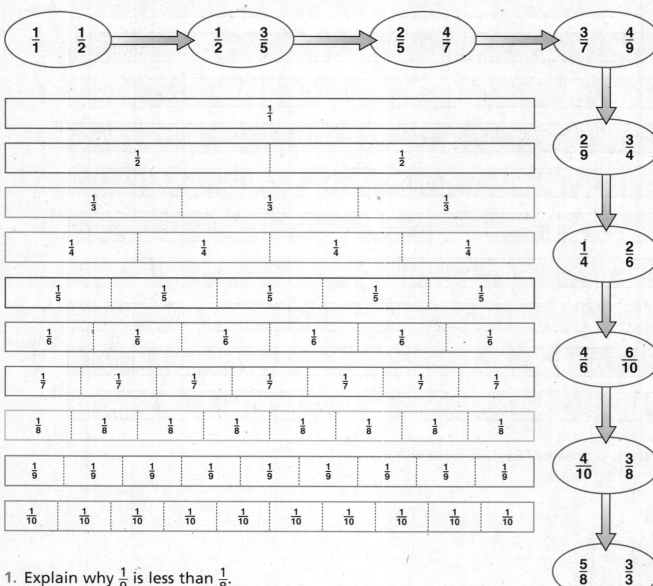

1. Explain why $\frac{1}{9}$ is less than $\frac{1}{8}$.

_____

_____

_____

Compare Fractions

Class Activity

Name _____   Date _____

Vocabulary

numerator
denominator

▶ Find Unknown Numerators and Denominators

The **numerator** of a fraction tells the number of pieces of the whole. The **denominator** of a fraction tells the divisions of the whole.

numerator
number of pieces
_____
denominator
divisions
→ $\frac{n}{d}$

Add or subtract.

1. $\frac{3}{5} - \frac{1}{5} =$ _____

2. $\frac{3}{9} + \frac{2}{9} + \frac{1}{9} =$ _____

Find n.

3. $\frac{2}{4} + \frac{1}{4} = \frac{n}{4}$

   $n =$ _____

4. $\frac{3}{6} + \frac{2}{6} = \frac{n}{6}$

   $n =$ _____

5. $\frac{5}{10} - \frac{4}{10} = \frac{n}{10}$

   $n =$ _____

6. $\frac{6}{7} - \frac{2}{7} = \frac{n}{7}$

   $n =$ _____

7. $\frac{4}{8} - \frac{3}{8} = \frac{n}{8}$

   $n =$ _____

8. $\frac{1}{12} + \frac{3}{12} + \frac{7}{12} = \frac{n}{12}$

   $n =$ _____

Find d.

9. $\frac{4}{7} + \frac{2}{7} = \frac{6}{d}$

   $d =$ _____

10. $\frac{7}{8} - \frac{2}{8} = \frac{5}{d}$

    $d =$ _____

11. $\frac{3}{d} + \frac{3}{d} + \frac{2}{d} = \frac{8}{9}$

    $d =$ _____

12. $\frac{1}{d} + \frac{1}{d} + \frac{1}{d} = \frac{d}{d}$

    $d =$ _____

13. $\frac{1}{d} + \frac{1}{d} + \frac{1}{d} + \frac{1}{d} + \frac{1}{d} + \frac{1}{d} + \frac{1}{d} = \frac{d}{d}$

    $d =$ _____

Which is greater?

14. $\frac{7}{8}$ or $\frac{5}{8}$ _____

15. $\frac{3}{d}$ or $\frac{6}{d}$ _____

16. $\frac{9}{d}$ or $\frac{4}{d}$ _____

17. What is d in this fraction bar? _____

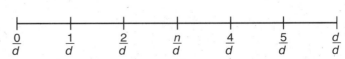

18. What is d in the number line?
    What is n? How do you know?

    $d =$ _____ $n =$ _____

    _____

    _____

▶ Real-World Fractions

Solve.

Show your work.

19. The Foster family bought a 1-pound (16-ounce) bag of popcorn kernels. On Sunday they popped 2 ounces, on Monday they popped 4 ounces, and on Tuesday they popped 3 ounces. What fraction of the popcorn have they popped so far? What fraction is left?

_____

20. Mrs. Reuben walked $\frac{9}{10}$ mile from home and then went back $\frac{1}{10}$ mile. How far from home is she now?

_____

▶ Summarize

Subtracting fractions means taking away fractions that are made of the same unit fraction (that have the same *d*).

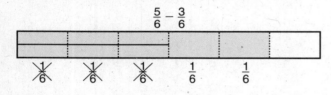
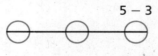

21. How is subtracting fractions like subtracting whole numbers? How is it different?

_____

_____

_____

22. How is subtracting fractions like adding fractions? How is it different?

_____

_____

Class Activity

Name _____ **Date** _____

▶ Find Addends That Total One

The numbers that you add to find the total in an addition expression are called **addends**.

1. What part of the fraction does not change when you add or subtract?

_____

$3 + 5 = 8$	$\frac{3}{9} + \frac{5}{9} = \frac{8}{9}$
The addends are 3 and 5. The total is 8.	The addends are $\frac{3}{9}$ and $\frac{5}{9}$. The total is $\frac{8}{9}$.

Add or subtract.

2. $\frac{3}{8} + \frac{4}{8} =$ _____

3. $\frac{2}{7} + \frac{3}{7} =$ _____

4. $\frac{5}{9} - \frac{2}{9} =$ _____

5. $\frac{1}{75} + \frac{1}{75} =$ _____

6. $\frac{3}{50} + \frac{3}{50} =$ _____

7. $\frac{9}{67} - \frac{5}{67} =$ _____

Find $\frac{n}{d}$.

8. $\frac{2}{5} + \frac{n}{d} = 1$

$\frac{n}{d} =$ _____

9. $\frac{3}{9} + \frac{n}{d} = 1$

$\frac{n}{d} =$ _____

10. $\frac{7}{12} + \frac{4}{12} = \frac{n}{d}$

$\frac{n}{d} =$ _____

11. $1 - \frac{7}{10} = \frac{n}{d}$

_____

$\frac{n}{d} =$ _____

12. $1 - \frac{8}{17} = \frac{n}{d}$

_____

$\frac{n}{d} =$ _____

13. $1 - \frac{18}{20} = \frac{n}{d}$

_____

$\frac{n}{d} =$ _____

14. $\frac{15}{30} + \frac{10}{30} = \frac{n}{d}$

$\frac{n}{d} =$ _____

15. $\frac{39}{40} + \frac{n}{d} = 1$

$\frac{n}{d} =$ _____

16. $\frac{70}{100} + \frac{n}{d} = 1$

$\frac{n}{d} =$ _____

Class Activity

▶ Unknown Addends in Real Life

Solve.

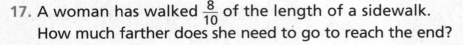

Show your work.

17. A woman has walked $\frac{8}{10}$ of the length of a sidewalk. How much farther does she need to go to reach the end?

_____

18. A man has walked $\frac{3}{10}$ of the length of the sidewalk. How much farther does he need to go to reach the end?

_____

19. A squirrel climbed $\frac{3}{8}$ of the way up a tree. How much higher does it need to go to reach the top?

_____

20. Another squirrel climbed $\frac{9}{16}$ of the way up the tree. How much farther does it need to go to reach the top?

_____

21. We ate $\frac{5}{12}$ of a watermelon at breakfast. At lunch we ate $\frac{7}{12}$ of the same melon. How much of the watermelon is left for dinner?

_____

22. The sailboat is $\frac{5}{9}$ of the way across the lake. How much farther does it have to go to reach the shore?

_____

23. The rowboat is $\frac{4}{17}$ of the way across the lake. How much farther does it have to go to reach the shore?

_____

24. I mowed $\frac{7}{12}$ of the lawn, and my friend mowed $\frac{3}{12}$. How much of the lawn do we still have to mow?

_____

Fractional Addends of One

Class Activity

▶ Explore Changing Wholes

Before you decide how much a fraction represents, you need to know how big the whole is.

1. Would you prefer to have $\frac{1}{2}$ of the large watermelon or $\frac{1}{2}$ of the small one? Why?

_____

_____

_____

2. Would you prefer to sweep $\frac{1}{3}$ of the gymnasium or $\frac{1}{3}$ of your classroom? Why?

_____

_____

What fraction of the whole is each shaded square?

3.   _____

4.  _____

5.   _____

6.   _____

7. 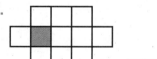 _____

8.   _____

9. The shaded squares in exercises 3–8 are all the same size. Why are the fractions different?

_____

_____

► Solve Problems With Changing Wholes

Solve.

10. Adrianne and Gabriél have 80 cherries. They need 50 cherries to make a pie, and they would also like a snack. Adrianne wants to eat $\frac{1}{2}$ of the 80 cherries, and Gabriél wants to eat $\frac{1}{4}$ of them. Will that leave enough cherries for the pie? Why or why not?

_____

_____

11. Sophia says she knows a way for Adrianne and Gabriél to eat $\frac{1}{2}$ and $\frac{1}{4}$ of the cherries and still have 50 left for the pie. First, divide the 80 cherries equally so that Adrianne and Gabriél each get the same amount. Adrianne eats $\frac{1}{2}$ of hers, and Gabriél eats $\frac{1}{4}$ of his. Will this leave enough cherries for the pie? Why or why not?

_____

_____

12. Why are your answers for problems 10 and 11 different?

_____

_____

_____

13. The 4 runners on a relay team all want to run the same distance in a race. The coach says that the first runner will go $\frac{1}{4}$ of the distance. Then the second runner will go $\frac{1}{3}$ of the remaining distance. The third runner will go $\frac{1}{2}$ of the distance that is left at that point. The fourth runner will finish the race. Will each runner run the same distance? Why or why not?

_____

_____

Relate Fractions and Wholes

Name

Date

Class Activity

Vocabulary

mixed number

▶ Represent and Add Mixed Numbers

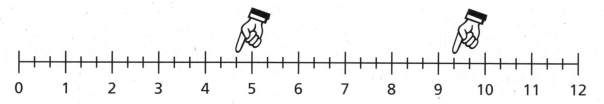

1. What fractional parts are shown on the number line?

_____

2. What **mixed numbers** do the fingers show?

_____

3. Where is $\frac{12}{3}$ on the number line?

_____

4. Where is $\frac{30}{3}$?

_____

5. Where is $\frac{31}{3}$?

_____

6. How can you add $4\frac{1}{3} + 1\frac{1}{3}$ on the number line?

_____

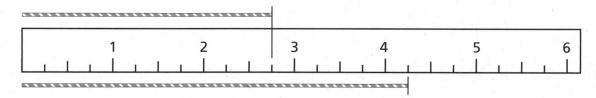

7. What fractional parts are shown on the inch ruler?

_____

8. How long is each string? _____

9. If you place the strings end to end, how long are they?

_____

Complete these equations.

10. $9\frac{5}{12} + 3\frac{1}{12} =$ _____

11. $7\frac{1}{8} + 2\frac{5}{8} =$ _____

Name _____ Date _____

▶ Add Mixed Numbers by Adding Separately

We can use our properties and definitions to prove that
$8\frac{1}{9} + 2\frac{4}{9} = (8 + 2) + \left(\frac{1}{9} + \frac{4}{9}\right)$.

Definition of a Mixed Number: $a\frac{n}{d} = a + \frac{n}{d}$

Commutative Property: $a + b = b + a$

Associative Property: $a + (b + c) = (a + b) + c$

---

12. Below is the math proof. Write the property or definition to justify each step.

a. $8\frac{1}{9} + 2\frac{4}{9} = \left(8 + \frac{1}{9}\right) + 2\frac{4}{9}$ _____

b. $\left(8 + \frac{1}{9}\right) + 2\frac{4}{9} = 8 + \left(\frac{1}{9} + 2\frac{4}{9}\right)$ _____

c. $8 + \left(\frac{1}{9} + 2\frac{4}{9}\right) = 8 + \left(\frac{1}{9} + \left(2 + \frac{4}{9}\right)\right)$ _____

d. $8 + \left(\frac{1}{9} + \left(2 + \frac{4}{9}\right)\right) = 8 + \left(\frac{1}{9} + \left(\frac{4}{9} + 2\right)\right)$ _____

e. $8 + \left(\frac{1}{9} + \left(\frac{4}{9} + 2\right)\right) = 8 + \left(\left(\frac{1}{9} + \frac{4}{9}\right) + 2\right)$ _____

f. $8 + \left(\left(\frac{1}{9} + \frac{4}{9}\right) + 2\right) = 8 + \left(2 + \left(\frac{1}{9} + \frac{4}{9}\right)\right)$ _____

g. $8 + \left(2 + \left(\frac{1}{9} + \frac{4}{9}\right)\right) = \left(8 + 2\right) + \left(\frac{1}{9} + \frac{4}{9}\right)$ _____

h. So we have proved that $8\frac{1}{9} + 2\frac{4}{9} = \left(8 + 2\right) + \left(\frac{1}{9} + \frac{4}{9}\right)$.

Now complete the addition problem. _____

Complete these equations.

13. $4\frac{1}{9} + 2\frac{1}{9} =$ _____

14. $5\frac{3}{8} + 2\frac{2}{8} =$ _____

15. $1\frac{1}{6} + 3\frac{4}{6} =$ _____

16. $4\frac{1}{3} + 6\frac{1}{3} =$ _____

17. $2\frac{1}{4} + 2\frac{3}{4} =$ _____

18. $3\frac{2}{7} + 2\frac{5}{7} =$ _____

Write each total as a mixed number.

19. $1\frac{3}{5} + 2\frac{4}{5} =$ _____

20. $40\frac{6}{7} + 22\frac{5}{7} =$ _____

21. $6\frac{8}{9} + 4\frac{7}{9} =$ _____

Add Fractions Greater Than One

Class Activity

▶ Solve Problems

The total length of the carrot is $9\frac{3}{8}$ inches.

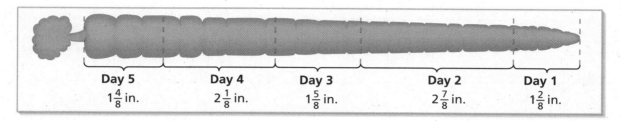

Day 5	Day 4	Day 3	Day 2	Day 1
$1\frac{4}{8}$ in.	$2\frac{1}{8}$ in.	$1\frac{5}{8}$ in.	$2\frac{7}{8}$ in.	$1\frac{2}{8}$ in.

This drawing shows how much of the carrot a rabbit ate each day until the carrot was gone.

Solve.

1. What was the length of the carrot when the rabbit started?

   _____

2. How long did it take the rabbit to eat the whole carrot?

   _____

3. Write and solve equations to determine how much of the carrot is left at the end of each day. Fill in the table as you find each answer. **Hint:** The length of carrot at the *beginning* of each day will be the same as the length of carrot at the *end* of the previous day.

	Length at Beginning of Day	Amount Eaten	Length at End of Day
Day 1	$9\frac{3}{8}$ in.	$1\frac{2}{8}$ in.	
Day 2			
Day 3			
Day 4			
Day 5			

4. **On the Back** If the last number in your table is 0, then you solved the problem correctly. Explain why you know this is true.

Subtract Mixed Numbers

Class Activity

Vocabulary

subtract
add on

► Compare Mixed Numbers

This inch ruler shows the lengths of four pencils.

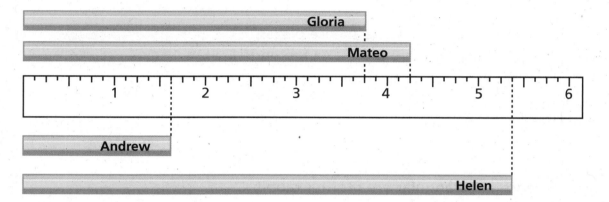

1. How long is Gloria's pencil? _____

   How long is Mateo's pencil? _____

2. How much longer is Mateo's pencil than Gloria's pencil?
   Hint: First, solve by **adding on** from the length of Gloria's
   pencil to make the length of Mateo's pencil. Then **subtract**
   the shorter length from the longer to see if you get the
   same answer. _____

3. How much shorter is Andrew's pencil than Helen's pencil?
   Hint: First, solve by adding on from the length of Andrew's
   pencil to make Helen's pencil. Then subtract the shorter length
   from the longer length to see if you get the same answer. _____

This number line shows how many miles three athletes traveled.

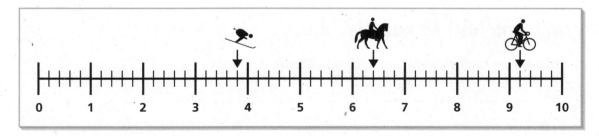

4. How much farther did the cyclist travel than the horseback rider? _____

5. How much farther did the horseback rider travel than the skier? _____

Name _____ **Date** _____

▶ Solve and Discuss Problems

Show your work.

Use what you know about adding and subtracting mixed numbers to solve each problem.

1. Kanesha ordered 6 pizzas for a party: 2 cheese pizzas, 2 Hawaiian pizzas, and 2 pepperoni pizzas. At the end of the party, $1\frac{3}{10}$ cheese pizzas, $\frac{5}{10}$ Hawaiian pizzas, and $1\frac{1}{10}$ pepperoni pizzas were left. How many pizzas were eaten altogether?

_____

2. Shing wants to fence a rectangular area for his rabbit. One side of the fence must be $8\frac{1}{4}$ feet long. Shing will use 28 feet of fencing. How long will the other side be?

_____

3. Ella needs to measure $2\frac{1}{4}$ cups flour, $1\frac{3}{4}$ cups oatmeal, and $\frac{3}{4}$ cups sugar for a recipe. Can she fit all these ingredients in a 4-cup measuring cup at the same time?

_____

4. Mr. Campbell can drive straight to Plainsville, or he can take a more scenic route by going through Riverdale. It is $12\frac{3}{8}$ miles to Plainsville. It is $6\frac{5}{8}$ miles to Riverdale. It is $7\frac{7}{8}$ miles from Riverdale to Plainsville. How much farther is it to go to Plainsville by driving through Riverdale?

_____

▶ Order Fractions and Mixed Numbers

Write these numbers in order from least to greatest.

5. $1\frac{1}{5}, \frac{8}{5}, \frac{5}{5}, 2\frac{4}{5}, \frac{3}{5}$ _____

6. $\frac{18}{8}, 2\frac{1}{8}, 2\frac{5}{8}, \frac{4}{8}, \frac{8}{8}$ _____

7. $\frac{6}{10}, 4\frac{2}{10}, \frac{20}{10}, \frac{10}{10}, \frac{9}{10}$ _____

Comparison Situations

Class Activity

Name _____ Date _____

► Correct a Solution

Dear Math Students:

There is a running path near our school that is $1\frac{1}{2}$ (or $\frac{3}{2}$) miles long. My friends and I want to run 3 miles every day. We are trying to figure out how many times we need to run the path to reach 3 miles. No matter how many times we add $\frac{3}{2}$, we never seem to reach 3. Here is our work:

Running 2 times: $\frac{3}{2} + \frac{3}{2} = \frac{6}{4}$ This is less than 3.

Running 3 times: $\frac{3}{2} + \frac{3}{2} + \frac{3}{2} = \frac{9}{6}$ This is less than 3.

Running 4 times: $\frac{3}{2} + \frac{3}{2} + \frac{3}{2} + \frac{3}{2} = \frac{12}{8}$ This is less than 3.

What have we done wrong?

Thank you for your help.

Puzzled Penguin

1. Write a response to Puzzled Penguin. Solve the problem and explain the mistake he and his friends are making in their solution strategy.

   _____

   _____

   _____

   _____

► Addition and Subtraction Word Problems

2. **On the Back** Write a word problem that can be solved by using fractions. Write the answer to your problem here.

   _____

Name _____   **Date** _____

Vocabulary
equivalent fractions

▶ Find Equivalent Fractions by Multiplying

You can use a number line to find **equivalent fractions**.

Circle the unit fractions up to $\frac{2}{3}$. Complete the number lines and equation boxes to find equivalent fractions for $\frac{2}{3}$.

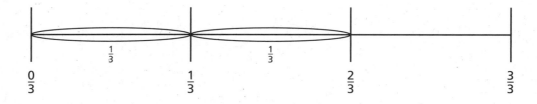

1. Sixths

$$\frac{2 \times \boxed{}}{3 \times \boxed{}} = \boxed{\frac{}{6}}$$

2. Ninths

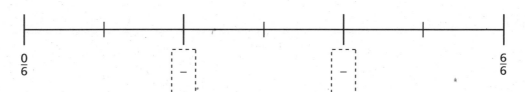

$$\frac{2 \times \boxed{}}{3 \times \boxed{}} = \boxed{\frac{}{9}}$$

Name _____ **Date** _____

Vocabulary

unsimplify

Circle the unit fractions up to $\frac{2}{3}$. Complete the number lines and equation boxes to find equivalent fractions for $\frac{2}{3}$.

3. Twelfths

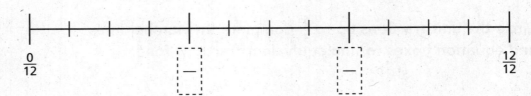

$$\frac{2 \times \square}{3 \times \square} = \frac{\square}{12}$$

4. Fifteenths

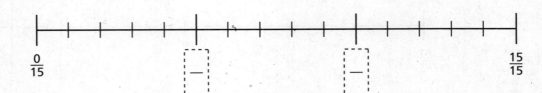

$$\frac{2 \times \square}{3 \times \square} = \frac{\square}{15}$$

5. Eighteenths

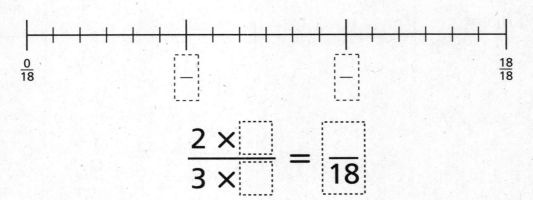

$$\frac{2 \times \square}{3 \times \square} = \frac{\square}{18}$$

6. When you **unsimplify** to make an equivalent fraction, you multiply the numerator and denominator by the same number to make more but smaller unit fractions. Discuss how that has happened for problems 1 through 5 on these two pages.

Discover Equivalent Fractions

Vocabulary

simplify

▶ Find Equivalent Fractions by Dividing

**Complete the number lines and equation boxes to show how
to simplify each fraction to $\frac{2}{3}$.**

7. Fifteenths

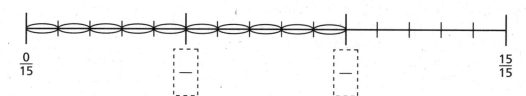

$$\frac{10 \div \boxed{}}{15 \div \boxed{}} = \frac{2}{3}$$

8. Twelfths

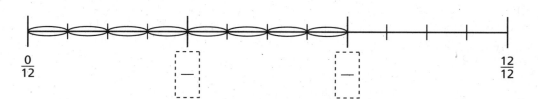

$$\frac{8 \div \boxed{}}{12 \div \boxed{}} = \frac{2}{3}$$

9. Ninths

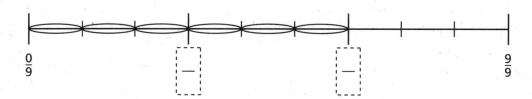

$$\frac{6 \div \boxed{}}{9 \div \boxed{}} = \frac{2}{3}$$

10. When you simplify to make an equivalent fraction, you
divide the numerator and denominator by the same
number to make fewer but bigger unit fractions. Discuss
how that has happened for problems 7 through 9 above.

11. Discuss how simplifying and unsimplifying are alike
and different.

▶ Solve Real-World Problems

Henri needs to make $\frac{2}{3}$ of his free throws in order to make the basketball team. Answer questions 12–14 about Henri's throws.

12. If he throws 12 times, how many baskets does he need? _____

13. If he throws 9 times, how many baskets does he need? _____

14. If he throws 15 times, how many baskets does he need? _____

▶ Practice Using Equivalent Fractions

Use the number lines to complete exercises 15–18.

Fifths

$$\frac{0}{5} \quad \frac{1}{5} \quad \frac{2}{5} \quad \frac{3}{5} \quad \frac{4}{5} \quad \frac{5}{5}$$

Tenths

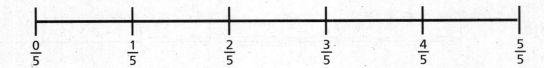

$$\frac{0}{10} \quad \frac{2}{10} \quad \frac{4}{10} \quad \frac{6}{10} \quad \frac{8}{10} \quad \frac{10}{10}$$

Fifteenths

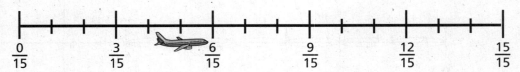

$$\frac{0}{15} \quad \frac{3}{15} \quad \frac{6}{15} \quad \frac{9}{15} \quad \frac{12}{15} \quad \frac{15}{15}$$

15. What fraction is marked by the car? _____

16. What fraction is marked by the airplane's wing? _____

17. If you worked $\frac{4}{5}$ of an hour, how many tenths of an hour did you work?

_____

18. Which is larger, $\frac{2}{5}$ or $\frac{4}{15}$? How do you know?

_____

Name   **Date**

Vocabulary
multiplication table

► Use the Multiplication Table to Find Equivalent Fractions

You can use these multiplication tables to find equivalent fractions.

×	1	2	3	4	5	6	7	8	9	10
1	1	2	3	4	5	6	7	8	9	10
2	2	4	6	8	10	12	14	16	18	20
3	3	6	9	12	15	18	21	24	27	30
4	4	8	12	16	20	24	28	32	36	40
5	5	10	15	20	25	30	35	40	45	50
6	6	12	18	24	30	36	42	48	54	60
7	7	14	21	28	35	42	49	56	63	70
8	8	16	24	32	40	48	56	64	72	80
9	9	18	27	36	45	54	63	72	81	90
10	10	20	30	40	50	60	70	80	90	100

×	1	2	3	4	5	6	7	8	9	10
1	1	2	3	4	5	6	7	8	9	10
2	2	4	6	8	10	12	14	16	18	20
3	3	6	9	12	15	18	21	24	27	30
4	4	8	12	16	20	24	28	32	36	40
5	5	10	15	20	25	30	35	40	45	50
6	6	12	18	24	30	36	42	48	54	60
7	7	14	21	28	35	42	49	56	63	70
8	8	16	24	32	40	48	56	64	72	80
9	9	18	27	36	45	54	63	72	81	90
10	10	20	30	40	50	60	70	80	90	100

$$\frac{3}{5} \quad \frac{6}{10} \quad \frac{9}{15} \quad \frac{12}{20} \quad \frac{15}{25} \quad \frac{18}{30} \quad \frac{21}{35} \quad \frac{24}{40} \quad \frac{27}{45} \quad \frac{30}{50}$$

$$\frac{4}{7} \quad \frac{8}{14} \quad \frac{12}{21} \quad \frac{16}{28} \quad \frac{20}{35} \quad \frac{24}{42} \quad \frac{28}{49} \quad \frac{32}{56} \quad \frac{36}{63} \quad \frac{40}{70}$$

1. Color rows 4 and 9 in the first table. Use the table to complete the equivalent fractions for $\frac{4}{9}$.

$$\frac{4}{9} = \underline{\quad} = \underline{\quad} = \underline{\quad} = \underline{\quad} = \underline{\quad} = \underline{\quad} = \underline{\quad} = \underline{\quad} = \underline{\quad}$$

2. Color rows 3 and 8 in the second table. Use the table to complete the equivalent fractions for $\frac{3}{8}$.

$$\frac{3}{8} = \underline{\quad} = \underline{\quad} = \underline{\quad} = \underline{\quad} = \underline{\quad} = \underline{\quad} = \underline{\quad} = \underline{\quad} = \underline{\quad}$$

Complete these equivalent fractions.

3. $\frac{1}{4} = \underline{\quad} = \underline{\quad} = \underline{\quad} = \underline{\quad} = \underline{\quad} = \underline{\quad} = \underline{\quad} = \underline{\quad} = \underline{\quad}$

4. $\frac{1}{3} = \underline{\quad} = \underline{\quad} = \underline{\quad} = \underline{\quad} = \underline{\quad} = \underline{\quad} = \underline{\quad} = \underline{\quad} = \underline{\quad}$

Class Activity

▶ Split Fraction Bars

Use the fraction bars to find equivalent fractions for $\frac{5}{6}$.

$\frac{5}{6}$

4.

$\frac{}{12}$

Multiplier = $\boxed{}$

$$\frac{5 \times \boxed{}}{6 \times \boxed{}} = \frac{\boxed{}}{12}$$

5.

$\frac{}{18}$

Multiplier = $\boxed{}$

$$\frac{5 \times \boxed{}}{6 \times \boxed{}} = \frac{\boxed{}}{18}$$

6.

$\frac{}{24}$

Multiplier = $\boxed{}$

$$\frac{5 \times \boxed{}}{6 \times \boxed{}} = \frac{\boxed{}}{24}$$

Use the fraction bars to find equivalent fractions for $\frac{3}{4}$.

$\frac{3}{4}$

7.

$\frac{}{8}$

Multiplier = $\boxed{}$

$$\frac{3 \times \boxed{}}{4 \times \boxed{}} = \frac{\boxed{}}{8}$$

8.

$\frac{}{12}$

Multiplier = $\boxed{}$

$$\frac{3 \times \boxed{}}{4 \times \boxed{}} = \frac{\boxed{}}{12}$$

Equivalent Fractions and Multipliers

Class Activity

Vocabulary

equivalent
simplify
unsimplify

▶ Find Unknown Numerators and Denominators

Find *n* or *d*.

1. $\frac{1}{4} = \frac{n}{12}$ $n = $ _____

2. $\frac{2}{5} = \frac{12}{d}$ $d = $ _____

3. $\frac{6}{36} = \frac{n}{6}$ $n = $ _____

4. $\frac{4}{20} = \frac{2}{d}$ $d = $ _____

5. $\frac{2}{9} = \frac{n}{45}$ $n = $ _____

6. $\frac{3}{8} = \frac{30}{d}$ $d = $ _____

7. $\frac{12}{16} = \frac{n}{4}$ $n = $ _____

8. $\frac{14}{35} = \frac{2}{d}$ $d = $ _____

9. $\frac{15}{25} = \frac{n}{5}$ $n = $ _____

10. $\frac{9}{36} = \frac{3}{d}$ $d = $ _____

11. $\frac{21}{28} = \frac{n}{4}$ $n = $ _____

12. $\frac{12}{20} = \frac{6}{d}$ $d = $ _____

Two fractions are **equivalent** if either can be changed into the other by multiplying or dividing the numerator and denominator by the same number.

To **simplify** a fraction, divide the numerator and denominator by the same number to make a *smaller* number of *larger* unit fractions.

To **unsimplify** a fraction, multiply the numerator and denominator by the same number to make a *larger* number of *smaller* unit fractions.

Use the words *multiply*, *divide*, *simplify*, and *unsimplify* to complete the statements.

13. To change $\frac{3}{5}$ to $\frac{18}{30}$, _____ the numerator

    and denominator by 6 in order to _____ the fraction.

14. To change $\frac{18}{30}$ to $\frac{3}{5}$, _____ the numerator

    and denominator by 6 in order to _____ the fraction.

Class Activity

▶ Solve Fraction Problems

Answer the questions about the table.

The Weather in April	
☀ Sunny Days	**10**
☁ Cloudy Days	**12**
🌧 Rainy Days	**8**

15. What fraction of the days were sunny? _____

    Simplify the fraction. _____

16. What is the advantage of simplifying the fraction?

    _____

    _____

17. What is the advantage of leaving the fraction unsimplified?

    _____

    _____

    _____

18. What fraction of the days were cloudy? _____

    Simplify the fraction _____

19. What fraction of the days were rainy? _____

    Simplify the fraction _____

Answer the questions about the bar graph.

20. What fraction of the vehicles are vans? _____

    Simplify the fraction _____

21. What fraction of the vehicles are cars? _____

    Simplify the fraction _____

22. What fraction of the vehicles are trucks? _____

    Simplify the fraction _____

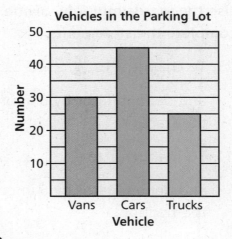

23. Do cars represent more or fewer than half of all
    the vehicles in the lot? _____ How do you know?

    _____

    _____

Solve Equivalence Problems

Vocabulary
common denominator

▶ Choose a Denominator

Find equivalent fractions for each fraction. To add them, they must have the same denominator. We call this a **common denominator**. Show below the number lines how to find the equivalent fractions numerically.

1.

| 1 whole |

| $\frac{1}{2}$ + $\frac{1}{3}$ | $\frac{1}{2}$ | $\frac{1}{3}$ |

$\boxed{—}$ + $\boxed{—}$ | $\frac{1}{6}$ | $\frac{1}{6}$ | $\frac{1}{6}$ | $\frac{1}{6}$ | $\frac{1}{6}$ |

$\dfrac{1\times}{2\times} = \dfrac{3}{6}$ $\dfrac{1\times}{3\times} = \dfrac{2}{6}$ The common denominator is _____.

2.

$\frac{1}{4}$ + $\frac{2}{3}$ | $\frac{1}{4}$ | $\frac{1}{3}$ | $\frac{1}{3}$ |

$\boxed{—}$ + $\boxed{—}$ | $\frac{1}{12}$ | $\frac{1}{12}$ | $\frac{1}{12}$ | $\frac{1}{12}$ | $\frac{1}{12}$ | $\frac{1}{12}$ | $\frac{1}{12}$ | $\frac{1}{12}$ | $\frac{1}{12}$ | $\frac{1}{12}$ | $\frac{1}{12}$ | $\frac{1}{12}$ |

$\dfrac{1\times}{4\times} = \dfrac{3}{12}$ $\dfrac{2\times}{3\times} = \dfrac{8}{12}$ The common denominator is _____.

3.

$\frac{1}{4}$ + $\frac{1}{2}$ | $\frac{1}{4}$ | $\frac{1}{2}$ |

$\boxed{}$ + $\boxed{}$ | $\frac{1}{8}$ | $\frac{1}{8}$ | $\frac{1}{8}$ | $\frac{1}{8}$ | $\frac{1}{8}$ | $\frac{1}{8}$ | $\frac{1}{8}$ | $\frac{1}{8}$ |

$\boxed{}$ + $\boxed{}$ | $\frac{1}{4}$ | $\frac{1}{4}$ | $\frac{1}{4}$ | $\frac{1}{4}$ |

Which common denominator would you use? _____

Why? _____

4. Does $\frac{1}{2} + \frac{1}{3} = \frac{2}{5}$? _____ Discuss why or why not.

▶ Choose a Denominator (continued)

Tell which common denominator you will use. Then find equivalent fractions and add.

5. _____ $\frac{7}{10} + \frac{1}{5} = \frac{n}{d}$ _____

6. _____ $\frac{3}{11} + \frac{1}{2} = \frac{n}{d}$ _____

7. _____ $\frac{1}{6} + \frac{3}{4} = \frac{n}{d}$ _____

▶ Compare Unlike Fractions

8. Tia and Carlos both ordered the same size pizza. Tia ate $\frac{9}{12}$ of her pizza. Carlos ate $\frac{5}{6}$ of his pizza. Who ate more pizza? How do you know?

_____

_____

9. Which spinner gives you a better chance of landing on a shaded space? Why?

A   B

_____

_____

10. East Bridge is $\frac{3}{5}$ mile long. West Bridge is $\frac{7}{10}$ mile long. Which bridge is shorter? How much shorter?

_____

11. Box A contains 14 marbles, and 8 of them are black. Box B contains 21 marbles, and 10 of them are black. If you had only one chance to draw a black marble, which box would you choose? Explain why.

_____

_____

▶ Add and Subtract Mixed Numbers

What error was made in each problem? Find the correct solution.

1. $3\frac{1}{2}$

   $+\ 6\frac{5}{7}$

   $\overline{\quad 9\frac{6}{9}}$

2. $8\frac{1}{5}$

   $-\ 2\frac{4}{5}$

   $\overline{\quad 6\frac{3}{5}}$

3. $2\frac{1}{6}$

   $+\ 1\frac{1}{9}$

   $\overline{\quad 3\frac{16}{54}}$

_____   _____   _____

_____   _____   _____

_____   _____   _____

Solve. Give your answer in the simplest form.

4. Dora the elephant eats $3\frac{3}{4}$ tons of food every month. Her baby eats $1\frac{1}{6}$ tons of food. How many tons of food do they eat together?

   _____

5. The tallest elephant, Leroy, can reach a branch $12\frac{1}{3}$ feet off the ground. Daisy can reach $10\frac{5}{6}$ feet. How much farther can Leroy reach than Daisy?

   _____

6. Speedy, the fastest elephant, can run $25\frac{1}{10}$ miles per hour. Squirt can run only $10\frac{3}{5}$ miles per hour. How many fewer miles can Squirt run in an hour than Speedy?

   _____

7. The truck that carries the elephants holds 10 tons. Which two elephants could travel together in the truck? Name all the possible pairs.

   _____

   _____

Dora	$5\frac{3}{4}$ tons
Leroy	$6\frac{1}{2}$ tons
Daisy	$4\frac{2}{3}$ tons
Speedy	$5\frac{2}{3}$ tons
Squirt	$3\frac{2}{3}$ tons

Going Further

Name _____ **Date** _____

▶ Solve Equations Involving Fractions

Find the missing addend. Write your answers in simplest form.

1. $2\frac{2}{3} + x = 3\frac{1}{6}$

   $x =$

2. $\frac{7}{8} + x = 1\frac{1}{4}$

   $x =$

3. $1\frac{19}{20} + x = 3\frac{1}{5}$

   $x =$

4. $x + 4\frac{5}{6} = 6\frac{5}{24}$

   $x =$

5. $x + \frac{1}{4} = \frac{7}{8}$

   $x =$

6. $x + \frac{5}{8} = 1\frac{1}{2}$

   $x =$

7. In the square below, each row, column, and diagonal has the same total. Copy your answers from exercises 1–6 into the square below. Find the total of one row and use it to fill in the missing entries in the square. Write the totals you find on the blanks.

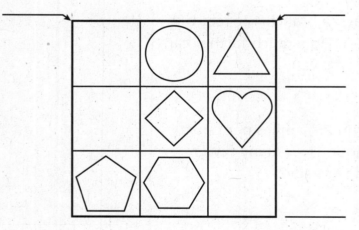

8. Mary Beth has some fabric for a patch quilt. She bought $\frac{3}{4}$ yd more. Now she has $2\frac{7}{8}$ yd of fabric. How much fabric did she start with? Write an equation to solve the problem.

_____

Solve With Unlike Mixed Numbers

► Rename and Ungroup Fractions

Dear Math Students,

I live in the town of Clear Springs. I am going on a hike with several of my friends next week. We would like to walk to Eagle Crest.

Clear Springs

Pine City

Eagle Crest

Clear Springs to Pine City = $9\frac{2}{5}$ miles

Eagle Crest to Pine City = $6\frac{7}{10}$ miles

The map tells us the whole distance to Pine City and it tells us the distance from Eagle Crest to Pine City. But it does not tell us the distance from Clear Springs to Eagle Crest. We know we can subtract the smaller distance from the larger to get our answer. But we don't know how to subtract these numbers.

Can you help?

Your friend,

Puzzled Penguin

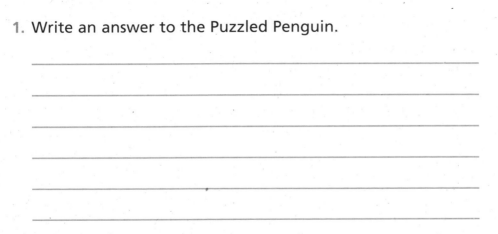

1. Write an answer to the Puzzled Penguin.

_____

_____

_____

_____

_____

Class Activity

► Choose How to Rename Fractions

The equations in each group have something in common.

Complete each equation.

Group 1	Group 2	Group 3
2. $\frac{9}{10} - \frac{2}{3} =$ _____	3. $\frac{9}{14} - \frac{2}{7} =$ _____	4. $\frac{5}{8} - \frac{1}{12} =$ _____
5. $4\frac{3}{5} + 2\frac{3}{4} =$ _____	6. $\frac{3}{28} + \frac{3}{4} =$ _____	7. $8\frac{5}{6} - 4\frac{3}{4} =$ _____
8. $\frac{2}{9} + \frac{1}{7} =$ _____	9. $3\frac{4}{18} - 1\frac{1}{3} =$ _____	10. $\frac{4}{9} + \frac{1}{6} =$ _____

11. How did you find a common denominator for the equations in Group 1?

   _____

12. How did you find a common denominator for the equations in Group 2?

   _____

13. How did you find a common denominator for the equations in Group 3?

   _____

14. Write one more equation that belongs in Group 1.

   _____

15. Write one more equation that belongs in Group 2.

   _____

16. Write one more equation that belongs in Group 3.

   _____

Practice With Unlike Mixed Numbers

Class Activity

Name _____   **Date** _____

► Use the Language of Probability

Use the words likely, unlikely, certain, or impossible to describe each event for the spinner.

1. Spinning a 2 _____

2. Spinning a 3 _____

3. Spinning a 5 _____

4. Spinning a number less than 5 _____

5. Which numbers are you equally likely to spin? _____

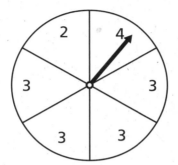

► Relate Probability to Fractions

6. What is the total number of sections for the spinner? _____

7. How many sections have a 2 on them? _____

8. What is the **probability** of spinning a 2? _____

9. How many sections have a 3 on them? _____

10. What is the probability of spinning a 3? _____

11. What is the probability of spinning a 4? _____

12. What is the total of the three probabilities in exercises 8, 10, and 11? _____

13. What is the probability of spinning a number less than 5? _____

14. What is the probability of spinning a 5? _____

► Solve Probability Problems

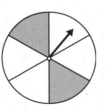

15. What is the total number of sections for the spinner? _____
    How many shaded sections are there? _____
    What is the probability that the spinner will stop on a shaded section? _____

    What is the probability that the spinner will stop on a white section? _____

16. Suppose you put the marbles in the box and take one out without looking.
What is the probability that you will get a white marble?

_____

What is the probability that you will get a black marble?

_____

What is the probability that you will get a gray marble?

_____

17. Ellen made this spinner with 4 white sections and 2 shaded sections. She says that the spinner is more likely to stop on a white section than a shaded section. Do you agree? Why or why not?

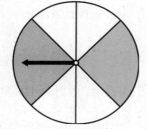

_____

_____

_____

▶ **Make Predictions**

Solve. Explain your reasoning.

18. Suppose you have a can that contains 100 nuts. The label says that there are about 20 pecans, 30 walnuts, and 50 almonds. If you take out 10 nuts, how many of each kind would you expect to get?

_____

_____

_____

19. Mark found a box in the attic labeled "72 clown noses, 2 sizes." He took out 8 noses. Five of them were large and 3 of them were small. Out of the 72 total noses, how many are likely to be large? _____
How many are likely to be small? _____

Probability and Equivalent Fractions

► Try These Problems

20. Tavia makes unusual dartboards like these.

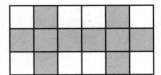

You want to try to hit one of the dark sections of one of the boards. Which board will you choose? Explain why.

_____

_____

21. Ryan and Steven were playing catch when they broke one pane in this window. Part of the window is clear glass. Part of it is valuable rose-colored glass. What is the probability that they broke the rose-colored glass?

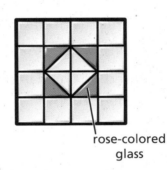

rose-colored
glass

_____

_____

22. Two horses will soon give birth. The farmer predicts that the 2 newborn horses will both be male. His son predicts that they will both be female. His daughter predicts that there will be one male and one female. His wife says that her daughter has the best chance of making the correct prediction. The farmer says that is not possible because there are 3 equal possibilities. Who is right? Explain why.

_____

_____

_____

_____

Going Further

▶ Read Data from a Line Plot

Vocabulary
frequency table
line plot

Two number cubes, labeled 1 to 6, were tossed 30 times. This **frequency table** shows the number of times each total occurred. You can organize data on a **line plot** to make the data easier to analyze.

Total of 2 cubes	Number of tosses
2	1
3	2
4	2
5	3
6	5
7	6
8	4
9	4
10	2
11	1
12	0

```
        ×     ×
  ×     ×     ×
├──┼──┼──┼──┼──┼──┼──┼──┼──┼──┼──┤
   2  3  4  5  6  7  8  9  10 11 12
```

1. The line plot has been filled in for tosses of 2, 3, and 4. Complete the rest of the line plot.

2. Based on this sample, describe the totals that are least likely to be thrown.

   _____

3. Based on this sample, describe the totals that are most likely to be thrown.

   _____

4. Why doesn't a total of 1 appear on the number line or the table?

   _____

   _____

Based on the data for the 30 tosses, what is each probability?

5. Tossing a total of 7 _____

6. Tossing a total of 2 _____

7. Tossing a total of 12 _____

Probability and Equivalent Fractions

Name _____   **Date** _____

Class Activity

▶ Fraction and Decimal Relationships

Below you can see that 100 pennies are equal to one whole dollar.

Fourths and Eighths

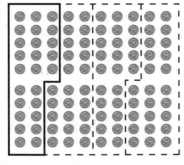
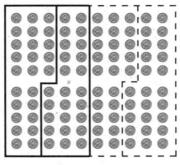
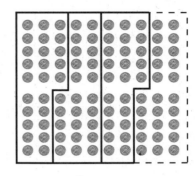

$\frac{1}{4} = 0.25 = \frac{2}{8}$ $\frac{1}{2} = \frac{2}{4} = 0.50 = 0.5$ $\frac{3}{4} = 0.75$

$\frac{1}{8} = 0.125$ $\frac{3}{8} = 0.375$ $\frac{5}{8} = 0.625$ $\frac{7}{8} = 0.875$

Fifths and Tenths

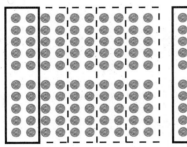
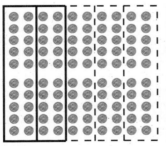
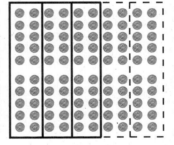
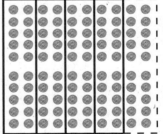

$\frac{1}{5} = 0.20 = 0.2 = \frac{2}{10}$ $\frac{2}{5} = 0.40 = 0.4 = \frac{4}{10}$ $\frac{3}{5} = 0.60 = 0.6 = \frac{6}{10}$ $\frac{4}{5} = 0.80 = 0.8 = \frac{8}{10}$

Thirds and Sixths

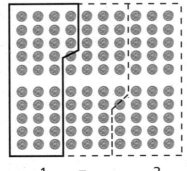
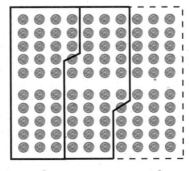

$\frac{1}{3} = 0.\overline{3} \underset{r}{=} 0.33 = \frac{2}{6}$ $\frac{2}{3} = 0.\overline{6} \underset{r}{=} 0.67 = \frac{4}{6}$

$\frac{1}{6} = 0.1\overline{6} \underset{r}{=} 0.17$ $\frac{3}{6} = 0.5$ $\frac{5}{6} = 0.8\overline{3} \underset{r}{=} 0.83$

▶ Identify Patterns Using Number Lines

Halves, Fourths, and Eighths

$1 = \frac{2}{2} = \frac{4}{4} = \frac{8}{8}$ — 1.000

$\frac{7}{8}$ — 0.875

$\frac{3}{4} = \frac{6}{8}$ — 0.750 = 0.75

$\frac{5}{8}$ — 0.625

$\frac{1}{2} = \frac{2}{4} = \frac{4}{8}$ — 0.500 = 0.50 = 0.5

$\frac{3}{8}$ — 0.375

$\frac{1}{4} = \frac{2}{8}$ — 0.250 = 0.25

$\frac{1}{8}$ — 0.125

$\frac{0}{4} = \frac{0}{8}$ — 0.000

Fifths and Tenths

$1 = \frac{5}{5} = \frac{10}{10}$ — 1.0 = 1.00

$\frac{9}{10}$ — 0.9

$\frac{4}{5} = \frac{8}{10}$ — 0.8 = 0.80

$\frac{7}{10}$ — 0.7

$\frac{3}{5} = \frac{6}{10}$ — 0.6 = 0.60

$\frac{5}{10}$ — 0.5

$\frac{2}{5} = \frac{4}{10}$ — 0.4 = 0.40

$\frac{3}{10}$ — 0.3

$\frac{1}{5} = \frac{2}{10}$ — 0.2 = 0.20

$\frac{1}{10}$ — 0.1

$\frac{0}{5} = \frac{0}{10}$ — 0.0

Thirds and Sixths

$1 = \frac{3}{3} = \frac{6}{6}$ — 1.00

$\frac{5}{6}$ — $0.8\overline{3}$
0.83

$\frac{2}{3} = \frac{4}{6}$ — $0.\overline{6}$
0.67

$\frac{3}{6}$ — 0.5

$\frac{1}{3} = \frac{2}{6}$ — $0.\overline{3}$
0.33

$\frac{1}{6}$ — $0.1\overline{6}$
0.17

$\frac{0}{3} = \frac{0}{6}$ — 0.0

▶ Practice Fraction and Decimal Equivalencies

Study Chart

Eighths	Fourths	Fifths and Tenths	Thirds and Sixths
$\frac{1}{8} = 0.125$			$\frac{1}{6} = 0.1\overline{6}$ 0.17
		$\frac{1}{5} = \frac{2}{10} = 0.2$	
$\frac{2}{8} = 0.250$	$\frac{1}{4} = 0.25$		
			$\frac{2}{6} = \frac{1}{3} = 0.\overline{3}$ 0.33
$\frac{3}{8} = 0.375$		$\frac{2}{5} = \frac{4}{10} = 0.4$	
$\frac{4}{8} = 0.500$	$\frac{2}{4} = 0.50$		$\frac{3}{6} = 0.5$
		$\frac{3}{5} = \frac{6}{10} = 0.6$	
$\frac{5}{8} = 0.625$			$\frac{4}{6} = \frac{2}{3} = 0.\overline{6}$ 0.67
$\frac{6}{8} = 0.750$	$\frac{3}{4} = 0.75$		
		$\frac{4}{5} = \frac{8}{10} = 0.8$	$\frac{5}{6} = 0.8\overline{3}$ 0.83
$\frac{7}{8} = 0.875$			
$\frac{8}{8} = 1.000$	$\frac{4}{4} = 1.00$	$\frac{5}{5} = \frac{10}{10} = 1.0$	$\frac{6}{6} = \frac{3}{3} = 1$

Fraction and Decimal Equivalencies

Class Activity

▶ Use Number Lines to Compare

Each tick mark on these numbers lines is missing a label for a fraction, a decimal, or both a fraction and a decimal. Write the missing fractions and decimals.

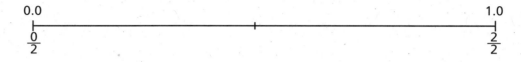

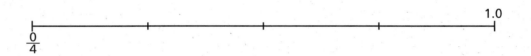

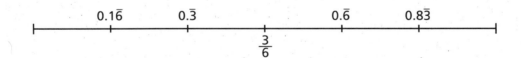

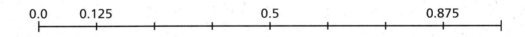

Class Activity

▶ Compare and Order Fractions and Decimals

Use estimation to decide where each number should be placed
on the number line. Then draw and label a point at those places.

1. $\frac{1}{2}$, $1\frac{3}{6}$, $1\frac{7}{16}$, $2\frac{5}{8}$

```
0                 1                 2                 3
├─────────────────┼─────────────────┼─────────────────┤
0                 4                 8                12
─                 ─                 ─                ──
4                 4                 4                 4
```

2. 0.6, $2\frac{5}{10}$, 3.25, 4.750

```
0      1      2      3      4      5
├──────┼──────┼──────┼──────┼──────┤
0.0    1.0    2.0    3.0    4.0    5.0
```

3. three-halves
   one and three-fourths
   twenty-five hundredths
   nine-tenths

```
0                    10                    20
──                   ──                    ──
10                   10                    10
├────────────────────┼─────────────────────┤
0.0                  1.0                   2.0
```

Write the numbers in order from greatest to least.

4. $\frac{3}{8}$, $1\frac{3}{4}$, $\frac{1}{2}$, $1\frac{7}{8}$, $\frac{5}{16}$ _____

5. $\frac{5}{6}$, $1\frac{2}{3}$, $\frac{7}{12}$, $1\frac{1}{2}$, $\frac{1}{3}$ _____

6. $\frac{15}{100}$, $\frac{1}{10}$, $\frac{10}{1,000}$, $\frac{1}{5}$, $\frac{10}{10}$ _____

Write the numbers in order from least to greatest.

7. $\frac{3}{4}$, $1\frac{1}{16}$, 0.8, $1\frac{1}{8}$, 1.25 _____

8. $\frac{5}{5}$, $0.\overline{6}$, $2\frac{1}{4}$, $\frac{5}{8}$, 1.75 _____

Compare and Order Fractions and Decimals

Name _____ **Date** _____

▶ Make Change

A $5 bill was used to purchase each item below. List the coins and bills that should be received as change.

1. paperback book
    $3.79 _____

2. pencil eraser
    35¢ _____

A $20 bill was used to purchase each item below. List the coins and bills that should be received as change.

3. outdoor basketball
    $12.61 _____

4. canvas book bag
    $6.95 _____

Use subtraction to make change for each situation.

5. Bought: jeans for $23.75
   Gave the clerk: one $50 bill

   Change: _____

6. Bought: groceries for $46.07
   Gave the clerk: three $20 bills

   Change: _____

Solve.

7. Hal has $70. After buying a hat for $9.50, mittens for $14.95, and a jacket for $36.50, does he have enough money to buy a pair of mittens for $15? Can Hal use an estimate to answer the question? Explain why or why not.

   _____

   _____

8. A customer purchased an item and received $8.00 in change after giving the clerk a $20 bill and a nickel. What was the cost of the item?

   _____

Going Further

▶ Compare and Order Money Amounts

Use >, <, or = to write a comparison statement for each pair of numbers.

9. $2.60, 2\frac{3}{4}$ _____

10. $\frac{5}{100}$, 0.050 _____

11. 1\frac{4}{5}$, $$\frac{17}{10}$ _____

12. $$\frac{15}{2}$, $7.49 _____

Solve.

13. Write the amounts below in order from greatest to least.

   $4.09 $3.96 $4.08 $3.89 _____

14. Write the amounts below in order from least to greatest.

   $106.45 $102.75 $106.08 $102.57 _____

15. Are the amounts below ordered from least to greatest or from greatest to least?

   3 quarters   16 nickels   9 dimes _____

Solve.

16. The students at Clinton Middle School participated in a school fundraiser. The amount of money each class earned is shown in the table at the right.

   The goal of the students was to earn $2,500. Did the students reach their goal? Explain how you can use an estimate to help decide.

Clinton Middle School Fundraiser	
Grade 4	$704.30
Grade 5	$410.75
Grade 6	$688.10

_____

_____

Compare and Order Fractions and Decimals

Class Activity

▶ Estimate Fraction Sums and Differences

A number line can be used to estimate the sum of two or more fractions.

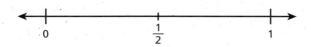

Decide if each addend is closer to 0 or closer to 1. Then estimate the sum or difference.

1. $\frac{1}{4} + \frac{7}{8}$

   Estimate: _____

2. $\frac{7}{16} - \frac{5}{12}$

   Estimate: _____

3. $\frac{5}{6} + \frac{9}{10}$

   Estimate: _____

Estimate by rounding each number to 0, 1, 2, or 3. Then add or subtract.

4. $5\frac{2}{3} - 3\frac{1}{6}$

   Estimate: _____

5. $1\frac{1}{4} + 2\frac{7}{10}$

   Estimate: _____

6. $3\frac{3}{8} - 1\frac{3}{16}$

   Estimate: _____

Use any method you wish to estimate the sums or differences.

7. Estimates of the sum $3\frac{7}{8} + \frac{5}{12} + 4\frac{3}{5}$ are shown below.

   Which student made the best estimate? Explain how you know.

   Jarvis: 8   Yolanda: 9   Ellis: 10

   _____

   _____

8. Estimates of the difference $9\frac{3}{16} - 2\frac{4}{5} - \frac{5}{8}$ are shown below.

   Which student made the best estimate? Explain how you know.

   Alyssa: $4\frac{1}{2}$ Jeong: $5\frac{1}{2}$ Brady: $6\frac{1}{2}$

   _____

   _____

Class Activity

Name _____

Date _____

▶ Check for Reasonableness

Solve each problem. Use an estimate to decide if your answer is reasonable. Show your work.

9. Nick estimated the difference $4.93 - 2.09$ to be 2. Did Nick make a reasonable estimate? Explain why or why not.

_____

10. Rochelle estimated the sum $\frac{3}{4} + \frac{3}{10}$ to be 1. Did Rochelle make a reasonable estimate? Explain why or why not.

_____

The list below shows a variety of cooking ingredients and amounts.

Ingredients and Amounts (c = cup)

wheat flour $1\frac{5}{8}$ c   white flour $\frac{3}{4}$ c   sugar $1\frac{1}{4}$ c   cornstarch $\frac{3}{8}$ c

Decide if each amount is closer to $\frac{1}{2}$ cup or $1\frac{1}{2}$ cups.

Then **estimate** the total of these amounts.

11. white flour + sugar _____

12. sugar + wheat flour _____

13. sugar + cornstarch _____

14. cornstarch + white flour _____

The list below shows a variety of packages and weights.

Packages to Be Shipped (lb = pound)

Package A 5.3 lb

Package B 6.6 lb

Package C 6.2 lb

Package D 5.8 lb

Decide if each weight is closer to a whole pound or to a half pound. Then **estimate** these combinations of weights.

15. A + B _____

16. C + B _____

17. B + D _____

18. D + A _____

19. What is a reasonable estimate of the total weight of all four packages? Explain your answer.

_____

Different Ways to Estimate

Class Activity

Vocabulary

Venn diagram

▶ Math and Social Studies

Yellowstone National Park and Grand Teton National Park are located in Wyoming. Suppose a group of park visitors was surveyed during the summer. The results are shown in the **Venn diagram** below.

Visitors to Two Wyoming National Parks

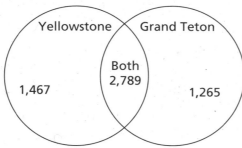

Yellowstone

Grand Teton

Both
2,789

1,467

1,265

Use the Venn diagram to answer the following questions.

1. How many people visited Yellowstone National Park?

_____

2. How many people visited Grand Teton National Park?

_____

3. How many people visited both national parks?

_____

4. How many people were surveyed in all?

_____

5. Suppose 100 more people were surveyed. 25 people visited Yellowstone National Park only, 35 visited Grand Teton National Park only, and the remaining people visited both parks. On a separate sheet of paper, draw the updated Venn diagram.

6. **Predict** Suppose another survey is taken in the winter. Do you predict these numbers will increase or decrease? Explain your reasoning.

_____

► Collect and Display Data

You are going to roll two number cubes. One number cube has the numbers 1 through 6. Another number cube has the numbers 7 through 12.

7. On a separate sheet of paper, make a table like the one shown on the right. The table should include all 11 possible sums from rolling the two number cubes.

Total of 2 Cubes	Tally Marks	Number of Tosses
8		
9		

8. Roll the two number cubes together 20 times and record the results in your table.

9. On a separate sheet of paper draw a line plot like the one shown below.

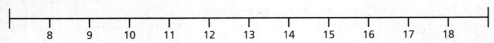

Use your data to complete your line plot.

10. Based on your collected data, describe the totals that are least and most likely to be thrown.

_____

_____

11. **Predict** If you rolled the numbers cubes a total of 40 times, predict the number of tosses for each total.

_____

_____

_____

Use Mathematical Processes

Add or subtract. Simplify your answers.

1. a. $\frac{3}{7} + \frac{2}{7} =$ _____

   b. $\frac{2}{3} - \frac{1}{9} =$ _____

2. a. $9\frac{1}{8}$
   $- 2\frac{7}{8}$
   $\overline{}$

   b. $2\frac{1}{4}$
   $+ 5\frac{3}{8}$
   $\overline{}$

3. Find d.

   $\frac{1}{d} + \frac{1}{d} + \frac{1}{d} + \frac{1}{d} = \frac{d}{d}$ $d =$ _____

4. Circle the greater fraction. Then write > or < between the fractions. Explain your thinking.

   $\frac{4}{9}$ $\frac{4}{10}$

   _____

   _____

   _____

   _____

5. Write the mixed number as an improper fraction. Show your work.

   $2\frac{1}{6} =$ _____

   _____

   _____

   _____

   _____

6. Write these fractions in order from **least to greatest**.

   $\frac{3}{8}$, $7\frac{1}{2}$, $\frac{4}{4}$, $\frac{8}{16}$, $\frac{5}{2}$

7. Write these numbers in order from **greatest to least**.

   $\frac{3}{5}$, 5.202, $\frac{100}{100}$, 0.7, $\frac{8}{5}$

8. Write the fraction that is equivalent to $\frac{9}{10}$. Show your work.

   $$\frac{32}{40} \qquad \frac{81}{100} \qquad \frac{36}{40}$$

   _____

   _____

Solve. Simplify your answer.   *Show your work.*

9. Kendra has 6 red marbles and 2 blue marbles in a bag.
   She reaches in and chooses one without looking. What
   is the probability that it is a blue marble?

   _____

10. **Extended Response** Terry worked in the garden for
    $\frac{3}{4}$ hour. Peter worked in the garden for $\frac{1}{6}$ hour more
    than Terry. How many hours did they work in the garden
    altogether?

    _____

    _____

    _____

    _____

    _____

    _____

    _____

Name _____   **Date** _____

Vocabulary
face
edge
rectangular prism
volume
cubic unit

▶ Describe a Cube

Use the cube to answer the questions below.

1. How many **faces** does a cube have? _____

2. How many **edges** does a cube have? _____

Write *true* or *false* for each statement.

3. All the edges of a cube are the same length. _____

4. All the faces of a cube are congruent squares. _____

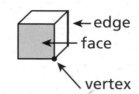

▶ Explore Volume

You can use cubes to build **rectangular prisms**.

5.

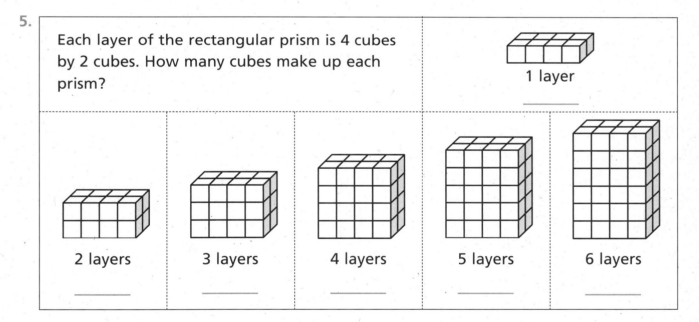

Each layer of the rectangular prism is 4 cubes by 2 cubes. How many cubes make up each prism?

1 layer _____

2 layers _____   3 layers _____   4 layers _____   5 layers _____   6 layers _____

The **volume** of a prism is the number of cubes needed to build the prism. Volume is recorded in **cubic units**.

Write the volume of the prism in cubic units.

6. 1 layer: $4 \times 2 \times 1 =$ ___ cubic units

7. 2 layers: $4 \times 2 \times 2 =$ ___ cubic units

8. 3 layers: $4 \times 2 \times 3 =$ ___ cubic units

9. 4 layers: $4 \times 2 \times 4 =$ ___ cubic units

10. 5 layers: $4 \times 2 \times 5 =$ ___ cubic units

11. 6 layers: $4 \times 2 \times 6 =$ ___ cubic units

▶ Develop a Formula

12. What is the volume of this rectangular prism?

_____

13. Write a formula for finding the volume of any
rectangular prism.

Volume = _____

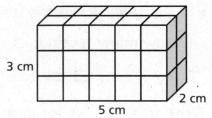

3 cm

5 cm   2 cm

▶ Share Solutions

Solve.

14. A box shaped like a rectangular prism is 4 dm long,
2 dm wide, and 3 dm tall. What is the volume of the box?

_____

15. When closed, the cargo area of a truck measures 3 m long by
2 m wide by 1 m deep. How many cubic meters of cargo
will fit in the closed area?

_____

16. A flower box is 3 feet long, 2 feet wide, and $\frac{1}{2}$ foot deep.
How many cubic feet of dirt can it hold?

_____

17. Cubes of fudge are arranged in 2 layers on a tray. Each layer
is 8 cubes long and 6 cubes wide. How many cubes of fudge
are on the tray?

_____

18. Todd used 8 small cubes and glue to build the cube shown
at the right. Then he painted the entire cube red. After the
paint dried, Todd broke the cube apart into the 8 smaller
cubes he started with. How many faces of the 8 smaller
cubes are *not* painted red?

_____

Dear Family,

Your child is learning about volume, capacity, and weight. Volume is a measure of the space that a three-dimensional figure, such as a box, occupies.

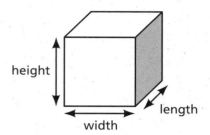

To find the volume of a box, you multiply the three dimensions of the box: length × width × height. Volume is measured in cubic units, such as cubic meters or cubic feet.

Capacity is a measure of the amount a container will hold. Capacity is measured in units such as liters or quarts.

Your child will also learn about units of weight and mass. Two objects with the same volume can have very different masses—for example, iron and wood. Weight is a measure of the pull of gravity on these objects: iron weighs more than wood. Weight is different on Earth and on the moon, but mass always stays the same.

Please help your child to continue to review and practice multiplications and divisions to keep those accurate and rapid. They will be used in the next unit.

If you have any questions or comments, please call or write to me.

Sincerely,
Your child's teacher

Estimada familia:

Su niño está estudiando el volumen, la capacidad y el peso. Su niño aprenderá que el volumen es una medida del espacio que hay dentro de una figura tridimensional, como una caja.

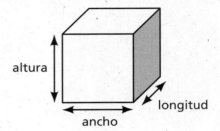

Para hallar el volumen de una caja, se multiplican las tres dimensiones: longitud × ancho × altura. El volumen se mide en unidades cúbicas, como metros cúbicos o pies cúbicos.

La capacidad es la medida de la cantidad que un recipiente puede contener. La capacidad se mide en unidades como litros o cuartos de galón.

Su niño también aprenderá acerca de las unidades de peso y de masa. Dos objetos que tienen el mismo volumen pueden tener masas muy diferentes; por ejemplo, el hierro y la madera. El peso es la medida de la fuerza de gravedad sobre esos objetos: El hierro pesa más que la madera. El peso en la Tierra es diferente al peso en la Luna, pero la masa siempre es la misma.

Por favor ayude a su niño a que continúe con el repaso y la práctica de las multiplicaciones y las divisiones para hacerlas con rapidez y precisión. Las usará en la siguiente unidad.

Si tiene alguna pregunta o comentario, por favor comuníquese conmigo.

Atentamente,
El maestro de su niño

Cubic Units and Volume

Class Activity

Name _____ **Date** _____

► Compare Length, Area, and Volume

Vocabulary

Length   one-dimensional
Area   two-dimensional
Volume three-dimensional

Length tells how wide, tall, or long something is. Finding length requires one measurement. Length is **one-dimensional** and is measured in length units.

Area tells how much surface a figure covers. Finding area requires two length measurements. Area is **two-dimensional** and is measured in square units.

Volume tells how much space an object occupies. Finding volume requires three length measurements. Volume is **three-dimensional** and is measured in cubic units.

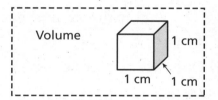

Length ⊢—⊣ 1 cm

Area 1 cm / 1 cm

Volume 1 cm / 1 cm / 1 cm

Tell if you need to measure for length, area, or volume. Then write the number of measurements you need to make.

1. How much water is in a swimming pool? _____

2. How tall are you? _____

3. How much carpet is needed for a floor? _____

4. How far is it from a doorknob to the floor? _____

5. How much sand is in a sandbox? _____

6. How much wallpaper is needed for one wall? _____

7. How long is a string? _____

8. How much space is there inside a refrigerator? _____

Class Activity

Name _____ Date _____

► Cubic Relationships

Solve.

The sides of a cube are 3 centimeters long.

Sides = 3 cm

9. What is the area of each face? _____

10. What is the volume of the cube? _____

A cube has a volume of 8 cubic meters.

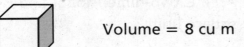
Volume = 8 cu m

11. What is the length of each edge? _____

12. What is the area of each of its faces? _____

One face of a cube has an area of 16 square inches.

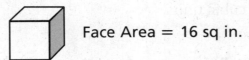
Face Area = 16 sq in.

13. What is the length of each edge? _____

14. What is the volume of the cube? _____

Describe a real-world situation for each.

15. measuring length

_____

16. measuring area

_____

17. measuring volume

_____

18. **Challenge** A box has a volume of 24 cubic inches.
Two of the faces of the box are squares. Its length
is 3 times its width. What are the dimensions of
the box?

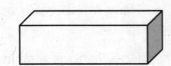

_____

Relate Length, Area, and Volume

Class Activity

Name _____ Date _____

▶ Double Two Dimensions of a Figure

Solve.

19. Luisa is making a quilt for Amanda. The quilt is 3 yards long and 2 yards wide. Amanda now wants the quilt to be twice as long and twice as wide.

    Luisa says that the quilt will be more than twice as large with the new dimensions. Amanda does not believe it. Who is right? Explain why.

    _____

    _____

    _____

    _____

3 yd

2 yd

▶ Double Three Dimensions of a Figure

20. Elbert keeps his CD collection in a box that is 3 dm long, 2 dm wide, and 1 dm high. His father is building him a new box that will be twice as long in every dimension.

    Elbert says that the new box will be twice as many cubic decimeters in volume as the old one. Is he right? Explain why or why not.

    _____

    _____

    _____

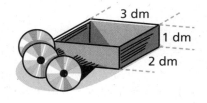

3 dm

1 dm

2 dm

21. A garden is shaped like a rectangle. What happens to the area of the garden if you double the length and the width of the garden? _____

22. A box is shaped like a rectangular prism. What happens to the volume of the box if you double _____ the length of each edge of the box?

Name _____   **Date** _____

Going Further

► Estimate and Solve

Carpeting comes in rolls that are 4 m wide. It is sold in whole meters. Shing's room is 3.2 m by 3.3 m.

1. How much carpeting does Shing need to buy to cover the floor of his room from wall to wall?

   _____

2. What is the area of the carpeting Shing will buy?

   _____

Solve.

3. A tetherball is attached to the end of a 3-meter rope. The rope is attached to a pole that is 5 cm in diameter. Estimate the greatest number of times the rope could wrap around the pole. Use 3 for π to make your estimate.

   _____

4. A baseball is about 3 inches in diameter. Estimate how many balls would fit in a box that is 6 in. by 12 in. by 9 in. Explain your estimate.

   _____

5. The floors of a 3-story building are $9\frac{1}{3}$ feet apart. Estimate the length of a ladder you would need to reach the roof.

   _____

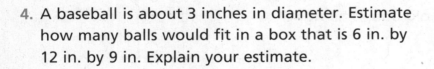

Relate Length, Area, and Volume

Class Activity

Vocabulary

capacity
liter
milliliter
kiloliter

▶ Decimals and Capacity

When you learned about volume, you learned that volume is a measure of the amount of space an object occupies.

Capacity is a measure of the amount a container can hold.

The chart shows the metric units that are used to measure capacity. **Liter** and **milliliter** are used most often. **Kiloliters** are sometimes used for large capacities, such as swimming pools.

kiloliter (kL)	hectoliter (hL)	dekaliter (dkL)	liter (L)	deciliter (dL)	centiliter (cL)	milliliter (mL)
1,000 L	100 L	10 L	1 L	0.1 L	0.01 L	0.001 L

× 10 ← × 10 ← × 10 ← → ÷ 10 → ÷ 10 → ÷ 10

Complete.

1. 1 kL = _____ L

2. 1,500 mL = _____ L

3. 3,000 L = _____ kL

4. 4.5 L = _____ mL

5. 2 kL = _____ L

6. 500 mL = _____ L

Solve.

7. Which is more, 500 liters or 0.5 kiloliters? Explain.

   _____

8. Kendall mixed 750 milliliters of orange juice with 750 milliliters of pineapple juice. How many liters of juice does he have?

   _____

9. Each of 5 water glasses has a capacity of 400 milliliters. How many liters of water do you need to fill all of the glasses? Explain.

   _____

   _____

► **Fractions and Capacity**

In the United States we measure in customary units.

Customary Units of Capacity						
1 gallon (gal)	=	4 quarts	=	8 pints	=	16 cups
$\frac{1}{4}$ gallon	=	1 quart (qt)	=	2 pints	=	4 cups
$\frac{1}{8}$ gallon	=	$\frac{1}{4}$ quart	=	1 pint (pt)	=	2 cups

Answer with a fraction in simplest form.

10. What fraction of 1 **gallon** is 3 quarts?

_____

11. What fraction of 1 **quart** is 1 **pint**?

_____

12. What fraction of 1 quart is 1 **cup**?

_____

13. What fraction of 1 gallon is 1 pint?

_____

Solve. Write your answers in simplest form.

14. A muffin recipe requires $2\frac{3}{4}$ cups of milk. What amount of milk do you need to make double the number of muffins?

_____

15. A recipe requires $\frac{3}{4}$ of a cup of water. Farha has a measuring cup that measures only ounces, but she knows that 8 ounces is 1 cup. How many ounces of water will she add to the mixture? Explain.

_____

_____

Measures of Capacity

Class Activity

Vocabulary
mass
kilogram
gram
milligram

► Decimals and Mass

Mass is the amount of matter in an object. Heavier objects have more mass. This table shows the metric units that we use to measure mass. We use **kilogram**, **gram**, and **milligram** most often.

kilogram (kg)	hectogram (hg)	dekagram (dkg)	gram (g)	decigram (dg)	centigram (cg)	milligram (mg)
1,000 g	100 g	10 g	1	0.1 g	0.01 g	0.001 g

× 10 ← × 10 ← × 10 ← → ÷ 10 → ÷ 10 → ÷ 10

Complete.

1. 1 kg = _____ g

2. 500 mg = _____ g

3. 2,000 g = _____ kg

4. 2.5 g = _____ mg

5. 4 kg = _____ g

6. 5,000 mg = _____ g

Solve.

7. Hiro has 5 kg of potatoes and 2 kg of onions. He plans to use 3 kg of potatoes and 0.5 kg of onions for a recipe. How many kilograms of each will not be used?

_____

_____

8. Javier estimates there are 2.5 kg of books in his book bag. Mavis estimates there are 1,500 g of books in her book bag. If the estimates are reasonable, who is carrying the heavier bag? Explain.

_____

_____

9. A United States nickel has a mass of 5 g. A cloth bag contains 1 kg of nickels. About how many nickels are in the bag? Explain.

_____

_____

Name _____ **Date** _____

▶ Fractions and Weight

Customary units of weight include **ounces**, **pounds**, and **tons**.

ounce (oz)	pound (lb)	ton (T)
1 lb = 16 oz	**1 lb**	1 T = 2,000 lb

10. The table below shows how to use fractions to compare ounces to pounds. Complete the table by writing each fraction in simplest form.

Ounces (oz)	1	2	4	8	12
Pounds (lb)	$\frac{1}{16}$	$\frac{1}{8}$			

Solve.

11. A book weighs $1\frac{1}{2}$ lb. What is the weight of the book in ounces?

_____

12. One package weighs 48 ounces. Another package weighs $3\frac{1}{4}$ pounds. Which package is heavier?

_____

13. A $\frac{1}{4}$ lb package of sunflower seeds costs 79¢. An 8-ounce package costs \$1.59. Which package represents the lower cost per ounce?

_____

14. A cargo truck is carrying three identical boxes. The weight of each box is $2\frac{1}{2}$ tons. Explain how to use mental math to find the total weight in pounds of the boxes.

_____

_____

_____

Measures of Mass and Weight

Class Activity

► Convert Measurements

Write *multiply by 1,000* or *divide by 1,000* to complete each sentence.

1. To change grams to kilograms, _____.

2. To change grams to milligrams, _____.

3. To change kiloliters to liters, _____.

4. To change milliliters to liters, _____.

Use the information in the table below to complete exercises 5–16.

Metric	Customary
kilo = 1,000 milli = $\frac{1}{1,000}$ 1 gram (g) = 1,000 milligrams (mg) 1 kiloliter (kL) = 1,000 liters (L)	1 pint (pt) = 2 cups (c) 1 quart (qt) = 2 pints 1 gallon (gal) = 4 quarts 1 pound (lb) = 16 ounces (oz) 1 ton (T) = 2,000 pounds

5. 3,040 mL = ___ L ___ mL

6. 1 gal = ___ pt

7. 72 oz = ___ lb ___ oz

8. 4 c = ___ qt

9. 4,300 g = ___ kg ___ g

10. 5 T = _____ lb

11. 1 g 1,000 mg = ___ g

12. 3 kL 1,000 L = ___ kL

13. 2 L 500 mL = _____ mL

14. 7 kg = _____ g

15. 2 qt 2 c = ___ pt

16. 1 gal = ___ c

17. Write an example to show that the statement below is true.

Multiplication is used to change a larger unit to a smaller unit.

_____

_____

18. Write an example to show that the statement below is true.

Division is used to change a smaller unit to a larger unit.

_____

_____

Class Activity

▶ Measurement Sums and Differences

Write an amount to complete each sentence.

19. One pound ungrouped to ounces = _____ ounces.

20. One kilogram ungrouped to grams = _____ grams.

21. One quart ungrouped to pints = _____ pints.

22. One ton ungrouped to pounds = _____ pounds.

23. One pint ungrouped to cups = _____ cups.

24. One gram ungrouped to milligrams = _____ milligrams.

25. One gallon ungrouped to quarts = _____ quarts.

26. One kiloliter ungrouped to liters = _____ liters.

27. **Discuss** When does a subtraction problem involve ungrouping?

28. **Discuss** When does an addition problem involve regrouping?

Add or subtract.

29.
```
   3 lb 10 oz
 − 1 lb 13 oz
```

30.
```
   4 L 500 mL
 + 2 L 600 mL
```

31.
```
    3 qt
 − 2 qt 1 pt
```

32.
```
   8 T 1,500 lb
 + 3 T 1,000 lb
```

33.
```
      1 c
 + 1 pt 1 c
```

34.
```
    9 gal
 − 5 gal 3 qt
```

35.
```
   12 lb 12 oz
 +  9 lb 15 oz
```

36.
```
    4 kg
 − 1 kg 300 g
```

37.
```
   9 L 250 mL
 − 3 L 650 mL
```

38.
```
   7 kL 1,000 L
 + 3 kL 1,000 L
```

39.
```
    5 T
 − 2 T 100 lb
```

40.
```
   3 qt 1 pt
 + 1 qt 1 pt
```

Working with Measurement Units

Name _____ \   **Date** _____

Vocabulary

degree Fahrenheit (°F)

► Solve Fahrenheit Temperature Problems

In the Customary System of Measurement, temperature is measured in **degrees Fahrenheit (°F)**. On the Fahrenheit scale, water freezes at 32°F and boils at 212°F.

Use the thermometer to solve the following problems.

1. What would you expect the temperature to be if many families were enjoying an afternoon at the beach?

   _____

2. Are you more likely to see rain or snow if the outside air temperature is 14°F? Why?

   _____

3. What is a comfortable room temperature in degrees Fahrenheit?

   _____

4. The high temperature of the day was 42°F. The low temperature of the day was 9° lower. What was the low temperature of the day?

   _____

5. The low temperature of the day was ⁻6°F. The high temperature of the day was 14° higher. What was the high temperature of the day?

   _____

6. The 5 A.M. temperature was ⁻9°F. The 5 P.M. temperature was 2°F. How many degrees did the temperature change from 5 A.M. to 5 P.M.? Was the change an increase or a decrease?

   _____

7. The 1 P.M. temperature was 8°F. The 9 P.M. temperature was ⁻2°F. By how many degrees did the temperature change from 1 P.M. to 9 P.M.? Was the change an increase or a decrease?

   _____

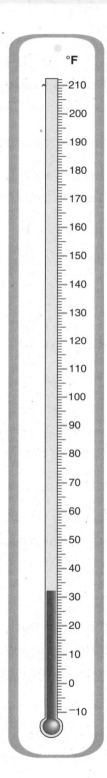

°F

210
200
190
180
170
160
150
140
130
120
110
100
90
80
70
60
50
40
30
20
10
0
−10

Name _____ **Date** _____

Vocabulary
degree Celsius (°C)

► **Solve Celsius Temperature Problems**

In the United States, we generally use degrees Fahrenheit to measure temperature. Most of the other countries in the world use **degrees Celsius (°C)**. On the Celsius scale, water freezes at 0°C and boils at 100°C.

Use the thermometer to solve the following problems.

8. The distance between two consecutive tick marks on the thermometer represents what number of degrees?

_____

9. What is a comfortable room temperature in degrees Celsius?

_____

10. Are you more likely to see rain or snow if the outside air temperature is 14°C? Why?

_____

11. The high temperature of the day was 24°C. The low temperature of the day was 5° lower. What was the low temperature of the day?

_____

12. The low temperature of the day was –2°C. The high temperature of the day was 5° higher. What was the high temperature of the day?

_____

13. The noon temperature was 31°C. The midnight temperature was 24°C. By how many degrees did the temperature change from noon to midnight? Was the change an increase or a decrease?

_____

14. The 6 A.M. temperature was ⁻8°C. The 6 P.M. temperature was 1°C. How many degrees did the temperature change from 6 A.M. to 6 P.M.? Was the change an increase or a decrease?

_____

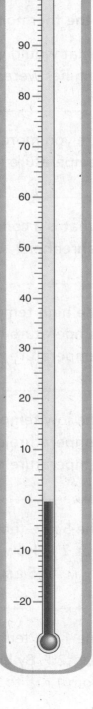

Temperature

Name _____ **Date** _____

▶ Estimate Temperatures

15. What is the freezing point of water in degrees Fahrenheit? in degrees Celsius?

_____

16. What is the boiling point of water in degrees Fahrenheit? in degrees Celsius?

_____

17. What is a comfortable room temperature in degrees Fahrenheit? in degrees Celsius?

_____

18. Many children are playing in the snow. What would you expect the temperature to be in degrees Fahrenheit? in degrees Celsius?

_____

19. Many families are enjoying an afternoon at the beach. What would you expect the temperature to be in degrees Fahrenheit? in degrees Celsius?

_____

20. a. Complete the table of corresponding Fahrenheit and Celsius temperatures.

°F	°C
104	
	30
68	
	10
32	

b. Discuss Use the data in the table to develop a *general* rule that can be used to change degrees Fahrenheit to degrees Celsius.

c. Discuss Use the data in the table to develop a *general* rule that can be used to change degrees Celsius to degrees Fahrenheit.

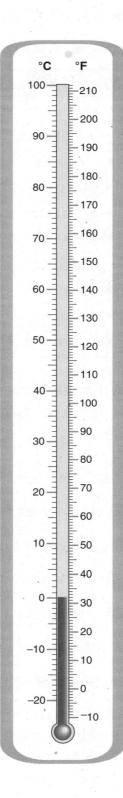

Name _____ **Date** _____

▶ Choose the Appropriate Tool and Unit

Look at these lists of measurement tools and units.

Measurement Tools
• centimeter ruler
• meter stick
• inch ruler
• yardstick
• protractor
• scale
• watch
• clock
• calendar
• thermometer

Measurement Units		
• grams	• milliliters	• millimeters
• ounces	• fluid ounces	• centimeters
• kilograms	• cups	• inches
• pounds	• pints	• feet
• tons	• quarts or liters	• yards or meters
• days	• gallons	• kilometers
• weeks	• seconds	• miles
• months	• minutes	• degrees (angles)
• years	• hours	• degrees (temperature)
• square units	• cubic units	

Write the name of the tool and the name of the unit you would use to make the following measurements.

21. the time that is needed to complete a quiz _____

22. the amount of storage space in a closet _____

23. the angles formed by intersecting lines _____

24. the weight of a book bag filled with books _____

25. the temperature during a summer day _____

26. the age of a tree in a forest _____

27. the amount of paint needed to paint a room _____

Discuss these situations.

28. Is it sensible to use seconds to measure the length of a school day? If so, explain why. If not, explain why not and name the unit you would use.

29. Would you use milliliters to measure the capacity of a swimming pool? Explain why or why not.

　　　　　　　　　　　　　　Temperature

► Stem-and-Leaf Plots

The stem-and-leaf plot below shows the average January
temperature in selected U. S. cities.

[data source: 2003 World Almanac page 175]

Average January Temperatures in Selected Cities (°F)	
Stem	Leaf
1	0 0 3 4 6 8
2	2 2 2 5 5 9 9
3	2 3 4 6 7 8
4	0 0 0 3 4 6 9 9
5	3 4 6 7 8
6	1 1
7	3

Legend: 5 | 3 means 53°F

Use the stem-and-leaf plot.

30. How many cities are represented by the data?

_____

31. What are the greatest and least temperatures?

_____

32. How many cities have an average January temperature that
    is less than the freezing temperature of water?

_____

33. How many cities have an average January temperature that
    is greater than 40°F?

_____

34. **Discuss** Which temperature is closest to the average January
    temperature where you live? Explain why you chose that
    temperature.

35. **Journal** Collect and record the daily high or low temperatures
    for a period of time. On a separate sheet of paper, display the
    data in a stem-and-leaf plot.

Name _____ **Date** _____

Going Further

▶ Integers on the Number Line

Integers include the set of whole numbers (1, 2, 3, …) and their opposites (⁻1, ⁻2, ⁻3, …) and 0. The number line below is an integer number line.

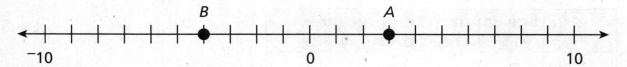

1. Label each tick mark with the integer it represents.

2. What integer represents the location of point *A*? _____

3. What integer represents the location of point *B*? _____

Plot the following points on the number line.

4. point *C* at 5   5. point *E* at ⁻1   6. point *F* at 9   7. point *D* at ⁻8

8. On a number line, an integer is to the right of another integer. Which integer is larger? Explain how you know.

_____

_____

9. Order the integers that represent the points in exercises 2–7 from least to greatest.

_____

Use the number line at the top of the page to compare these integers. Write >, <, or =.

10. 2 $\bigcirc$ 6   11. 4 $\bigcirc$ ⁻1   12. ⁻7 $\bigcirc$ 3   13. ⁻2 $\bigcirc$ ⁻10

14. ⁻8 $\bigcirc$ ⁻7   15. ⁻5 $\bigcirc$ ⁻5   16. 6 $\bigcirc$ ⁻6   17. ⁻3 $\bigcirc$ 0

Temperature

Class Activity

Name _____   Date _____

Vocabulary

analog clock
digital clock

► Compare Different Clocks

An **analog clock** uses an hour hand and a minute hand to display time. Some analog clocks also have a second hand, and most are circular with faces numbered from 1 to 12.

A **digital clock** uses a colon (:) to separate numbers that represent hours (h) from numbers that represent minutes (min). Some digital clocks also have another colon to separate minutes from seconds (s). Digital clocks also display A.M. or P.M.

1. **Discuss** How are analog and digital clocks alike? How are they different?

2. **Discuss** How can you remember which hand is the hour hand and which hand is the minute hand on an analog clock?

3. **Discuss** How can you remember which direction is clockwise and which direction is counterclockwise on an analog clock?

4. **Discuss** Is it easier to see how many minutes have passed using an analog clock or a digital clock?

How much time has passed since 12:00 A.M.?

5.

6.

7.

_____   _____   _____

► Calculate Units of Time

8. 2 h = _____ min

9. 5 min = _____ s

10. $\frac{1}{2}$ h = _____ min

11. 120 s = _____ min

12. $\frac{3}{4}$ h = _____ min

13. 10 min = _____ s

14. $\frac{1}{4}$ h = _____ min

15. 180 min = _____ h

16. $1\frac{1}{2}$ h = _____ min

► Solve Elapsed-Time Problems

Solve.

17. Afternoon recess at Darla's school begins at 1:20 P.M. and ends at 1:35 P.M. How many minutes long is the afternoon recess?

_____

18. The school library is open for 2 hours 30 minutes each afternoon. What time does the library open if it closes at 3:45 P.M.?

_____

19. What time should Trevor get up in the morning if it takes him 45 minutes to get ready for school and he wants to leave home at 7:50 A.M.?

_____

20. A movie that is 94 minutes long is scheduled to begin at 6:20 P.M. What time does the movie end if it begins 1 minute late?

_____

21. After school on Friday, Rojean began doing her homework at 4:12 P.M. She finished at 5:24 P.M. Between those times, she took a 10-minute break.

What length of time did Rojean spend doing her homework on Friday?

_____

22. A two-act theater play begins at 8:00 P.M. and ends at 11:25 P.M., including an intermission period. The play is 3 hours and 5 minutes long.

How long is the intermission period between Act 1 and Act 2?

_____

23. The times that the school day begins and ends at three different schools are shown below. Use the times to answer the questions that follow.

Jefferson School	Lakeside School	Adams School
Start: 8:15 A.M.	**Start:** 8:05 A.M.	**Start:** 8:40 A.M.
End: 3:35 P.M.	**End:** 3:10 P.M.	**End:** 3:50 P.M.

a. Which school has the longest school day? _____

b. Which school has the shortest school day? _____

24. What time does the day begin at your school? What time does it end? What is the length of a day at your school?

_____

The Passing of Time

Class Activity

► Calculate Elapsed Time

Complete.

25. 1 hour is ungrouped as _____ minutes.

26. 1 minute is ungrouped as _____ seconds.

27. 60 minutes is regrouped as _____ hour(s).

28. 60 seconds is regrouped as _____ minute(s).

Write each time as it would appear on a 24-hour clock.

29. 1:00 P.M. _____

30. 4:09 P.M. _____

31. 6:45 P.M. _____

32. 10:00 P.M. _____

Solve.

33. How much time will elapse from 8:30 P.M. to 7:15 A.M.?

_____

34. How much time will elapse from 10:55 A.M. to 6:25 P.M.?

_____

35. An extra-inning professional baseball game began at 8:17 P.M. and ended at 12:06 A.M. What was the length of the game in hours and minutes?

_____

36. On Saturday night, the late showing of a movie began at 11:40 P.M. and ended at 2:05 A.M. What was the length of the movie in hours and minutes?

_____

37. Victor's favorite shift to work is the third shift, and he often works overtime. The times Victor worked last week are shown in the table at the right. Use the data to answer the following questions.

a. On which day did Victor work the greatest amount of time?

_____

b. On which day did work the least amount of time?

_____

Day	Time
Monday	Start: 11:45 P.M. End: 8:10 A.M.
Tuesday	Start: 10:50 P.M. End: 9:20 A.M.
Wednesday	Start: 11:15 P.M. End: 7:35 A.M.
Thursday	Start: 10:40 P.M. End: 8:30 A.M.
Friday	Start: 11:55 P.M. End: 9:05 A.M.

c. How much time altogether did Victor work last week?

_____

► Solve Time Problems

Complete.

38. 1 year = _____ weeks   39. 1 week = _____ hours   40. 1 day = _____ minutes

41. 1 hour = _____ seconds   42. 2 days = _____ hours   43. 4 weeks = _____ days

44. 14 days = _____ hours   45. 15 years = _____ months

46. 3 days 12 hours = _____ hours   47. 7 weeks 5 days = _____ days

48. 8 hours 20 minutes = _____ minutes   49. 4 years 10 months = _____ months

50. Serena played soccer for 1 hour 45 minutes on Saturday morning and for 3 hours 10 minutes on Saturday afternoon. What is a reasonable estimate of the length of time she played soccer on that day?

51. On Sunday, Jeremy studied from 11:40 A.M. to 12:30 P.M., from 1:55 P.M. to 3:45 P.M., and from 6:15 P.M. to 7:20 P.M. What is a reasonable estimate of the length of time he studied on Sunday?

_____   _____

52. Explain how to find the number of decades in a century, and then name that number of decades.

_____

_____

53. There are 1,000 years in a millennium. Explain how to find the number of centuries in a millennium, and then name that number of centuries.

_____

_____

54. What is a reasonable estimate of your age in months? In days?

_____

Find the volume of each prism.

1.

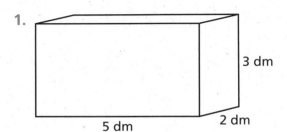

3 dm

5 dm   2 dm

_____

2.

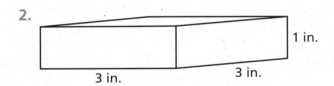

1 in.

3 in.   3 in.

_____

3.

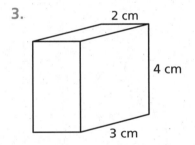

2 cm

4 cm

3 cm

_____

4. **Find each elapsed time.**

a. Lisa took a long nap and slept from 3:15 P.M. to 5:30 P.M. How long did she nap?

_____

b. The movie started at 10:45 A.M. and was 2 hours 20 minutes long. What time did the movie end?

_____

Solve.

5. A box top is 24 sq cm in area. The volume of the box is 240 cu cm. What is the height of the box?

_____

6. Cardiss made punch with 1,500 mL of ginger ale and 600 mL of cranberry juice. How many liters of punch did Cardiss make?

_____

7. A recipe for one batch of muffins requires $1\frac{1}{3}$ cups of flour. Kazuo has $1\frac{1}{2}$ cups of flour. Is that enough flour to make the recipe?

_____

8. Pauline has 3 kg of potatoes and 3 kg of meat. She plans to use 1.5 kg of potatoes and 500 g of meat to make a stew. How many grams of each will not be used?

_____

_____

9. A refrigerator is 3 ft wide, 2 ft deep, and 6 ft high. How much floor space does it cover? _____
What is its volume? _____

10. **Extended Response** One package weighs 36 ounces. Another package weighs $2\frac{3}{4}$ pounds. Which package is heavier? Explain your answer.

_____

_____

_____

_____

Glossary

acre A measure of land area. An acre is equal to 4,840 square yards.

acute angle An angle whose measure is less than 90°.

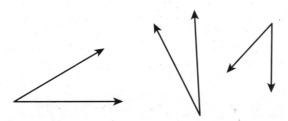

acute triangle A triangle with three acute angles.

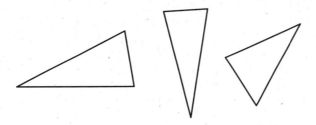

addend One of two or more numbers added together to find a sum.

Example:

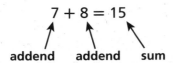

$$7 + 8 = 15$$

addend addend sum

Add On Method for Subtraction Find the difference between two numbers by adding to the lesser number to get the greater number.

adjusted estimate A new estimate that is made using the Digit-by-Digit method of dividing when an overestimate or underestimate has been initially made.

analog clock A clock that uses an hour hand and a minute hand to display time. Most are circular and have a face numbered from 1 to 12. Some analog clocks also have a second hand.

angle A figure formed by two rays or line segments with a common endpoint.

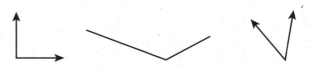

apex The vertex of a cone.

area The amount of surface covered by a figure measured in square units.

array An arrangement of objects, symbols, or numbers in equal rows and equal columns.

Associative Property of Addition Changing the grouping of addends does not change the sum.

Example:
$$3 + (5 + 7) = (3 + 5) + 7$$

Associative Property of Multiplication Changing the grouping of factors does not change the product.

Example:
$$3 \times (5 \times 7) = (3 \times 5) \times 7$$

average (See **mean**)

axis A line, usually horizontal or vertical, that is labeled with numbers or words to show the meaning of a graph.

axis of rotation A line about which a figure is rotated.

Glossary (Continued)

B

bar graph A graph that uses bars to show data.

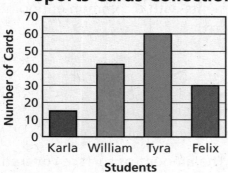

Sports Cards Collection

base of a figure For a triangle or parallelogram, a base is any side. For a trapezoid, a base is either of the parallel sides. For a prism, a base is one of the congruent parallel faces. For a pyramid, the base is the face that does not touch the vertex of the pyramid.

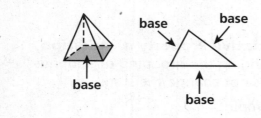

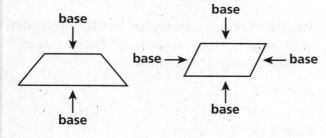

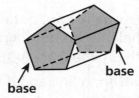

base of a power The number that is used as a factor when evaluating powers.

Example: In 10^3, the 10 is the base.

basic ratio A ratio in simplest form.

Example: The ratio 12 to 8 simplifies to 3 to 2.

billion One thousand million.
1,000,000,000

billionth One thousandth of a millionth.
0.000000001

C

capacity A measure of how much a container can hold.

categorical data Data expressed as words that represent categories.

Example: Color (red, blue, yellow, and so on)

Celsius The metric temperature scale. Water freezes at 0°C and boils at 100°C.

centimeter A unit of measure in the metric system that equals one hundredth of a meter. 1 cm = 0.01 m

1 cm

change minus A change situation that can be represented by subtraction. In a change minus situation, the starting number, the change, or the result will be unknown.

Example:

Unknown Start	Unknown Change	Unknown Result
$n - 2 = 3$	$5 - n = 3$	$5 - 2 = n$

change plus A change situation that can be represented by addition. In a change plus situation, the starting number, the change, or the result will be unknown.

Example:

Unknown Start	Unknown Change	Unknown Result
$n + 2 = 5$	$3 + n = 5$	$3 + 2 = n$

circle A plane figure that forms a closed path so that all the points on the path are the same distance from a point called the center.

circle graph A graph that uses parts of a circle to show data.

Zak's Book Collection

circumference The distance around a circle.

clockwise The direction in which the hands of a clock move.

collection situations Situations that involve putting together (joining) or taking apart (separating) groups.

column A part of a table or array that contains items arranged vertically.

•
•
•

combination situation A combination situation is one in which pairs or sets are counted. Tables can be used to show combinations.

Types of Sandwiches			
	Cheese	Peanut Butter	Tuna
White	W + C	W + PB	W + T
Wheat	Wh + C	Wh + PB	Wh + T

common denominator A common multiple of two or more denominators.

Example: 6 could be used as a common denominator for $\frac{1}{2}$ and $\frac{1}{3}$.

$$\frac{1}{2} = \frac{3}{6} \quad \frac{1}{3} = \frac{2}{6}$$

so $\frac{1}{2} + \frac{1}{3} = \frac{3}{6} + \frac{2}{6} = \frac{5}{6}$

Commutative Property of Addition Changing the order of addends does not change the sum.

Example: $3 + 8 = 8 + 3$

Commutative Property of Multiplication Changing the order of factors does not change the product.

Example: $3 \times 8 = 8 \times 3$

comparison situation A situation in which two amounts are compared by addition or by multiplication. An additive comparison situation compares by asking or telling how much more (how much less) one amount is than

Glossary (Continued)

another. A multiplicative comparison situation compares by asking or telling how many times as many one amount is as another. The multiplicative comparison may also be made using fraction language. For example, you can say, "Sally has one fourth as much as Tom has," instead of saying "Tom has 4 times as much as Sally has."

complementary angles Two angles having a sum of 90°.

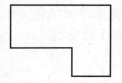

complex figure A figure made by combining simple geometric figures like rectangles and triangles.

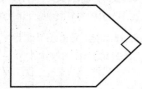

composite number A number greater than 1 that has more than one factor pair. Examples of composite numbers are 4, 15, and 45. The factor pairs of 15 are: 1 and 15, 3 and 5.

cone A solid figure with a curved base and a single vertex.

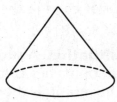

congruent Exactly the same size and shape.

Example: Triangles *ABC* and *PQR* are congruent.

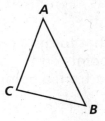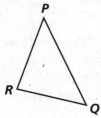

continuous data Data that represent an accumulation without interruption. Each data point is related to the data point before and after it.

Example: Temperature reading over a 24-hour period: 45°, 47°, 52° and so on.

coordinate A number that determines the position of a point in one direction on a grid.

coordinate plane A system of coordinates formed by the perpendicular intersection of horizontal and vertical number lines.

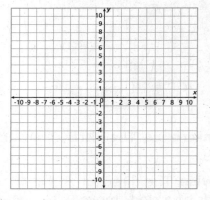

counterclockwise The direction opposite to the direction the hands of a clock move.

counterexample An example that proves that a general statement is false.

cube A rectangular prism that has 6 faces that are congruent squares.

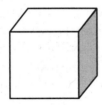

cubic centimeter A metric unit for measuring volume. It is the volume of a cube with one-centimeter edges.

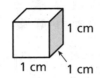
1 cm
1 cm   1 cm

cubic meter A metric unit for measuring volume. It is the volume of a cube with one-meter edges.

cubic unit A unit of volume made by a cube with all edges one unit long.

Example: Cubic centimeters and cubic inches are cubic units.

cup A U.S. customary unit of capacity equal to half a pint.

cylinder A solid (three-dimensional) figure with two curved, congruent bases.

D

data Pieces of information.

decimal number A representation of a number using the numerals 0 to 9, in which each digit has a value 10 times the digit to its right. A dot or decimal point separates the whole-number part of the number on the left from the fractional part on the right.

decimeter A unit of measure in the metric system that equals one tenth of a meter. 1 dm = 0.1 m

degree A unit for measuring angles. Also a unit for measuring temperature. (See Celsius and Fahrenheit.)

denominator The number below the bar in a fraction. It tells the number of unit fractions into which the 1 whole is divided.

Example: 4 is the denominator.

$\frac{3}{4}$ ◄— denominator

diagonal A line segment connecting two vertices that are not next to each other.

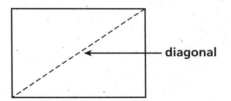
diagonal

diameter A line segment from one side of a circle to the other through the center. Also the length of that segment.

difference The result of a subtraction.
Example: 54 − 37 = 17
└─ difference

digit Any of the symbols 0, 1, 2, 3, 4, 5, 6, 7, 8, or 9.

Glossary (Continued)

digital clock A clock that has a colon (:) separating digits representing hours from digits representing minutes. Some digital clocks also have another colon to separate minutes from seconds. Digital clocks also display A.M. or P.M.

Digit-by-Digit A method used to solve a division problem.

Example:

Put in only one digit at a time.

```
        5              54              546
    7) 3,822        7) 3,822        7) 3,822
      - 3 5           - 3 5           - 3 5
        32              32              32
                       - 28            - 28
                         42              42
                                       - 42
```

dimension The height, length, or width.

Examples:

A line segment has only length, so it has *one* dimension.

A rectangle has length and width, so it has *two* dimensions.

A cube has length, width, and height, so it has *three* dimensions.

discrete data Data that involve counting. In a set of discrete data, each number is exact and the numbers are not related to each other.

Example: The heights of five trees: 18 ft, 35 ft, 20 ft, 40 ft, 28 ft.

Distributive Property You can multiply a sum by a number, or multiply each addend by the number and add the products; the result is the same.

Example:

$$3 \times (2 + 4) = (3 \times 2) + (3 \times 4)$$
$$3 \times 6 = 6 + 12$$
$$18 = 18$$

divisible A number is divisible by another number if the quotient is a whole number with no remainder.

Example: 15 is divisible by 5 because $15 \div 5 = 3$

dot array An arrangement of dots in rows and columns.

double bar graph Data is compared by using pairs of bars drawn next to each other.

Number of Rainy Days in Florida and Texas

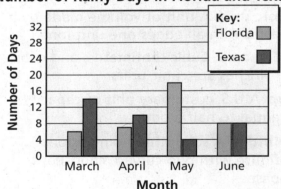

Key:
Florida
Texas

E

edge A line segment that forms as a side of a two-dimensional figure or the part of a three-dimensional figure where two faces meet.

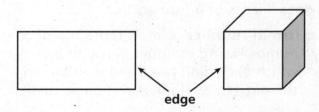

edge

elapsed time The amount of time that passes between two times.

equal groups Groups that have the same number of objects.

equation A statement that two expressions are equal. An equation always has an equals sign.

Example: $32 + 35 = 67$
$50 = 75 - 25$
$1 + 10 + 40 = 53 - 2$

equilateral Having all equal sides.

Example: An equilateral triangle

equivalent Representing the same number or amount.

equivalent fractions Two or more fractions that represent the same fractional part of 1 whole.

estimate Find *about* how many or *about* how much. A reasonable guess about a measurement or answer.

evaluate To substitute a value for a letter and then calculate to simplify the expression.

even number A whole number that is a multiple of 2. An even number ends with a 0, 2, 4, 6, or 8.

Example: 68 is an even number because it is a multiple of 2; $2 \times 34 = 68$.

example A specific instance that demonstrates a general statement.

expanded form A way of writing a number that shows the value of each of its digits.

Example: Expanded form of 835:
$800 + 30 + 5$
8 hundreds + 3 tens + 5 ones

Expanded Notation A strategy used to solve multiplication and division problems.

67×43

$43 = 40 + 3$ $\longrightarrow$
$\times 67 = 60 + 7$

$60 \times 40 = 2{,}400$	43
$60 \times 3 = 180$	$\times 67$
$7 \times 40 = 280$	2,400
$7 \times 3 = 21$	180
2,881	280
	21
	2,881

$3{,}822 \div 7$

Show the zeros in the places.

$$\begin{array}{r} 500 \\ 7\overline{)3{,}822} \\ -3{,}500 \\ \hline 322 \end{array}$$

$$\begin{array}{r} 40 \\ 500 \\ 7\overline{)3{,}822} \\ -3{,}500 \\ \hline 322 \\ -280 \\ \hline 42 \end{array}$$

$$\begin{array}{r} 6 \\ 40 \hspace{0.5em})546 \\ 500 \\ 7\overline{)3{,}822} \\ -3{,}500 \\ \hline 322 \\ -280 \\ \hline 42 \\ -42 \end{array}$$

expression A combination of one or more numbers, variables, or numbers and variables with one or more operations.

Examples: 4
$6n$
$6n - 5$
$7 + 4$
$2(3 + 4)$

exponent The number in a power that tells how many times the base is used as a factor.

Example: In 10^3, the 3 is the exponent.

F

face A flat surface of a three-dimensional figure.

Glossary (Continued)

factor One of two or more numbers multiplied together to make a product.

Example:

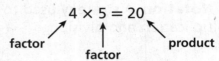

4 × 5 = 20

factor · factor · product

Factor Puzzle A two-by-two table that is made from the cells in two rows and two columns of the Multiplication Table. It can be used to solve proportions. The unknown number in the ○ will be 5 × 3 = 15.

	3	7	
2	6	14	2
5	○	35	5
	3	7	

Fahrenheit The temperature scale used in the United States. Water freezes at 32°F and boils at 212°F.

floor plan A scale drawing of a room as seen from above.

foot A U.S. customary unit of length equal to 12 inches and $\frac{1}{3}$ yard.

fraction A number that is the sum of unit fractions, each an equal part of a set or part of a whole.

Examples: $\frac{3}{4} = \frac{1}{4} + \frac{1}{4} + \frac{1}{4}$

$\frac{5}{4} = \frac{1}{4} + \frac{1}{4} + \frac{1}{4} + \frac{1}{4} + \frac{1}{4}$

front-end estimation A method of estimating that uses the left-most digit in each number and replaces all of the other digits with zeros.

Example:

$$4,588 \longrightarrow 4,000$$
$$-2,616 \longrightarrow -2,000$$
$$2,000 \text{ estimated difference}$$

function A consistent relationship between two sets of numbers. Each number in one of the sets is paired with exactly one number in the other set. A function can be shown in a chart, or as a set of ordered pairs.

Example: The relationship between the number of yards and the number of feet.

$$f = 3y$$

Yards	1	2	3	4	5	6	7
Feet	3	6	9	12	15	18	21

G

gallon A U.S. customary unit of capacity equal to 4 quarts, 8 pints, and 16 cups.

gram The basic unit of mass in the metric system.

greater than (>) A symbol used when comparing two numbers. The greater number is given first.

Example: 33 > 17
33 is greater than 17.

greatest Largest.

growing pattern A number or geometric pattern that increases.

Examples: 2, 4, 6, 8, 10…
1, 2, 5, 10, 17…

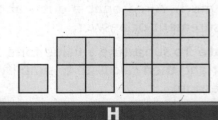

H

half turn A 180° rotation.

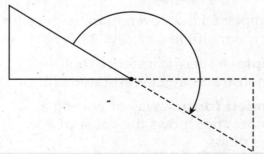

height The perpendicular distance from a base of a figure to the highest point.

hexagon A six-sided polygon.

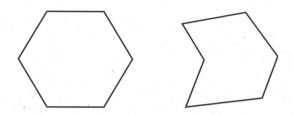

histogram A graph in which bars are used to display how frequently data occurs between intervals.

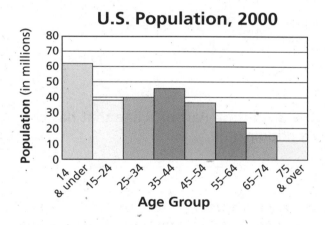

hypothesis A statement used as the basis of an investigation.

I

Identity Property of Multiplication The product of 1 and any number equals that number.

Example: $10 \times 1 = 10$

image The new figure that results from the translation, reflection, or rotation of a figure.

improper fraction A fraction whose numerator is greater than or equal to the denominator.

Example: $\frac{3}{2}$

inch A U.S. customary unit of length. There are 12 inches in 1 foot.

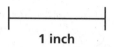

1 inch

inequality A statement that two expressions are not equal.

Examples: $2 < 5$
$4 + 5 > 12 - 8$

integer The set of integers includes the set of positive whole numbers (1, 2, 3, …) and their opposites (–1, –2, –3, …) and 0.

inverse operations Opposite or reverse operations that undo each other. Addition and subtraction are inverse operations. Multiplication and division are inverse operations.

Examples: $4 + 6 = 10$, so $10 - 6 = 4$
$3 \times 9 = 27$, so $27 \div 9 = 3$

isosceles trapezoid A trapezoid with one pair of opposite congruent sides.

isosceles triangle A triangle with at least two congruent sides.

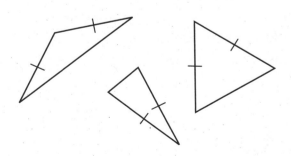

Glossary (Continued)

K

key A part of a map, graph, or chart that explains what symbols mean.

kilogram A unit of mass in the metric system that equals one thousand grams. 1 kg = 1,000 g

kiloliter A unit of capacity in the metric system that equals one thousand liters. 1 kL = 1,000 L

kilometer A unit of length in the metric system that equals one thousand meters. 1 km = 1,000 m

L

least Smallest.

least common denominator The least common multiple of two denominators. **Example:** 6 is the least common denominator of $\frac{1}{2}$ and $\frac{1}{3}$.

length The measure of a line segment, or of one side or edge of a figure.

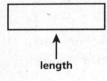
length

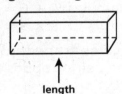
length

less than (<) A symbol used when comparing two numbers. The smaller number is given first.

Example: 54 < 78
54 is less than 78.

line A straight path that goes on forever in opposite directions.

Example: line *AB*

A   B

line graph A graph that uses a broken line to show changes in data.

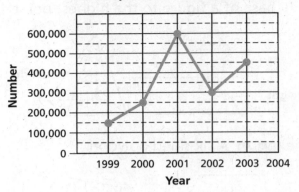

Deer Population in Midland Park

line plot A diagram that shows the frequency of data on a number line.

line of symmetry A line such that if a figure is folded on that line, the two parts will match exactly.

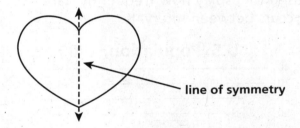
line of symmetry

line segment Part of a line that has two endpoints.

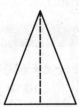

line symmetry A figure has line symmetry if it can be folded along a line to create two halves that match exactly.

Linked Multiplication Column Table A Multiplication Column Table that also has a column showing the unit that links the terms in each ratio.

Example: This table shows the ratios of two rates, $3 per day and $5 per day, and the linking unit, days.

Days	Noreen ③	Tim ⑤
0	0	0
1	3	5
2	6	10
3	9	15
4	12	20

liter The basic unit of capacity in the metric system.

M

mass The measure of the amount of matter in an object.

mean (average) The size of each of n equal groups made from n data values. The mean can be found by adding the values in a set of data and dividing by the number of such values.

Example: 75, 84, 89, 91, 101
   $75 + 84 + 89 + 91 + 101 = 440$,
   then $440 \div 5 = 88$. The mean is 88.

measure of central tendency The mean, median, or mode of a set of numbers.

median The middle number in a set of ordered numbers. For an even number of numbers, the median is the number halfway between the two middle numbers.

Examples: 13   26   34   47   52
   The median for this set is 34.
   8   8   12   14   20   21
   The median for this set is 13.

meter The basic unit of length in the metric system.

milligram A unit of mass in the metric system that equals one thousandth of a gram. 1 mg = 0.001 g

milliliter A unit of capacity in the metric system that equals one thousandth of a liter. 1 mL = 0.001 L

millimeter A unit of length in the metric system that equals one thousandth of a meter. 1 mm = 0.001 m

misleading A comparing sentence containing language that may trick you into doing the wrong operation.

Example: John's age is 3 *more* than Jessica's. If John is 12, how old is Jessica?

mixed number A number represented by a whole number and a fraction.

Example: $4\frac{2}{3}$

mode The number that appears most frequently in a set of numbers.

Example: 2, 4, 4, 4, 5, 7, 7
   4 is the mode in this set of numbers.

Multiplication Column Table A table made of two columns from a multiplication table.

Days	Dollars
0	0
1	3
2	6
3	9
4	12
5	15
6	18
7	21
8	24
9	27

multiplication table A table that shows the product of each pair of numbers in the left column and top row.

multiplier The factor used to multiply the numerator and denominator to create an equivalent fraction.

Example: A multiplier of 5 changes $\frac{2}{3}$ to $\frac{5 \times 2}{5 \times 3} = \frac{10}{15}$.

Glossary (Continued)

N

negative number A number less than zero.

Examples: −1, −23, and −3.5 are negative numbers.

net A flat pattern that can be folded to make a solid figure.

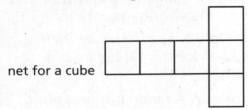

net for a cube

non-unit fraction A fraction with a numerator greater than 1.

Examples: $\frac{3}{4}$ or $\frac{4}{8}$ or $\frac{10}{8}$.

number sentence Describes how numbers or expressions are related to each other using one of the symbols =, <, or >. The types of number sentences are equations and inequalities.

Examples: 25 + 25 = 50
13 > 8 + 2

numerical data Data that consist of numbers.

numerator The number above the bar in a fraction.

Example: The numerator is 2.

$\frac{2}{3}$ ← numerator

It tells how many unit fractions there are: 2 of the $\frac{1}{3}$.

O

oblique lines Lines that are not parallel or perpendicular.

obtuse angle An angle greater than a right angle and less than a straight angle.

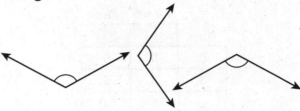

obtuse triangle A triangle with one obtuse angle.

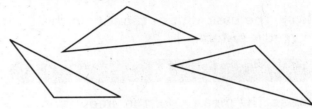

odd number A whole number that is not a multiple of 2. An odd number ends with 1, 3, 5, 7, or 9.

Example: 73 is an odd number because it is not a multiple of 2.

one-dimensional Having only length as a measure. A line segment is one-dimensional.

operation A mathematical process. Addition, subtraction, multiplication, division, and raising a number to a power are operations.

Order of Operations A set of rules that states the order in which operations should be done.
1. Compute inside parentheses first.
2. Simplify any exponents.
3. Multiply and divide from left to right.
4. Add and subtract from left to right.

ordered pair A pair of numbers that shows the position of a point on a coordinate grid.

Example: The ordered pair (3, 4) represents a point 3 units to the right of the *y*-axis and 4 units above the *x*-axis.

origin The point (0, 0) on a two-dimensional coordinate grid.

ounce A unit of weight or capacity in the U.S. customary system equal to one sixteenth of a pound or one eighth of a cup.

outlier A number or numbers whose values are much less or much greater than the other numbers in a data set.

overestimate An estimate that is greater than the actual amount.

Example: A shirt costs $26.47 and a pair of jeans cost $37.50. You can make an overestimate by rounding $26.47 to $30 and $37.50 to $40 to be sure you have enough money to pay for the clothes.

P

parallel The same distance apart at every point.

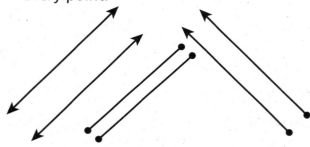

parallelogram A quadrilateral with both pairs of opposite sides parallel.

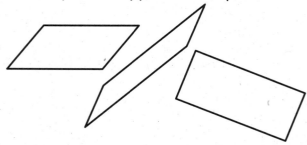

parentheses Symbols used to group numbers together.

$$7 + (3 \times 4) = 19$$

parentheses

partial products Products of the smaller problems in the Rectangle Sections method of multiplying.

Example: The partial products are highlighted.

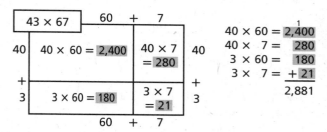

pentagon A polygon with five sides.

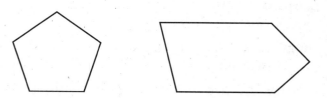

percent Percent means out of a hundred or per hundred. The numerator of a fraction that has 100 as the denominator is followed by the % sign: 50% is $\frac{50}{100}$ or a value equivalent to $\frac{50}{100}$.

perimeter The distance around a figure.

perpendicular Lines, line segments, or rays are perpendicular if they form right angles.

Example: These two lines are perpendicular.

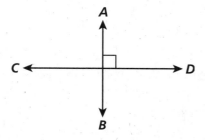

pi A number equal to the circumference of a circle divided by its diameter, or about 3.14. Pi is often represented by the symbol π.

Glossary (Continued)

pint A U.S. customary unit of capacity equal to half a quart.

place value The value assigned to the place that a digit occupies in a number.

Example: 235

The 2 is in the hundreds place, so its value is 200.

plane A flat surface that extends without end.

polygon A closed plane figure with sides made of straight line segments.

pound A unit of weight in the U.S. customary system.

pre-image A figure before its transformation.

prime factorization A whole number written as the product of prime factors.

Example: Prime factorization of 30: 2 × 3 × 5

prime number A number greater than 1 that has 1 and itself as the only factor pair. Examples of prime numbers are 2, 7, and 13. The only factor pair of 7 is 1 and 7.

prism A solid figure with two congruent parallel bases.

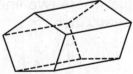

pentagonal prism

probability A number between 0 and 1 that represents the chance of an event happening.

product The result of a multiplication.

Example: 9 × 7 = 63

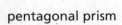

product

proof A demonstration of the truth of a general statement.

proportion An equation that shows two equivalent ratios.

Example: 6 : 10 = 9 : 15

pyramid A solid with a polygon for a base whose vertices are all joined to a single point.

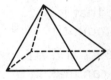

Q

quadrilateral A two-dimensional figure with four sides.

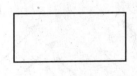

quart A U.S. customary unit of capacity equal to $\frac{1}{4}$ gallon or 2 pints.

quarter turn A 90° rotation.

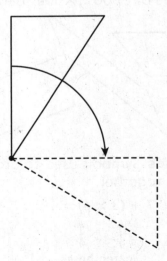

radius A line segment that connects the center of a circle to any point on that circle. Also the length of that line segment.

range The difference between the greatest and the least number in a set.

ratio A comparison of two or more quantities in the same units.

Ratio Table A table that shows equivalent ratios.

Example: This table show ratios equivalent to the basic ratio, 3 : 5.

③	⑤
0	0
3	5
6	10
9	15
12	20
15	25
18	30
21	35
24	40

ray A part of a line that has one endpoint and extends without end in one direction.

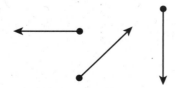

rectangle A parallelogram with four right angles.

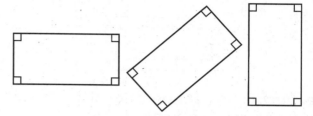

Rectangle Rows A method used to solve multiplication problems.

Example:

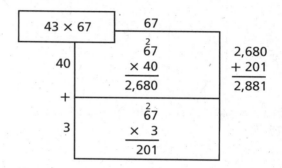

Rectangle Sections A method used to solve multiplication and division problems.

Example:

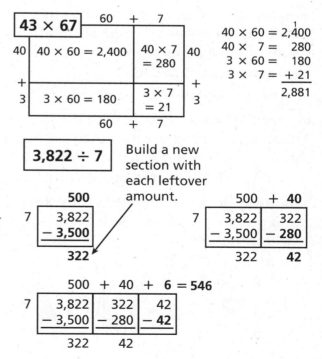

Glossary (Continued)

rectangular prism A solid that has congruent rectangular bases.

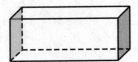

reflection A transformation that flips a figure onto a congruent image. Sometimes called a *flip*.

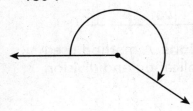

reflex angle An angle greater than 180°.

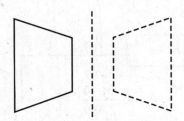

remainder The number left over after dividing a number by a number that does not divide it evenly.

Example: 43 ÷ 5 = 8 R3

The remainder is 3.

Repeated Groups Groups with the same number of objects are Repeated Groups.

Example: 2 + 2 + 2 = 6

There are 3 repeated groups of 2.

repeating pattern A pattern consisting of a group of numbers, letters, or figures that repeat.

Example: 1, 2, 1, 2, …

A, B, C, A, B, C, …

rhombus A parallelogram with congruent sides.

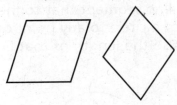

right angle An angle that measures 90°.

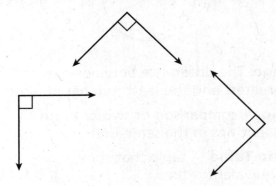

right trapezoid A trapezoid with at least one right angle.

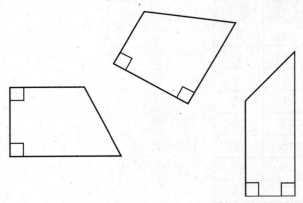

right triangle A triangle with one right angle.

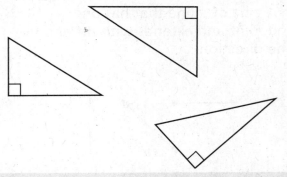

rotation A turn. A transformation that turns a figure so that each point stays an equal distance from a single point, the center of rotation.

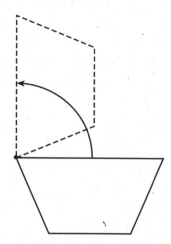

rotational symmetry The property of a figure that allows it to fit exactly on itself in less than one full rotation.

round To find the nearest ten, hundred, thousand, or some other place value.

Example: 463 rounded to the nearest ten is 460.
463 rounded to the nearest hundred is 500.

row A part of a table or array that contains items arranged horizontally.

• • • • •

S

scale Numbers or marks arranged at regular intervals that are used for measurement or to establish position. In a scale drawing, the scale tells how the measurements in the drawing relate to the actual measurements.

scale drawing A drawing that is made in proportion to the size of a real object.

scalene triangle A triangle with no equal sides is a scalene triangle.

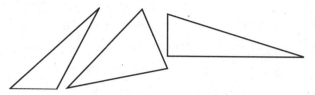

Short Cut Method A method used to solve multiplication problems.

Example: 43 × 67

Step 1	Step 2	Step 3	Step 4	Step 5
$\overset{2}{4}3$	$\overset{2}{4}3$	$\overset{2}{4}3$	$\overset{1}{\underset{2}{4}}3$	$\overset{1}{\underset{2}{4}}3$
× 67	× 67	× 67	× 67	× 67
1	301	301	301	301
		0	2,580	2,580
				2,881

short word form A way of writing a number that uses digits and words.

Example: Short word form of 12,835: 12 thousand, 835

shrinking pattern A number or geometric pattern that decreases.

Example: 15, 12, 9, 6, 3,…
25, 20, 16, 13, 11,…

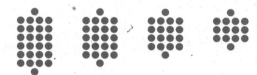

similar Having the same shape but not necessarily the same size. The lengths of the corresponding sides are in proprotion.

similar figures

Glossary (Continued)

simplest form A fraction is in simplest form if there is no whole number (other than 1) that divides evenly into the numerator and demominator.

Example: $\frac{3}{4}$ This fraction is in simplest form because no number divides evenly into 3 and 4.

simplify To find a result. To rewrite a fraction as an equivalent fraction with a smaller numerator and denominator.

Example: $\frac{3}{6} = \frac{1}{2}$

situation equation An equation that shows the action or the relationship in a problem.

Example: $35 + n = 40$

slant height The height of a triangular face of a pyramid.

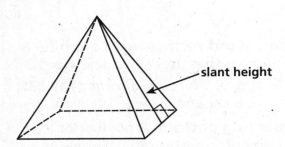

solution equation An equation that shows the operation to perform in order to solve the problem.

Example: $n = 40 - 35$

square A rectangle with four congruent sides.

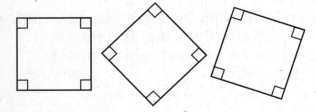

square number The product of a whole number and itself.

Example: $3 \times 3 = 9$
9 is a square number.

square root The square root of a number n is a number that when multiplied by itself equals the number n.

Examples: 4 is the square root of the number 16.

square unit A unit of area equal to the area of a square with one-unit sides.

Examples: square meters and square inches

square yard A unit of area equal to the area of a square with one-yard sides.

standard form The form of a number written using digits.

Example: 2,145

stem-and-leaf plot A display that uses place value to organize a set of data.

Central College Team
Points Scored

Stem	Leaf
5	5
6	
7	0 3 4 5
8	0 1 1 2 2 2 4 5 6 6 8
9	1 2 7 8

9 | 2 means 92

straight angle An angle of 180°.

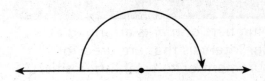

sum The result of an addition.

Example:

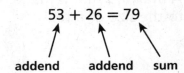

$$53 + 26 = 79$$

addend   addend   sum

supplementary angles Two angles having a sum of 180°.

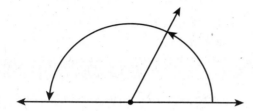

surface area The total area of the two-dimensional surfaces around the outside of a three-dimensional figure.

T

table Data arranged in rows and columns.

term in a pattern A number, letter, or figure in a pattern.

Example: The second term in this number pattern is 10.

5, 10, 15, 20, 25,…

three-dimensional Having length measurements in three directions, perpendicular to each other.

ton A unit of weight or mass that equals 2,000 pounds.

tonne A metric unit of mass that equals 1,000 kilograms.

transformation Reflections, rotations, and translations are examples of tranformations.

translation A transformation that moves a figure along a straight line without turning or flipping. Sometimes called a *slide*.

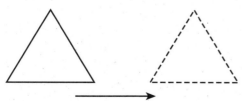

trapezoid A quadrilateral with exactly one pair of parallel sides.

triangle A polygon with three sides.

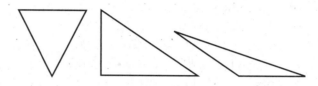

two-dimensional Having length measurements in two directions that are perpendicular to each other.

U

underestimate An estimate that is less than the actual amount.

Example: A shirt costs $26.47 and a pair of jeans cost $37.50. If you brought $60 to pay for the clothes because you rounded $26.47 to $25 and $37.50 to $35, you made an underestimate and did not have enough money.

ungroup Rewrite a mixed number with a different whole number and fraction part or rewrite a whole number with different numbers in the places.

Example: $4\frac{2}{3} = 3\frac{5}{3}$ or $100 + 20 + 3 = 90 + 30 + 3$

unit Something used repeatedly to measure quantity.

Examples: Centimeters, pounds, inches, and so on.

unit fraction A fraction with a numerator of 1.

Examples: $\frac{1}{2}$ and $\frac{1}{10}$

Glossary (Continued)

unsimplify Rewrite a fraction as an equivalent fraction with a greater numerator and denominator.

Examples: $\frac{1}{2} = \frac{3}{6}$

V

variable A letter or symbol that represents a number.

Venn Diagram A diagram that uses overlapping circles to show the relationship between two (or more) sets of objects.

Example: This Venn diagram shows that of 25 students surveyed, 12 like the color blue, 10 like the color orange, and 3 like both colors.

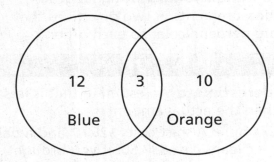

vertex A point that is shared by two arms of an angle, two sides of a polygon, or edges of a solid figure. The point of a cone.

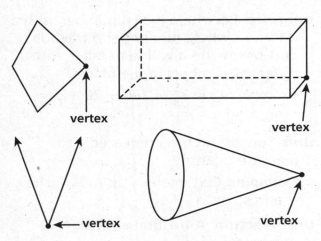

view A two-dimensional representation of what a three-dimensional figure looks like from the front, side, or top.

volume The measure of the amount of space occupied by an object.

W

width The measure of one side or edge of a figure.

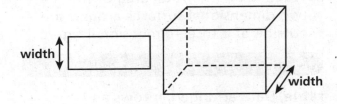

word form The form of a number written using words instead of digits.

Example: Six hundred thirty-nine

X

x-axis The horizontal axis of a two-dimensional coordinate grid.

x-coordinate A number that represents a point's horizontal distance from the *y*-axis of a two-dimensional coordinate grid.

Y

y-axis The vertical axis of a two-dimensional coordinate grid.

yard A U.S. customary unit of length equal to 3 feet or 36 inches.

y-coordinate A number that represents a point's vertical distance from the *x*-axis of a two-dimensional coordinate grid.

The New
Transition Handbook

The New Transition Handbook

Strategies High School Teachers Use that Work!

by

Carolyn Hughes, Ph.D.
Vanderbilt University
Nashville, Tennessee

and

Erik W. Carter, Ph.D.
Vanderbilt University
Nashville, Tennessee

·P A U L·H·
BROOKES
PUBLISHING Cº ®

Baltimore • London • Sydney

Paul H. Brookes Publishing Co.
Post Office Box 10624
Baltimore, Maryland 21285-0624

www.brookespublishing.com

Typeset by Auburn Associates, Inc., Baltimore, Maryland.
Manufactured in the United States of America by
Sheridan Books, Inc., Chelsea, Michigan.

Library of Congress Cataloging-in-Publication Data

Hughes, Carolyn, 1946–
   The new transition handbook: strategies high schocl teachers use that work! / by Carolyn Hughes, Ph.D.,
Vanderbilt University, Nashville, Tennessee, and Erik W. Carter, Ph.D., Vanderbilt University, Nashville,
Tennessee.
     pages   cm
   Includes bibliographical references and index.
   ISBN-13: 978-1-59857-199-8 (pbk.)
   ISBN-10: 1-59857-199-0 (pbk.)
   1. Youth with disabilities—Education (Secondary)—United States.   2. Youth with disabilities—Education
(Middle school)—United States.   3. Youth with disabilities—Services for—United States.   4. School-to-work
transition—United States.   5. Community and school—United States.   I. Carter, Erik W.   II. Title.
   LC4019.H83 2012
   371.9'0473—dc23   2012007855

British Library Cataloguing in Publication data are available from the British Library.

2016   2015   2014   2013   2012

10   9   8   7   6   5   4   3   2   1

Contents

Contents of the Accompanying CD-ROM

About This CD-ROM

About the Authors

Carolyn Hughes, Ph.D., Professor of Special Education, PMB 228, Peabody College, Vanderbilt University, Nashville, Tennessee 37203

Dr. Hughes's research program extends more than 25 years in the areas of transition to adult life, self-determination, support strategies for students with intellectual disabilities and autism, and social interaction among general education high school students and their peers with disabilities. She has been principal investigator or coprincipal investigator on multiple research grants funded by the U.S. Department of Education, including the Metropolitan Nashville Peer Buddy Program. She also has managed multiple master's and doctoral personnel preparation grants at Vanderbilt University funded by the U.S. Department of Education. Currently, Dr. Hughes is principal investigator or coprincipal investigator on research grants funded through the Organization for Autism Research, the Dan Marino Foundation, and Autism Speaks to study a peer-mediated model for teaching social interaction skills to high school students with autism spectrum disorders and a federal grant to develop and validate an instrument to assess the support needs of children with intellectual and developmental disabilities.

Dr. Hughes has published numerous books, chapters, and articles addressing social interaction and self-directed learning skills among high school students. She is on the editorial board of many journals in the developmental disabilities field and is Associate Editor of *Research and Practice for Persons with Severe Disabilities.* In addition, for more than 10 years, Dr. Hughes taught general and special education classes in public schools in Montana and inner-city New York City.

Erik W. Carter, Ph.D., Associate Professor of Special Education, PMB 228, Peabody College, Vanderbilt University, Nashville, Tennessee 37203

Dr. Carter's research and teaching focus on evidence-based strategies for supporting access to the general curriculum and promoting valued roles in school, work, and community settings for children and adults with intellectual and developmental disabilities. Prior to receiving his doctorate, he worked as a high school teacher and transition specialist with youth with significant disabilities. He has published widely in the areas of educational and transition services for children and youth with intellectual disabilities, autism, and other developmental disabilities. His recent books include *Peer Support Strategies for Improving All Students' Social Lives and Learning* (with L.S. Cushing & C.H. Kennedy; Paul H. Brookes Publishing Co., 2009), *Peer Buddy Programs for Successful Secondary School Inclusion* (with C. Hughes; Paul H. Brookes Publishing Co., 2008), and *Including People with Disabilities in Faith Communities: A Guide for Service Providers, Families, and Congregations* (Paul H. Brookes Publishing Co., 2007). He lives in Goodlettsville, Tennessee, with his wife, Sharon, and three children, Mason, Madeleine, and William.

Foreword

It is my distinct pleasure to endorse *The New Transition Handbook!* This book first appeared by Carolyn Hughes and Erik W. Carter in 2000 as *The Transition Handbook*, and as good as it was then, I think it may have been a book that was ahead of its time. My first reaction when I saw the original book was that this is a brilliant idea: They are marrying the concepts of support and transition together; what a perfect strategy. Now, this well-updated version takes the *Handbook* to a whole new level. This is an absolutely essential, "must-read" book for any transition practitioner. The materials in this book take the teacher step by step through the process of implementing transition programs for student with disabilities. There are highly useful forms for each chapter that illustrate concepts in the book. I will discuss more of this a bit later, but first it will be useful to discuss the context for this handbook.

In the early 1980s, the concept of support grew from supported employment as a viable alternative paradigm to providing services in center-based programs such as sheltered workshops and adult activity centers. The center-based approach was closely aligned with a hospital-medical model to "fix" the person and then send him or her out into the world. Supported employment challenged that premise. The model of supported employment drew on the concept of utilizing a trained employment specialist who worked with the individual client on the job site. This idea was built on the groundbreaking work of the applied behavioral experts in the field and directly influenced by these experts, such as Lou Brown, Doug Guess, Wayne Sailor, and Marc Gold, as well as the philosophical giants who were pushing for community integration, such as Wolf Wolfensberger and Robert Perske. The whole paradigm changed from center based to community or business based in the 1980s. This paradigm shift that emphasizes supports would subsequently influence residential programs, special education, federal policies, and laws and even redefine terms and definitions for the American Association on Intellectual and Developmental Disabilities.

At the same time, in the mid-1980s, Madeleine Will, as the Assistant Secretary of Special Education and Rehabilitative Services in the U.S. Department of Education, was promoting not only supported employment but also transition from school to work. Both of these initiatives became huge federal priorities in the disability world and gave great hope to parents and families of young children growing up and looking for more than placement in a segregated adult day program. Transition includes the rehabilitation counselor, teachers, the student, families, related-services personnel, social security representatives, one-stop centers and businesses—all working together to help young people leave school for meaningful lives in work and the community. It requires the understanding of how to provide blended and braided funding of resources. It sounds easy, but it isn't. If it were easy, 40%–50% of special education students would not graduate and exit school unemployed.

Hence, in the 1990s many authors wrote articles and books about transition and employment, sharing this helpful and useful new information with other professionals in the field. However, *none* of these books blended the two concepts together: *transition*, or movement for youth from schools to adulthood (e.g., how to plan, who is involved, what to do, what it will cost), and *support* (e.g., what kind of support, how much, who delivers the support, when to deliver it, where). These two key concepts finally were brought together by Hughes and Carter. The authors' intuitions then, and even more so now, are creative and brilliant. The ideas and suggestions in the current book are timely, relevant, and evidence based—something their earlier book could not provide as higher quality research had not yet been performed.

In the current book, the authors take us down a wonderful trail of assessment and how to develop supports to enhance participation. Then, saving the best for last, the authors provide four detailed chapters full of forms and "how-to-do-it" instructions on self-determination training, social skills instruction, access to the general curriculum, and career development. The beauty of this book is that it goes beyond work, internship, and employment—it gives us the whole picture of what the young person needs to succeed. The model described in Chapter 1 will provide the blueprint educators need to know about how to best integrate these critical concepts: transition + support = success.

In short, repeating what was raised earlier, I see this as being a highly valuable handbook that needs to be on the desk of *every* teacher who is interested in maximizing the best transition outcomes for each of their students. Those graduate students in training will now have the handbook to guide them through the individual transition planning process.

The authors have done the field a service by doing the hard work involved in making this an outstanding resource. I am sure thousands of families and professional will benefit from its publication

Paul Wehman, Ph.D.
Professor of Physical Medicine and Rehabilitation
Chairman, Division of Rehabilitation Research
Director of VCU-RRTC
Medical College of Virginia
Virginia Commonwealth University, Richmond
http://www.worksupport.com

Acknowledgments

We wish to acknowledge the many contributors to this volume and its previous edition, *The Transition Handbook* (Paul H. Brookes Publishing Co., 2000). This book would not exist without the many researchers and practitioners who gave us input as we developed the Transition Support Model, as well as the countless secondary transition teachers who shared their transition support strategies with us. We are also grateful for the hundreds of transition teachers who have invited us into their classrooms, worksites, and recreational settings to see firsthand how they put transition support into action.

Our mentors and colleagues from Illinois—Marty Agran, Jim Martin, Frank Rusch, and many others—have guided and supported us through the process of writing a book from beginning to end. Montrose Wolf, as a muse, reminded us how important it is to always ask people what they think and value rather than assume we know. Paul Wehman, as an advocate, has always encouraged us to think about the importance of our work and the Transition Support Model to the secondary transition field.

We are grateful to the U.S. Department of Education and the Tennessee Developmental Disabilities Council, who funded us and our students throughout the development of the Transition Support Model and *The Transition Handbook*. And we have untold gratitude toward our students, who toiled along with us conceptualizing and categorizing mounds of data—both quantitative and qualitative.

We are also grateful to Rebecca Lazo, our editor at Paul H. Brookes Publishing Co., and her assistant, Steve Plocher. Rebecca has been insightful in guiding us in the changes needed to update the new edition of *The Transition Handbook,* and Steve has been irreplaceable in the process of preparing the new edition and helping us envision the layout of the book. We appreciate the support of both of them as well as all the editorial and production staff at Brookes.

And, finally, we have great appreciation for Rebecca Hendrix of the Department of Special Education at Vanderbilt University, who invested many long hours assisting us with preparing this edition.

*To all the teachers who so freely contributed
their experience and ideas that make up this book—
we are deeply grateful*

Introduction to *The New Transition Handbook*

The New Transition Handbook

A Model of Transition Support

In this chapter, you will learn

- Why we need a model of transition support
- How we developed the Transition Support Model
- What is new and unique about *The New Transition Handbook*
- How to use *The New Transition Handbook*

Case Study 1.1 *Wesley Hopkins*

Wesley Hopkins attended a large, rural, consolidated high school during his freshman year. Things just did not seem to click for him there. Back in his hometown of Sharon Springs, he had attended a small elementary school where he knew all the students. He felt comfortable there, and kids did not make fun of him for some of the words he mispronounced or stumbled over in class. School was hard, and his grades were never good, but there was always recess and gym, where he excelled at kickball and base-ball. Nobody hit a homer like Wesley. That is when he really shone and could feel good about himself. It got tougher in middle school, though. Classes were harder, he was always in trouble at home because of his grades, and he did not know all of the kids at school anymore. And then there was the teasing every time he gave a botched answer in class or failed another test. It was getting to the point where he did not even want to play sports anymore. Maybe the kids would make fun of him there, too.

Wesley certainly was not looking forward to attending Randolph High School when he finished eighth grade. It was all the way across the valley and brought students from five rural middle schools together. He knew he would be lost. And speaking up and making friends was not really something Wesley felt he knew how to do, especially when he had to change classes and classmates every 50 minutes. Just as he had suspected, Wesley's grades started slipping even more. He was already failing four of his seven classes by the end of the first grading period in October. One of his teachers was talk-ing about referring him to special education, but what was the sense in going to school anyway? It

(continued)

Case Study 1.1   *(continued)*

didn't seem worth the effort. Sometimes in the morning, instead of getting on the school bus at the end of the road by his house, Wesley started hiding in the shed behind the barn and staying all day until school was over. After a while, he never got on the bus to go back to school at all.

THE NEED FOR A MODEL OF SUPPORT THAT WORKS

Open the front section of any local newspaper or talk to any high school teacher or principal and you are reminded that Wesley's story, unfortunately, is not unusual. For many students, high school is not a positive experience leading to a successful transition to adult life. A promising career, satisfying personal relationships, a comfortable home, enjoyable leisure time activities—the expectations many of us hold for adulthood—do not materialize for a sizable number of students who leave high school.

Secondary and Postschool Life Outcomes of Students with Disabilities

Secondary education has not resulted in a successful transition to adulthood for many students, despite growing attention in federal policy, research, and the media (Newman, Wagner, Cameto, & Knokey, 2009). Unemployment or underemployment, financial dependence, limited social relationships, segregation, and poverty are the outcomes faced by many students as they leave high school and enter their adult lives (Hughes & Avoke, 2010). For example, Newman et al. (2009) reported that only 31% of youth with intellectual disabilities are employed (primarily part time) after leaving high school, only 7% attend postsecondary education as their sole postschool activity, only 14% live independently or semi-independently, only 26% have a checking account, and only 11% participate in a community group, such as a sports team or church club. Students with disabilities from low-income households also fare more poorly across these same postschool indicators than do their peers from higher income homes. In addition, white youth with disabilities (63%) are more likely to be employed than their black (35%) or Hispanic (54%) counterparts; they are also more likely to hold a skilled labor job and have a checking account (Newman et al., 2009). Unfortunately, job training programs for people with disabilities often target low-paying, part-time, entry-level jobs that offer few benefits or opportunities for promotion or advancement (Metzel, Boeltzig, Butterworth, Sulewski, & Gilmore, 2007), further relegating young people to a life of poverty.

Legislative Initiatives Supporting Secondary Transition

Since the 1990s, key pieces of legislation have addressed the need for improving postschool outcomes for students with disabilities. Three legislative acts with particular relevance for youth with disabilities are the Individuals with Disabilities Education Improvement Act (IDEA) of 2004 (PL 108-446), the Elementary and Secondary Education Act (ESEA) of 1965 (PL 89-10), which was reauthorized in 2001 as the No Child Left Behind (NCLB) Act (PL 107-110), and the Americans with Disabilities Act (ADA) of 1990 (PL 101-336).

Individuals with Disabilities Education Act

IDEA 2004 reiterated the requirement of the Individuals with Disabilities Education Act (IDEA) of 1990 (PL 101-476) and its 1997 amendments (PL 105-17) that students' individualized education programs (IEPs) include a statement of needed transition services before students exit school services. Although the student's age at which this statement must be included in the IEP has fluctuated in the legislation (it is now "not later than the first IEP to be in effect when the child is 16," IDEA 2004, § 614), this requirement was substantial because, for the first time, high school teachers were mandated to address students' postschool outcomes, goals, and needed services beginning years before students actually left school (Stodden & Roberts, 2008).

As defined in IDEA 2004, *transition services* is a coordinated set of activities designed "to facilitate the child's movement from school to postschool activities, including postsecondary education, vocational education, integrated employment (including supported employment), continuing and adult education, adult services, independent living, or community participation" (§ 602). Accordingly, secondary transition personnel must address a wide gamut of postschool outcomes for students across multiple settings—including home, school, work, and employment as appropriate for each student. Furthermore, IDEA 2004 stipulates that transition services must focus on improving students' "academic and functional achievement" (§ 602) and must be based on each student's individual needs, strengths, preferences, and interests. Therefore, not only must educators begin early to address a wide range of student outcomes, but they must also provide transition services that are individualized for each student and responsive to each student's own interests and strengths—implying that students must have a voice in designing their own education programs. Finally, under IDEA 2004, secondary personnel are required to provide a summary of performance to a student who is exiting the education system due to graduating from high school or exceeding the age eligibility. The summary describes the student's achievements and provides recommendations for assisting the student in meeting postsecondary education and employment goals. Under IDEA 2004, therefore, schools are held accountable just short of the actual postschool success of exiting students (Rusch, Hughes, Agran, Martin, & Johnson, 2009).

More important, IDEA 2004 also calls for public schools to be responsive to the changing demographics of the public school population and the disparate in-school and postschool outcomes found across racial, ethnic, and cultural groups. White students represent just 56% of public school students; by 2020, the majority of public school students are estimated to be black, Hispanic, Asian, Native American, or other ethnicities (National Center for Education Statistics, 2006, 2010). In addition, at least 20% of the school population is reported to speak a language other than English at home (National Center for Education Statistics, 2007). Overidentification for placement in special education programs and high dropout rates persist for some racial and ethnic groups and English language learners, however (U.S. Department of Education, 2009). Students of color and those from low-income households also face lower employment and attendance in postsecondary education than their peers from white, middle-class households (Newman et al., 2009). Responding to these challenges, a stated purpose of IDEA 2004 is to ensure equitable allocation of resources, opportunities, and services to improve postschool outcomes for all students with disabilities.

Elementary and Secondary Education Act

A major focus of the ESEA was to improve educational and postschool outcomes for students who were underserved or growing up in poverty. The act was reauthorized in 2001 as the NCLB Act (with stated purposes of "meeting the educational needs of low-achieving children in our Nation's highest-poverty schools" and "closing the achievement gap between high- and low-performing children, especially the achievement gaps between minority and nonminority students, and between disadvantaged children and their more advantaged peers" [§ 1001]). In addition, ESEA legislation includes students with disabilities as a target population whose needs must be addressed and who are required to participate in statewide assessments—resulting in an increased call for alignment between special education curricula and state and local standards. Indeed, teachers and administrators are held accountable for the achievement of all students because schools must document increases in assessment scores and graduation rates for all subgroups of students, including English language learners, members of racial and ethnic groups, students from high-poverty backgrounds, and students with disabilities. In addition, in concert with IDEA 2004, NCLB authors argued that educational services and supports for students with disabilities are most effective when provided in the general education class and when school personnel hold high expectations for all students.

Americans with Disabilities Act

The ADA, enacted in 1990 and amended in 2008 (PL 110-325), affirmed the basic civil rights of people with disabilities by stating that "physical or mental disabilities in no way diminish a person's right to fully participate in all aspects of society" (ADA 2008, § 12101) while arguing that individuals had systematically been denied the opportunity to exercise their rights because of discrimination, prejudice, and segregation. Similar to IDEA 2004 and NCLB, which describe the diminished outcomes experienced by students with disabilities and other groups in part due to unequal opportunities, the ADA states that "census data, national polls, and other studies have documented that people with disabilities, as a group, occupy an inferior status in our society, and are severely disadvantaged socially, vocationally, economically, and educationally" (ADA 2008, § 12101). Consequently, the stated purpose of the ADA is to provide a national mandate to eliminate day-to-day discrimination of children and adults with disabilities. Consistent with IDEA 2004 and NCLB, the ADA of 2008 seeks to correct past inequities with regard to equal treatment and opportunity of people with disabilities and other high-need groups to ensure "equality of opportunity, full participation, independent living, and economic self-sufficiency" (§ 12101).

Transition Support Models

The legislation is explicit in calling for the services and supports needed to improve in-school performance and postschool outcomes of students with disabilities. Positive postschool outcomes are elusive for many, however, despite more than 20 years of transition legislation addressing secondary students with disabilities (Migliore & Butterworth, 2008; Sanford et al., 2011). The premise of this book is that these students require more support than typically is provided by a traditional secondary school curriculum to achieve the adult outcomes that many of us take for granted, such as a job, community involvement, transportation, or a safe and satisfying place to live. The importance of providing support for students as they make the transition from school to adult life has been advocated since the mid-1980s (Halpern, 1985; Will, 1984). Support models that have received attention in the literature include Will's (1984) "bridges" model of school to employment proposed by the Office of Special Education and Rehabilitative Services (OSERS); Halpern's (1985) model of school to "community adjustment"; IDEA 1990, which initially mandated support for the transition from school to a range of postschool adult outcomes; and the School-to-Work Opportunities Act of 1994 (PL 103-239), which addressed employment experiences for youth with and without disabilities.

The Transition Service Integration Model (Certo et al., 2003, 2008) is a more contemporary example of a transition support model in which students with disabilities are served during their final school year by an adult service agency subcontracted with the public schools and authorized to continue to provide postschool support after students leave school, creating a seamless transition from school to adult life. Consistent with the model, students spend their final school year in the community, immersed in work and functional skill-related instruction delivered by a coordinated set of adult service agencies and community employers in collaboration with the school district. During the first 5 years of implementation of the program (1998–2002), 261 of the 293 students served during their final school year (89%) exited with continued support provided by the same adult agency that served them in school. In addition, 60% of students left school already employed (Certo et al., 2008).

The New Transition Handbook: **A Model of Transition Support**

Although the scope of the previous models differs, each was designed to match the type and intensity of support to students' individual needs. The models are based on the assumption that students need varying amounts of support to fully participate in general education and the community during their transition from school to adult life (Thompson, Wehmeyer, & Hughes, 2010). For example, support strategies might include a co-worker giving a student a ride to work, a peer helping a student with limited use of her hands to eat lunch, or a vocational rehabilitation counselor assisting a student to develop a résumé. In *The New Transition Handbook,* we define *support strategies* as any assistance or help provided directly to a student to promote a successful transition from school to adult life.

Research offers some insight into factors that may promote successful student outcomes, such as paid work experiences during high school, family involvement, social skills instruction, inclusion in general education, and community-based instruction (Test et al., 2009). The field cannot ignore findings, however, that show that secondary education has not led to successful adulthood for many special education students. In an era of shrinking funding allocated for disability programs (Klein, 2011), it is important to provide teachers with effective strategies to improve postschool outcomes for their students. *The New Transition Handbook* provides a model of support for secondary students designed to improve their outcomes after high school. A unique feature of *The New Transition Handbook* is that it contains only transition support strategies that are both research based and teacher tested. Although the type and intensity of support that students need to make a smooth transition to adult life will differ according to individual needs, such as a personal care attendant for a person with quadriplegia or a communication book for a student who is nonverbal, there are strategies appropriate for every student. In addition, the transition support strategies included are those that can be initiated and implemented by one educator in collaboration with others who are interested in a student's life and well-being.

INNOVATIVE FEATURES OF THE TRANSITION SUPPORT MODEL

The New Transition Handbook provides an innovative approach to the transition process by focusing on both the supports and skills a student needs to experience successful outcomes in adult life. It represents a new approach to the way educators think about students with diverse abilities and students at risk of poor postschool outcomes. Educational supports, which are services and assistance individually tailored to promote successful educational outcomes for students, is a concept that is just coming of age in the field. The emphasis is on maximizing the "fit" between the student and the environment by providing the supports needed for a student to meaningfully participate in everyday life activities both in and outside of school (Thompson et al., 2010).

The New Transition Handbook is an iteration of the first edition of the book, *The Transition Handbook* (Hughes & Carter, 2000). The development of *The Transition Handbook* was a 5-year process involving both researchers and practitioners (Hughes, Hwang, et al., 1997; Hughes & Kim, 1998; Hughes, Kim, et al., 1997). Evidence-based transition practices were identified from a comprehensive review of the transition literature and arranged as a proposed model of transition support. A national survey of the transition research community established the acceptability of the model by the field. Secondary transition teachers throughout the state of Tennessee were then asked to provide input on the practicality of the model. An updated version of the Transition Support Model that resulted is shown in Table 1.1. Teachers also provided more than 500 ways they implemented the support strategies in their own transition programs. These strategies were then compiled and became *The Transition Handbook.*

Table 1.1.   Transition Support Model

Developing supports that enhance participation	Teaching skills that promote success
Increasing support within school and community settings	Promoting independence and self-determination
Increasing social support and promoting acceptance	Promoting social participation and teaching social skills
	Promoting functional skills and access to the general curriculum
	Teaching employment skills and promoting career development

Why a New Edition of *The Transition Handbook?*

Much has happened in education since the first publication of *The Transition Handbook.* New legislation has had profound effects on secondary transition, including an increased emphasis on accountability, postschool outcomes, academic performance, access to general education, and basic civil rights of students with disabilities. Furthermore, the demographics of public schools have radically changed to a more racially, ethnically, economically, and culturally diverse student population. Teachers face growing challenges accommodating increasing numbers of students from high-poverty backgrounds. High school reform movements—from small learning communities to online classes in strip malls—have changed the very nature of the high school day for many students and teachers. In addition, the research base has continued to grow, providing additional insights into transition practices demonstrated to work for youth with disabilities (e.g., Cobb & Alwell, 2009; Test et al., 2009). Although the first edition of *The Transition Handbook* continued to be well received, we felt strongly that we needed to update the text to address the changes that have occurred since 2000. The result is *The New Transition Handbook,* which incorporates current legislative initiatives, educational movements and reforms, and recent research.

What Is Unique About *The New Transition Handbook?*

Unique features of the Transition Support Model and *The New Transition Handbook* are as follows.

- We have written *The New Transition Handbook* with many readers in mind: preservice teachers, middle or high school teachers, students, parents and family members, friends, employers, job coaches, and service providers of students who need support in making the transition from school to adult life.

- The strategies teachers shared are applicable for the breadth of students attending today's schools, including those with disabilities, such as physical impairments, intellectual disabilities, emotional/behavior disorders, autism, or sensory impairments. They also are relevant for students at risk for poor school performance or school dropout; students from high-poverty backgrounds; students who are ethnically, racially, and culturally diverse; and students who are English language learners.

- *The New Transition Handbook* is hands on, user friendly, and solution oriented. Practical examples, case studies, and reproducible forms are provided to illustrate the hundreds of easy-to-use secondary transition strategies embedded throughout. Blank copies of all forms are provided on the accompanying CD-ROM for readers' own use. We chose a presentation format from which teachers, in collaboration with others, may pick and choose strategies to use based on a student's individual support needs, strengths, and preferences.

- The Transition Support Model is the product of more than 5 years of model program development involving both researchers and teachers. The strategies composing the model are unique because they are both research based and drawn directly from teachers practicing in the field.

- Strategies in *The New Transition Handbook* can be implemented by individual teachers themselves in collaboration with family members, employers, service providers, and others who are important in a student's life. The transition strategies do not require a major financial investment or education reform to implement.

LAYOUT AND ORGANIZATION OF THE BOOK

The New Transition Handbook is organized according to the Transition Support Model, which comprises two main goals: 1) developing supports that enhance participation and 2) teaching skills that promote success. Six areas of student support fall under these two goals and provide a conceptual framework for the teacher-suggested support strategies that compose the model. These strategies are arranged in *The New Transition Handbook* according to the six areas of student support. *The New Transition Handbook* is also organized into three main sections designed for easy access for readers.

Section I

Section I introduces *The New Transition Handbook* and Transition Support Model approach to secondary transition. Chapter 1 describes the need for and development of the Transition Support Model. It also describes the innovative and unique features and organization and use of *The New Transition Handbook.* Chapter 2 presents an overview of the assessment and planning process used to identify student supports and skills within the framework of the Transition Support Model.

Section II

Section II contains support strategies related to the first main goal of the Transition Support Model—developing supports that enhance participation. Fortunately, a deficit model of student support, in which a student must be "fixed" in response to demands of the environment, is losing favor within the field of education. This model is being replaced by a more social-ecological approach in which the environment is adapted and naturally occurring support is maximized in response to the full array of an individual's needs, strengths, interests, and preferences (e.g., Thompson et al., 2010). Research shows that much support is available in most environments (Hagner, Butterworth, & Keith, 1995). In addition, acceptance of individual differences can be promoted in an everyday setting at work, in school, or in the community, particularly when people with disabilities are viewed as competent (Siperstein, Parker, Bardon, & Widaman, 2007). The strategies in Section II allow teachers to gain access to and maximize support in an environment, as well as develop social support and acceptance in settings in which they are lacking, in order to promote students' full participation in daily activities both in and outside school.

Chapter 3 discusses strategies for increasing environmental support. These include gaining access to existing environmental support, developing environmental support plans, and modifying settings to promote meaningful participation. Chapter 4 contains strategies for increasing social support, such as developing social support plans, communicating social support needs, and gaining access to existing social support. This chapter also presents strategies for promoting social acceptance by communicating an attitude of acceptance, promoting diversity awareness, and teaching skills that promote acceptance.

Section III

Section III contains four chapters related to the second main goal of the support model—teaching skills that promote success. Competence relates to skill performance—individuals are more readily accepted into school, work, and community settings when they are viewed as competent by performing expected skills (Walker et al., 2011; Wolfensberger, 1983). Being competent also allows people to have access to many benefits, such as job advancement, educational opportunities, and satisfying relationships. Competence is judged within the context of an environment, which is consistent with a social-ecological model of human behavior (Thompson et al., 2010). Being considered competent in one context, such as consistently hitting home runs on a baseball team, does not mean that the same person would be considered competent in another context, such as being a member of a spacecraft launching crew. Skill performance and competence must be promoted, supported, accepted, and maintained within an environment (Agran, Wehmeyer, Cavin, & Palmer, 2010). The strategies in Section III help teachers to build the competence of students within everyday settings and to teach skills and arrange environments to support and promote skill maintenance.

Chapter 5 describes strategies for increasing students' independent performance and self-determination by teaching self-determination skills and incorporating self-determination opportunities into daily life. This chapter also contains strategies for increasing students' choice and decision making. Chapter 6 focuses on strategies for teaching social interaction skills and promoting relationships with peers in school, on the job, in college, or in recreational settings. Chapter 7 provides strategies for enhancing students' academic performance and functional skill repertoire. This chapter includes methods for increasing students' active participation in general education classes and activities. Chapter 8 emphasizes strategies for teaching employment and work-related skills and skills that promote students' full participation in the community.

SUMMARY

Our intent in writing *The New Transition Handbook* is that it be solid and research based yet accessible to and maximally useful to readers. Our primary audience is teachers, family members, service providers, and others interested in providing support to secondary students as they make the transition from school to adult life. Ultimately, however, our primary focus is young people like Wesley Hopkins, who are not experiencing the outcomes all people value—a meaningful career, close relationships, and everyday enjoyment—when they leave high school.

It is our hope that all students who need it will be served by the Transition Support Model found in *The New Transition Handbook*—one that develops support in a student's environment and increases a student's individual skills and competence so that all students will experience productive, satisfying, and healthy adult outcomes.

CHAPTER 2

Assessment and Planning

Identifying Supports and
Skills that Enhance Success

In this chapter, you will learn how to

- Ensure the role of assessment in the transition planning process

- Choose appropriate assessments for students

- Use observational, informal, and formal assessments to collect data

- Develop a summary of performance and communicate information to others

OVERVIEW

Everyone possesses strengths in various areas, such as academics, sports, leadership, character, social relationships, and/or career performance. IDEA 2004 stresses that students' IEPs emphasize students' strengths rather than limitations. The move from deficit-based educational programming reflects the belief that all students can and should be maximally included in everyday school, work, and community settings (Thompson et al., 2010). Students gain opportunities to learn new skills, expand their competence, and develop valued relationships when they are actively participating in inclusive settings and are provided with needed social and environmental supports.

Identifying students' individual strengths and the areas in which they need support is one of the first steps in building their skills. Teachers can pinpoint these strengths and needs by observing students' involvement in a variety of school, work, and community activities and by systematically recording and evaluating these observations. It is important to observe students in many different environments because people's strengths and needs vary according to the demands of a particular setting (Alberto & Troutman, 2009). Because observing students in different settings can be time consuming, teachers can use alternative approaches to gather information not easily accessible through direct observation, including a variety of informal and formal assessments. In addition, information can be obtained by collaborating with family members, peers, community members, co-workers, and other individuals who see the student regularly as well as by talking to the student herself.[1] When a student's strengths and needs have been accurately identified and communicated with others, instruction should target those skills in a student's repertoire that need support (Sitlington, Neubert, & Clark, 2009).

This chapter contains four main groups of strategies that teachers may use to identify students' strengths and areas needing support to promote successful student outcomes. It includes such strategies as ensuring the role of assessment in the transition planning process, choosing appropriate assessments, using a variety of assessments to collect data, and developing a summary of performance and communicating information with others.

Case Study 2.1   *A New Student at Washington High*

Carlos Santanora was somewhat of a surprise. Autumn was already revealing itself in the leaves of the maple trees outside Washington High School, where students had been in classes for almost 2 months. Halfway through Mr. Kleeb's math lesson, Carlos hesitantly walked through the door, accompanied by his father and the school secretary. After asking his coteacher to continue with the lesson, Mr. Kleeb, a consulting special education teacher, walked over and greeted his unexpected guests. Mr. Santanora shook hands and politely apologized for his "difficulty with English." He explained that he and his family had just moved to the United States after he had received a job promotion with a large computer company. The sudden move meant a new classroom, school, and country for Carlos. Mr. Kleeb, knowing how apprehensive Carlos must have felt, assured him that he would do everything he could to assist him in his transition to his new community. Mr. Santanora added that he knew little about the types of educational services Carlos had received at his old school but stated that he did hope his son would "make some new friends, pick up English, and learn to do more things on his own." With that, Mr. Santanora thanked Mr. Kleeb, hugged Carlos, and left for work. Mr. Kleeb stood at the door with a confused smile—glad to have a new student in his class but unsure of exactly where to begin with him. How long would it be before Carlos's files arrived from his former school? When (and if) they did arrive, would they provide Mr. Kleeb with helpful information about Carlos's educational program and his individual strengths and support needs? What should Mr. Kleeb do in the meantime? Where should he begin?

ENSURING THE ROLE OF ASSESSMENT IN THE TRANSITION PLANNING PROCESS

LEGISLATION

IDEA 2004 requires local education agencies (LEAs) to "use a variety of assessment tools and strategies to gather relevant functional, developmental, and academic information, including information provided by the parent" (§ 614) in determining the content of students' IEPs. Educators cannot "use any single measure or assessment as the sole criterion" (§ 614) in determining the appropriateness of a student's educational program. In addition, they must select and administer assessments free of racial or cultural discrimination "in the language and form most likely to yield accurate information on what the child knows" (§ 614). The IEP team must review existing assessment data, including information provided by parents and derived from observations conducted of the student, when evaluating a student. Furthermore, beginning at age 16 or earlier, students' IEPs must include "appropriate measurable postsecondary goals based upon age-appropriate transition assessments related to training, education, employment and, where appropriate, independent living skills" (§ 614).

---

[1]We alternated the use of *his* and *her* per chapter for ease of readability.

The transition planning process for every student begins with good assessment. Educators begin by assessing students' interests, preferences, needs, and strengths in relation to students' current goals, performance, and desired postschool outcomes. Assessment findings are then incorporated into students' IEPs and transition programs. As educators implement students' educational programs, they should conduct ongoing assessment to evaluate students' progress toward achieving IEP and transition goals. Transition assessment is meant to inform educators, family members, and service providers. But it should also help students get to know more about themselves, their strengths and interests, their goals for the future, and the pathways through which they might reach these goals (Fowler, Walker, & Rowe, 2010).

Assumptions of the Transition Assessment Process

Evidence-based practice in transition assessment implies several assumptions (Hughes & Carter, 2002). First, students must be actively involved in the process because one purpose of transition assessment is to assist them in making meaningful decisions by becoming aware of their strengths, interests, and preferences in relation to current and future environments (Sitlington & Clark, 2007). For example, students can contribute to decisions about where to conduct observations, which assessment approaches might be used, and the implications of any findings (Thoma, Bartholomew, & Tamura, 2010). Increasing student involvement may provide a fuller picture of students' strengths, preferences, and support needs and is consistent with IDEA 2004's call for student involvement in educational programming. Second, as described in Chapter 1, the student population of U.S. public schools is becoming increasingly racially, ethnically, culturally, and economically diverse. One in five students speaks a language other than English at home and just over one half of students are white (National Center for Education Statistics, 2007, 2010). Teachers are likely to have students in their classes from cultural backgrounds very different from their own. As affirmed by IDEA 2004, educators must encourage close communication with families and be sensitive to the cultural values that influence students and their families when conducting assessments.

RESEARCH

Promoting Student Involvement in Transition Education

The heightened emphasis on supporting students' self-determination in all aspects of transition education has led to the development and evaluation of a number of different approaches for engaging students more actively in their own transition planning. Students may be more motivated—and more likely—to strive toward and accomplish their personal goals when they are more actively involved in planning for their own future. Yet, students often need instruction and support on how best to participate in meaningful and effective ways—particularly within the context of the annual IEP meeting. According to the National Longitudinal Transition Study–2 (NLTS–2), teachers reported that 6% of youth with disabilities did not attend their planning meeting; 25% were present but provided little input; 58% were moderately active participants; and only 12% were reported to have taken a leadership role (Cameto, Levine, & Wagner, 2004).

A number of strategies and curricular approaches have been designed to prepare youth with disabilities for their IEP meeting (Test et al., 2004). For example, the *Self-Directed IEP* (Martin, Marshall, Maxson, & Jerman, 1993), *Whose Future Is It Anyway?* (Wehmeyer et al., 2004), *TAKE CHARGE for the Future* (Powers, Ellison, Matuszewski, & Turner, 2004), and *Next S.T.E.P.* (Halpern, Herr, Doren, & Wolf, 2000) have all been evaluated in at least one study involving youth with disabilities. Although each of these approaches has some evidence of promise for increasing participation in transition planning, it is important to consider carefully whether and how these approaches might be tailored to meet the individualized needs of students, including students from culturally and linguistically diverse backgrounds (Griffin, 2011).

Third, collaboration is the key to meaningful assessment. Including the perspective of students, families, community members, employers, college instructors, and service providers in relation to a student's goals, strengths, interests, and support needs results in a more comprehensive and complete portrayal of a student. Collaborating with others in the assessment and resulting transition planning process is consistent with IDEA 2004 and is likely to result in postsecondary goals that align with families' and others' desired postschool outcomes for students (Carter, Trainor, Sun, & Owens, 2009). Fourth, transition assessment must be ongoing and occur in the actual settings in which students participate (Clark, 2007). Opportunities and demands vary across locations requiring that assessment be responsive to the contextual features of the different settings in which a student spends time. In addition, students themselves change over time. They learn new skills, acquire new interests, achieve and form new goals, and spend time in new settings. Support needs also evolve as students develop and change (Thompson et al., 2010). Assessment should be fluid, ongoing, and responsive to student changes over time.

CHOOSING APPROPRIATE ASSESSMENTS FOR STUDENTS

This section overviews an eight-step, evidence-based model for 1) choosing appropriate assessments and procedures, 2) modifying existing assessments, and 3) using assessment results in the transition planning process. Each step is also displayed in Table 2.1.

Step 1: Determine the Purpose of Assessment

First, determine the purpose for assessment. For example, you may want to know how well a student is accepted at a job or in a general education classroom. Or, a parent may want to know

Table 2.1.   Eight-step assessment process

Step	Example
1. Determine the purpose of assessment	Joshua's transition team would like to find out the extent to which Joshua is accepted by peers in a recreational setting.
2. Identify student behavior and settings	To assess Cynthia's choice-making skills at school, her teacher will target how often Cynthia makes a choice independently in her general education classes when given the opportunity to choose.
3. Seek input to validate Steps 1 and 2	Tomika's teacher will discuss with Tomika's parents whether they agree with their daughter's goal of attending postsecondary education after high school.
4. Choose appropriate assessments	Direct observation may be appropriate for assessing how long it takes Carey to complete his chores, whereas a formal assessment would be appropriate for assessing his math skills.
5. Modify assessments as needed	Abdul's teacher will read aloud the questions on a social studies test rather than have Abdul take a paper-and-pencil test independently.
6. Conduct assessments	Because Lionel's teacher wants to assess Lionel's shopping skills, assessment will be conducted at a local mall.
7. Use assessment findings in the transition planning process	At Hugh's transition planning meeting, his teacher communicated all assessment findings to the transition team members.
8. Develop transition plans to achieve goals	Together members of Julia's transition team—and Julia as a member of the team—agreed on the general education classes and job and community experiences she would have during the year in order to achieve her transition goals.

what recreational opportunities exist in the neighborhood that match her son's interests. The dimensions of a student's life and educational experiences that could be a focus of assessment are virtually unlimited—social skills, career interests, choice-making skills, academic performance, or opportunities for community involvement (Clark & Patton, 2006). Assessment can focus on the student (e.g., What strengths does a student have in relation to a particular task or setting?), the setting, (e.g., What natural supports exist in a setting?), or the transition program or services (e.g., To what extent does a student's program address her postschool goals?).

Step 2: Identify Student Behavior and Settings

Next, identify student behaviors and settings related to the purpose of the assessment. For example, if you want to learn the extent to which a student is self-directed, you could target choice-making or problem-solving skills for assessment (Field & Hoffman, 2007). Of course, you should assess these skills in the settings in which they are expected to be used. If a goal is to increase a student's greetings to general education classmates, then assessments should occur in the student's general education classes. It is also important to consider the context of each setting. For example, sometimes a no-talking rule is in effect in class (e.g., when taking a test), during which time greeting classmates would be inappropriate. Consider future settings in which a student may participate, such as a college classroom or student center.

Step 3: Seek Input to Validate Steps 1 and 2

Your next step is to seek input from students and family members to see if assessment decisions made in Steps 1 and 2 reflect their priorities and values. Input from other transition team members can also help confirm the validity of the conclusions you have drawn (Carter, Trainor, Sun, et al., 2009). It may be that you determined that going straight to employment after high school was a priority for a student, but communication with the student and her family revealed her postschool goal was attending a college certification program in child care. Or, it may be that you assumed that a student's loud vocalizations in the hallway were a problem for classmates, but input from students revealed that they liked it when Kevin sang "Rocky Top" in his baritone voice on the way to the cafeteria.

Step 4: Choose Appropriate Assessments

The decision to use a particular assessment procedure should be based on the purpose of the assessment, the behaviors and settings of concern, and input of important people in the student's life. Luckily, a variety of assessments is available and selection should be based on the information needed (Sitlington & Clark, 2007). The primary types of assessment include direct observation (e.g., observing how long it takes a student to begin a task), informal assessment (e.g., interviewing a student to determine her recreational preferences), and formal assessment (e.g., having a student complete an aptitude test). Consistent with IDEA 2004, a variety of age-appropriate assessments should be used to gather information across a range of domains relevant to a student's life, such as social interaction, self-determination, academic and functional skills, and college and career goals.

Step 5: Modify Assessments as Needed

Many students with disabilities have unique needs and forms of communicating. After selecting an appropriate assessment, you may need to modify assessment procedures based on characteristics of the student and relevant settings. For example, you may need to have an interpreter accompany you when you interview parents for whom English is a second language. Or, you may need to read questions on a paper-and-pencil test to students with limited reading skills and allow them to answer orally. IDEA 2004 requires that assessments are administered in the language and form most likely to yield accurate information about a student.

Step 6: Conduct Assessments

Now you are ready to conduct the assessments you have chosen and possibly modified. If you are using direct observation, then observe in the settings in which you expect the behavior to occur. If you are using informal assessment, then seek input from the student and important people in that student's life in a particular setting, such as a student's home or workplace. Be sure to provide appropriate accommodations when conducting a formal assessment to allow a student to yield accurate information about herself.

As you conduct assessments, be sure to focus consistently on the established purpose of the assessment, the chosen behaviors, and relevant settings. If you are conducting assessments over time, then it is especially important to stay true to the original intent of the assessment and to continue to seek input from others to ensure the validity and relevance of findings. It is important that your procedures are not intrusive or stigmatizing to a student when you conduct assessments in shopping malls, worksites, recreation centers, or college campuses.

Step 7: Use Assessment Findings in the Transition Planning Process

Assessment is not an end in itself. Use the information gathered during the assessment process to inform the transition team, including the student, in setting goals and making decisions related to instruction, services, and supports (Sitlington & Clark, 2007). To assist team members, communicate information in ways that are readily understandable, including findings about a student's preferences, strengths, and support needs in relation to both her current and expected future environments. Areas identified in which students' skills—such as increasing attendance at school or work—need to be increased or supports developed or enhanced should be targeted as potential transition goals. Ultimately, all team members should work together collaboratively to prioritize transition goals and instructional objectives.

Step 8: Develop Transition Plans to Achieve Goals

The final step is to identify relevant educational experiences that address a student's identified transition goals. Consistent with IDEA 2004, transition plans must be individualized for each student, based on assessment findings related to students' strengths, needs, preferences, and projections of future performance, rather than on preestablished educational policies. Educational experiences should occur in inclusive settings to the maximum extent possible, such as general education classes and activities, service-learning experiences (Dymond, Renzaglia, & Slagor, 2011), community-based instruction (Walker, Uphold, Richter, & Test, 2010), job training sites, and college campuses (Grigal & Hart, 2010). For example, a student with a goal of identifying her career interests may enroll in several career development classes and sample multiple community jobs to identify her employment preferences. Finally, conduct ongoing assessment to determine if students are making progress toward their transition goals and if they and important people in their lives are satisfied with the educational program.

USING OBSERVATIONAL, INFORMAL, AND FORMAL ASSESSMENTS TO COLLECT DATA

LEGISLATION

IDEA 2004 stipulates that the LEA or state agency must conduct a full and individual initial evaluation before special education and related services can be provided to a student who is identified as eligible for services. The LEA must use a variety of assessment tools and strategies when conducting the evaluation in order to gather relevant functional information, including behavioral factors, to assist in determining an appropriate educational program for the student.

Now that you are familiar with a process for choosing appropriate assessments to use in the transition planning process, more information is provided about the types of assessments available for teachers—direct observation and informal and formal assessments.

Observing Students' Performance

Observing a student's performance within a given setting and systematically collecting data allow a teacher to target the specific strengths and needs of a student within the context and demands of that particular setting. Many students' strengths will remain unidentified until students are given the opportunity to try new activities. Untapped strengths may be more likely to emerge when students participate across an entire spectrum of school, work, and community events, rather than only in those that typically are available in separate settings. By observing a student as she participates in a new activity, teachers are able to identify those skill areas needing supports to increase a student's competence and participation. Creating an accurate picture of a student's competence within a given context helps you identify ways to build on a student's strengths and areas of needed support. Be a good observer and a good listener while you follow these suggestions from teachers.

- Observe your students in the actual environments in which they will be participating. Artificial environments, such as simulated grocery stores, separate gym classes, or mock worksites, cannot accurately replicate the demands of the environment and do not give the student the opportunity to demonstrate strengths in related areas of behavior. Instead, observe a student's social skills while she is interacting with co-workers, or observe a student's problem-solving skills when materials with which to complete an assignment are missing.

- Remember that few people are proficient at skills they are trying for the very first time. Give students opportunities to practice new skills and routines, observing them periodically to see how their skills develop.

- Look for multiple examples of students' strengths. Task performance in the workplace is only one of several areas that a teacher should observe. Other areas in which a student may demonstrate strengths include social relationships, self-care skills, communication abilities, and job-related skills such as punctuality or dependability.

- Incorporate students' preferences into the activities in which they are involved as you observe them. People are better at tasks they enjoy and select themselves.

"I go to jobsites and observe students' social behavior and work skills. I make written notes on my observations and talk to the supervisor. I also observe students during their recreation and community activities and note their behavior."

Teacher, Farragut High School

Assessing Outcomes: How to Collect Data

ASSESSMENT

Collecting information on a student's strengths and needs is critical to developing educational programs for all students. Knowing what information you want and actually gathering it both require a series of interrelated decisions. After all, there are many ways to record data on any particular student behavior. For example, you may want to identify a student's strengths and needs at a new job-training site. You could record the number of faucets she repairs (frequency), how many are fixed each hour (rate), how long each takes to repair (duration), how long it takes before she starts on her repairs (latency), the proportion of faucets she fixes correctly (percentage), and so forth. Deciding which method to use will depend on two factors: 1) the target behavior, such as starting to work on the job, and 2) the information wanted, such as how long an employee takes after punching a time card. The following section illustrates three types of observation systems that you can use to collect information about students' strengths and needs—event recording, interval recording, and task analysis.

Event Recording

How often does a student do something? Event recording can help you answer this question. You can either observe as a behavior occurs (e.g., the number of times a student sneezes in class or scores a basket in a game) or observe the outcome of a particular behavior after it happens (e.g., the number of math problems solved correctly, the number of clothes folded independently). Form 2.1 is an Event Recording Datasheet that can be used to observe more than one behavior at a time. Different behaviors are listed at the top of each of the columns and the times of day are displayed at the start of each row. Every time a behavior was observed, the teacher tallied it in the appropriate cell. A blank, reproducible form is included on the accompanying CD-ROM.

FORM 2.1.
Event Recording Datasheet

Student: **Emily Raptor**   Date: **March 25**

Location: **Lagner's Department Store**   Observer: **Ms. Roberts**

Activity: **Job training in the women's clothing section**

Time	Greeted others	Asked for assistance	Provided assistance	Items folded correctly	Items folded incorrectly
9:00–9:15	III	II	II	HHT II	I
9:15–9:30	II	III	IIII	IIII	HHT
9:30–9:45	—	II	I	HHT	—
9:45–10:00	IIII	I	—	HHT HHT II	III
Total	1 hour	9	8	7	28	9

Comments

Emily greeted only employees she knew well and greeted very few customers. She increased the number of items she folded correctly by almost 10 over her last effort. She seems to really enjoy working around her friend Jane.

Form 2.1.   Event Recording Datasheet for Emily Raptor. (A blank, photocopiable version of this form is included on the accompanying CD-ROM.)

FORM 2.2.
Interval Recording Datasheet

Students: Jeff and Andy   Date: April 12

Location: Charlemonte Bar & Grille   Observer: Mr. Gabel

Activity: Hosting during the lunch shift

Interval: minutes	On task (Jeff)	On task (Andy)	Socializing (Jeff)	Socializing (Andy)	Smiling (Jeff)	Smiling (Andy)
:10	✓	✓	—	—	✓	—
:20	—	✓	✓	—	✓	—
:30	—	✓	✓	—	✓	—
:40	—	—	✓	—	✓	—
:50	✓	✓	✓	—	✓	—
1:00	—	✓	✓	—	✓	—
1:10	—	✓	—	—	✓	—
1:20	✓	—	✓	✓	✓	✓
1:30	✓	✓	✓	—	✓	✓
1:40	—	✓	✓	—	✓	—
Total	4	8	8	1	10	2
Percentage of intervals	40%	80%	80%	10%	100%	20%

✓ = Occurrence   — = Nonoccurrence

Comments

Andy worked almost constantly but didn't talk with any of the other employees or customers—he seemed a bit uncomfortable (few smiles). Jeff was a "social butterfly" but completed very little work.

Form 2.2. Interval Recording Datasheet for Jeff and Andy. (A blank, photocopiable version of this form is included on the accompanying CD-ROM.)

Interval Recording

Does a student perform a particular behavior for a long enough time (e.g., preparing for a class presentation) or short enough time (e.g., taking a break between tasks)? You can use interval recording to estimate how long a student does something. By dividing an observation period into equal intervals (e.g., 10 seconds or more), you can identify those intervals in which a behavior occurs. Form 2.2 is an Interval Recording Datasheet that can be adapted for use in a variety of work, school, home, or community settings. The teacher has listed critical work behaviors for two students, Jeff and Andy, across the top of each column. Each row represents a 10-minute interval during which the occurrence or nonoccurrence of each behavior is noted. A blank, reproducible form is included on the accompanying CD-ROM.

Task Analysis

You may want to know what aspects of an activity a student does particularly well (or needs support to perform). You can observe each step of a student's performance and determine whether support is needed by listing all of the steps of an activity using a task analysis. Form 2.3 is a Task Analysis Observation form that can be used in a variety of settings in which the student may participate. A blank, reproducible form is included on the accompanying CD-ROM.

"I have noticed the following behavior when students are comfortable and competent on a job. They will stop looking at me or the job coach for prompts and put all of their attention into the job."

Transition teacher, Nashville Public Schools

Teachers recommend the following strategies for observing students' behavior across a variety of settings.

- Develop a checklist or inventory of skills and behaviors, such as social skills or study skills, that are important for successful participation in a specific setting. Use the checklist as a guide for evaluating the student's performance.

- Job sampling (i.e., providing a student with a variety of employment training experiences) allows you to observe students across a range of employment sites that represent both the students' career interests and the types of jobs actually available in the community. The Work Performance Evaluation (see Form 3.2 in Chapter 3) allows you to conduct a situational vocational assessment of a student's skills, and the Student Job History Form (see Form 8.3 in Chapter 8) allows you to track skill development across multiple work experiences. Both forms can be adapted for different situations, such as participating in classroom activities or eating in a restaurant.

- Observe students in many different settings because people's strengths and needs vary according to the demands and opportunities in different contexts. Visit students at home to observe their morning routine, at work to watch as they interact with customers, or at the mall to survey their shopping and money skills.

- Observe students in different settings with varying degrees of "pressure." Situations that require a high speed or production rate will affect individuals differently than those that require a slower pace. You may find that a student appears agitated, aggressive, or anxious in a high-pressure job, such as customer service, or in a class where students are frequently expected to respond orally. Try changing the student's job or classroom tasks to some with less pressure to determine whether her behavior relates to the task or the situation itself. Use this information to help determine career or college placement for the student.

ASSESSMENT

Assessing Outcomes: Conducting Comparative Observations

Observing a student is one thing, but how do you know how well the student should be performing? How do you know what the "norm" is within a particular setting? For example, if a student is responsible for filing medical records in a doctor's office or answering multiple-choice questions in class, then how do you know how fast the student should be going? A simple solution is to compare the student's performance with that of co-workers, classmates, or peers who are proficient at the same tasks in the

Task Analysis Observation

Student: __Marcus Anderson__

Setting: __Leitermann Corporation employee cafeteria__

Goal: __Marcus will complete every step independently on three consecutive trials by 4/12. His goal is to obtain a__
__total score of 76.__

Coding:
  4 = Independent response
  3 = Verbal prompt
  2 = Gestural prompt
  1 = Physical prompt

	Steps	Trial									
		1	2	3	4	5	6	7	8	9	10
20	—	—	—	—	—	—	—	—			
19	Leave the lunch line.	3	3	2	3	3	4	3			
18	Pick up lunch tray.	1	1	2	2	2	4	4			
17	Sign credit card receipt.	2	2	2	3	4	3	4			
16	Give cashier credit card.	2	2	3	3	3	3	4			
15	Move to cashier station.	1	1	2	2	3	3	3			
14	Place beverage on tray.	2	2	3	2	2	3	3			
13	Locate preferred beverage.	1	2	2	3	2	3	3			
12	Move to beverage station.	2	3	3	3	3	3	3			
11	Repeat Steps 9 and 10 (meat, vegetable, bread).	1	1	1	2	2	2	3			
10	Indicate preference.	1	1	1	1	2	2	3			
9	Ask what food choices are available.	1	1	1	1	2	4	3			
8	Move to food station.	3	4	3	3	4	4	4			
7	Pick up napkin and place on tray.	1	2	3	3	3	4	4			
6	Pick up spoon and place on tray.	3	4	4	4	4	4	4			
5	Pick up knife and place on tray.	2	3	4	3	4	4	4			
4	Pick up fork and place on tray.	2	3	4	3	4	3	4			
3	Place lunch tray on rails.	2	3	2	3	3	2	3			
2	Pick up lunch tray.	1	1	2	2	2	4	3			
1	Enter beginning of lunch line.	4	4	3	4	4	4	4			
	Total	35	43	47	50	56	63	66			
	Date	4/1	4/2	4/3	4/4	4/5	4/8	4/9			

Note: List the first step of the task on the bottom line (i.e., Step 1).

Form 2.3.   Task Analysis for Marcus Anderson. (A blank, photocopiable version of this form is included on the accompanying CD-ROM.)

same settings. This creates a standard by which to evaluate a student's performance as well as a goal to aim for in instructional programs. Follow these four steps to compare a student's performance.

1. Begin by identifying at least one peer in a particular setting who is proficient at performing the same routines, activities, or tasks as the student.

For example, you may choose to select another cashier at a student's worksite, a teammate in her basketball league, a roommate from her apartment, a fellow soprano from the community choir, or a classmate in school. If possible, identify several peers because people vary in their performance.

Mr. Roehler, one of James's teachers, noticed that James was very quiet at lunch. He hardly seemed to talk to anyone. Mr. Roehler wondered whether increasing conversational initiations should be one of James's IEP goals. He did not know, however, how much a typical high school student talked at lunch. He decided to do a comparative observation. He picked three general education peers who ate nearby in the same cafeteria as James and who frequently talked to their peers.

2. Observe the identified peers as they perform the target behavior, and record their performance.

Observe each peer's performance at least three to five times because everyone's behavior varies from day to day. Compile the information, compute the average performance, and then allow some flexibility to establish a range of performance that would be expected for the target behavior.

Mr. Roehler recorded the peers' performance over a 2-week period. It really was not difficult to do because he ate in the lunchroom every day anyway. James's peers initiated conversation at an average of three times per minute. Mr. Roehler decided to choose the range of two to four times per minute as a standard for James's initiating behavior.

3. Next, observe the student performing the same target behavior.

Observe at least three to five times to establish an average and range for the student's performance. Then compare the student's performance with the range you established for the peers. Is there a substantial difference? If so, you may want to target the behavior for instruction and support. If not, the student may already be performing within the expectations of the environment.

As Mr. Roehler had suspected, there was a big difference between James's observed behavior and his peers' standard. In fact, it was worse than he had thought: During all five observations, James never initiated conversation once. Occasionally, he responded when spoken to, but that was all. It seemed that increasing initiations was a behavior that should be targeted in James's IEP.

4. Obtain input from others.

Although you have been able to demonstrate through comparative observations that there is (or is not) a difference in the student's performance and the expected levels of performance, you still need to find out whether other individuals in the same setting agree with your findings. Even if your data show that there is a difference in performance, others may not believe that there is a problem (or vice versa). Be sure to ask others' opinions before initiating an instructional program; this will help you prioritize educational goals for a student.

Mr. Roehler discreetly asked James's peers in the lunchroom, his other teachers, lunchroom staff, and James's parents whether they believed that James's lack of conversation during social times was a problem. They all agreed that it was. Everyone liked James, but, as one student put it, "He's like in a shell. He'll answer when I talk to him, but I really wish he'd joke around with me more and ask me about myself." Mr. Roehler was convinced. He would show his data to the other members of the IEP team and propose to include the goal to "increase conversational initiations" on James's IEP.

Collecting Data and Reviewing Students' Evaluations

"I make on-site observations of students at places where they go for recreation, school, work, and other activities. Then I compare what they do with others in those settings."

Teacher, East High School

According to IDEA 2004, the IEP team must review existing evaluation data as part of an initial evaluation of a student (if appropriate) and as part of any reevaluation. These data must include classroom-based assessments and observations, teachers' and related services providers' observations, psychological reports, and evaluations and information obtained from parents.

"To assess a student's skills and needs, first do the task yourself. Then have a general education peer do the task. Then have the student do the task him- or herself. Compare performance using a task analysis. This will point out the student's strengths and needs."

Teacher, Warren County High School

Collecting data is critical in identifying strengths among your students. In addition to helping teachers target those aspects of a routine that students perform well, data gathered can be used as a basis for communicating with others about a student's skills. In fact, employers, parents, and others who are important to the student may be pleasantly surprised when they see documentation that a student is performing certain tasks better than they realized. Teachers suggest the following strategies for collecting student data.

- Complete a task analysis of the activity or skill that you are observing the student performing, such as cooking breakfast. Recording the student's performance for each step of the task analysis will assist you in determining in which aspects of a routine a student is proficient and which areas may require future instruction and support (see Form 2.3).

- Data that are collected on only one occasion are not likely to be representative of a student's actual skills. Performance often varies over time. Allow the student time to adapt while you take periodic data over time, especially when a student is participating in a new activity or setting, such as a new school, club, or class.

- As one person, you cannot be present in all of the settings in which a student participates throughout the day. Luckily, as stated in IDEA 2004, other individuals in the setting can assist with collecting data. For example, a co-worker could record the number of aisles stocked, a peer could note a student's progress on math problems, a baseball coach could keep track of a batting average, or a parent could indicate the time it takes to complete a chore.

- Videotape or photograph a student at several points across time. The videotapes and photographs can be used to evaluate and document a student's progress over time. You can also use them for a teaching tool for the student or other students who are learning to perform the same or similar task.

- Collecting data provides you with a reference point against which to compare later improvements in a student's performance. In addition to academic and school-related areas, information should be recorded in work, community, and residential environments. Students' performance varies according to the context of an environment.

"I use the student's psychological evaluation in combination with classroom behavioral observations to determine a student's need for additional supports. I also consider the observations of parents, co-workers, peers, and the students themselves."

Teacher, Hillcrest High School

Case Study 2.2 *Gathering Data*

Mr. Kleeb had been teaching for several years and was used to having new students join late in the year. Usually, he would speak with their parents and former teachers, examine the students' IEPs, and look through their student files to determine where to begin. Carlos's situation, however, was different—no teachers to consult, no IEP, and no student records. Mr. Kleeb knew he would have to begin by identifying Carlos's individual strengths and areas in which he needed support. Doing so would require observing Carlos's interactions in a variety of school, work, and community settings and carefully recording his findings.

Many of the students with whom Mr. Kleeb worked were already involved in activities throughout the school and community. Each week, he helped students learn important skills through purchasing food for the culinary arts class, depositing money in the bank for the athletic department, and buying school supplies for the central office. As Carlos participated in these activities, Mr. Kleeb used a task analysis to identify skills at which Carlos excelled and to determine where he might need additional supports. Mr. Kleeb discovered that although Carlos had never used (or seen) an automated teller machine, he knew exactly how to deposit and withdraw money from the bank. Moreover, he was familiar with how to purchase items at a store, and he even taught Mr. Kleeb the best way to pick out ripe fruit. Mr. Kleeb looked at more than just Carlos's participation in certain activities. He also watched for less visible strengths, such as how Carlos interacted with strangers, when he appeared confident or hesitant, how he dealt with unexpected problems, and to whom he turned for assistance.

Mr. Kleeb arranged for Carlos to gain some work experience at several community businesses. As a result, he was able to observe Carlos's performance across a variety of different jobs. Because two other students also worked at the same businesses, Mr. Kleeb asked a co-worker to evaluate Carlos's work skills against a checklist of skills he and the store manager had developed. Mr. Kleeb quickly discovered that Carlos loved working with people and was very successful at it. Before long, Carlos was working almost independently and had made several new friends.

Almost 1 month later, a worn package arrived in the mail, covered with foreign postage stamps. Mr. Kleeb, full of curiosity, opened the package and discovered a collection of documents from Carlos's former school. With a little help from a translator, Mr. Kleeb read through the entire contents of Carlos's educational program. Former teacher observations gave Mr. Kleeb some good ideas about some interests and activities Carlos might enjoy and do well at. He was surprised, however, to discover that, in many ways, he didn't recognize the student described in those files: "Skill deficits in communication, functional academics, and social skills." "Emphasis placed on prevocational skills." The Carlos he had observed was an outgoing, excited student who demonstrated numerous strengths and talents. How could two people view a student so differently? Mr. Kleeb stepped back for a moment, glad that he had not relied solely on others' perceptions of Carlos but had observed and documented his strengths for himself.

"A good checklist or logbook is helpful. I reverse how it's usually done by looking only for strengths or job match skills instead of problems. I list skills on the checklist that are needed for certain jobs. For example, is endurance most important or is work rate?"

Transition teacher, Nashville Public Schools

LEGISLATION

Students have benefited from the instruction and supports of many teachers and individuals by the time they reach high school. Their records are likely to contain a wealth of useful information regarding their experiences, performance, and strengths. You are required by IDEA 2004 to review current and existing evaluation data in determining a student's educational and related services needs, the IEP, and appropriate program modifications to allow the student to be involved in and progress in the general curriculum.

ASSESSMENT

Assessing Outcomes: Evaluating Students' Data

- Communicate frequently with general education teachers regarding your students' grade reports rather than waiting until the end of the grading period or semester. Doing so will keep you abreast of collaborating teachers' perceptions of students' work and will allow you to identify curriculum areas in which they are performing strongly or need supports or program modifications.

- Student files are frequently filled with past observations, teacher and parent interviews, assessment results, and former IEPs. Combine this information with current evaluations to identify students' areas of strength and needed supports.

- Keep track of your students' daily school and work attendance and behavior. This information can help you identify days that tend to be problematic for a student. Then adapt the daily schedule to accommodate the student's needs. For example, a student may be consistently sleepy and late to school on Mondays because she visits her grandmother on the weekends. Try to have community-based instruction for the student in the afternoon on Mondays, and start the day at a slower pace.

"At his job-training site, a student was gathering aluminum cans for recycling. By observation, we noticed that he would drain the cans in the trashcan properly, but sometimes he would take trash out of the garbage to keep for himself: large bags, papers, and plastic 2-liter bottles. After instructing him not to remove trash from the cans, we periodically would pair him with another student to monitor his behavior."

Teacher, Pearl-Cohn High School

Using Informal Assessment Methods

"I use a home–community activities inventory that has a checklist of tasks and is filled out at every IEP meeting with the parent. I use systematic data collection to determine steps on a task analysis that cause difficulty. I use student profiles to facilitate information sharing with the vocational rehabilitation counselor and general education teacher feedback forms for information on integrated classrooms. I use employer evaluations to assess vocational training."

Teacher, Karns High School

Informal assessment has many advantages. It allows you to assess a student's skills within the context of the particular settings in which a behavior is expected to be performed. Rather than assess a student on a generic set of skills, such as job readiness, which may have no immediate relevance in the current setting, you can assess only those skills needed in your students' everyday lives. For example, one of your students may have trouble ordering her favorite meal, a grilled chicken sandwich, at a local sit-down restaurant. It is not necessary to assess every restaurant skill she has—only the skills she needs to order the sandwich. Informal assessment allows you to focus on only those skills that count in a particular student's daily life.

ASSESSMENT

Assessing Outcomes: Behavior Checklists

Behavior checklists help you focus on particular behaviors of interest and can be generated by the teacher or commercially prepared. Teacher-generated checklists have the advantage of reflecting only the skills that are important in a student's environment. Commercially prepared checklists are ready-made and save you time. In either case, information can be obtained quickly by either observation or interviews. Form 2.4 can be used to evaluate an employee's social skills on the job. For each skill listed on the form, the job coach notes how well the student performs the skill and adds any comments that might inform the design of instruction or delivery of supports. A blank, reproducible form is included on the accompanying CD-ROM. Different forms can be devised for other behaviors important in clubs, classrooms, or community activities.

"Pretesting, oral reading, and chalkboard activities provide much information about students' strengths and needs. Discreetly questioning students privately one to one helps clarify puzzling cases in which students are having problems."

Teacher, Fairley High School

It is important to involve as many people who work with the student as possible when assessing a student's strengths. Doing so will provide teachers and others with information they do not have the time or opportunity to gather because they do not see the student in a particular setting. In addition, incorporating the perspectives of others into an assessment will help eliminate any bias that may occur when only one person completes a student's assessment (Carter, Trainor, Sun, et al., 2009). Teachers can use contact "logs" for maintaining communication between themselves and others who work with a student and for keeping ongoing assessments across different environments. One suggested strategy is to ask parents, general education teachers, employers, and others to record information about a student's performance in a spiral notebook, planner, calendar, or tablet computer (whichever a student prefers or can access) that accompanies the student throughout the day and is exchanged among all parties.

RESEARCH

Collaborating on Transition Assessment

Although meaningful assessment has long been considered an essential element of the transition planning process, specific legislative mandates to directly connect postsecondary goals with assessment data did not appear until IDEA 2004. Without a strong linkage between assessment findings and transition planning, the relevance of transition programming may be limited for a student. Indeed, according to the NLTS–2, only 39% of youth with disabilities received educational programming that school staff perceived to be "very well suited" for meeting the students' transition-related goals (Cameto et al., 2004).

Employee Social Skills Checklist

Student: __Lyndon Shakespeare__   Interview/observation date: __3/22__

Work environment: __Computer Universe on Blanco Road__

Skill	Always	Sometimes	Never	N/A	Comments
Does the student greet co-workers when arriving to or leaving work?	☑	☐	☐	☐	Lyndon especially likes greeting Karen!
Is the student punctual and on time?	☑	☐	☐	☐	
Does the student look approachable (e.g., smiling, well-groomed)?	☐	☑	☐	☐	Sometimes Lyndon needs to be reminded to tuck in his shirt.
Is the student polite (e.g., jokes, uses social amenities)?	☑	☐	☐	☐	Extremely courteous!
Does the student greet/interact with customers in an acceptable way?	☑	☐	☐	☐	
Does the student greet/interact with co-workers in an acceptable way?	☑	☐	☐	☐	
Is the student meeting expected work performance goals?	☐	☑	☐	☐	Lyndon often gets so wrapped up in talking with others that he doesn't finish his work.
Does the student turn to co-workers for assistance when needed?	☐	☑	☐	☐	
Does the student give and receive directions/instructions well?	☐	☑	☐	☐	Lyndon can get upset when his supervisor gives him work feedback.
Does the student give and receive praise/criticism well?	☐	☑	☐	☐	
Does the student get along well with his or her peers?	☑	☐	☐	☐	
Does the student seem to fit in with a social group at work?	☑	☐	☐	☐	Lyndon has several great friends at work!
Does the student spend break or lunch with co-workers?	☑	☐	☐	☐	Sometimes he tries to go on break with co-workers even when it isn't his turn.
Does the student interact with co-workers outside of work?	☑	☐	☐	☐	

Form 2.4.   Employee Social Skills Checklist for Lyndon Shakespeare. (A blank, photocopiable version of this form is included on the accompanying CD-ROM.)

Incorporating the perspectives of multiple people who know a student well into the assessment process is one way to increase the relevance of transition programming (Carter, Owens, Trainor, Sun, & Swedeen, 2009). After all, different people sometimes hold different perspectives on what should be addressed within the transition plan. For example, Carter, Trainor, Sun, et al. (2009) examined the transition competencies of 160 students with emotional/behavior disorders and/or learning disabilities by inviting special educators, parents, and youth to complete the Transition Planning Inventory (Clark & Patton, 2006). Youth often differed from their teachers and parents in their views of their own transition-related strengths and needs. This should not be surprising as each team member has a different vantage point from which to view a youth's strengths and needs across different settings.

In addition, a student can be paired with a peer during school, work, and recreational activities, and the peer can evaluate the student's performance on important tasks. Doing so allows teachers an opportunity to work with other students and provides a peer's perspective on the student's strengths. For example, if a student's goal is to increase positive self-statements, then the peer can keep a simple tally of occurrences. Finally, the students themselves are one of the best sources of information regarding their strengths. Students may have more insight into their own performance than others realize. It is critical to give students regular opportunities to evaluate their own performance and to suggest areas of supports. Additional strategies for conducting informal assessments include the following.

- The Work Performance Evaluation (see Form 3.2 in Chapter 3) is an informal vocational assessment that can be modified to reflect the skills required in your students' actual work environments. Save yourself some work by keeping a log of the forms you develop so that you can reuse them in the same environment with different students.

- You simply cannot follow your students around all day to find out how they are doing in every setting they encounter. Collaborate with others, such as parents and employers, to develop a checklist of important student skills, knowledge, and behaviors. Let others use the checklist across different settings as a guide for assessing students' strengths and needs. Get together over lunch and compare outcomes while you socialize.

- Ongoing assessment is the key to effective instruction and support. You need to keep on top of your students' progress. Practice may result in a student mastering a skill that was once difficult, whereas changes in jobs, people, or activities may result in a student being challenged in an activity that was formerly routine. Expect and adjust for change in performance.

"Provide job sampling—observe students in various job settings. Do interest surveys with students. Informal testing and checklists can also provide additional information on students' strengths and needs."

Teacher, Whites Creek High School

Evaluating Outcomes: Conducting a Home Inventory

ASSESSMENT

Parents know their children best. Moreover, individuals who live with the student on a day-to-day basis (e.g., parents, siblings, relatives, support staff, roommates) are in a position to observe strengths and needs that cannot be witnessed by a teacher in school and work settings (Carter, Owens, et al., 2009). Asking these individuals to help a student complete home inventories of a student's activities and involvement can assist teachers in developing instructional programs and opportunities that meet a student's needs. They also allow parents an opportunity to express their preferences and personal values. Form 2.5, the Home Inventory Form, gives you a chance to discuss

Student: Jared Hutchinson   Age: 20   Interview date: September 24

Where do you live? ____ House   ✓ Apartment   How long have you lived there? 11 months

Who lives with you? Two roommates (Michael and Samuel)

Do you have relatives who live near you? Yes   Who? Brother, parent, aunt, and uncle

Likes and Dislikes

	What do you like?	What do you dislike?
Foods (snacks, treats, special diet)	Fast food—Burger Hut, McRey's Popcorn Chinese food—egg rolls, fried rice	Seafood Dairy products (allergic)
Activities (hobbies, sports, places, events)	Working in workshop with father Wichicumba Redbirds baseball games Computer games/Internet Watching movies	Bowling
Work (jobs, chores, volunteer events)	Working at Sheare's Hardware Landscaping, working in the garden Volunteering with Habitat for Humanity Anything outdoors	Cleaning jobs—mopping, bathrooms Working alone

Concerns

Are there issues that keep you from enjoying community events
(e.g., toileting accidents, hitting others, loud screaming)?

What issues?	Where do they occur?	What is the result?
Afraid to take bus alone	Downtown	Stay home, miss the Redbirds
Get angry at work	At the hardware store	Yell at Mr. Sheare

Your Community

A "map" of your community will help develop a picture of where neighbors live, work, and play.
Make sure to fill this out completely.

	Which streets in your neighborhood do you use frequently?	How do you use them?			Are there...	
		Walk	Car	Bus	Signals	Crosswalks
Streets	Neese Drive	✓				
	Nolensville Boulevard	✓			✓	✓
	Twin Oaks Parkway		✓		✓	✓
	Antioch Drive	✓				✓

(page 1 of 4)

Form 2.5. Home Inventory Form for Jared Hutchinson. (From Allen, W.T. [2000]. *Read my lips: It's My choice.* St. Paul, MN: Governor's Council on Developmental Disabilities, Department of Administration; adapted by permission of Allen, Shea & Associates.) (A blank, photocopiable version of this form is included on the accompanying CD-ROM.)

Family and friends

Whom do you visit?	How far away?		How do you get there?			How often do you visit?			
	1–5 blocks	5 or more blocks	Walk	Car	Bus	Daily	Each week	Each month	Other
Mom and Dad		✓		✓			✓		
Brother	✓		✓						Three times per week
Aunt and Uncle		✓		✓				✓	
Friend (Richard)	✓		✓			✓			
Friend (Hank)		✓		✓			✓		

Community activities

Where do you go?	How do you get there?			When?		How often do you go?			
	Walk	Car	Bus	Week-day	Week-end	Daily	Each week	Each month	Other
Redbirds games			✓		✓			✓	
Church		✓		✓	✓		✓		
McLane's grocery store		✓		✓			✓		
Work (Sheare's Hardware)	✓			✓		✓			
Hobby shop and computer store	✓			✓	✓		✓		
Library		✓		✓	✓			✓	
Movies		✓			✓		✓		
Volunteer activities		✓			✓			✓	

Strengths and Training Needs
Here is an opportunity to talk about what you like to do, the talents that you have,
and which supports might help you become more independent in the community.

Circle area: (Community)   Recreation/leisure   Home   Work   Other

Strengths

What activities do you do?	What is involved in that activity?
Go to the community library on Nolensville Boulevard	Find books using computer, read magazines, socialize
Barber shop	Get haircut, pay, and tip; talk with barbers; read magazines
McLane's grocery store	Find ride, buy groceries with roommate
Crestwood Outlet Megamall	Find ride, get money from ATM, find bargains
Video rental store (in convenience store)	Walk to store, browse, choose movie, pay
Dentist's and doctor's offices	Wait and read magazines, tell doctor problem, pay bill
Superplex movie theater	Find ride, purchase tickets/snacks, talk after
Various restaurants	Walk/find ride, order from menu, eat, pay bill, talk

(page 2 of 4)

Training Needs	
What things would you like to learn to do?	What things get in the way?
Sometimes go places alone (grocery store, mall)	Don't know how to use the bus or call a cab
Go to the YMCA	Don't know how to get membership or what is there
Attend more Redbirds baseball games	Lack of money, don't always have a ride
Go to the dance club with friends	Never danced before, don't know what is there

Potential supports

Instruction can focus on travel training. Family member or roommates could take Jared to the YMCA one evening to show him the courses and equipment they offer. Help arrange for Jared to work a few extra hours and/or find where Jared can get discount game tickets—see if co-worker might want to join him.

What do we know...

. . . about your community?
Jared lives near several busy streets, which he walks down. He gets rides to several of his relatives' homes and walks to others. He is very active in the community, getting rides to activities throughout the week.

. . . about your likes and dislikes?
Jared loves eating out, especially at fast-food restaurants. He is allergic to dairy products. Jared loves computers, baseball, movies, and woodworking. He likes working with others outdoors and working with tools but doesn't like bowling or jobs that require cleaning.

. . . about your strengths?
Jared is already very involved in many community activities and enjoys trying new experiences. He gets along well with others and seeks help when he needs it.

What things have you decided you would like to work on with us?

Community	• Travel training, including riding the bus and taxi
	• Learning how to write checks and use debit card
	• Trying some new activities (e.g., dance club, YMCA)
	•
Recreation/ leisure	• Getting involved in some community classes, such as woodworking and cooking
	• Joining a community or work baseball/softball team
	• Learning how to develop an exercise program
	•

(page 3 of 4)

FORM 2.5. *(continued)*

Home	• Budgeting for monthly expenses
	• Getting along with my roommates (conflict resolution)
	• Making certain meals and snacks
	• Programming my DVD player
Work	• Getting faster at the work I do (improving productivity)
	• Making more friends at work
	• Getting a promotion
	•
Other	• Learning how to stand up for myself (self-advocacy skills)
	•
	•
	•

(page 4 of 4)

the advantages of community-based transition programs and be responsive to parents' viewpoints. A blank, reproducible form is included on the accompanying CD-ROM.

It is best to have as many family members as possible participate in answering the queries on the form. Ideally, you will be able to visit the family and help family members respond.

Using Formal Assessment Methods

The assessment that is most appropriate for high school transition students is informal and is often teacher designed and specific to a particular work, school, or community environment (Sitlington & Clark, 2007). For example, a teacher may develop a checklist for monitoring a student's reaction to anger-provoking situations. Formal, or standardized, assessment can augment the information derived from informal assessments to aid in developing educational programs, evaluating student progress, determining eligibility for programs, and developing support needs (Mazzotti et al., 2009; Thompson et al., 2010). Formal assessment provides information about a student in relation to a standardized norm, typically national or statewide. Types of formal assessments include adaptive behavior and independent living assessments, aptitude tests, interest inventories, intelligence tests, achievement tests, personality assessments, and measures of self-determination (Fowler et al., 2010). For example, a student's language development could be compared with that of a national sample of general education students. Teachers provide the following recommendations when using formal assessments with transition-age students.

- Although you should never rely solely on commercially prepared assessment instruments, developmental scales and adaptive behavior tests can provide valuable insight into a student's strengths and needs.

- Keep in mind that you are trying to get as much information as you can about a student's strengths and support needs. This means that you will need to use a variety of formal and informal assessments, each of which reveals different types of information about a student.

- Formal assessments typically provide less information about a particular student in the context of a specific setting than informal assessments. Formal assessments do have advantages, however. For example, they can save you time because they are already prepared. Also, by following the directions, a paraprofessional or school staff member may be able to administer some assessments that do not require a professional evaluator.

- Standardized tests are just that—standardized. Consequently, the results of a standardized assessment, such as an adaptive behavior scale, usually can be easily communicated to and interpreted by other professionals. Communicating information about a student makes collaboration among providers easier.

- Formal assessments that teachers have found helpful for secondary students include the AAMR Adaptive Behavior Scales (Lambert, Nihira, & Leland, 1993), the Brigance Transition Skills Inventory (Brigance, 2011), the Quality of Life Questionnaire (Schalock & Keith, 1993), and the Woodcock Reading Mastery Tests (Woodcock, 2011). More information about these and other formal assessments is in the resources section at the end of the chapter.

LEGISLATION

IDEA 2004 states that students with disabilities are to be included in general state- and districtwide assessment programs with accommodations, where necessary. Accommodations provided for students should directly address their individual needs. For example, you could change the setting in which a student takes the assessment; vary the format of the test; allow a student to respond in a different way, such as speaking rather than writing; extend the amount of time a student has to complete the test; or provide an alternative assessment.

"I assess a student's competence in at least two ways: By evaluating their progress on academic and vocational goals in their IEPs and by measuring their performance on a variety of standardized tests."

Teacher, Treadwell High School

DEVELOPING A SUMMARY OF PERFORMANCE AND COMMUNICATING WITH OTHERS

"Talk to any general education classroom teachers that the student may have. Ask them to describe to you the problems that they see with the student. Then, incorporate teaching solutions or ways to deal with the problems while the student is in the resource class."

Teacher, McEwen High School

Developing a Summary of Performance

LEGISLATION

IDEA 2004 requires that when a student exits special education services due to graduating from high school with a regular diploma or exceeding the age limit for services under state law, the LEA will "provide the child with a summary of the child's academic achievement and functional performance, which shall include recommendations on how to assist the child in meeting the child's postsecondary goals" (§ 614).

When young people with disabilities are still in high school, they are entitled to free and appropriate services and supports based on their individual needs. Until the IDEA 2004 legislation required that a summary of performance accompany each student who is graduating or aging out of high school, there was no available documentation of a student's disability to show eligibility for disability-related services in postschool settings. The summary of performance is designed as a bridge between high school and adult life to provide documentation of a disability in accordance with Section 504 of the Rehabilitation Act of 1973 (PL 93-112) and ADA 2008 in order for a student to gain access to accommodations and supports after leaving school (Kochhar-Bryant & Izzo, 2006). As its title indicates, the summary of performance summarizes a student's current level of functioning upon leaving school, including information about the student's disability, eligibility for services and accommodations, and recommendations for how best to support the student in postschool life.

The summary of performance must be completed during a student's final year in high school. The document comprises five sections and follows a prescribed template (Kochhar-Bryant & Izzo, 2006).

1. *Demographic information:* This section includes the student's background and school information, the student's primary and any additional disabilities, and a list of assessments conducted. In addition, this section includes a copy of the most recent formal and informal assessment reports documenting the student's disability and information to assist in postschool planning.

2. *Student's postsecondary goals:* This section indicates the setting in which the student intends to enter upon completing high school, such as postsecondary education or employment. This information should already be included in the student's IEP.

3. *Summary of performance:* In this section, the student's current level of performance—including grade level, standard scores, strengths, and needs—is summarized in three areas—academic, cognitive, and functional. Information relevant to the student is required within each area, such as reading and math skills, problem solving, communication, social and independent living skills, and self-determination. In addition, teachers are required to describe all accommodations, modifications, or assistive technology that were essential to a student's progress in each of the areas.

4. *Recommendations:* This section provides suggestions for assisting the student in meeting her postsecondary goals as derived from the previous sections. These suggestions can include accommodations, support services, adaptive equipment, or other supports to enhance success across school, home, work, and community settings.

5. *Student input:* The summary of performance is strengthened by including input from the student with respect to how her disability affects her performance, supports that have been effective in promoting her success, and her view of her own strengths and needs in relation to postschool goals.

If teachers have adhered to the systematic assessment procedures described in this chapter, then developing the summary of performance should not be difficult. By the time a student is getting ready to leave school, a teacher will have collected a range of assessment data across behaviors and settings relevant to the student's current and projected settings, tasks, and demands. The summary of performance is a valuable document that can provide a bridge to a student's future adult life comprising information on a student's achievements, postschool goals, and recommendations for achieving these goals (Kochhar-Bryant, 2007; Richter & Mazzotti, 2011). The summary of performance can be regarded as the ultimate document in the transition assessment and planning process. In summary form, information can be readily shared with those with whom a student will spend the majority of her time after leaving school. If teachers enter assessment information into the summary of performance in an ongoing fashion rather than waiting until just prior to school exit, then the accuracy and utility of the summary of performance in communicating information to others will be increased (Sitlington & Clark, 2007).

Communicating with Parents, Teachers, and Others

"Communication between the people who supervise, assist, and care for the student should be ongoing. Identify what areas the student needs help in, and implement how to get needed changes made."

Teacher, Cookeville High School

LEGISLATION

Communication with parents must be ongoing. According to IDEA 2004, IEPs must include statements of how teams will measure student progress on annual goals and how the students' parents "will be regularly informed (by such means as periodic report cards), at least as often as parents are informed of the nondisabled children's progress" (§ 614). By informing parents of their child's strengths and needs, teachers encourage parents' involvement in students' educational programs.

"I assess students' strengths and needs through formal testing and by observing throughout the day. I also ask other teachers for frequent feedback on a student to assure me that I am not biased in my observations."

Teacher, Huntington High School

Student information obtained through observation and assessment has only limited use if it is not shared with others. The next step is to share the information you assembled. Teaching is a team effort requiring that information be shared across all team members. It is critical to communicate and collaborate with parents, fellow teachers, and others who are important to the student to develop educational programs that are based on shared information from all parties involved (Cobb & Alwell, 2009). Collecting student data is not an end in itself—the purpose of data is to communicate information. Share your data with and seek input from others who are important to the student. You may find that a parent is less interested in his daughter's improvement in telling time and more impressed with her increase in social interaction.

Collaborate with employers and community leaders when developing checklists of skills that you think are critical in their settings (Carter & Wehby, 2003). You may find that what you thought was a survival skill in a setting may be considered irrelevant by others in that setting. It is wise to be specific when you convey student information gathered through observation and assessment. For example, to say that "Jason does pretty well at work" is not as helpful to an employer as, "Jason independently performs the first nine steps of his cleaning task but needs partial assistance for the final two steps."

"Involvement of others in the selection and learning process of activities ensures that they are relevant to the student and those around him or her."

Teacher, Volunteer High School

"I help students achieve competence by asking others what skills are important, and then I find means of supporting these skills in order to raise the individual's level of independence."

Teacher, Volunteer High School

LEGISLATION

Developing a student's IEP on the basis of information specifying a student's strengths and areas of need is a collaborative team effort. IDEA 2004 stipulates who should be included on the IEP team. Team members include the student's parents, at least one general education teacher and one special education teacher, a representative of the LEA, an individual who can interpret the instructional implication of evaluation results, other individuals at the discretion of the parents or LEA, and the student, if appropriate.

Teachers suggest the following strategies for communicating and collaborating with others.

- Develop written profiles of the students with whom you work to share with employment and career counselors and potential employers and co-workers.

- Ask parents what chores their child does well at home and what areas need more work.

- Ask parents to complete an inventory of their child's independent skills at home and in the community.

- Consult weekly with the student's job supervisor. Include identified problem areas in instructional and support programs.

- Keep a checklist of expected student behaviors and have teachers, co-workers, and peers fill it out. Share it with the student and have the student complete one as well.

"I believe that satisfaction from others is very important to students [with disabilities] just as with anybody. Often, their self-esteem is very low, and they need all the support they can get. All of my students attend their IEP meetings so they can hear me discuss with their family all of their academic and vocational accomplishments."

Teacher, Pearl-Cohn High School

Interviewing Students and Others

By observing and assessing a student, you will have compiled important information about a student's strengths. But as only one person, you will never have direct access to everything you need to know about a student. It is critical to learn to ask for information from others. Employers, parents, students, and others usually are very willing to be interviewed by you; after all, they too are interested in a student's success and well-being. Teachers suggest using the following strategies in interviewing students and others important to the student.

- Interview individuals who regularly interact with the student but who typically are not consulted during IEP team meetings or assessments. Cafeteria workers, bus drivers, store owners, neighbors, and teammates all can provide information about a student's strengths and support needs.

- Look for ways that work, school, and community activities can be modified so that areas of need can become areas of strength for a student. Interview teachers, work supervisors, peers, and community members to determine how flexible a particular job or activity is and ideas for modifying it.

- Assessment and observation do not tell all. By meeting one to one with others who spend time with a student, you can learn their perspective on the strengths they think a student has. What you thought was a liability may be viewed as an asset by others.

- The best source of information about a student's strengths may be the student herself. Take time to talk with your students regularly. You may be surprised to find out how much insight they have into their own strengths and needs. Use alternative modes of communication with students who are nonverbal (see Chapter 5).

LEGISLATION

The importance of collaboration is made explicit in the law. IDEA 2004 states that research and practice have demonstrated that "Systemic change benefiting all students, including children with disabilities, requires the involvement of States, local educational agencies, parents, individuals with disabilities and their families, teachers and other service providers, and other interested individuals and organizations to develop and implement comprehensive strategies that improve educational results for children with disabilities" (§ 650).

RESOURCES

Brigance, A. (2011). *Brigance Transition Skills Inventory.* North Billerica, MA: Curriculum Associates.

This tool can be used to assess independent living, employment, and other postsecondary skills for adolescents with disabilities.

Fowler, C.H., Walker, A.R., & Rowe, D. (2010). *Age-appropriate transition assessment guide* (2nd ed.). Charlotte, NC: University of North Carolina at Charlotte, National Secondary Transition Technical Assistance Center.

This free, online guide addresses the purpose of transition assessment, provides an overview of sample instruments, and discusses how to conduct age-appropriate assessment.

Sitlington, P.L., Patton, J.R., & Clark, G.M. (2007). *Informal assessments for transition: Postsecondary education and training.* Austin, TX: PRO-ED.

This book addresses numerous informal assessment approaches for evaluating the postsecondary needs, opportunities, and participation of students with disabilities.

Synatschk, K.O., Clark, G.M., & Patton, J.R. (2007). *Informal assessments for transition: Independent living and community participation.* Austin, TX: PRO-ED.

This book includes an array of assessment approaches for exploring a student's community participation and independent living skills.

Synatschk, K.O., Clark, G.M., Patton, J.R., & Copeland, L.R. (2007). *Informal assessments for transition: Employment and career planning.* Austin, TX: PRO-ED.

This book reviews a range of tools and strategies for assessing the career development of youth with disabilities.

Woodcock, R.W. (2011). *Woodcock Reading Mastery Tests* (3rd ed.). Circle Pines, MN: American Guidance Service.

This instrument can be used to assess students' reading readiness and reading achievement.

Developing Supports that Enhance Participation

CHAPTER 3

Increasing Support within School and Community Settings

In this chapter, you will learn how to

- Identify existing supports and potential barriers
- Assess students' environmental support needs
- Develop individual support plans
- Gain access to existing environmental supports
- Enhance environments to promote participation

OVERVIEW

For many students, the success of their transition to adult life depends on the amount of environmental support they receive. Fortunately, most settings provide a variety of supports that exist naturally (Hughes, 2001; Lakin & Stancliffe, 2007). When teachers, college professors, job coaches, employers, and others learn to identify this support, they can begin to match it to the needs, preferences, and strengths of individual students. Whether it is a clock signaling the beginning of class, a sign reminding employees to wash their hands, or aisle markers in the college bookstore telling a student where to find a text for a class, environmental supports help a student achieve greater independence on the job, in the classroom and school, and around the community. Visiting a site and conducting a survey of naturally occurring supports and potential challenges is the first step in identifying environmental supports (Griffin, Hammis, & Geary, 2007). Additional information gained through observing the student and interviewing both the student and others is included to build a support plan for the student. Teachers, job coaches, family members, and service providers familiar with different settings a student encounters will be helpful in gaining access to existing environmental supports. They may also have ideas for modifying the setting to increase support, such as propping a door open for wheelchair users or providing shoes that do not require tying for individuals who have limited fine motor coordination. Environmental support may also be promoted by increasing community awareness and interagency collaboration and by increasing access to services and resources. By doing so, students gain access to a supportive environment that encourages rather than discourages their success.

This chapter contains five groups of strategies that teachers may use to increase environmental support for a student. It includes strategies such as identifying existing supports by conducting site visits and observations, gaining access to and communicating environmental support needs, developing individual support plans, gaining access to existing environmental support, and enhancing the environment to promote full participation. Fortunately, many supports need not be costly or intrusive. Environmental supports can be something as simple as a naturally occurring cue in the setting, such as a street sign or illustrated cookbook, that can be used to support a student in initiating and completing an expected and desired behavior.

Case Study 3.1   *Elisha Goes to College*

Ms. Earndale's View

Ms. Earndale had many dreams for her daughter—a paying job, a circle of friends, an apartment in the community—but college was definitely not one of them. Elisha had been an outgoing and active student while in high school, but college would be a different story. Elisha had always received such wonderful support from a constellation of people—classmates, peer buddies, general and special education teachers, and a variety of service providers. Where would her support come from in college? Besides, higher education was all about academics and intellectual pursuits. Wouldn't a student with physical and learning disabilities simply feel out of place?

Elisha's View

If you were to ask Elisha, she would tell you that she absolutely loves her job. Working in the student union of the local community college allows her to earn money and hang out with her new friends, two of her favorite activities. Sitting in her wheelchair behind the coffee counter, she is famous for providing the best cup of java on campus. Still, Elisha wants more than anything to enroll—along with her friends—in classes that interest her. As with most new endeavors, many questions swirl around in Elisha's head: How would I find my classes? What should I do when I get there? Would the classrooms accommodate my wheelchair?

Ms. Miranda's View

Ms. Miranda was so proud of how independent Elisha had become at her job at the community college after just 3 short months. As Elisha's transition teacher, Ms. Miranda had worked hard to find opportunities for Elisha to be successful in the community. So when Elisha mentioned that she would like to take classes such as Theater Arts along with the friends she had made at the college, Ms. Miranda thought it was an awesome idea. As Ms. Miranda began to brainstorm ideas for including Elisha in community college courses, she focused her thoughts on ways of providing supports that were as typical as possible. She realized that having a special assistant in class would be awkward for Elisha. Besides, so many potential environmental supports were already available to Elisha. There were signs in the bookstore indicating which text to purchase for a class, maps that could guide Elisha around campus, and friends to help adapt assignments for her. And Elisha already knew how to use her tablet computer to schedule her daily activities. In fact, if they tapped into many of the supports that were already available within the campus environment, they would have to add very few additional supports that would be atypical.

IDENTIFYING EXISTING SUPPORTS AND POTENTIAL BARRIERS

For many students, a gamut of opportunities opens up upon their graduation from high school. With careful planning and support, you can help ensure that these opportunities will be available to all students. The first step is to conduct a site visit to survey those likely settings in which your students will live, work, study, and recreate after graduation to help you identify supports that will assist your students in gaining access to these opportunities and to enhance full participation in adult life.

"Surveying the particular environment will help you identify what resources may be available to the student. Then, use these resources to help support a student."

Teacher, Maplewood High School

Conducting a Site Visit

You will begin by visiting and observing each setting in which a student will participate during postschool life following graduation or school exit. Your job is to uncover all signs of support, such as friendly co-workers, accessible buildings, or posted bus routes, as well as possible barriers requiring modification within the settings a student is likely to frequent, such as a worksite, library, or restaurant. As you visit, be sure to complete an environmental survey, such as the Job Analysis Survey (Form 3.1), to identify the demands of the setting and its potential supports. You will then use the survey findings as you observe your student to check how well he is doing in relation to these demands and to match supports to his individual needs.

After completing the survey in the selected settings for your student, prioritize the demands required at a job, community site, or college campus, and place them in order of importance. Focus on the most critical demands first. For example, if is important to be neat and clean on the job but this is a problem for a student, then you likely should focus on hygiene first. Remember to also ask family members, employers, and others about the unique requirements of a particular setting, many of which may not be apparent at first glance. For example, you thought production rate was the most important consideration at a worksite, but, instead, accuracy is actually valued more. Teacher-recommended strategies for conducting environmental surveys include the following.

- You can easily modify the Job Analysis Survey to use at school, in the community, or at home. For example, the "job task requirements" item on the survey can be changed to "academic task requirements," and "co-worker support" can be changed to "peer support" for use in the classroom.

- It is not always necessary to develop or modify environmental surveys on your own. A number of published assessments already exist that you may or may not need to modify. (See Resources at the end of the chapter.)

- As you complete the last page of the Job Analysis Survey, which asks you to break down a required task—such as navigating from the cafeteria to world history class—into its component steps, jot down potential sources of support for each step of the task. For example, a student could learn to use the school counselor's office door as one of a series of guides on the way to class, or a restaurant may have pictures of salad choices on a menu for a student to use when ordering a meal.

- Employment, educational, residential, and recreational personnel may be unaware of restricted accessibility that may exist, such as narrow hallways, stairs, or the small type that

Worksite: __Donaldson's Food and Drug Store__   Date: __November 17__

Basic Information

1. General job type or position: __Stock person__

2. Job tasks involved in the position: __Tasks include examining shelves for empty slots, reading shelf tags, writing__ down low-count/missing items, locating items in storeroom, reading box labels, loading boxes on cart, cutting open boxes, matching items to shelf tags, stocking items on shelves, blocking shelves, breaking down boxes, and returning waste and materials to proper places.

Three most time-consuming job tasks: __Locating items in storeroom, loading boxes, and stocking items__

3. Worksite location and access to public transportation: __Site is located on Reed Street, in Millner Shopping Center__ (walking distance from the classroom). During the day, Joseph's job coach will transport him back and forth to the site 2 days per week. Joseph will also be able to use the public bus system. There is a bus stop in front of the store and within 1 mile of Joseph's home. As the distance between his home and the store is not large, a taxi would also be a financially reasonable option.

Task Characteristics

Job task requirements: __Worker must recognize areas in need of stocking, use reading/writing abilities (or alterna-__ tive way of recording low-count and missing items), reach high shelves, understand the storeroom's organization, lift boxes and place them on cart, match item numbers and names to shelf numbers/names, place items on the shelf in a neat manner, reorganize messy shelves, locate out-of-place items, break down boxes, clean up area, initiate work, and ask for help.

General mobility requirements: __Worker must have a method for moving up and down aisles, a method for reaching__ high shelves (through reaching or assistive device), a method for reaching low shelves, the ability to use arms and hands, a method for lifting boxes of light to heavy weight and moving them to a cart, and a method for pulling a cart from the storeroom to the floor.

Physical demands—gross motor: __Demands include bending down, reaching up, balancing, moving up and down__ aisles, lifting full and broken-down boxes, pushing boxes aside in the storeroom, pulling all items simultaneously to the front of a shelf, opening large boxes, and pushing carts.

Physical demands—fine motor: __Demands include using pencil/paper to record items, using a box cutter, opening__ boxes, placing items on or removing items from shelves (grasping), stacking items, shuffling items on shelves, and balancing on the balls of the feet.

(page 1 of 4)

Form 3.1.   Job Analysis Survey for Donaldson's Food and Drug Store. (From Renzaglia, A., & Hutchins, M. [2005]. Materials developed for *A model for longitudinal vocational programming for students with moderate and severe disabilities.* Grant funded by the U.S. Department of Education, Office of Special Education and Rehabilitation Services; adapted by permission.) (A blank, photocopiable version of this form is included on the accompanying CD-ROM.)

Length of work tasks: Stocking shelves is a continuous process. The length of time to finish isolated tasks varies depending on the items being stocked, the condition of the storeroom, and the day of the week (trucks deliver inventory on Tuesday and Thursday). For a given aisle, time required to identify missing items is about 8 minutes. Time required to locate and gather items for that aisle is about 15 minutes. Time required to stock those items is as much as 40 minutes. Cleanup takes 5 minutes.

Variability of daily job tasks: Although the routine is generally the same from day to day, the items to be stocked vary considerably each day. Certain items, however, must be restocked at least every day (e.g., milk, eggs, specials). Variability is highly determined by the section of the store to which the employee is assigned.

Problem-solving requirements: Worker must have the ability to recognize which shelves need additional items, determine how to shift items in the storeroom to retrieve boxes on the bottom of stacks, determine the stocking pattern for individual shelves, and decide what should be done with extra items that shelves can't accommodate. Worker needs a method for working quickly without damaging items; the ability to stack boxes on a cart without crushing them; and the ability to creatively reorganize shelves in appropriate ways.

Production rate requirements: Worker must be able to work continuously on task for the duration of the shift. Although variability makes it difficult to attach an exact number on production rate, the average worker completes approximately 20 boxes per hour. Employer's main concern is that empty shelves and specials are restocked immediately and that old stock is put out prior to new stock arriving.

Work product quality requirements: All items should be stocked until shelves are full. All shelves should be blocked (all items pulled forward so shelves appear full). All items must match shelf tags. All shelves should have a neat appearance and design. All materials should be returned upon completion, and the storeroom should be kept neat and orderly.

Continuous working requirements: Worker will continuously stock shelves, except during designated work breaks and trips to the storeroom to reload a pull-cart. Worker will continuously place items on shelf until each box is emptied.

Task-Related Characteristics

Co-worker presence/task-related contact: Except for brief interactions with other employees (particularly other stock people), the worker will work alone. Other employees are almost always within sight or hearing distance and will frequently walk past the area in which the student is working. Most interaction with other stock people occurs in the stockroom.

Non–task-related social contacts while working: Occasionally, another stock person will be working on the same aisle as the student, during which non–task-related interactions are appropriate (as long as it is not overly loud or of an inappropriate subject). Student will also have breaks during which he will likely interact with other store employees.

Social atmosphere of worksite: ___As the worker will be working the majority of the time on the floor of the store, he will be in the presence of scores of customers who are shopping and a few other employees as they work (often stock people and courtesy clerks).___

Interactions with customers: ___Interactions with store customers are likely to be frequent. He will have to move out of the way of many customers and will probably be asked to help others locate particular items.___

Supervisory contact: ___Initially, the job coach/trainer will work closely with the student, gradually fading his or her presence and checking in on the student about every 10–15 minutes. His actual job supervisor will be another, more experienced stock person, who will check on his work approximately every 30–45 minutes initially.___

Environmental Characteristics

Distraction level (noise/visual): ___The noise and visual levels vary depending on time and day of the week. Busy times in the store can get extremely noisy, and the aisles get especially crowded. Most of the stocking is done at relatively quiet times of day, however, with few distractions.___

Comfort factors (temperature, space available, lighting, odor, sensory): ___The temperature is comfortable throughout the store, except in the frozen foods, dairy, produce, and meat sections of the store. There is usually little work space available as the aisles tend to be crowded with customers. The lighting is artificial but more than adequate. Odor factors are only an issue near the seafood and florist sections and when certain food containers break.___

Equipment/tool use requirements: ___Worker will use one pull-cart, box cutter, milk crate/stepladder, pad of paper, and pencil/pen.___

Natural Supports

Environmental support: ___Weekly and daily job schedules are posted above time clock. Shelf tags tell employees where items are located and how many fit on a shelf. Labels on boxes can be matched to shelf tags. Storeroom is organized to match the store's aisles. Pull-carts are available to avoid heavy lifting. Milk crate/stepladders are available for reaching high locations. Clocks are located throughout the store. City bus stop is located outside the store.___

Supervisor and co-worker support: ___New employee training is typically carried out by co-workers. Employees typically work in pairs when stocking particular aisles. Co-workers often carpool to work together. Supervisors are always on-site to provide assistance and answer questions. Job tasks are flexible and supervisor is very willing to rearrange assignments. Numerous opportunities for socialization exist (e.g., during break time, after work, employee softball team).___

Job Task Analysis

	Approximate times	Tasks performed
1	10 seconds	Clock in.
2	30 seconds	Gather all necessary supplies (box cutter, notepad, pen).
3	2 minutes	Find and ask supervisor with which aisle to begin.
4	1 minute	Go to assigned aisle.
5	10 seconds	Look for first empty/near-empty shelf space on right side.
6	20 seconds	Read shelf label, locate item number, and record item number on notepad.
7	4 minutes	Repeat Steps 5 and 6 until all empty/near-empty spaces on right are located.
8	4 minutes	Repeat Steps 5 and 6 for all empty/near-empty spaces on left of aisle.
9	1 minute	Go to storeroom.
10	30 seconds	Bring pull-cart to area where needed items are stored.
11	1 minute	Locate box containing the first item on the list.
12	15 seconds	Place box on pull-cart.
13	15 minutes	Repeat Steps 11 and 12 for each subsequent item on the list until pull-cart is full.
14	2 minutes	Bring loaded pull-cart to assigned aisle.
15	15 seconds	Remove first box from cart and read item number.
16	1 minute	Match item number to shelf tag number.
17	15 seconds	Open the box.
18	2 minutes	Remove items and place them on the shelf.
19	1 minute	Block shelf area that has just been stocked.
20	15 seconds	Break down empty box.
21	40 minutes	Repeat Steps 15–20 until all items on the pull-cart have been stocked.
22	2 minutes	Gather all empty boxes and place them on the pull-cart.
23	2 minutes	Bring pull-cart back to storeroom.
24	2 minutes	Dump cardboard in the trash area.
25	—	Repeat Steps 10–24 until all items on the list have been stocked.
26	—	Repeat Steps 3–24 until shift is completed.
27	10 seconds	Clock out.

Emily George

Person completing the form

Leslie Erikson

Signature of employer or supervisor

appears on instructional materials. By sharing the results of your environmental survey and student observations, you may discover that many businesses, schools, and organizations are willing to make modifications.

Completing a Job Analysis Survey

"Finding time to visit worksites and community settings is difficult. Because I don't have time to visit all areas and write down my findings, I develop a checklist of environmental features that assistants or others can use to observe."

Teacher, Gallatin High School

ASSESSMENT

Assessing Outcomes: Job Analysis Survey

Throughout high school, students with diverse abilities should be provided with opportunities to sample a variety of different job or career exploration experiences (Carter, Austin, & Trainor, 2011). Once a potential worksite has been identified for a student, the next important task is to acquire information about the environmental, social, and task characteristics of the worksite. By identifying potential supports available in the work environment, students' opportunities for independence and success on the job are increased (Cimera, 2007). Furthermore, by pinpointing these supports early, teachers, employers, or job coaches can incorporate them into on-the-job training from the beginning. The following steps should be followed when conducting a Job Analysis Survey.

- Begin by identifying several potential worksites, taking into consideration factors such as distance from home or school, the number of students that the site can accommodate, the number and variety of jobs available, and the projected availability of such jobs after graduation.

- After identifying several initial training sites, select a site that differs from what your students have previously experienced in terms of the task and social and environmental characteristics. This will allow students to have a wide variety of job experiences and enable them to find a job or career opportunity that matches both their preferences and their skills.

- Use the Job Analysis Survey to record information regarding the task, social and environmental characteristics of the site, and sources for support. Form 3.1 is a completed Job Analysis Survey for Joseph, the young man who will be described in Case Study 3.2. A blank, reproducible form is found on the accompanying CD-ROM.

- The Job Analysis Survey is divided into six sections. The first section, Basic Information, asks questions related to the job position, job tasks, and location of the particular job being surveyed. The second section, Task Characteristics, is a detailed analysis of the tasks required for the job, such as fine and gross motor skill demands and problem-solving requirements. Task-Related Characteristics relate to the social aspects of the work setting being surveyed, such as opportunities to interact with co-workers or customers and level of supervisory contact. The Environmental Characteristics section requires observing physical conditions of the work setting, such as temperature, lighting, and noise level that may affect a worker. To complete the Natural Supports section, observe or ask the student or others in the work setting to identify naturally occurring supports that exist for a worker, such as posted schedules or employee training programs, even if the student is not currently gaining access to these supports. The final section, Job Task Analysis, requires observing a worker completing a required task and breaking the task into its component parts. Alternately, you can complete the task yourself as you write down each step as you perform it.

- Information for the Job Analysis Survey can be obtained from several sources. For example, managers or immediate supervisors can readily share job characteristics and expectations. Observing other employees performing the job can also provide important information. Finally, job coaches and teachers can perform the job themselves.

Case Study 3.2 *Joseph Gets a Job*

Joseph, a recent graduate of Woodcock High School, has been a student in the district's community-based transition classroom for a little more than 5 months. After sampling several jobs around the community, Joseph indicated he had an interest in working at a local grocery store. He just seemed to get excited every time he went shopping or whenever he "faced cans" at his job-training site at the store. In preparation for job placement and training, Joseph's job coach, Ms. George, spent one morning talking with and observing employees working on a variety of tasks at Donaldson's Food and Drug Store. Next, she completed a Job Analysis Survey, noting many of the potential supports that would be available. Finally, she had the store manager look through the survey, filling in missing information. The process allowed her to identify the store manager's expectations while identifying supports that would provide Joseph with a greater opportunity for success and independence.

"When looking for sources of support for a student, you must check all environments: school, home, and work. At school, you must check that the classroom is located near other general education classes, the lunchroom, and break area. The home will require home visits. While you are visiting the home, find out what is important to the family. For example, our community is known as the 'Nursery Capital of the World.' If a student's family is in the nursery business, find out whether the family wants this for their child and whether this is what the child wants.

Also, you must check to determine whether the home is accessible to the child. For example, one student requires an electric wheelchair at school for transportation, but the home is not accessible. In this case, get vocational rehabilitation or the state agency that serves people with intellectual disabilities to build a ramp so that the chair can be used at home and in the community.

The work situation must be safe for the student, too. For example, one student with pica (a condition that causes him to eat anything he sees) eats out of the toilet. You could ask an employee to check the bathroom each day and clean and remove from the bathroom anything that might be harmful before the student uses the bathroom."

Teacher, Warren County High School

ASSESSING STUDENTS' ENVIRONMENTAL SUPPORT NEEDS

"I use observations that have been completed by school staff, employment personnel, and family members to identify support available in an environment. Also, I ask them to identify support needed and suggestions for modifying the environment."

Teacher, Riverside High School

Observing Students' Performance

After identifying the demands and available supports at a particular job, community site, or classroom, it is important to observe your students' behavior in those settings. Completing a Work Performance Evaluation (Form 3.2) in conjunction with the Job Analysis Survey will assist you in identifying your students' strengths, needs, and preferences and the supports available to your students in order to build an effective support plan for them. As with the Job Analysis Survey, a Work Performance Evaluation can be adapted for any setting. For example, items such as "general mobility requirements" or "variability of daily tasks" apply as readily to a classroom setting as to a worksite.

"To observe my students' performance, I get them involved in many school and community activities, such as clubs. Then I observe them to find out how they get along and ways in which they participate."

Teacher, South Side High School

ASSESSMENT

Assessing Outcomes: Work Performance Evaluation

After completing the Job Analysis Survey, the next step is to observe the student actually performing the specific job or task. The Work Performance Evaluation is used to summarize how the student performs under the various environmental, social, and task demands of the job in relation to available supports. Each step of the targeted job routine and features of the environment are recorded in the first of three columns using information derived from the Job Analysis Survey. In the next (middle) column titled Performance, indicate the student's observed performance level in relation to the job requirements. Finally, in the last column (Implications), record the implications of the student's performance and potential supports available to the student that may enable him to complete the routine more independently and successfully. Such supports can include those that are typically available to other employees (natural supports) or those that must be created or modified by the teacher, employer, or job coach.

The Work Performance Evaluation can easily be adapted for use in a school, community, or home setting to assess a student's performance, strengths, preferences, and support needs. For example, all settings can be surveyed to identify naturally occurring supports and physical characteristics, such as lighting or visual distractions. Follow these steps to use the Job Analysis Survey with the Work Performance Evaluation to assess your students' environmental support needs.

- Use the Job Analysis Survey you completed as a checklist of skills to observe as your student performs required job tasks. The survey will guide you to identify a range of skills that are required on most jobs, such as fine and gross motor skills, problem-solving skills, ability to vary order of tasks, and getting along with co-workers or customers.

- Carefully record those areas in which students demonstrate skill strengths and areas in which students need support. For example, you may find out that a student can work continuously on required tasks without being distracted but "falls apart" when there are variations in task requirements. Breaking down a job into its specific requirements can help you identify exactly where a student's strengths and needs lie.

- Using observations completed by school staff, employers, and family members is an excellent way to supplement the information you gather. Because you cannot be present in all settings, teach others what to look for in a student's performance, and learn to rely on their observations and perceptions in addition to the information you have gathered.

- As you watch a student, also note the different types of resources that are available, such as social support, environmental supports, or job modifications. If your observations reveal the

FORM 3.2

Work Performance Evaluation

Student: __Joseph__   Date: __January 9__

Worksite: __Donaldson's Food and Drug Store__   Evaluator: __Emily George__

Job task requirements	Performance	Implications
Recognize areas needing stocking	Joseph easily pointed out shelves that were clearly empty but had trouble with half-empty shelves.	Teach Joseph to understand all of the information on the shelf tag, especially the information that indicates number of items per box.
Basic reading/writing abilities	His reading/writing abilities are adequate. He relies too much on visual comparison for item placement rather than on reading labels.	Provide Joseph with a written routine to help remind him to read labels and shelf tags prior to placing items.
Means for reaching high shelves	Joseph is of average height and can't reach the back of top shelves without help. When he tries, he knocks items over.	Show Joseph how to safely use a milk crate or small stepladder to stock high items.
Understand storeroom organization	Because Joseph is still new, he doesn't yet understand the storeroom's organization.	The storeroom is well organized and easy to understand. It won't be hard for him to learn.
Lift boxes/place them on carts	He complains that boxes are too heavy but has no difficulty lifting them.	Teach Joseph to lift only one box at a time and to use his safety belt.
Match items to correct shelf tag	Joseph says reading the tags is a waste of time when he can just match the items.	Show Joseph how to evaluate the accuracy of his work.
Place items on shelf neatly	Joseph is extremely neat, but it affects his work rate.	Show him how to balance quality with speed.
Reorganize messy shelves	Joseph likes "fixing up the shelves nice" and does an excellent job.	Joseph seems to like organizing things.
General mobility requirements	Performance	Implications
Method for moving up and down aisles	Joseph can walk up and down the aisles.	He can work long periods of time without getting tired.
Method for reaching high shelves	Joseph tried to reach shelves he clearly couldn't reach and knocked items over.	Teach Joseph to use adaptive equipment such as ladders or milk crates.
Method for reaching low shelves	Joseph's back became extremely tired.	Show him basic safety techniques.
Method for lifting boxes and moving to cart	Joseph complained about the heavy boxes.	Avoid jobs requiring heavy lifting in future.
Method for pulling carts from storeroom	Joseph performs this job in the same way as other employees.	Joseph said he liked to do jobs "like other people do them." Fitting in is really important to Joseph.

(page 1 of 5)

Form 3.2.   Work Performance Evaluation for Joseph. (From Renzaglia, A., & Hutchins, M. [2005]. Materials developed for *A model for longitudinal vocational programming for students with moderate and severe disabilities.* Grant funded by the U.S. Department of Education, Office of Special Education and Rehabilitation Services; adapted by permission.) (A blank, photocopiable version of this form is included on the accompanying CD-ROM.)

Physical demands—gross motor	Performance	Implications
Bending down	His back got tired toward the end of the shift. He quickly gave up on bottom shelves.	Future jobs requiring frequent bending over should be avoided.
Reaching up	No problems	
Balancing	No problems	
Moving up and down aisles	Joseph can walk up and down aisles on his own.	It appears Joseph enjoys jobs where he can walk around. He dislikes stationary tasks.
Lifting full/broken-down boxes	When the distance required to lift a full box was short, Joseph complained very little.	Help show Joseph how to unload his cart as he moves down the aisle, rather than having to transfer items from one end to the other.

Physical demands—fine motor	Performance	Implications
Using paper/pencil to record items	He has good writing skills.	To save time, show Joseph some shorthand.
Using a box cutter	He doesn't follow safety rules.	Emphasize safety rules at the workplace.
Opening boxes	No problems	This skill will be useful for him at other jobs.
Placing/removing items on/from shelves	Joseph has excellent control and can work well in small areas.	Future jobs requiring strong fine motor abilities should remain open for Joseph.
Stacking items	He is able to stack food items up to four high.	Future jobs requiring strong fine motor abilities should remain open for Joseph.
Shuffling items on shelves	No problems	
Balancing on balls of feet	No problems	

Length of work tasks	Performance	Implications
Stocking shelves continuously	Joseph has a difficult time staying on task. He stocked about half a box on his own before finding something else he was interested in.	Joseph doesn't perform well in highly distractible jobs. Also, the initial novelty of any job will likely result in difficulty for Joseph to stay on task.
Recording needed items	Joseph takes about twice as long to record items.	Teach him time-saving techniques to improve his work pace.
Locating/gathering items in storeroom	Joseph was initially slow, but he is picking it up quickly.	He learns quickly when things are organized.
Cleaning up	Joseph usually cleans up very quickly.	

Variability of daily job tasks	Performance	Implications
Routine is generally the same day to day	The routine of stocking is very predictable for Joseph. He is currently focusing on a small section of the store before moving on to other areas. Joseph enjoys the variety of patterns, items, and displays on which he gets to work.	Less variability certainly makes Joseph work more quickly. He really seems to enjoy novel things, however, and likes to ask questions about "unknowns." An ideal future job would definitely balance the predictability of routine with the novelty of variety.

Problem-solving requirements	Performance	Implications
Recognizing shelves needing stocking	He easily pointed out clearly empty shelves but had trouble with half-empty shelves.	Teach him to read information on shelf tags that indicates the number of items a shelf holds.
Means for shifting boxes in storeroom	Joseph knocked several boxes over while trying to pull out the bottom box.	Show Joseph how to move boxes in safe and effective ways.
Determining stocking patterns for shelves	He followed the established shelf patterns.	Joseph does very well when he has a model.
Deciding what to do with extra items	Joseph asked a co-worker for help.	Joseph asks the same questions repeatedly and has some difficulty generalizing advice.
Stacking boxes	No problems	

Production rate requirements	Performance	Implications
Works continuously on task for the entire shift	He had a very difficult time staying on task. He was constantly finding items he wanted to look at. He would stock about half of a box before stopping to look at something else.	Joseph doesn't perform well in highly distractible jobs.
Average of 20 boxes per hour	Initially, he was slow, but he is improving his pace with more experience.	The main concern is keeping Joseph on task. Jobs that require a lot of independent work will require a lot of initial supervision.

Work product quality requirements	Performance	Implications
Stock items until shelves are full	No problems	
Block shelves neatly	No problems	
All items match shelf tags	Because he matches items, he often puts similar looking items in the wrong place.	Teach Joseph to evaluate the quality of his work.
All shelves have neat design/appearance	Joseph is extremely neat and careful to make sure the shelves look nice.	
All materials returned upon completion	He did a great job.	
Storeroom kept neat and orderly	Joseph makes very little mess in the storeroom.	It is actually someone else's job to keep this area clean.

Continuous working requirements	Performance	Implications
Continuously stock shelves (except for breaks and trips to storeroom)	As previously mentioned, Joseph has a difficult time staying on task. He is very distracted by things and people around him.	Joseph doesn't perform well on highly distractible job tasks. He is more likely to be successful at jobs with consistent, understandable routines.

Co-worker presence/task-related contact	Performance	Implications
The job is primarily one in which the employee works alone.	Joseph had a difficult time working alone when he was supposed to. Instead, he would go to other co-workers and bombard them with numerous questions.	Although asking for help is a good quality, knowing when not to is also important. Joseph may have trouble staying on task in environments that involve working too closely with another employee. Moreover, Joseph tends to prevent other employees from doing their jobs effectively.
Non–task-related social contacts while working	**Performance**	**Implications**
Only occasional interactions with co-workers outside of breaks	Joseph has had little opportunity to interact socially with other co-workers because he has had to return to the transition classroom upon completion of his work.	Joseph says that the thing he enjoys most about work is talking to his co-workers. Future jobs that offer such opportunities would likely be enjoyed most by Joseph.
Social atmosphere of worksite	**Performance**	**Implications**
Employee works in the presence of numerous customers	The areas in which Joseph worked were constantly entered by customers and other employees. He greeted very few of them.	Joseph needs to be taught appropriate ways to interact with customers (socially acceptable behavior) and may need help overcoming some of his shyness with them.
Interactions with customers	**Performance**	**Implications**
Interactions with customers are quite frequent	Numerous customers entered the area in which Joseph was working, but he initiated no conversations and offered few greetings.	Again, Joseph needs to be taught appropriate ways to interact with customers (socially acceptable behavior) and may need help overcoming some of his shyness with them.
Supervisory contact	**Performance**	**Implications**
Supervisor checks in approximately every 30–45 minutes	Joseph is quick to ask for assistance for every problem he encounters (big or small), often monopolizing the time of his supervisors.	More experience on the job should reduce the large number of questions Joseph has. He is well liked by his supervisor, and he would likely work well with supervisors at future jobsites.
Distraction level	**Performance**	**Implications**
Noise levels Visual distractions	No problems As mentioned before, Joseph was distracted by all of the food items that he had questions about. This keeps him off task for a large percentage of time.	Joseph might work better in a place with fewer visual distractions or when he is given opportunities prior to or after work to ask questions.

Comfort factors	Performance	Implications
Temperature	No problems: Joseph is working in neither the frozen foods nor refrigerated sections.	
Space available	Joseph tends to spread out a little more than space will allow, making it difficult for customers to get around him.	Teach Joseph to make better use of his workspace by organizing his materials more efficiently.
Lighting	No problems	
Odor/sensory	No problems, except in the produce section.	

Equipment/tool use requirements	Performance	Implications
Pull-cart	No problems	
Box cutter	Joseph had no problems using the cutter but didn't adhere to safety rules.	Supervisor will need to emphasize safety rules at the workplace.
Milk crate/stepladder	Joseph is able, but reluctant, to use them.	Show Joseph the benefits of certain adaptive equipment and the ways in which they can make his job easier.
Pad of paper/pen	No problems	

Environmental support	Performance	Implications
Job schedules	Joseph picked up using his schedule fairly quickly.	
Shelf tags	Joseph is able to read them, but prefers not to use them.	Teach Joseph to use shelf tags to evaluate his work.
Box labels	No problems	
Stockroom organization	Joseph is learning to navigate the stockroom.	
Pull-carts	Joseph has some trouble stacking items.	Provide specific instruction regarding how to use the equipment correctly.
Time clocks	Joseph has difficulty reading the clocks.	Provide instruction on reading time.

Supervisor and co-worker support	Performance	Implications
Training carried out by co-workers	Joseph really enjoyed his trainer—a college student around his age.	In future jobs, Joseph would likely prefer to be trained by his co-workers rather than solely by a job coach.
Co-worker carpool	Joseph rides the community bus.	
Supervisor presence	Joseph asks numerous questions of his supervisor throughout his shift.	Joseph would do well at jobs in which the supervisor is frequently present and willing to answer questions.
Opportunities for socialization	Joseph loves hanging out in the break room.	Encourage frequent opportunities for Joseph to meet with co-workers.

(page 5 of 5)

student is not performing according to the expectations of the job, then you will already have identified potential sources of support that could be introduced to assist the student.

- See Observing Students' Performance in Chapter 2 for additional ideas.

Form 3.2 is a completed Work Performance Evaluation for Joseph, the student involved in community-based training at a grocery store. A blank, reproducible version is included on the accompanying CD-ROM.

LEGISLATION

In completing an environmental assessment, such as the Job Analysis Survey and the Work Performance Evaluation, you are in compliance with the requirements of IDEA 2004 for conducting "age appropriate transition assessments related to training, education, employment, and, where appropriate, independent living skills" (§ 614). This requirement means that you must evaluate a student's performance on the job and in other contexts in relation to the demands and environmental conditions of the worksite, home, and other relevant settings.

"If a job task has several pieces and can be arranged on a table in front of the worker, watch to see how that individual performs the job. Then make changes, if needed, so the worker is not wasting time on each movement."

Transition teacher, Nashville Public Schools

Interviewing Families and Important Others

Interviewing individuals involved in the lives of students allows you to create a comprehensive picture of the supports currently available in these students' everyday settings. Establishing open lines of communication with important others is imperative for acquiring critical information about support at the worksite, in the classroom, or in the community that is not available through direct observation (Sitlington & Clark, 2007). Meeting with family members may be the only way to determine what they value and what their attitudes are regarding their child's future employment, social, recreational, and residential possibilities. Without knowing what parents think, you may be in danger of assuming that you always know what is best for a student—particularly with students from cultures that differ from yours.

"I think it is important to take the time to explain to people about our purpose in helping students with the transition from school to the working world. We need to answer their questions and assist them in understanding our program."

Teacher, Pearl-Cohn High School

Interviewing family members can help you determine a student's preferences, as well as the types of supports he is already provided at home. Families may have developed a communication system using pictures or symbols, which you could use at school or in the community, or they may have taught a student to use a timer and a checklist while completing his homework. Or you may find out that the student really does not like pizza, which you had been trying to use as reinforcement for getting his work done.

Conversations with employers and community agencies can help others in a setting think about a student's support needs and potential solutions of which they may not have been aware. For example, you may assume a student's college instructor is not concerned if a student is having difficulty hearing a lecture, but it may be that the instructor does not know this is a challenge for the student. Brainstorming with the student and instructor can produce potential solutions to address the situation, such as preprinted lecture notes. Communication is the answer to many challenges—interviews may even allow you to apply available resources to student needs in other environments. For example, adaptations that parents say they use for helping their child complete chores at home, such as an adapted broom or picture schedule, could be used at a potential job-training site.

Developing Cultural Sensitivity

When communicating with your students' families, you are likely to encounter many people who have different perspectives from yours, who are English language learners, or who are from different cultural or economic backgrounds. Students from racially and ethnically diverse groups make up an increasing proportion of the public school population. In the South and several western states, White students are now in the minority (National Center for Education Statistics, 2007; Suitts, 2010). By 2020, most U.S. public school students are expected to be of color and from low-income families (National Center for Education Statistics, 2006; Suitts, 2010). IDEA 2004 requires you, as a teacher, to be responsive to the growing needs of an increasingly diverse society and school population. A first step is simply to practice listening with an open mind to another's point of view. The Home Inventory (Form 2.5) in Chapter 2 is useful as a guide in conducting interviews with family members.

"In communicating with community members, the first priority should be to promote what the student with special needs can give to the community. Focus on the positive. As a result, positive change and support will follow."

Teacher, Cleveland High School

DEVELOPING INDIVIDUAL SUPPORT PLANS

Environmental support plans are the product of environmental assessments and communication with individuals who are important to the student. These plans give focus and direction to instruction in the community, in school, on the job, or across a college campus. At the same time, they assist a student in becoming as independent, successful, and happy as possible. Support plans must be designed to address the individual characteristics of students and their work, home, or community settings. By recognizing that supports designed for one context or individual may not be effective for another context or individual, teachers and job coaches can devise plans that meet the unique needs of each student.

Developing Effective Support Plans

"In order to identify environmental support, you need to make a home visit. You must find out about family members' attitudes toward having the student work. Will they support it? If not, why not? Do they work? It may be that there is not anyone to help the student get up every morning to go to work—an alarm clock may be needed. The student may also need to learn to fix a simple breakfast. You must also visit the worksite to identify needed changes. For example, you may find there is a better place for the student to sit or stand to prevent potential problems from occurring. Moving a student's workstation so that it is not by a large window or door will help cut down on distractions if the student is easily distracted."

Transition coordinator, Metro Nashville Public Schools

As with all instructional programs, environmental support plans must be based on an assessment of the individual and his unique needs, strengths, and preferences as consistent with IDEA 2004. Remember to ask the student what he thinks about his own support needs. All support plans should be a product of site visits, student observations, and interviews, as previously discussed in this chapter. Using the information you have derived from these sources, you can be assured that you are building a support plan that is specific to a student and the settings in which he spends time, as well as reflects the values and preferences of the student and his family.

After identifying which supports are necessary, prioritize them in order of importance. Because you will not be able to address every need immediately, it is necessary to decide which are the most important. For example, if a young man is having toileting accidents in his auto tech class, you will need to address this issue before focusing on the legibility of his handwriting. The following strategies will be helpful in developing individually tailored support plans for your students.

- Environmental supports should be as similar as possible to those already present at a worksite. The more familiar the supports are, the fewer the differences that will exist between co-workers or classmates and students with varying abilities. For example, if co-workers are already using a "jig" to fold papers neatly, then why devise a new tool if this one also works for a student?

- Design support plans that include multiple settings, addressing a student's needs in school, at work, at home, and within the community. For example, if a student uses a wheelchair, then he will need accessible entrances, walkways, and hallways in all of these contexts. Another student may have time management needs and will need to have environmental cues, such as watching to see when his classmates leave for lunch, established across all environments.

- Survey the student's immediate neighborhood to learn what resources are available, such as an accessible bus route, a book club that meets at a local bagel shop, or a nearby self-service laundry. Keep a record of what you find, take the student to visit the places, and provide telephone numbers, addresses, a map, or a tablet computer to help the student use these resources.

- You will find the section called Developing Individual Social Support Plans in Chapter 4 helpful in incorporating social support—such as a cue from a bus driver when approaching a student's designated stop—into students' individual support plans.

LEGISLATION Developing an individual environmental support plan is consistent with the requirements of IDEA 2004 for the IEP. Specifically, the IEP must contain "a statement of the special education and related services and supplementary aids and services, based on peer-reviewed research to the extent practicable, to be provided to the child, or on behalf of the child, and a statement of the program modifications or supports for school personnel that will be provided for the child" (§ 614).

Case Study 3.3 *Jerome Gets a Support Plan*

Jerome Baxter had been looking forward to his support team meeting all week. This was his sophomore year at McClintock High, and already he had had three support team meetings just this year. What Jerome really liked about the meetings was that he was the one who got to do a lot of the talking. Mr. Blackstone, his special education teacher, and Jerome had been practicing what he was going to say. First, he would introduce himself and the members of his support team—even his mom and dad. Because he couldn't say all their names (or remember them, for that matter), each team member would sit where his or her name tag was displayed at the table. Then, when Jerome pointed to the members, they would hold up their name tag (with their picture and their name, of course) and say their name. Jerome would even hold up his name tag to introduce himself. Next, Jerome would present the support goals that he and the team had developed and had been working on this quarter. (Form 3.3 is Jerome's completed Individual Support Plan.) Jerome and Mr. Blackstone had been looking at each goal, deciding if it had been met or needed to be adjusted. When Jerome presented the goals at the meeting, he would hold up a card describing each goal in words and pictures. First, he would talk about his progress toward the goal, and then he would give everyone else a turn to give their input.

The goal Jerome was really excited to talk about was "Jerome will develop friendships in his classes and at work." When Jerome first started going into general education classes and to his community jobsites last year, it was true that he didn't feel like he had any friends. Those were not very happy days for Jerome—he felt like all he would do was sit by himself while everyone around him seemed to be talking to each other and having a good time. But now, Adam, Scott, and Ricardo helped him get from class to class, helped him do his work when they were in the same class, hung out with him in class and around school, and introduced him to their friends. Sometimes, they even did things after school or on the weekends together, such as going to the mall or the movies, watching McClintock's basketball games, or playing soccer. Last time, Jerome got to play goalkeeper and even made a "save" by catching the ball before it went through the goal posts. At his community jobsite at Marcino's Ice Cream Parlor, Mr. Owens was helping Jerome set up and clean the customers' tables. He even took Jerome to the break room when it was break time. They liked to sit around and joke with the other employees. Jerome also had been working on the goal "Jerome will sample jobs and express his preferences," and together he and Mr. Blackstone had decided that he would switch to an office job next semester. Jerome would miss Marcino's, but he liked trying different jobs so that he could decide which one he liked best by the time he was ready to leave high school.

Jerome had been practicing communicating all his other support goals too and he knew he could do a good job at his support team meeting. He was excited about sharing his progress and hearing what the team members had to say. Jerome was also looking forward to presenting a new goal that he and Mr. Blackstone had been developing together: "taking the bus downtown alone." Getting a ride with mom was okay, but Jerome really thought he was ready to go on his own. He loved going to Escapade Music to look for used CDs and posters but going with his mom just wasn't that "cool." Learning to transfer buses all by himself was Jerome's next big support goal. For a while he would have to go with his older brother to learn the route, but Jerome knew that, with a little support in the beginning, he would be ready to go to Escapade all on his own really soon.

From RUSCH, FRANK R., BEYOND HIGH SCHOOL: PREPARING ADOLESCENTS FOR TOMORROW'S CHALLENGES, 2nd Edition, © 2008. Adapted by permission of Pearson Education, Inc., Upper Saddle River, New Jersey.

Individual Support Plan

Support strategy	Goal	Action steps
Develop support in the setting		
Promote social acceptance	Jerome will be accepted as an equal participant in school and the community.	• Mr. Blackstone will observe and assess the extent to which Jerome is accepted in his classes and other school settings and in his community placements. • Mr. Blackstone will model including Jerome as an equal participant, as needed. • Mr. Blackstone will provide disability awareness information, as needed.
Increase environmental support	Jerome will learn to use exit signs and other markers to find his way.	• Adam, Scott, and Ricardo (Jerome's peer buddies) will help Jerome to use signs and markers to find his way around school and the community. • The peer buddies will fade their assistance as Jerome learns to find his way independently across different settings.
Increase social support	Jerome will develop friendships in his classes and at work.	• Adam, Scott, and Ricardo will help Jerome get to his classes, do his work in class, and befriend him in class. They also will attend school, extracurricular, and outside school events together. • Mr. Owens will help Jerome set up and clean tables at Marcino's Ice Cream Parlor. He will also take Jerome to the break room at break time and help him get to know and interact with his co-workers.
Increase student's competence		
Identify and promote student's strengths	Jerome will learn to ride the city bus downtown to shop by himself.	• Mr. Blackstone will provide Jerome with a color-coded bus schedule and map with pictures of destinations and transfer stations. • Jerome's brother, Matt, will accompany Jerome on his bus routes, decreasing his instructional assistance until Jerome can ride independently without getting lost.
Increase student's self-determination	Jerome will identify and communicate his support goals.	• Jerome will complete a goal-setting and evaluation sheet with his parents and Mr. Blackstone on a quarterly basis throughout the school year. • Jerome will role play communicating his support goals with Mr. Blackstone using pictures cards in order to present his goals at his support team meetings.
Increase student's choice and decision making	Jerome will sample three to five different jobs during his sophomore year and express his preferences.	• Mr. Blackstone will arrange a variety of community jobs for Jerome during the year that require different job skills. • Using a pictorial job preference assessment, Mr. Blackstone will assist Jerome in evaluating his job experiences and expressing his preferences.

(page 1 of 2)

Form 3.3. Jerome's Individual Support Plan. (From *RUSCH, FRANK R., BEYOND HIGH SCHOOL: PREPARING ADOLESCENTS FOR TOMORROW'S CHALLENGES. 2nd Edition,* © 2008. Adapted by permission of Pearson Education, Inc., Upper Saddle River, New Jersey.)

FORM 3.3. *(continued)*

Support strategy	Goal	Action steps
Promote student's social interaction	Jerome will increase his social interaction skills.	• Jerome will interact socially with his peer buddies, Adam, Scott, and Jerome, on a daily basis. They will also introduce Jerome to their friends and promote interactions among them. • Jerome's peer buddies will assist him in using his communication book in his classes, the lunchroom, and during extra-curricular activities. The peer buddies will also help Jerome learn to say new words.

(page 2 of 2)

Communicating Environmental Support Needs to Others

"Establish lines of communication with people significant to the student. Speak to parents, classroom teachers, students, co-workers, and employers to assess the levels of support that exist for the student."

Teacher, Hillcrest High School

LEGISLATION

Communicating with parents and others who are important to the student is part of your job. IDEA 2004 requires teachers to "assist parents to better understand the nature of their children's disabilities and their educational, developmental, and transitional needs; to communicate effectively and work collaboratively with personnel responsible for providing special education, early intervention services, transition services, and related services; and to obtain appropriate information about the range, type, and quality of options, programs, services, technologies, practices, and interventions based on scientifically based research, to the extent practicable, and resources available to assist children with disabilities and their families in school and at home" (§ 671).

Supports that are either available or needed will become much more evident when assessing both a student's performance and the demands of a particular setting. In preparation for building an individual support plan, teachers must communicate with others concerning ways of gaining access to and modifying those supports. Remember to talk with family members and teachers about the kinds of supports they are already providing to students. You may find out some ingenious and creative ideas, such as putting together socks of the same color in a drawer for a student with a visual impairment or having a student with an intellectual disability carry a photograph of the bus stop nearest home when riding the bus.

If necessary, suggest ways of strengthening or enhancing supports suggested by others. By ensuring that family members and others who are important to the student are active members of the assessment process from the beginning, you will increase the likelihood that they will be supportive of support plans developed by the IEP team. Keep families informed about your ideas; family involvement is critical to a student support plan (Cobb & Alwell, 2009; Povenmire-Kirk, Lindstrom, & Bullis, 2010). Additional strategies recommended by teachers for promoting communication about students' support needs include the following:

- Developing a support plan with parents and employers that can be carried out at home and work will ensure consistency in support in all of the settings in which a student is involved. It is more likely that the plan will be carried out when you let others have input in what is included and feel some ownership of the plan.

- Let others know about a student's needs. For example, an employer may not know that a student with learning disabilities has difficulty prioritizing tasks and needs assistance in organizing his day. Suggest ways in which others can help make the student's experiences more successful and satisfying.

- Encouraging all members of the student's IEP team—family members, general education teachers, job coach, employer, physical therapist, and so forth—to provide input into the support plan will help ensure that a complete picture of the student's needs is created. You cannot expect everyone to know everything about a student.

- Ask a student's general education peers for their ideas on modifying an environment to make it more accessible or supportive for the student. Their creative ideas may surprise you, such as a new style of backpack that helps a student organize his belongings or an easier way for a student to get from world history to commercial art class that avoids using the stairs.

- Regularly communicate a student's support needs to staff at vocational rehabilitation, the state agency that serves students with disabilities and other community agencies that provide support to the student. Interagency collaboration is the key to addressing all of a student's support needs.

GAINING ACCESS TO EXISTING ENVIRONMENTAL SUPPORTS

From the moment job- or community-based training begins for a student, attention should be focused on fading the involvement of the job coach or teacher (Cimera, 2007). Durable, natural supports should be introduced to lessen trainer assistance (Luecking, 2009). A variety of supports already exist in abundance throughout community, school, and work settings. Identifying and gaining access to these supports will result in more independence and acceptance of students with differing abilities.

Many individuals and agencies are available to provide this continued support. Using these services will allow a student to gain continued long-term success, independence, and acceptance on the job. Many of the supports that students need are not directly related to their job or academic performance but are critical to their personal satisfaction and quality of life. Examples of services you may need to help students find are transportation, personal care, a recreational program, or support staff. A first step is to secure a list of service providers available in the community. Often, supports are available from organizations that do not work solely with individuals with disabilities. These can include Rotary, Elk, Moose, Civitan, and Optimist organizations; the YMCA; Big Brothers and Big Sisters; local congregations; and Boys' and Girls' Clubs. Whenever possible, identify and use supports that are already available in worksite, community, or postsecondary education settings. Doing so ensures that supports will be as similar as possible to those that all people receive, such as an employee carpool, mentorship programs, or a campus recreation facility.

Establishing Interagency Collaboration

Ensuring the successful transition of a student from school to adult life often requires a large constellation of efforts. Fortunately, a number of organizations and agencies are designed to assist in this transition. IDEA 2004 requires that collaboration between school and community agencies ensures that all of a student's transition needs are met. Specifically, Section 612 of IDEA 2004 calls for interagency coordination to ensure that services are provided that deliver a free appropriate public education (FAPE) for all students with disabilities. These collaborative relationships can be helpful resources when identifying and gaining access to environmental supports in community and employment settings. Teachers suggest the following strategies for promoting collaboration.

- One step in building collaborative relationships is to assist community agencies in sharing information regarding the services they provide. You can help distribute brochures to families, schools, businesses, and community organizations; post information on a web site; or compile information into a short handbook.

- Involve agencies, such as vocational rehabilitation and other adult services, in the planning and implementation of students' support plans. If you expect these agencies to assist in the support process, then you need to involve them "up front" in the planning process.

- Members of community agencies can be excellent resources when identifying the steps required to achieve certain employment or career outcomes, such as learning a new trade. To the maximum extent possible, involve these people in the IEP meetings of students well before graduation.

- Vocational rehabilitation services may be a resource for acquiring funding for assistive devices used to support a student with diverse abilities in employment or postsecondary education. Be sure to check whether a student is eligible for services; if the student is not eligible, then begin the referral process immediately.

Incorporating Environmental Supports into Instruction

"In setting up a support plan, I replicate practices within each environment so that all are similar—this helps to promote generalization. I send home a survey for parents to fill out, and I visit the home, group home, or other residential placement and the workplace. Then I plan programming and materials so that all aspects are as similar as possible. For example, the washing machine at school and in the school's training apartment is the same model, and the table settings at home and school are the same. At school, we use the same time cards and clocks as do many of the businesses in town."

Teacher, Karns High School

If teachers, family members, service providers, and employers are not careful, then students may learn to depend on others for direction and assistance in the community and on the job. Teachers, job coaches, and others can expect students to become more independent by incorporating environmental supports into instruction (Luecking, 2008). In addition, using environmental supports during instruction will assist in the generalization of new skills, even in the teacher's absence (Stokes & Baer, 1977; Wehmeyer, Agran, et al., 2007).

Teaching students methods they can use for adapting their own environments can make a task easier and result in greater independence on the job or college campus and in the community. For example, if a young man with a physical disability has trouble reaching across a table to use the copy machine at work, then he could figure out how to rearrange the table. Or a college student with visual impairments could learn to enlarge the font on a computer to make instructional materials more accessible. Because responsibilities and expectations are likely to be changing constantly, reevaluation of an individual's support plan should be ongoing. In addition, a student's support needs will change over time as he learns new skills and faces new challenges, such as moving to a new neighborhood or applying for college. Teachers recommend the following strategies for incorporating supports into instruction.

- Try to make in-school instruction and materials as similar as possible to those in community-based and on-the-job training. For example, if teachers at school use photographs to help a student learn new task sequences, then it likely would be a good idea to do the same at work, at a community recreational site, or on the college campus.

- At work, support students in receiving the same training their co-workers receive, such as using a computer or e-mail program. Rather than introduce a new training program at a site, adapt programs that already exist, such as a worksite orientation program.

- Remember to inform parents, employers, and others what instructional supports are in use so that they can use them also.

ENHANCING ENVIRONMENTS TO PROMOTE PARTICIPATION

A worksite or school or community setting may need to be modified to promote optimal participation by a student. Doing so may mean introducing supports or materials or adapting the physical setting to promote student participation.

Providing Needed Materials

Providing appropriate materials to employees with differing abilities can assist them in completing their job more efficiently and successfully in a manner similar to that of their co-workers. These materials will assist a student in becoming a more active participant in daily life, whether in the community, on the college campus, or at home. Using materials that are typical of and valued naturally in these settings may decrease the need for outside assistance, further promoting the acceptance of the student (Nisbet & Hagner, 2000).

Identifying appropriate materials should be determined by matching the requirements of the setting (from the Job Analysis Survey) to the supports needed by the student (from the Work Performance Evaluation). For example, if you determine that a student is required to do considerable heavy lifting and bending on a job but does not have the physical strength, then you may decide to place heavy materials on a table rather than on the floor to make the job easier. Keep a student's social needs in mind as you decide which materials to provide a student in work or community environments. Any modified materials should promote social interactions, not hinder them. If using a shopping cart to deliver mail in an office makes a student stand out from his peers, then try for an adaptation that fits in better in the setting, such as a smaller pushcart. Or if students in a history class communicate with each other when at home by texting on their cell phones when working on a group project, teach your student the same skill on a cell phone so he can participate in the group.

Fortunately, many materials that are relatively inexpensive or homemade can act as effective adaptations (Job Accommodation Network, 2011). An electric stapler, a counting box, or a picture restaurant menu may be all that is necessary to allow a person increased independence. It is often not necessary to spend a lot of money for adaptations. Many companies provide common—or even ingenious—adaptive equipment and materials. Browsing through their catalogs can give you great ideas for making your own adaptations, or maybe you would like to purchase some already made. A wealth of information about adaptations can be found on the Job Accommodations Network web site listed in the resources section at the end of the chapter.

In addition, teachers report that they have used the following environmental modifications.

- Provide desks at the right height for each student. Have appropriate desks for people who are left-handed writers.

- If tables at a local restaurant are not high enough for wheelchairs to fit underneath, then work with the restaurant owners and help them adapt the eating areas.

- Provide a switch to students with multiple disabilities so that they can listen to CDs and watch DVDs. Learning how to use a switch to turn their music or movies on or off can help them control part of their environment.

- Use higher tables that accommodate students' wheelchairs to allow them to have access to computers.

- Provide wider spaces between office cubicles to accommodate students with physical impairments who may require assistance, such as those who use a cane or a wheelchair.

- Develop a nonstigmatizing jig or counting box so that students can count the correct number of items for packaging on the job, such as ceramic tiles or salt packages.

- Teach students to use applications on a tablet computer to gain access to menus for a favorite restaurant and to figure out the total cost of a meal before ordering.

TECHNOLOGY Technology is an increasingly important and prominent part of people's everyday lives. For youth with disabilities, these new and emerging technologies hold great promise for supporting them to participate more fully in the classroom, on the job, and at home. Research suggests that this promise is still only beginning to be fully realized. Wehmeyer, Palmer, Smith, Davies, and Stock (2008) reviewed 81 studies in which technology was implemented with individuals with intellectual disabilities. They identified 19 different types of technologies used in these studies, which they grouped into nine categories: 1) computers, 2) augmentative and alternative communication devices, 3) electronic and information technology (e.g., cell phones), 4) auditory prompting systems, 5) video-based systems, 6) handheld computers, 7) switches, 8) voice-recognition software, and 9) home appliances. Overall, these various approaches were fairly effective at improving outcomes across a range of settings.

Making Environmental Modifications

"We suggest that students in wheelchairs carry water bottles so they don't have to worry about drinking fountains they can't get to. We check with general education classroom teachers to discuss ways to modify the setting to adapt for students in wheelchairs. Sometimes they need assistance transferring to a regular chair; sometimes a specific table in the classroom can be used. Peers in the general education classroom are often very creative in adapting materials."

Teacher, Rutledge High School

LEGISLATION ADA 2008 states that, "individuals with disabilities continually encounter various forms of discrimination, including outright intentional exclusion, the discriminatory effects of architectural, transportation, and communication barriers, overprotective rules and policies, failure to make modifications to existing facilities and practices, exclusionary qualification standards and criteria, segregation, and relegation to lesser services, programs, activities, benefits, jobs, or other opportunities" (§ 12101). In response, ADA 2008 requires employers and operators of public services and accommodations to make "reasonable accommodations" for individuals' needs.

Environmental modifications typically have been used at the worksite for a variety of reasons, including increasing an employee's work rate or quality. Environmental modification, however, can also be used to increase an employee's independence and acceptance on the job as well as an individual's participation in everyday life in the community, such as dining at a restaurant, taking public transportation, or going to a concert (Cimera, 2007; Luecking, 2009).

In addition, IEPs for students must include a statement of the

> Supplementary aids and services, based on peer-reviewed research to the extent practicable, to be provided to the child, or on behalf of the child, and statement of the program modifications or supports for school personnel that will be provided for the child. (IDEA 2004, § 614)

Such supports should be used to assist students in attaining their annual goals and in achieving greater participation in general education and extracurricular activities. All decisions to modify the environment should be made in partnership with the individual using the modifications and other individuals in the setting to promote acceptance of the modifications. For example, if an employer changes the position of equipment in a computer repair shop to meet the needs of a student, then this modification will also affect co-workers in the shop. If the changes make their job more difficult, then this may be a problem for the entire repair shop crew.

Involving Others

In addition to the student, involve co-workers, peers, recreational staff, and others in brainstorming ways to adapt a setting. For example, at the worksite, co-workers are most likely to know the job best. Therefore, they may have practical ideas about alternative ways to complete a task or short cuts that will assist the student without compromising job performance. Ask people who are familiar with tools and hardware for help when devising environmental modifications across students' everyday life activities at home or school or in the community. For example, you could ask a carpenter, a plumber, an electrician, or a mechanic for ideas on how to build jigs, ramps, switches, or other adaptive equipment to assist a student in daily living activities.

One reason that the ADA was crafted was to make employment and other settings more accessible to individuals with differing abilities. A number of sources, including the Job Accommodation Network, provide free information about job accommodations to businesses and individuals. In addition, teachers have made the following suggestions.

- Job carving is one means of modifying a job to accommodate a worker's skills by devising alternative ways of completing job tasks at a workplace. Be careful, however, not to create new tasks that result in segregating a student from other employees.

- It may be easier to modify existing jobs than to attempt to create new jobs. Job modification should result in a student performing tasks that are typical of those already present in the workplace, thereby promoting the acceptance of the student.

- If a student is having trouble gaining access to a building or room, then contact some of the volunteer agencies in town. Many organizations will send volunteers to build a ramp.

- For students who have visual impairments or who are easily distracted, such as those with attention disorders, arrange their desks so that they are closer to the board and the front of the room. Have students with hearing impairments sit where they can see others' faces.

- Leave the door to your classroom open, if possible, for easy access to students. Students with visual impairments could sit close to the door so that they have fewer obstacles to meet in finding a seat and leaving the room.

- Provide a homework area within a general education classroom where students can receive assistance from peers and not have to be separated from the rest of the class.

"I noticed one of my students had difficulty picking up litter on a jobsite. I made him a stick with a nail in the end so he could 'spear' the litter and then put it in his trash bag."

Teacher, Hillsboro High School

LEGISLATION Making modifications to a setting is not the sole responsibility of the special education teacher. IDEA 2004 states, "a regular education teacher of the child, as a member of the IEP Team, shall, to the extent appropriate, participate in the development of the IEP of the child, including the determination of appropriate positive behavioral interventions and supports, and other strategies, and the determination of supplementary aids and services, program modifications, and support for school personnel" (§ 614).

WEB RESOURCES

Job Accommodation Network, http://askjan.org/index.html

The Job Accommodation Network is an extensive web-based resource that provides expert and confidential guidance on workplace accommodations and disability employment issues.

Office of Disability Employment Policy, http://www.dol.gov/odep/

The mission of the Office of Disability Employment Policy is to provide national leadership by developing and influencing disability employment-related policies and practices affecting an increase in the employment of people with disabilities.

PRINT RESOURCES

Fowler, C.H., Walker, A.R., & Rowe, D. (2010). *Age-appropriate transition assessment guide* (2nd ed.). Charlotte, NC: University of North Carolina at Charlotte, National Secondary Transition Technical Assistance Center. Available at http://www.nsttac.org

This free, printable guide addresses the purpose of transition assessment, provides an overview of sample instruments, and discusses how to conduct age-appropriate assessment.

Sitlington, P.L., Patton, J.R., & Clark, G.M. (2007). *Informal assessments for transition: Postsecondary education and training.* Austin, TX: PRO-ED.

This book addresses numerous informal assessment approaches for evaluating the postsecondary needs, opportunities, and participation of students with disabilities.

Synatschk, K.O., Clark, G.M., & Patton, J.R. (2007). *Informal assessments for transition: Independent living and community participation.* Austin, TX: PRO-ED.

This book includes an array of assessment approaches for exploring a student's community participation and independent living skills.

Synatschk, K.O., Clark, G.M., Patton, J.R., & Copeland, L.R. (2007). *Informal assessments for transition: Employment and career planning.* Austin, TX: PRO-ED.

This book reviews a range of tools and strategies for assessing the career development of youth with disabilities.

CHAPTER 4

Increasing Social Support and Promoting Acceptance

In this chapter, you will learn how to

- Develop social support plans

- Foster accepting attitudes and promote greater disability awareness

- Gain access to existing social support

- Equip others to provide social support

- Increase students' social participation

OVERVIEW

Social relationships and belonging are important to both a high quality of life and successful postschool outcomes (Rubin, Bukowski, & Laursen, 2009; Test et al., 2009). In fact, promoting meaningful social connections and inclusion in the mainstream of everyday life have long been considered central to recommended transition and secondary education practices (Carter & Hughes, in press; Halpern, 1985). IDEA 2004 states "that the education of children with disabilities can be made more effective by having high expectations for such children and ensuring their access to the general education curriculum in the regular classroom to the maximum extent possible." This statement affirms that inclusive learning environments can provide rich opportunities for students to gain access to natural social supports and develop relationships with their peers. Indeed, educational planning teams must now provide a strong explanation for the extent to which students will not participate alongside their peers without disabilities in general education classes and other school activities. This emphasis on fostering social connectedness and inclusion is prominent in legislative and policy initiatives focused on the community and workplace. For example, the Rehabilitation Act Amendments of 1992 (PL 102-569) state that "individuals with disabilities, including individuals with the most significant disabilities, have demonstrated their ability to achieve gainful employment in integrated settings if appropriate services and supports are provided" (§ 100), placing clear emphasis on fostering inclusive workplaces.

In our view, social integration means fully participating in the interactions and relationships occurring within a classroom, club, workplace, or community activity 1) to a similar extent as do others who are also involved in those same settings and 2) in ways that lead to a sense of belonging. By participating fully in the numerous interactions taking place in any given setting, students gain access to many benefits, such as supportive friendships, opportunities to learn new skills, and personal satisfaction. One indicator of social integration is apparent when individual differences are accepted and individual strengths are maximized and supported.

Not only is it critical that secondary transition instruction occurs in the settings in which students will ultimately live their lives—such as in the community, in the home, and on the job—and that all students be included in school activities and classes alongside their peers without disabilities, but it also is important that students be accepted and welcomed within these settings as full participants and real members of the community. Physical proximity—that is, simply being present in a classroom, club, cafeteria, or company—does not mean that a student is considered an active and equal participant. Teachers, paraprofessionals, and others can be instrumental in promoting acceptance of students as valued members of their school, workplace, and neighborhood communities.

This chapter contains five clusters of strategies teachers may use to foster social support and promote belonging across school and community settings. It includes strategies focused on developing social support plans, fostering accepting attitudes and greater awareness, gaining access to existing social support, equipping others to provide social support, and increasing students' social participation. The relationships students develop during adolescence and the social support they receive from their peers, co-workers, teachers, and others can be instrumental in promoting successful school transitions and a sense of belonging.

Case Study 4.1 *Meet Kenneth Cartwright*

Kenneth Cartwright is 18 years old and attends Pecan Valley High School. He is dependable, hardworking, and easygoing. Kenneth also has an intellectual disability and extensive support needs. He walks unassisted, although somewhat unsteadily; communicates with usually one or two words; and completes daily personal tasks (e.g., shaving, preparing his lunch) with reminders and occasional help. At school, Kenneth spends his mornings in a special education life skills class and several career preparation classes. Kenneth has developed few friendships, even though he participates in many school activities with other students during the day. Usually he sits alone in a class or walks by himself in the halls. When spoken to, Kenneth usually responds. Yet, he rarely starts conversations with his classmates.

In the afternoon, Kenneth participates in his school's transition employment training program. Each day, he takes a bus from school to his part-time job at a large, nearby hotel. Kenneth works in the housekeeping department, where he collects used towels and sheets from the hotel rooms and transports them in a bin to the basement laundry facility. Kenneth is reliable at his job, remains on task, and rarely misses picking up a sheet or towel from a hotel room. On the elevator or in the halls, however, Kenneth rarely speaks to hotel residents or co-workers. Some customers have actually complained to the hotel management about Kenneth because they feel uncomfortable when they meet him in the hall and he does not greet them. Kenneth's co-workers feel somewhat uncomfortable as well, and many have started to avoid Kenneth because he does not hang out with them, joke around during breaks, or acknowledge their presence when they are working in the same area. Kenneth has been warned several times by his manager that in the hotel business it is important to be friendly, especially to customers. If Kenneth is not responsive to these concerns, then his manager is afraid he may have to fire him. Otherwise, the hotel may start losing customers.

LEGISLATION IDEA 2004 requires that formal and informal assessment strategies be used to inform key elements of a student's IEP and determine the most appropriate educational programming. The information provided by such assessments can help planning teams identify a student's social-related strengths, preferences, and needs. It can help teams identify annual goals that focus on social participation and belonging and address how the student will be supported within general education classes and other school activities. And it can help teams identify key transition experiences that might expand the relationships and connections available to the student.

DEVELOPING INDIVIDUAL SOCIAL SUPPORT PLANS

As students advance through high school and approach graduation, the opportunities available to them rapidly expand—new job possibilities, new avenues for community involvement, new expectations for civic engagement, new considerations about where and how to live, and new avenues to develop friendships emerge. Each new opportunity brings both the challenge and excitement of learning about and adapting to new experiences. As students encounter these emerging opportunities, the amount of social support they receive can influence the degree of success and satisfaction that they experience. Fortunately, students do not have to navigate these experiences on their own. Most schools, workplaces, and community settings have rich sources of social support available. Opportunities to interact socially, engage in relationships, and receive social support abound in every aspect of our lives.

Social support can manifest in a variety of ways. For example, some students may need assistance with learning a new job or hobby, obtaining transportation, meeting new people, managing time, fulfilling responsibilities, finding housing, or solving personal problems. Peers, co-workers, teachers, family members, and others can be instrumental in helping students with disabilities to navigate these and other areas of their lives. In addition, the intensity of social support needed will differ from one person to the next (Thompson et al., 2010). Whereas one student may need only an occasional reminder or encouraging word, another student may benefit from ongoing assistance and support. Of course, people's support needs can change over time. The key point here is that the need for social support is universal. Indeed, everyone is a recipient (and hopefully a provider) of a certain amount of social support to someone else. For youth with disabilities, however, it may be particularly important to be intentional about identifying and connecting students to these naturally available sources of support.

Strategies that teachers can use to identify social support in a setting and match it to a student's needs are similar to those for identifying environmental supports (see Chapter 3). Teachers should visit, observe, and analyze the settings in which students are (or eventually will be) participating; develop a meaningful support plan; and communicate those support needs to others. Social support may come from a variety of sources, such as friends of a student's sibling or from someone who happens to wait at the same bus stop on the way to work. Sometimes students must learn skills to gain access to social support that exist in a particular setting; other times peers or co-workers may benefit from learning to better communicate with or offer assistance to students.

Identifying Social-Related Support Needs

Assessing the specific social-related strengths and needs of a student is the starting point for developing an effective social support plan. Carefully aligning social supports to meet the individualized needs of a student increases the likelihood of long-term success. Too often, assessment information is gathered only when a student is having difficulty fitting into a particular setting. In addition to providing information concerning how to address challenging social situations in a classroom or community settings, social support assessments can also provide insight into the types of support helping to create a successful experience for a student.

Direct Observations

One of the most direct and accurate ways to identify existing and needed social supports for a student is to observe as she interacts with others in and across settings. As you observe a student, you may find that relatively few social supports or opportunities for interaction are available. For example, a student enrolled in a community art class may be the only Spanish-speaking member of the group, or a worker employed as a night maintenance person may not have any co-workers to talk with on her shift. Record specific areas of need for which you can later brainstorm solutions with other members on the team. For other students, you may notice interactions that either enhance or impede their acceptance or competence in relation to the demands of the environment. Because all students respond in unique ways to the different demands of a particular environment, note those areas in which individual students could benefit from additional social support. For example, a student may benefit from learning how to gain access to the social supports already present in a setting, such as learning acceptable ways of asking a co-worker or supervisor for assistance.

"I follow closely the interactions of students when they are in community and general education settings. I watch how they interact with others at school dances, parties, or lunch or during recreational times. Casual conversation with others can also give insight."

Teacher, Northside High School

Consider the following strategies identified by transition teachers when carrying out observations of students across important school and community settings.

- Casually observe students as they interact with their peers without disabilities outside the classroom, such as at school assemblies, while participating on the school track team, during lunch, or within after-school clubs and other activities. Are students laughing and joking with their peers? Do they seem to enjoy spending time with one another?

- Use the job task analysis from the Job Analysis Survey (Form 3.1) as a checklist of skills to observe. As the student performs each step, record the social supports (e.g., peers) the student draws on, as well as those supports that are available to—but not used by—the student (e.g., supervising or maintenance staff).

- Whether at work, in school, or around the community, begin by observing others in the same setting to determine the types of support they are receiving (e.g., checking in with a supervisor or co-workers periodically about the quality of her work) and the kind of social support they may be able to provide to a student (e.g., showing the student how to request help). This will provide insights into the natural supports already available within a setting and the extent to which a student is already gaining access to those social supports.

- As you visit the different settings in which a student is (or eventually will be) participating, note the people who live close by or come in contact with or work with the student, such as a student's favorite cousin or a friendly neighbor. These people represent potential sources of social support to the student.

- As you notice specific challenges encountered by the student, indicate areas in which a student may benefit from specific social-related instruction in conjunction with additional social support (see Chapter 6). Quite often, efforts to enhance access to supports must be accompanied by efforts to teach new skills.

"I observe others who are involved in a student's environments, noting any possible ways they may be able to provide support. In addition, I ask others about the types of support they are able to provide."

Teacher, Pearl-Cohn High School

Interviewing Others

Interviewing key stakeholders is a second approach for identifying social-related support needs. The real authorities on the social demands and social supports in a given environment are those individuals who are already successfully participating in that environment. Collaborate with these experts—which may include peers, teachers, co-workers, family members, and community members—who know exactly what the social expectations are of a particular environment. Getting input from others who are involved in these settings has a twofold purpose. First, it can lead to suggestions and ideas you may not have initially thought about. Second, it can help encourage greater ownership by others of a newly developed support plan.

- Interview parents, employers, paraprofessionals, and fellow teachers occasionally to learn how well they think a student is fitting in within a particular setting. If they identify a problem (e.g., a student sits at home all weekend without spending time with friends, has few conversations with co-workers, seems uncomfortable interacting with customers), then be sure to address it even if you do not agree or have not seen the problem at school. Continue to check with them to determine whether their perceptions change over time.

- Do not automatically assume that the types of support provided to one student will necessarily be valued by the family or community of another student. In this diverse society, it is especially important that teachers make home visits to determine the types of social supports that are available to, needed by, and valued by a student's family (see Form 2.5 in Chapter 2).

- Social supports can come in all different forms. Interviewing the student who will be the recipient of the supports will allow you to match the support preferences and needs of the student to the breadth of supports available within a setting.

"Make all people involved in the student's life aware of how they can provide support to the student. Sometimes we take for granted that we all have the same definition of support."

Teacher, Cleveland High School

ASSESSMENT

Assessing Outcomes: Getting Feedback from Others

Determining how fully a student is accepted within a particular classroom, club, or community setting is fairly straightforward. Be observant, be a good listener, and keep careful records. Because it can sometimes be difficult to visit every setting in which a student is participating as well as talk to all of the stakeholders who encounter the student there, explore creative ways to gather information from these individuals across contexts. For example, you might provide employers, paraprofessionals, peer supports, or general education teachers a quick checklist to fill out that addresses behaviors generally expected within a particular setting. Form 4.1 is a Behavior Checklist used to evaluate the acceptance of a student's conversational interactions in a high school. A blank, reproducible form is

FORM 4.1
Behavior Checklist

Person completing checklist: __Arthur Luga__   Date: __October 28__

Student: __Anderson Blackwell__

	Strongly disagree	Somewhat disagree	Do not feel strongly either way	Somewhat agree	Strongly agree
The student has good conversational skills.	1	2	3	④	5
The student acts like most high school students when they eat lunch in a school cafeteria.	1	2	③	4	5
Most high school students would probably act like the student in this conversation.	1	②	3	4	5
The student's conversational behavior looks acceptable to me.	1	2	3	④	5
Most high school students would likely enjoy having a conversation with someone who acts like the student.	1	2	3	④	5
	1	2	3	4	5
	1	2	3	4	5

Comments

The conversation was okay—I just wish that Anderson would talk about something else besides the Dallas Cowboys!

Form 4.1. Behavior Checklist for Anderson. (A blank, photocopiable version of this form is included on the accompanying CD-ROM.)

included on the accompanying CD-ROM. Down the left column of Anderson's Behavior Checklist, the teacher has listed social-related behaviors important to participation in a particular setting (e.g., a cafeteria). Individuals who are familiar with the student and the expectations of the setting then rate the extent to which each statement reflects their perceptions of the student.

Developing Social Support Plans

There is often a discrepancy between the supports available in a particular school, job, or community setting and the supports a student is currently using. The process of developing an individual social support plan involves helping students gain access to the supports available in the setting that match her individual needs. Social support plans can incorporate the information derived from site visits, observations of the student, and collaborations with others who are important in the student's life into a step-by-step blueprint for actively involving the student in everyday life in ways that are productive and satisfying.

Case Study 4.2 *Living on My Own*

Yvonne thought that it was about time that she got her own apartment. After all, living at home with seven brothers and sisters would be considered a challenge for even the toughest of people. Besides, she was 18 years old, had graduated from high school, and had just started job training as a library assistant. Yvonne had been enrolled in the district's 19- to 22-year-old community-based program for just more than 1 year, and her teacher, Mr. Carpenter, was working hard toward helping Yvonne realize her dreams of independence and involvement in the community. A new apartment seemed to be the next natural step.

Yvonne's high school friend Anna had recently lost a roommate and was looking for a replacement. Mr. Carpenter visited the apartment and spoke with Anna about the different expectations she had for her new roommate. Anna mentioned the types of chores that needed to be completed each week and the bills that had to be paid each month. In addition, she described her typical weekly routine, which included activities such as shopping, working, visiting with friends, going to church, and doing volunteer work. She indicated that she was eager to have a new roommate but was worried that her busy schedule might not allow her much time to help Yvonne with many of her physical needs. Mr. Carpenter reassured Anna that many people would be involved in supporting Yvonne and that she shouldn't worry that all of the responsibility would be on her.

Several weeks later (and aided by nine family members), Yvonne moved into her new apartment. Even her classmates showed up to offer her help and congratulations. The excitement that everyone displayed was overwhelming. Mr. Carpenter and Ms. Malonee, a representative of a supported living agency, visited Yvonne once a week for the first month to observe how she adapted to her new living environment. They noted that Yvonne had already established supportive relationships with several of her neighbors and that she and Anna were getting along quite well. Anna, however, expressed concern that Yvonne was having trouble completing all of her chores, and Ms. Malonee observed that Yvonne was still not very involved in the community, despite her new residence.

Mr. Carpenter decided to gather together the individuals who were on Yvonne's planning team to discuss ways of providing support to Yvonne in her new home or neighborhood. In addition, he hoped to develop a social support plan that would be carried out by the various members of the team. At the meeting, Yvonne began by explaining her vision for her life in the community. Next, several of her family members shared strategies they had used to support Yvonne when she was living at home. After Ms. Malonee explained the supports that her agency was willing to provide, Yvonne's work supervisor told the group that his company already had several programs in place that could address those same needs, including a carpool, a mentoring program, and a financial advisor who could meet with Yvonne. Before long, the blackboard was overflowing with more suggestions than Mr. Carpenter ever could have thought of himself. After arranging all of the supports into a plan for Yvonne, the group adjourned, excited to return in 1 month to reevaluate the effectiveness of the plan. Little did they know how much Yvonne would surprise them.

A student's transition goals and objectives as stated in the IEP are a starting point for identifying some of the social supports already provided to the student and for developing and evaluating a comprehensive support plan. It may be helpful, however, to incorporate several additional components within a social support plan. These elements include the student's social support needs, the specific strategies used to address those needs, the person(s) responsible for implementing each strategy, the anticipated outcomes, and the methods that will be used

FORM 4.2

Individual Social Support Plan

Student: __Alfred Otawba__   Age: __20__   Date: __September 8__

	Support needs	Support strategy	Person or agency responsible	Outcome	Target date	Evaluation method
Employment	Improved job performance at the bike shop	Pair Alfred with another employee for continued job training.	Vocational counselor will help co-worker adapt training	Alfred's job output will increase 20%.	11/15	Co-worker will record the number of bikes Alfred builds each week.
	Accepting criticism from supervisors	Job coach and co-workers will model expected behavior.	Co-worker Job coach Adult service agency	Alfred will say, "Thank you for the help," when given job feedback.	10/15	Direct observation and student interviews
Community involvement	Transportation training—needs way to get to store, work, and various community activities	Teacher/family will show Alfred how to use public transportation. Friends provide rides. Co-workers provide ride to worksite.	Special education teacher Parents Peers Co-workers	Alfred will use public transportation to get to a desired location.	11/15	Log books and direct observation
				Alfred will contact and ride with a co-worker to his worksite.	10/15	Direct observation and communication with co-workers
Independent living	Planning meals that address Alfred's diet needs	Nurse trains roommate to help Alfred plan meals that meet his dietary needs.	Nurse Alfred's roommate	With the assistance of a roommate, Alfred will plan weekly meals that meet his dietary needs.	12/1	Examine weekly menu of meals that Alfred plans.
	Budgeting for monthly expenses	Teacher will provide classroom instruction. Parents will help Alfred.	General and special education teachers Parents	Alfred will complete a monthly budget.	12/1	Direct observation and communication with parents

(page 1 of 2)

Form 4.2. Individual Social Support Plan for Alfred. (A blank, photocopiable version of this form is included on the accompanying CD-ROM.)

FORM 4.2. *(continued)*

	Support needs	Support strategy	Person or agency responsible	Outcome	Target date	Evaluation method
Education and college	Involvement in an extracurricular activity	Peer joins Alfred when attending extracurricular activity of his choice.	Peers	Alfred will participate in at least one extracurricular activity.	10/1	Direct observation and conversation with peers
	Increased class involvement during general education classes	Peer can model behavior. Teacher provides more chances for involvement.	General education teacher Educational assistant	Alfred will increase his active involvement in class by 50%.	11/1	Direct observation and conversation with teacher

(page 2 of 2)

to evaluate those outcomes. Form 4.2 is an Individual Social Support Plan for a 20-year-old student named Alfred Otawba. A blank, reproducible form is included on the accompanying CD-ROM. Remember to address the student's social support needs in each setting in which she now participates (or will eventually participate). Notice that each row on the form focuses on a different domain typically addressed within transition planning: employment-related support needs, community-related support needs, independent living support needs, and education-related support needs. Other areas important to a student can readily be added. Each column addresses the key elements previously noted.

Developing a support plan should be a collaborative endeavor. Consider the following additional strategies suggested by teachers for building such support plans in coordination and cooperation with others.

- Ultimately, students and their families determine whether proposed social supports harmonize with their personal values, daily routines, and cultural expectations. Their views may be quite different from yours. Be certain to involve them throughout the planning process.

- All members of the IEP team, including community agencies, should be involved in developing the student's social support plan. For example, the student's parents, employer, and supporting agencies should work together to help a student experience success on the job. Similarly, a paraprofessional, club sponsor, and peers might brainstorm together ways to involve a student more fully within an after-school model rocket club.

- Bring together all individuals involved in a student's life to provide input into developing a complete picture of social support available to the student. It may be that others will learn about supports successfully being used in one area of a student's life (e.g., an interpreter, notetaker, peer support) that could be introduced in another area.

- Holding individual meetings with a student's family, friends, and co-workers can give you an opportunity to help them see how they can support the student. People may be surprised at the ways in which they can provide support. For example, a co-worker may help a new worker to better enjoy a baseball game they are attending together by explaining the rules of the game.

- Involving peers, family, employment staff, and community members as sources of social support, rather than just you alone as teacher or job coach, ensures those supports and efforts will continue long after high school when the student leaves the classroom or job-training site.

- It is both natural and desirable that students receive support from their friends and classmates, that employees receive support from their co-workers, and that community members receive support from neighbors or fellow businesspeople. Be sure to supplement, not replace, supports already provided in the natural environment whenever introducing additional supports.

"I think that as part of the transition effort we should heavily involve the family of the individual in the planning process. Involvement with the employer should continue after the student has graduated."

Teacher, Treadwell High School

LEGISLATION

The ability and freedom to make important life choices is valued by many people. IDEA 2004 acknowledges this principle and stresses that the transition services provided to students be based on the individual student's needs, taking into account the student's strengths, preferences, and interests. Allowing students to determine with which social supports they would be most comfortable and how they would prefer them to be delivered allows them to exercise that choice. Strategies for identifying a student's needs and personal preferences can be accomplished by talking with the student and others who know the student well.

Case Study 4.3   *It Is Great to Have Friends*

Yvonne's apartment wasn't the biggest or fanciest one in town. It didn't even have the nicest furnishings. But it was hers, and that made it the best. Anna and Yvonne had been roommates for just more than 2 months, and the two women were already getting along extremely well. Yvonne's weeks were full of work and community activities, which kept her busier than ever. Still, Yvonne occasionally found time to curl up on the living room couch and listen to her favorite bands before Anna got home from work.

Soon, the planning team gathered together again to listen to Yvonne share how her second month had gone and to determine whether her support plan had been effective or needed fine-tuning. Yvonne described the types of social supports she had received in different areas of her life

Transportation Supports

Because Yvonne did not have a driver's license, getting around could have been difficult, but a co-worker living in the next apartment complex drove her to and from work each day. Yvonne's brother picked her up for church each Sunday morning, and another church member drove her home when there was choir practice. Finally, Anna rode the bus with Yvonne to her community training program for the first couple of weeks until Yvonne had memorized the route. Just in case, Anna talked with the bus driver, asking him to remind Yvonne when she needed to get off.

Recreation/Leisure Supports

Yvonne met several friends through Anna at the apartment complex pool. Pretty soon, Yvonne had found companionship with three women with whom she went out to eat, shop, and dance. Her participation in the church choir also resulted in meeting several additional friends. She enrolled in a knitting class at the neighborhood yarn shop and was already knitting a scarf for her niece.

Employment Supports

Yvonne went through the same job-training program as the other new employees, and Mr. Carpenter helped the library supervisor find ways to adapt some aspects of the training to meet Yvonne's needs. In addition, Yvonne was paired with a mentor, an experienced employee, who helped her adjust to the job and provided her with emotional support. Yvonne knew she could always call on Mr. Carpenter, but she quickly learned to turn to her co-workers or work supervisor first.

Personal Supports

If Yvonne kept a messy apartment, then Anna was even worse. The two decided to pay a housekeeper to visit their place twice per month for an "overhaul." In between, Anna showed Yvonne how to do some basic house cleaning and repairs. Yvonne met with a volunteer at the library to help her begin a budget. At the same time, Mr. Carpenter emphasized money management skills during community-based instruction.

Everyone was excited about the success that Yvonne was experiencing; the social supports they had planned for her were beginning to work. Yvonne was learning how rewarding living on her own could be and thanked everyone on her team for all of their assistance. Yvonne's family, teachers, and friends chuckled because they realized that they hadn't helped her in ways that were different or unusual. They hadn't even really gone too far out of their way to provide supports. But they did support Yvonne's desire to be independent. To Yvonne, that made them the best.

Communicating Students' Social Support Needs to Others

The active involvement of teachers, family members, service providers, and others in pinpointing the social support available to and needed by a student can greatly enhance the effectiveness of any individual support plan. By soliciting the suggestions and input of others when identifying social support, you are more apt to create a comprehensive picture of a student's needs, as well as foster communication of those needs to others who are involved in activities with the student. The more involved others are in designing the support plan, the more familiar and fluent they will be in ensuring those supports are provided in those contexts in which they spend time with the student.

At the same time, it is important to communicate to others who work with and spend time with a student with a disability how they can play a role in supporting that student socially in the classroom and beyond the school campus. Transition planning teams have a responsibility to provide school and community members with information regarding the strengths, skills, and support needs of students with disabilities. When others have accurate information, they may be more likely to be accepting of differences and hold more realistic expectations of students with disabilities.

"I would help people to understand the needs of the student and allow them to see how they can help students to have successful experiences."

Teacher, Cookeville High School

Teachers have recommended a variety of strategies for sharing the social-related support needs identified on a student's support plan.

- Discuss the goals of a student's career development program at an employee meeting. For example, co-workers might not know that a student's goals are to make decisions independently and accept work-related criticism without getting defensive. Encourage employees to communicate any questions, concerns, or suggestions they may have about a student's program.

- Brainstorm with classmates or clubmates ways they could interact with a student to help meet her goals. For example, rather than step in and do an assignment for a student when she is having difficulty, a peer could help the student problem-solve how to do the assignment independently. Doing so not only will help the student but also will reward the classmate for having helped someone learn a new skill.

- Emphasize that all people—not just people with disabilities—have both strengths and limitations. For example, stress to an employer that a worker has perfect attendance and a great performance record, even if she has her own way of performing job tasks. Help others have realistic expectations of students who have different abilities.

- Encourage youth programs and community organizations to consider the many types of social support they could provide to students, such as carpooling, mentors, or team-based activities. Assure them that these supports can be used to benefit all of the youth who are involved in the activity.

- Share with others that the rationale for using particular social supports (e.g., peer buddies, Best Buddies, Big Brother or Big Sister) is not to make less work for paraprofessionals, teachers, or parents, but to increase a student's social participation, friendships, and interdependence.

When teachers communicate with family members, employers, community members, fellow teachers, and others who are important to the student, they multiply the number of strategies they have available to draw on in supporting a student. Providing social support for a student is a collaborative endeavor. IDEA 2004 requires teachers to collaborate with other members of the IEP team

LEGISLATION to gain access to the experience, expertise, and support of others who know the student well.

FOSTERING ACCEPTING ATTITUDES AND GREATER DISABILITY AWARENESS

The attitudes and limited knowledge teachers, employers, community members, peers, and others possess about inclusion and the specific support needs of youth with disabilities are frequently cited as salient barriers to full participation and social integration. Since the 1990s there has been greater awareness and inclusion of people with disabilities, but barriers of attitude and expectations unfortunately still endure (Siperstein, Norins, & Mohler, 2007). For example, classmates, co-workers, or others may initially express uncertainty about how to interact with or support someone who has a disability, communicates in somewhat different ways, or requires extensive assistance. Sometimes, a lack of acceptance of students with disabilities originates from a lack of information. Other times, people have simply had limited opportunities and experiences getting to know young people with disabilities. By providing students, teachers, and community members with knowledge about the skills, strengths, and contributions of people with disabilities, new opportunities and experiences for including all students equally may emerge. Such efforts can create contexts in which social support becomes more readily available to youth with disabilities.

"Interview family members, employers, and co-workers to determine attitudes toward workers with disabilities. Identify key support personnel based on the interviews."

Teacher, Central High School

> ### Case Study 4.4   *Ms. Lewis's First Day*
>
> Ms. Lewis proudly entered King High School and quickly walked up the stairs to her very first classroom. The past 4 years of consuming textbook after textbook had finally paid off just 3 months ago when she received her teacher's certification in special education. Full of ideas and plans for her students, she began to think about the ways she would help them become important members in their school, workplace, and community. She knew that general class participation would be important, so she made a mental note to talk to several of the teachers on her wing. She remembered hearing about peer buddy programs in a college class and decided to speak with someone in administration about beginning one. And she marveled about the friends her students would make as she found ways to help them fit in with a peer group. What a great first year it was going to be.
>
> The next day, Ms. Lewis discovered that King High School was not quite ready for such "radical" thinking. Mr. Feagan, the science teacher, expressed his "concern" that having a student who used a wheelchair in his lab might pose a safety risk. Mrs. Ross felt that the other students would end up losing out if she were expected to include students with disabilities in her social studies classes. And Coach Boyette excitedly explained that she already taught a separate physical education class for students with disabilities. The meeting with the administration was also puzzling. The principal said that the idea of a peer buddy program sounded tolerable, but she believed students would benefit more from experiences such as being an office worker or library assistant. Anticipating that students would certainly be more receptive to her students, Ms. Lewis approached a group of adolescents in the lobby. Four of the students didn't realize King High School had any students with disabilities. The other two stated that they felt uncomfortable when the students did "weird things."
>
> Frustrated and spent, Ms. Lewis went back to her classroom and sat down to reflect on the day. She thought about legislation such as the ADA and IDEA 2004 and realized that it takes much more than laws to change how people view individuals with diverse abilities. Moreover, she began to understand that negative attitudes aren't unique to just students but also can be present in both teachers and administrators. Pulling out a pen and a piece of paper, Ms. Lewis began to make a careful list of strategies that she believed would help promote diversity awareness at King High School, leading to the social acceptance of students with diverse abilities.

Among Teachers and Other School Staff

Although students with disabilities are spending increasingly more of their time in general education classes, clubs, and school activities than ever before, inclusion in many secondary schools remains uneven, more often the exception rather than the norm (U.S. Department of Education, 2009). Many general educators, special educators, paraprofessionals, and administrators are committed to inclusive practices and strive to design learning environments that address the needs of all students. But attitudes and expectations are not uniform across or within schools—some teachers will be more confident and comfortable than others (Carter & Hughes, 2006). To foster more socially supportive school contexts, it is critical to help school staff become more aware of the benefits of and strategies for including students with disabilities in all of the activities that make up everyday secondary school life.

"Talk with the individuals with whom a student will be interacting. A casual conversation can go a long way toward evaluating a level of acceptance and promoting an attitude of acceptance."

Teacher, Hunters Lane High School

Some teachers focus on broad efforts to foster greater awareness and acceptance by holding informational or training sessions for all school staff. For example, you might discuss the goals of high school transition programs and the benefits of including all students in the mainstream of school life at an in-service or faculty meeting. Indeed, many general educators and vocational educators may not be aware of the purpose of secondary transition programs for students with disabilities. Or you might invite general education teachers to a breakfast or lunch prepared and served by your students. At the breakfast, share information about your program, describe your goals and plans for the year, and give teachers a chance to get to know your students better. Consider the following strategies recommended by teachers.

- Try to ease into the process of building acceptance and support of new programs and inclusion in your school. Include school personnel in decision making, such as where a classroom should be located or how to modify a class assignment. Other staff and administration members will be more likely to support and accept new ideas when they feel that they have ownership in and input into program development.

- Discuss the benefit to general education students of having students with disabilities in their clubs, activities, and classes. For example, research suggests that inclusive experiences can foster increases in self-esteem, acceptance of others, and the building of new friendships (Hunt & McDonnell, 2007).

- Make yourself available to other staff members for information and assistance regarding individual students' needs and skills. Visit the classrooms in which students are included. Talk with general educators on a regular basis, or communicate by using memos or checklists to promote an open line of communication. Discuss discrepancies between their perceptions of a student's performance and your perceptions. Do not wait for report card day to find out how a student is doing.

Case Study 4.5 *Getting the Word Out*

Ms. Lewis was a little nervous as she entered the cafeteria for her first faculty in-service session. She had spent the past week trying to establish rapport with the general education teachers, particularly Mr. Boeing, an experienced teacher who was popular with many of the faculty. Knowing that teachers wouldn't be open to her students if they didn't know who she was, she tried to remain as visible as possible, hanging out in the faculty lounge and by the mailboxes and attending the first school football game and pep rally of the year. Ms. Lewis also spoke with the principal and convinced her not to hold separate in-service sessions for general and special education teachers. In addition, she asked if she could have some of the meeting time to introduce her fellow teachers to her special education program.

By lunchtime, the in-service session had been going on for nearly 3 hours. Looking around at the faces of the faculty, Ms. Lewis knew that one more lecture might not be well received. When the principal called her up, Ms. Lewis began her "pitch." Ms. Lewis, joined by Mr. Boeing, began by inviting the rest of the staff to take part in a disability awareness activity that involved reflecting on the accessibility of the school campus. Ms. Lewis explained to the teachers that the barriers at King High School weren't only physical but also attitudinal. She then shared the numerous strengths that each of her students possessed and challenged the teachers to find ways of allowing the students to demonstrate those strengths in the general education classrooms.

Next, she talked excitedly about the benefits that general education students might receive—increased academic performance, more positive attitudes, improvements in self-concept, and new friendships. Dispelling the myth that teachers would have to focus much of their instructional time on the few students with diverse abilities, she shared with the teachers the instructional support she would be able to provide to them. Mr. Boeing then discussed some of the possibilities he saw for students in his classroom.

Back in her classroom, Ms. Lewis wondered whether the activity had been effective. She knew that having Mr. Boeing join her in speaking was a good idea as teachers appeared to appreciate hearing from a general educator. She knew that today was just a first step, but she hoped she had planted ideas in the heads of the faculty. Her next step would be to sow the idea in the heads of students.

Among Peers without Disabilities

Peers represent perhaps the most widely available source of natural social support in any school (Hughes & Carter, 2008). The students enrolled in any given school represent the future employers, civic leaders, and neighbors in that community. The opportunities they have to meet, learn alongside, and develop friendships with their classmates with disabilities can have a long-term impact on the opportunities, expectations, and attitudes youth with disabilities encounter into adulthood. Therefore, it is important to find ways to foster greater awareness and interaction opportunities among students with and without disabilities. Indeed, students will become better citizens in their communities as they learn from their interactions with each other.

A number of approaches exist for fostering accepting attitudes and greater awareness among peers. You might work with other teachers at your school to incorporate information about students with disabilities into existing units in classes such as social studies, civics, literature, teen living, and so forth. Some schools hold initial orientation activities for peers who will be working closely in supporting a classmate or clubmate with a disability. Such meetings typically involve discussing the strengths and support needs of the students with whom they will work, strategies for providing effective support, and ideas for encouraging social connections and relationships (Carter, Cushing, & Kennedy, 2009). For example, it can be helpful for peers to know that a student with a learning disability may benefit from having help organizing her daily assignments or that a student who has autism communicates best when using an augmentative or alternative communication device. Other schools focus on broader awareness activities aimed at reaching the entire school body. For example, a school might host an assembly in which an invited speaker or a panel of young adults discuss their experiences with having a disability, sponsor a film screening and follow-up discussion addressing the topic of inclusion, involve students in launching a schoolwide campaign to promote greater acceptance (e.g., "End the *R* Word" Campaign), or schedule events as part of National Inclusive Schools Week each December. Peers who get to know their classmates with disabilities may be more accepting of differences, have an increased appreciation of diversity, and possess a greater understanding of the beliefs and feelings that underlie others' behavior.

"Before I joined the program, I really did not understand people with disabilities. I felt sorry for them. Now I know that each one has his or her limits and abilities. It's like becoming friends with anyone else."

Peer buddy, McGavock High School

Communicating an Attitude of Acceptance: One Teacher's Story

"I do many things to communicate an attitude of acceptance in my high school. I teach a peer tutoring course to general education students that includes special education legislation, types and characteristics of disabilities, and instructional methods. The course is taught prior to any interaction with special education students. I also teach disability units in general education health classes and hold discussions with English classes when they are assigned to read books about people with disabilities. I have general education peers coach and train athletes in Unified Sports events. I also make announcements in school and community newspapers about current events or competitions taking place in my special education program.

Prior to integrating my students into general education classes, I discuss expectations with the teachers and students in these classes. I also help raise community awareness and acceptance by providing instruction in the community using the grocery store, bank, and so forth. Community-based job-training sites allow my students' work to 'speak for itself.'

This past year, I had more than 40 peer tutors involved in my special education transition program and had to turn down more than 100 other students who wanted to be involved in the program. In addition, all my students, even those with very severe disabilities, are included in general education classes, eat lunch, and ride the school bus with their general education friends. My students also participate in many extracurricular activities, watch plays and ball games, and go to dances with their general education peers. I am very fortunate to be in an environment with tremendous support for and acceptance of my transition program."

Teacher, Karns High School

Case Study 4.6 *Letting the Community Know*

Ms. Lewis's first semester as a teacher had been quite challenging, but she was extremely pleased with the progress she was beginning to see. Her fellow teachers and administrators had really gotten excited about the programs that she had proposed. Two general education teachers were already working with a number of students to put together a lunch bunch program. The ball had begun rolling. Ms. Lewis knew, however, that her students would need to be prepared for life in the community after graduation. In addition, the community would need to be prepared to receive these graduates.

As Ms. Lewis thought about the difficulties that students with diverse abilities frequently face in finding employment after high school, she realized that she would need to provide job-training opportunities before her students graduated. She created a simple flier that described her students and the types of services they could provide. After distributing it to more than 20 local businesses, she waited for the calls to pour in. The telephone never rang.

Ms. Lewis was baffled. Why weren't businesses knocking at her door to gain access to student volunteers? Why weren't they eager to have her students as trainees? In talking with other teachers, Ms. Lewis realized that it wasn't a lack of work that prevented employers from calling her but rather a lack of experience with her students. Whereas students and school staff had frequent opportunities to see students with differing abilities demonstrate their strengths and abilities, community members had fewer chances to be involved with these students. Undeterred, Ms. Lewis resolved to start out a little slower. She would begin by involving just one worksite in her community-based program for her students. Once established, she would use that as a springboard for involving other community businesses in her transition program.

Among Employers and Co-workers

Connecting youth with disabilities to early career development experiences is strongly advocated as an important element of high-quality transition education. Increasing acceptance and promoting awareness in the workplace, therefore, is an important element of supporting meaningful employment experiences for these youth. Employers and co-workers may be more confident in working with, supporting, and getting to know employees with disabilities when they feel that support, information, and assistance are readily available. Sometimes co-workers or customers are initially hesitant or uncertain interacting with youth with disabilities simply because they do not know them and do not know what to expect of them. Communicating an attitude of acceptance can help people move beyond perceived differences and invest time getting to know each other. Thus, the efforts you make to develop socially supportive work environments hold great potential to improve the quality and impact of students' community work experiences.

Efforts to foster greater awareness begin when first approaching local businesses and organizations about hiring youth. Consider the following strategies for increasing employers' understanding of the benefits of hiring youth with disabilities.

- Inform employers about the myriad advantages of hiring employees with diverse abilities, including the benefits of enthusiastic, well-trained, reliable employees and employer tax incentives (Luecking, 2008; U.S. Chamber of Commerce, 2005).

- Encourage potential employers to visit established community job-training sites. For example, in your own community, there may be a chain of drugstores or supermarkets that have been especially successful at hiring students from high school transition programs. Seeing the success of a business's job-training program might be an incentive for employers to consider establishing a similar endeavor at their location.

- Design a brochure or web site that includes photographs of your students at work, a list of the jobs and services they can perform, and potential benefits for employers who partner with the high school. Some employers may be surprised to find out what your students and program can offer.

- Solicit information from community leaders and employers about the needs of local businesses. You may find that employee shortages exist in certain areas of the job market. By equipping your students to perform these much-needed services, you may increase the likelihood that they will find meaningful full-time employment upon graduation.

"An employer complained that one of my students wouldn't follow directions. He had told the student to sign his name on a time card but didn't realize that the student couldn't read. The student was too embarrassed to tell the employer. I discussed the problem with the employer, and together we figured out another system the student could use for filling out his time card."

Teacher, Nashville Public Schools

It can be helpful to meet personally with co-workers, supervisors, and others when a student is offered a new position in order to raise awareness of the ways in which they can support their new employee. Hold an orientation meeting to answer questions and concerns from prospective co-workers before training begins at a worksite. Discuss the importance of co-worker relationships and social acceptance to the student's success on the job. Emphasize that although a student may complete tasks or interact somewhat differently, she also has many strengths and ways to contribute to a job and a workplace. For example, although an employee's production rate may be slower than her co-workers' speed, she may make up for it by never missing or being late to work. Another student may have such a positive attitude that working alongside her puts everyone on the job in a good mood. Finally, talk with employees and supervisors regularly to promote understanding and open communication. Discuss any discrepancies between their perceptions of a student's performance and your perceptions. For example, a supervisor may believe that a young man is taking long breaks and is hardly ever at his desk in his office. As the job coach, however, you have been keeping track of the young man's hours and can point out that he actually is at his desk more often than any other worker in the office.

"Promote your students' abilities to other employees. Display enthusiasm and professionalism toward your students. I have found that when I treat my students with respect and fairness, other employees observe this and will usually follow the same pattern."

Teacher, Whites Creek High School

In addition, secondary transition teachers have recommended the following strategies for sharing your efforts with employers more broadly.

- Use the local newspaper to thank employers who have supported your program. Employers will appreciate the exposure, and other businesses may wish to join in.

- Develop a web site for your job-training program. Include pictures of your students at work and in the community. Your students and their peer supports can help you.

- Create short videos about your program that can be shared via social media sites.

LEGISLATION

Using technology and media not only is an effective way to promote acceptance of your program but also is supported by the law. An intent of IDEA 2004 is to ensure that appropriate technology, media products, and activities are accessible to students, parents, and personnel and are integrated in the educational process. Plus, you are modeling technologically adept behavior by using innovative technology and media.

Case Study 4.7   *Going Public*

The students huddled anxiously around the television. The commercial break was almost over, which meant that they would be on next. Ms. Lewis watched the excitement from the back of the classroom, glad so many of her students would appear on the program. She was thankful for the television station's willingness to showcase her job-training program during the "Community Happenings" segment of the midday news. Although only a few minutes in length, the program would feature students working around town, brief interviews with employers, and an invitation for other businesses to participate in the program. Ms. Lewis was certain that this type of publicity would open up new opportunities for her students.

In the Community

As more students with and without disabilities grow up learning, working, and recreating alongside one another, community attitudes toward and expectations for youth and young adults with disabilities are certainly changing. Laws such as ADA 2008 and court cases such as the Supreme Court's Olmstead decision (1999) have also been instrumental in increasing access to and supports within all aspects of the community. Yet, there is an enduring need to help communities more fully understand the support needs and potential contributions of young people with disabilities.

Teachers have undertaken and recommended a variety of strategies for promoting community awareness, including the following.

- Speak at club and community events about the various community contributions of organizations made up of people with diverse abilities, such as the local People First or Self-Advocates Becoming Empowered chapter.

- Host social gatherings for community support personnel and parents. Getting to know each other informally helps to build a collaborative spirit.

- Have small discussion groups with parents and community members to discuss communication, expectations, misunderstandings, levels of acceptance, and methods for promoting acceptance among all people.

- Invite and involve a variety of community members in transition and multidisciplinary team meetings to meet the full range of your students' needs.

- Invite community members to visit your school's programs and see the types of educational and career development experiences you are providing. They may discover that your students are well trained in their particular area of business.

- Develop informational programs about your students that can be delivered at various meetings attended by community members. Conduct regular information presentations with community members. A slide show or video can be a useful tool to communicate the goals and objectives of a transition program and the skills and talents of the students involved.

- Make a list of potential participants who will be involved in ongoing public awareness activities. Include people such as family members, representatives of local business organizations that have successfully hired students, or local talk show hosts. Host a luncheon prepared by students during which you brainstorm with participants how to increase public awareness of your transition program.

- Help other teaching staff plan an in-service session that informs community members and employers about interacting with people with diverse abilities. You may find that some of the participants volunteer to become involved with your students as mentors.

Regularly involving students in community events and activities can make the task of promoting acceptance even easier. As the community has the opportunity to meet and interact with young people with disabilities in supportive contexts, they will come to see those students in terms of their individual personalities, strengths, and contributions. Encourage and support your students to be engaged in community life. And help them take visible roles at public events so that community members see the contributions of students with diverse abilities without having to come to the school. For example, a student could serve as an usher at a city play, serve on a neighborhood cleanup committee, or work at the local chamber of commerce.

Clearly, the task of building community support for a school's transition program can be overwhelming for just one person. Fortunately, many avenues exist for getting the word out broadly. Television, newspapers, radio, social media, and the Internet all provide effective means of informing the public about the contributions that students with diverse abilities can make to the community. For example, consider the following strategies teachers have used to maximize the reach of their awareness efforts.

- Many television and radio stations broadcast community calendars that highlight community programs and events. Call them well in advance so that they can include events that are taking place in your classroom.

- Talk to your local television or radio news station about doing a brief segment on your program. Many news stations broadcast human interest programs.

- Solicit community support through articles in the school newspaper, parent newsletter, or local newspaper. Parents can be excellent resources for program ideas.

- Make initial contacts with community members to inform them about public awareness programs by using introduction letters and local newspapers and radio and television stations.

Modeling is one of the most powerful ways to promote greater awareness and acceptance. Awareness efforts do not always have to be explicit. Teachers, students, employers, or community members may have had few opportunities to interact with students with diverse abilities. By modeling appropriate interaction, increasing opportunities for interaction, and providing basic instruction in social interaction skills, people will begin to see that all people are more alike than different. In addition, set a positive example by interacting frequently yet casually with students with diverse abilities at your school. Model an attitude of acceptance in the workplace and build rapport with personnel at the worksite. Employers, co-workers, and customers will follow your lead. For example, you can show people at a bank how easy and enjoyable it is to talk with a worker who uses a communication board. Or you might show them how you discuss sports events at a hardware shop with a worker who has a visual impairment—just like you would with anyone else. They will learn that they can do it, too.

"Education is the key. The community must understand people with different abilities and how they and we can adapt so they can be accepted into society."

Teacher, Cookeville High School

ASSESSMENT

Assessing Outcomes: Identifying Social Support

Strategies teachers can use to identify existing sources of social support in a classroom, work, or community setting are similar to those for identifying environmental supports. The natural supports section of the Job Analysis Survey (see Form 3.1 in Chapter 3) provides an assessment tool for developing a comprehensive picture of the social supports available at a given worksite. By observing other employees performing the same job, interviewing supervisors and co-workers, and surveying the workplace, teachers can pinpoint those sources of social support that will enhance a student's job performance and promote her acceptance at work. The Job Analysis Survey can also be modified to identify supports in other settings. For example, instead of recording information about Job Task Requirements, a teacher can note the task-related expectations of a particular classroom or community activity. Instead of addressing a student's interactions with a customer, a teacher can note how well a student interacts with her clubmates, other volunteers, or teammates. Tips for using the form include the following.

- Observe a student across various settings by "hanging out" and being visible without being intrusive. Ask a lot of questions because you might miss something or misinterpret someone's actions.

- As you complete the form, think about ways a co-worker or peer can support a student in adapting to the demands and environmental characteristics of a setting, such as taking notes for a student during a lecture. Ask for input from others in the setting.

- Social supports, such as co-workers or employee assistance programs, that naturally occur in a setting generally are better accepted than supports introduced from outside a home, work, or community environment, such as paid employment specialists. Record social supports that are typically occurring in the natural supports section of the Job Analysis Survey.

TECHNOLOGY

The explosion of new social technologies is introducing many new ways to meet, support, and connect one another. For example, online communities and social network sites are changing the ways in which youth and young adults stay in touch and communicate with one another. Although these technological connection points hold promise, there is a growing technology gap that means many students with disabilities are missing out on these new avenues for social participation. Work with students and families to identify appropriate and valued technologies that might increase students' social supports and connections. Teach students the skills they need to gain access to these venues effectively and safely. Peers are often the experts in using these technologies and can be instrumental in helping teach these 21st century skills.

GAINING ACCESS TO EXISTING SOCIAL SUPPORT

Students often need access to a variety of social supports to become active and meaningful participants in community and school activities. After crafting a compelling social support plan and fostering accepting school, work, or community contexts, attention can turn toward connecting students to the individualized social supports they will need to be successful. Drawing on already available social supports is also likely to enhance students' sense of belonging and inclusion in that setting.

"To help students gain access to social supports, I encourage them to initiate conversation with their co-workers on topics such as their families, pets, clothes, transportation, and so forth. I also encourage co-workers to do the same. I make an effort to effect an air of openness at the jobsite."

Teacher, McGavock High School

Other individuals in settings in which a student is participating can sometimes be reluctant to interfere with the instruction or decisions of the student's teacher. They may inadvertently get the message that they should defer responsibility for providing support to outside professionals, such as a special educator, related services provider, or job coach. Yet, peers, co-workers, and others in a setting are often quite willing to provide social support when they are given opportunities to participate in the planning process or when they are personally encouraged to do so. By talking candidly with these individuals, teachers can encourage others to share involvement in the student's program, while also gaining important "inside" information regarding available social supports. In the workplace, a variety of co-worker supports are naturally available. Conversations with supervisors and co-workers about how they can support the student can often generate new and creative ideas. For example, for a student who is having difficulty returning from break on time, a co-worker who shares the same break could prompt the student to return to work. A delivery driver at a pizza place or fast-food delivery service could drop off a fellow employee at home when they are out making deliveries. Or a student could be linked with a mentor at work during initial training and orientation to the job. After all, this is the way most people learn on the job.

"Acknowledge the student's efforts toward a goal. Stress that all individuals possess both strengths and limitations in varying mixtures and to different degrees."

Teacher, Melrose High School

As your planning team decides which supports will be drawn on by the student, always consider using the least intrusive supports available in an environment, such as a family member or neighbor rather than a paid staff person. In a school, this might mean involving peers before paraprofessionals and general educators before specialists. For example, peers could encourage and join students in participating in school activities, such as assemblies, dances, sporting events, theater productions, and extracurricular clubs. Not only will the student enjoy it, but the peers also will appreciate having developed new friendships and will feel better about their contributions toward an inclusive school. Peers can also be instrumental in supporting students to gain access to general education classes (Carter, Moss, Hoffman, Chung, & Sisco, 2011). For example, a student enrolled in a culinary arts class could work alongside one or two peers who provide social and academic support. Without this support (or with support from a paraprofessional), a student may be physically present but not socially included. Similarly, peers could volunteer to help with the lunch tray of a student with multiple disabilities. This is less stigmatizing to a student than having a teacher or paraprofessional provide that same help. Using natural social supports should have the effect of bringing individuals into contact with each other rather than isolating them. Make sure that the supports you provide do not result in a student's being unnecessarily "singled out."

By keeping in frequent contact with parents and other family members, you can ensure planned social supports are introduced across different areas of a student's life beyond the school day or work shift. Use the following strategies to remain engaged with families.

- Provide support to parents, too, as you encourage them to involve their children in social activities in and out of school. For example, parents can provide information about hobbies or interests that are seen only by them.

- Encourage parents to get involved in promoting students' social participation with peers. Have parents provide transportation so that a student and her peers can attend games together. Doing so also enables parents to meet a student's friends.

- If a student has no independent means of transportation to and from work, then a Plan to Achieve Self-Support (PASS) could be written to pay family members (or co-workers) to provide her with transportation.

For some students, however, simply identifying potential social supports in a particular setting will not be enough. Teachers may need to help students learn how to gain access to this support. Learning to gain access to social supports is a valuable skill for any student. For example, a student with a learning disability may not know whether it is appropriate to ask for a time extension on a quiz; a student with autism may be uncertain how to recruit assistance related to a particular job expectation; or a student with emotional or behavioral disabilities may wonder whom to turn to for help solving a personal problem. Teachers can increase students' opportunities for acceptance, success, and personal satisfaction by incorporating these supports into instruction.

For example, students might be taught to first request assistance from fellow classmates, co-workers, or fellow sports team or club members before requesting it from you, the teacher, or job coach. Support from these individuals is more natural and easily available and is more likely to be present over the long term. Occasionally, students may need instruction on accepted social skills in a given environment. Or a student might be taught to initiate and respond in conversations with peers or discuss more appropriate conversational topics, helping her to develop her own social supports as well as make her interactions more enjoyable for everyone involved. Teachers can also help a student compile a resource list of social supports to turn to for assistance. The list might include peers in a general education class who could provide assistance on an assignment or in getting to the next class or include people who usually ride on the student's bus and who could inform her when her stop is coming up. Next, students should be taught how and when to use such supports. If you are unsure how to do this, then invest time observing how others in the same setting gain access to support for themselves. For example, observe how co-workers request assistance at a worksite. Then, teach the student similar ways to request assistance, if needed, to complete a job task. For example, co-workers may ask each other for help in some work environments. At other jobs, it may be more appropriate to ask a supervisor or administrative assistant.

"A female student works at a grocery store. She is allowed to lift only 15 pounds at a time. As a courtesy clerk, this can cause a problem with items such as dog food. She has informed her co-workers, and they know to help her when she asks. She also confides in a co-worker about her boyfriend."

Teacher, Central High School

Helping students with disabilities gain access to social support is an important endeavor. Remember the following points when undertaking these efforts. First, consider introducing similar social supports across all of the different settings in which a student participates. Research shows that students are more likely to generalize their skills across similar instructional supports. For example, if a student has been taught to seek assistance by handing a peer a card at school, then teach her to use the same support in a store or on a bus. Second, remember that students (and the activities in which they participate) will change over time. Identify sources of support that will be available to the student both now and in the future, such as long-time residents of a community or a well-established social club, when observing home, work, school, and community settings. Third, think carefully about the breadth of supports a student will need in a setting. Task-related social supports are important to consider in the workplace, but so are social supports not directly related to job performance, including providing emotional support, helping a student get along socially, answering questions, or getting a meal after work. Finally, put your public relations skills to work as you help the individuals who provide a student's social support learn to collaborate with each other. Doing so will demonstrate that the whole is more than the sum of its parts when it comes to working together to provide support for a student.

"Provide varied opportunities for students to be involved in the community—teaching social interaction, independent living, and recreation/leisure skills. This is the best way to increase their social acceptance and participation in everyday life."

Teacher, Greeneville High School

ASSESSMENT

Assessing Outcomes: How Natural Are a Student's Supports?

Providing a student with social support in the classroom, workplace, or other setting is important in helping the student experience success and social acceptance. External supports, however, may unintentionally decrease natural supports and opportunities for social interaction available to the student if not designed carefully. Natural supports may promote a student's acceptance and competence by providing assistance in ways that are routine and valued by others in the work environment (Jorgensen, 1992). Ask yourself the following questions as you observe the students with whom you work across settings. Answering "yes" to the first four questions and "no" to the last three questions indicates that your students are likely receiving supports in a way that is both natural and nonstigmatizing.

1. Does the work supervisor or teacher spend as much time interacting with the student as with other employees or students in the classroom?

2. Does the teacher or job coach keep sufficient distance from the student, except when providing direct instruction?

3. Do co-workers or peers talk directly to the student instead of talking through the job coach or teacher?

4. Do teachers and job coaches direct co-worker and peer questions away from themselves and toward the student?

5. Would other employees or peers be embarrassed by the attention that the student receives from her teacher or job coach?

6. Has the teacher or job coach ever been mistaken for the student's parent because of his or her constant presence?

7. If a minor crisis arises with the student, do other employees or peers call for the job coach or paraprofessional instead of the supervisor or classroom teacher?

"I have planned social support for students, and often it is superficial and 'short-lived.' I have even made it a requirement of the peer-tutoring course I instruct. Friendships and social supports that are created by the student are far better, more stable, and usually nonsuperficial."

Teacher, Karns High School

EQUIPPING OTHERS TO PROVIDE SOCIAL SUPPORT

In addition to connecting students to needed social supports and teaching them to recruit natural supports on their own, people who interact regularly with your students may benefit from learning how to provide social support themselves. For example, this may involve teaching a co-worker to modify certain job tasks, helping a classmate find just the right way to provide encouragement, or assisting a peer to teach a new leisure skill to a student. Do not assume that others will automatically know how or feel confident to provide this support. Some initial guidance or extra encouragement from you may be just the thing they need to feel comfortable serving in this role. At the same time, it is important to know that some classmates, co-workers, and neighbors will be quite adept at providing social-related supports once they know it is acceptable for them to do so.

"Sometimes students at work get too much assistance from their co-workers. To give students opportunities to learn to complete their work more independently, we discuss with co-workers how to modify the task or environment. Often they are very helpful. Sometimes I use the same strategies with peers in class and in the school cafeteria."

Teacher, Rutledge High School

Peer buddy programs in middle and high schools are an especially promising approach for equipping peers without disabilities to provide social, academic, and personal supports to their classmates with disabilities (Hughes & Carter, 2008). Students receive initial information and guidance related to their new roles in the form of orientation sessions led by special educators, school counselors, or paraprofessionals. Peer buddies then provide daily or weekly class times when participating students with and without disabilities can spend time together and get to know one another. By interacting and providing support, general education peers help students with diverse abilities become actively involved in the mainstream of middle and high school life. Participating general education students, in turn, report that they are building new friendships and learning new social interaction skills. They also say that they have increased their appreciation of diversity, improved their communication skills, and improved their understanding of themselves and others. A variety of approaches for implementing peer support programs exist (e.g., Bond & Castagnera, 2006; Carter, Cushing, et al., 2009). Form 4.3 is a checklist of seven steps to consider when launching a credit-based peer buddy program in your school. (A blank, reproducible form is included on the accompanying CD-ROM.) In most schools, the starting point will be a conversation with administrators about the logistics of and steps in starting a new course and recruiting students (Step 1; Hughes & Carter, 2008). After inviting peers to become involved and matching them to students with disabilities (Steps 2 and 3), attention should turn toward orienting students to their new support roles (Step 4). As students begin working together, it is essential to assess the extent to which the program is accomplishing its intended goals (Step 5) and, if so, to explore ways of drawing in new students (Step 6). Finally, an advisory board can be established to provide support, feedback, and guidance as efforts are undertaken to grow the program (Step 7). Of course, you can adapt them to start a program in your own school, evaluating your progress by checking off each step as you go.

"'Peer tutoring, huh?' That was my first reaction to this class. The first day of school, I received my schedule and didn't know what the class was about. Of course, I had heard about the class from former peer tutors but didn't know what to expect. Like many others, I had already made my assumptions about the class. Since that time, I have come to realize that these assumptions were incorrect. I thought that the Life Skills students would be helpless, but this is not the case. As the first couple of weeks went by, I began to see that many of the students were not much different from me. A lot of the students enjoy many of the same games and activities that I do, such as Bingo, UNO, Connect Four, and even basketball. As time has gone by, the majority, if not all, of the students and I have become good friends, especially the boys. I often begin basic conversations with them as with any other person on subjects or events that I feel we might have in common. Peer tutoring has been a wonderful experience for me. It has allowed me to make new friends who have slight differences, but with more similarities than you could imagine!"

Peer buddy, Maplewood High School

RESEARCH

Impact of Peer-Mediated Support Strategies

There is strong research support for a wide variety of peer-mediated support strategies such as peer buddy programs and peer networks (see Carter, Sisco, Chung, & Stanton-Chapman, 2010). These strategies offer some clear benefits for students with disabilities—especially those with intellectual disabilities, autism, or multiple disabilities—rather than relying entirely on support provided by paraprofessionals, special educators, or job coaches. For example, peer support strategies have been shown to increase students' academic engagement, promote access to general education curricular content, enhance academic achievement, and help students meet their individualized goals. Socially, students with disabilities benefit as well. For example, research has shown that students can increase their communication skills, peer interactions, social networks, and friendships through working with their peers without disabilities. And students may develop greater self-determination and independence when they do not turn first to adults for help (Wehmeyer, Agran, et al., 2007).

Seven Steps to Starting a Peer Buddy Program

Step 1: Develop a one-credit course

☑ Incorporate a peer tutoring course into your school's curriculum that allows peer buddies to spend at least one period each day with their partners in special education.

☑ Begin building a base of support with the administration, guidance personnel, and teachers in your school for the inclusion of students receiving special education services in general education activities.

☑ Follow the established procedures of the local and state educational agencies when you apply for the new course offering.

☑ Include the course description in your school's schedule of classes.

Step 2: Recruit peer buddies

☑ Actively recruit peer buddies during the first year. After that, peer buddies will recruit for you.

☑ Include announcements, posters, articles in the school newspaper and PTA newsletter, videos on the school's closed-circuit television, and peer buddies speaking in school clubs and classes.

☑ Present information about the new program at a faculty meeting.

☑ Start slowly while you establish the course expectations.

Step 3: Screen and match students

☑ Have guidance counselors refer students who have interest, good attendance, and adequate grades.

☑ Arrange for students to interview with the special education teachers.

☑ Have students provide information regarding their past experience with students with diverse abilities and about clubs or activities that they are involved in and that their partners could join.

☑ Allow students to observe in the classroom to learn about the role of a peer buddy and whether they would be an appropriate match for the class.

Step 4: Teach peer buddies to use instructional strategies

☑ Model the use of prompting and reinforcement techniques.

☑ Conduct a peer buddy orientation that includes the concept of "people-first language," disability awareness, communication strategies, and suggested activities.

☑ Communicate teachers' expectations for the peer buddy course, including attendance and grading policies.

☑ Provide suggestions for dealing with inappropriate behavior, setting limits, and modifying activities.

Step 5: Evaluate the program

☑ Schedule observations and feedback sessions with peer buddies to address their questions or concerns.

☑ Provide feedback on their interaction skills, time management, use of positive reinforcement, and activities engaged in with their partners.

☑ Have peer buddies keep a daily journal of their activities and reflections, which should be reviewed weekly by the classroom teacher.

☑ Establish a peer buddy club, which allows students to share experiences and ideas as well as gives the teacher an opportunity to offer ongoing training and feedback.

(page 1 of 2)

Form 4.3. Seven Steps to Starting a Peer Buddy Program. (*Source:* Hughes et al., 1999.) (A blank, photocopiable version of this form is included on the accompanying CD-ROM.)

FORM 4.3. *(continued)*

Step 6: Hold a lunch bunch

☑ Invite peer buddies to join students in special education for lunch in the cafeteria.

☑ Encourage the peer buddies to invite their other friends to join the group, increasing social contacts for their partners.

☑ Remind general education students who are unable to enroll in the course because of class conflicts to join the lunch bunch.

Step 7: Establish an advisory board

☑ Develop an advisory board that includes students (peer buddies and partners), students' parents, participating general and special education teachers, administrators, and guidance counselors.

☑ Include community representatives to expand the peer buddy program to community-based activities, such as work experiences.

☑ Meet at least once each semester to obtain insight and suggestions for evaluating and improving the program. Thank all members for their participation.

(page 2 of 2)

The benefits are not limited only to students with disabilities, however. In fact, peers without disabilities also have much to gain from their involvement in these programs and support approaches. For example, peers have been shown to be as or more engaged academically when they provide support within inclusive classrooms (Cushing & Kennedy, 1997; Shukla, Kennedy, & Cushing, 1999). Having regular opportunities to work with and get to know their classmates with disabilities may also diminish attitudinal barriers, promote personal growth, and foster greater appreciation of diversity (Copeland et al., 2004; Siperstein, Norins, et al., 2007).

In addition to launching structured peer support initiatives such as peer buddy programs, consider the following strategies for equipping others to provide social support as recommended by teachers.

- Although some families are already familiar with the array of supports available to their child within and beyond the school, other families may not have access to these forms of social capital (Trainor, 2008). For example, parents with limited English proficiency may not know how to find a mentoring program for their child, such as Big Brothers or Big Sisters. Work with other staff at your school to identify ways of sharing information about available home and community supports with all families represented in your school.

- Encourage students with disabilities to become peer tutors in their skill areas. For example, a student may be especially knowledgeable about special effects in movies or an expert on the saxophone. In addition, encourage students to participate in clubs and classes on the basis of their interests, skills, and preferences.

- Offer training and information regarding positive behavior support procedures to staff, parents, and peers of students with disabilities, when appropriate. For example, peer buddies will need to know what to do if a student presents challenging behavior, such as aggression, or how to encourage a student who is shy to hold her head up and talk.

- Hold a discussion session with general education peers about the ways in which they can increase social and learning opportunities for students with disabilities at their school. For example, encourage general education students to help students with disabilities get involved on sports teams as a player, equipment manager, coach, or spectator.

- Let employers and co-workers know that you are available to discuss any questions or concerns that they may have about an employee. Have regular hours that you are available on the job, or give them your office, classroom telephone, or pager number. Worksite personnel will feel more comfortable if they know you are readily available if they have a question, such as what to do if a student misses the bus or if a student gets sick.

"Participating in a peer buddy program has been one of the most insightful experiences about life and about myself. I have learned that every student is unique, so you have to treat each person differently just as you would anybody else."

Peer buddy, Glencliff High School

Assessing Outcomes: Assessing Social Support Involvement

Evaluating the extent to which social supports are accessed by students does not have to be difficult. Consider the following strategies used by teachers.

ASSESSMENT
- Use the Work Performance Evaluation (see Form 3.2 in Chapter 3) to compare the social support available in a setting and the extent to which a student is actually using the support. Pinpoint reasons why a student may not be using particular supports, such as Friday potlucks at work, and brainstorm how to get the student more involved.

- Directly observe others in the classroom or workplace as they interact with a student. People's expressions or the way they interact with a student can tell you a lot about the relationship. Are they smiling and laughing with the student, or are they looking around and seeming distracted by and more interested in others? How is the student responding during the interactions?

- Schedule regular visits or conversations with people frequently involved with a student, such as a fellow member of the basketball team or chess club. Ask directly what sort of supports a student receives, or infer from their conversations about the support in the environment.

- Interview the student. She may be the best judge of the supports that she is receiving. For example, she may report that peers in her general education classes are making fun of her. Check the student's judgment by direct observation. It may be that she is correct or that her peers are actually joking with her as they do with the rest of their friends. In either case, be sure to address the student's perceptions.

"One of my students is very 'antisocial.' I called a meeting with the employer, co-workers, job coach, and parents and explained the skills I wanted to work on and told them the methods I had tried and what worked and what didn't. I asked for their ideas—others are often more willing to support me if they have input into the problem. For example, we wanted a student to learn to wave 'hello' when he entered a store. The employer and employees helped develop a plan. As a result, not only did they get to know the student and his family, but, to this day, when he enters the store, they will greet him openly and reach out to make his hand wave back if he does not respond independently."

Teacher, Warren County High School

INCREASING STUDENTS' SOCIAL PARTICIPATION

Everybody loses when students with and without disabilities have few opportunities to get to know and learn from one another. Students in general and special education alike miss out on the chance to develop social acceptance and appreciation of others. We ensure that all students will lead more socially fulfilling lives when students with diverse abilities have opportunities to interact frequently throughout the day and participate in all aspects of school and everyday life. Yet, many students with disabilities—particularly students with more extensive support needs—have diminished involvement in the numerous social and learning opportunities that exist within every school (Simeonsson, Carlson, Huntington, McMillen, & Brent, 2001; Wagner, Cadwallader, Garza, & Cameto, 2004).

Begin by reflecting on the breadth of social opportunities already available in your school or community (Swedeen, Carter, & Molfenter, 2010). What are all of the various places and activities in which students typically spend time together? Think beyond the classroom, considering not only the coursework (both required and elective) students take, but also the career development activities, extracurricular offerings, fine arts programs, social events, and informal settings (e.g., cafeterias, hallways, courtyards) in which students participate. Now, observe whether the students with whom you work are also participating in this same breadth of activities in similar ways. Assessing Outcomes (see below) includes several strategies for carrying out these observations. You may discover that some students are woven in tightly to the social fabric of their school and/or community. Other students, however, may remain on the peripheries of everyday activities and have few durable friendships.

Your next step is to identify and remove barriers that may be standing in the way of students' social participation. Increased opportunities for social support frequently can result from making modifications to certain settings. For example, adjusting work schedules will permit co-workers to take a break together, rearranging a classroom lab will encourage two students to share a computer, and building a ramp will allow a student access to a church youth group. Physically placing students in mainstreamed environments is not enough. A student may be in an integrated environment but have no social participation at all. Create opportunities, such as cooperative learning projects and peer buddy programs, that promote all students' active involvement in academic and social activities.

LEGISLATION

Full participation in school, at work, and in the community is both the letter and the spirit of the law. IDEA 2004 states, "Disability is a natural part of the human experience and in no way diminishes the right of individuals to participate in or contribute to society. Improving educational results for children with disabilities is an essential element of our national policy of ensuring equality of opportunity, full participation, independent living, and economic self-sufficiency for individuals with disabilities" (§ 601). Our national policy reflects a commitment to ensuring that all citizens—including individuals with disabilities—have rich opportunities to participate meaningfully in the life of their community.

ASSESSMENT

Assessing Outcomes: Observing Students' Social Participation

How much are students really participating in social activities throughout the day? It is important to know because it may be that they are simply in proximity of their peers but not interacting socially with them. Here are some ways to evaluate how much students actually interact with each other in everyday school settings.

- Observe a student's opportunity for and participation in community activities during a 1-month period using a simple tally sheet. (Form 4.4 is a Community Activity Participation Form. A blank, reproducible form can be found on the accompanying CD-ROM.)

FORM 4.4
Community Activity Participation Form

Student: __Antonio London__   Month: __April__

Activity	Monday	Tuesday	Wednesday	Thursday	Friday	Weekends	Total
Exercise at the YMCA		III				II	5
Church activities			III			IIII	7
Volunteer at nursing home				II			2
Softball league	III			I			4
Shopping at the mall					I	II	3
Movies with friends					II		2
Grocery shopping		IIII					4
Concerts/fairs				I	I	II	4
Other	I		I			II	4

Form 4.4. Community Activity Participation Form for Antonio. (A blank, photocopiable version of this form is included on the accompanying CD-ROM.)

- Keep a record of a student's attendance in a journalism, computer, or social studies class. Check with a peer buddy to determine the extent to which the student is participating in classroom activities and interacting with classmates.

- Ask a student to identify the social activities in which she participates outside school on a regular basis. Also, ask about which activities she would like to do but has not had the chance to do. Ask for parents' input as well.

- Use interest surveys and activity sampling to pinpoint students' interests. Then, on the basis of students' interests, arrange community and employment opportunities that allow students to work and interact with their general education peers, co-workers, and peers in the community.

LEGISLATION

All students should have the opportunity to learn and enjoy leisure activities with their peers both in and outside the classroom. Many students, however, will need support to assist them in taking full advantage of this opportunity. Students' IEPs must include a statement of the supports that will be provided for them to "be involved and progress in the general curriculum and to participate in extra-curricular and other nonacademic activities" (IDEA 2004, § 614).

Social connections at work are also important factors contributing to job satisfaction and success. Promoting high levels of participation and involvement with co-workers increases a student's chances of successful long-term employment and personal satisfaction, both on and off the job. Encourage and support students in becoming involved with other workers on the job and outside work, too. For example, support students to attend company picnics and/or other work-related social activities. If they are hesitant, then an interested co-worker could pick them up and accompany them to the event. Arrange for students to take breaks with their co-workers at work, recognizing that you may need to prompt students to talk to their co-workers. Or try asking a willing co-worker to sit down at the same table with a student and start a conversation. Getting games or conversations going in the break room is another way to encourage social participation. Set up social opportunities during or after work hours to include all employees. For example, have basketball shoot-outs in a company's gym during lunch or an after-work social hour at a local pizza place. Finally, provide opportunities for students to sample as many worksites as possible before they graduate from high school. Remind them to consider the opportunities for social interaction that occur at a worksite when they make decisions about where to work after graduation. Help students get involved in the community through participation in activities at community parks and recreation centers. Encourage parents to provide transportation and get peer buddies involved. You could even start an after-school program, such as swimming at the YMCA.

For students with differing abilities, simply possessing the right set of job or daily living skills may not be enough to ensure their full participation in community life after high school. Opportunities for demonstrating and putting those skills to use must be made available. Community members, however, are often unaware of the need to create such opportunities. Introducing community members to students through visits and participation in transition programs will show the potential contributions these students can make to the community.

- Include peers in all activities in which a student is involved throughout the day. For example, integrate students into production teams with their co-workers. In the community, include peer buddies in a student's activities to model appropriate behaviors and provide support when learning new skills, such as using an automated teller machine.

- Include recreation and leisure training in a student's educational program. Having skills that allow a student to participate in recreational activities with peers will provide the student with opportunities to build friendships and become connected to social supports around the community, such as at the YMCA, a singles club, or a women's (or men's) support group.

- Do not leave participation in after-school and community activities to chance. Your students and their families may need a "nudge." Send home calendars of social events, such as community dances, and arrange for carpooling if they do not have a ride to an event.

- Find a peer who has similar interests as a student, and make time for them to get together for activities outside school. For example, students who like French could join the French club and go on club outings together, or students who like to volunteer could join the local Red Cross and do community volunteer activities together.

"Encourage social interaction through a network of peer tutors at school and work. Assign peer tutors activities that carry over into the student's community and family life when possible."

Teacher, Riverdale High School

WEB RESOURCES

The Disability History Museum, http://www.disabilitymuseum.org/dhm/index.html

The Disability History Museum web site hosts a searchable library, posts education curricula, and showcases museum exhibits aimed at fostering research and study about the historical experiences of people with disabilities and their communities.

Inclusive Schools Week, http://www.inclusiveschools.org

Inclusive Schools Week is an annual event held each year during the first week in December. Free materials and resources for hosting activities are available on this web site.

Spread the Word to End the *R* Word Campaign, http://www.r-word.org/

The web site for this campaign to end use of the word *retard(ed)* includes downloadable resources, videos, and an online pledge form.

Teaching Skills that Promote Success

CHAPTER 5

Promoting Independence and Self-Determination

In this chapter, you will learn how to

- Educate students and others about self-determination

- Teach self-determination and self-management skills

- Assess opportunities for self-determination and choice making

- Collaborate with others to promote opportunities for self-determination in daily life

OVERVIEW

Simply put, *self-determination* means that students set personal goals, speak up for themselves, and make and act on their own educational and lifestyle choices. The focus on self-determination dates to the normalization movement of the 1970s, which held that the patterns and conditions of everyday life experienced by members of society should be available to all people with disabilities (Nirje, 1972). Implicit in the concept of self-determination is the notion that other people take into account a person's choices, preferences, and aspirations so the person can experience the respect and autonomy to which every human being is entitled. Skills that promote self-determination include self-management, self-advocacy, choice making, problem solving, decision making, self-awareness, and goal setting (Wehmeyer, Agran, et al., 2007).

LEGISLATION

Legislation supporting self-determination includes IDEA 1997 and 2004 and the Rehabilitation Act Amendments of 1992, which require incorporating self-determination into educational and rehabilitation programs. IDEA 2004 requires that students' strengths, preferences, and interests as well as considerations for their cultural backgrounds be incorporated into their IEPs.

Research shows that transition-age students often have little opportunity to make choices or advocate for themselves (Agran & Hughes, 2008; Carter, Owens, et al., 2009; Washington,

Hughes, & Cosgriff, in press). For example, students may have little say in developing their own educational goals and may be placed in classes or on a career track not of their own choosing. Unfortunately, limited opportunity to choose or act independently may continue into adulthood. Too often, decisions about everyday living—such as what to wear or eat, how to spend free time, or where to live or work—are made by family, teachers, or service providers, even after students leave school.

Educators should learn to assess environments to determine what opportunities exist to exercise self-determination skills (Field & Hoffman, 2003). If opportunity to practice self-determination is limited, then students likely will not develop goal-setting, choice-making, or other skills. Consequently, students will need to be taught how to set goals, guide their own behavior, and speak up for themselves. Educators should also learn to support students in making decisions and being responsible for their own behavior. Teachers can learn to expand opportunities for students to choose, make decisions, and self-advocate across many aspects of their lives (Martin et al., 2006). Not only are self-determination and involvement in developing one's own educational program legal mandates, but they also can have many benefits for students. For example, students may learn more about themselves, their strengths, and their interests by choosing to try new experiences.

This chapter comprises four groups of strategies for educators to use to promote students' self-determination, self-advocacy, and greater independence. These strategies include educating students and others about self-determination, teaching self-determination and self-management skills, assessing students' opportunities to use choice-making and self-determination skills, and collaborating with others to support students' self-determination.

Case Study 5.1 *Few Choices for Angelo*

Angelo Rust used to get his hair styled at a salon called Choices. What a joke, he thought. Today, he had no choices. Whether to get up or just stay in bed all day was about the extent of his choices. When he used to have money, well, maybe then he had choices. But that was before he got busted for selling drugs. Before that, he could buy whatever he wanted. He wore jewelry around his neck and wrists, had new shirts and shoes, and had his hair styled every day. But still, he thought, looking up at the ceiling from where he lay on his mattress on the floor, even then he was a just a workhorse for his business. It's not like he could just take off work for the weekend and go to the lake or even go to the movies. He always had to be ready to answer a text or a call, make a deal, or hide from the cops. Really, what kind of choices were those? What he really had wanted back then was just the chance to sit on a park bench in the sun, watching his nieces play in the sand and the men play chess at the tables under the trees. Now he had all the time in the world to do that since he dropped out of school 2 years ago at age 15, and now he hardly ever had work. Without even a general equivalency diploma or any kind of legitimate work experience, he never could find a job worth anything. So, what choice did he have now anyway but to sit on his mattress and wait for the next 24 hours to roll around?

All right, so maybe one time he did have choices. Maybe he did choose to start hanging out with the drug crowd, and maybe it was his idea to start selling drugs for some quick cash. And maybe he did decide to quit school. But let's face it: He hated school. He never had any choices there, that's for sure. For one thing, his counselor stuck him in auto tech classes all the time, and he hated working on cars. Dirty, greasy work, he thought. What he really had wanted to do, to tell you the truth, was to enroll in the child care classes they had at school and someday become a preschool teacher. He loved little kids, just like his nieces, and he had wanted to teach them that they could have a better life and make better choices than he did. But nobody listened to him, and, finally, one day, he just quit going to school. And the only choice now was either to get up or to stay in bed. (See Case Study 8.3 in Chapter 8 for a different view of Angelo's life, had he been given career choices.)

"Self-determination is

- Having a choice
- Knowing more about ourselves
- Having dreams and goals and going after them
- Being in control
- Making your own decisions
- Spending money our way"

Southern Collaborative of Self-Advocates, People First of Tennessee, Georgia, and Alabama

EDUCATING STUDENTS AND OTHERS ABOUT SELF-DETERMINATION

LEGISLATION

IDEA 2004 clearly supports students' self-determination. The amendments require that students are involved in developing their educational programs as members of their own IEP teams and that they attend their IEP meetings as active participants when appropriate. The amendments also state that students' educational programs must be based on their preferences and interests. One year before students reach the age of majority, they must also be informed of their rights that will transfer to them when reaching their majority. These requirements put considerable responsibility on students. Educators must support students in learning new self-determination and self-advocacy skills in order for them to fulfill these requirements.

"I give my students as much independence as possible so that they can make their own choices and experience the consequence of these choices—at work, at school, and in social situations. I let them experience the consequence of a poor choice, too—such as when selecting the wrong item from a vending machine."

Itinerant transition teacher, Nashville Public Schools

Educating Students About Self-Determination

Sometimes the student is the first person you must convince about self-determination. Students are likely to have learned to "let someone else do it," even when doing so might go against their own preferences or interests, after many years of having few opportunities to make choices or decisions and to act on those choices. Students should learn they can set goals, monitor and reward their own performance, speak up for themselves, and solve problems on their own. Letting students and others know that self-determination is every person's right and responsibility is often an important first step.

Teachers recommend beginning the process by discussing the importance of setting goals. Together, a teacher and students—individually or as a small group—can brainstorm examples of goals, such as raising a grade in class or reading a new book every month. Students then need actual opportunities to set their own educational goals, which should be embedded in their daily activities. For example, a student who is learning to expand his social skills may set a goal of greeting five peers before lunch each day. Because students are just learning to set goals, teachers will need to use direct instruction to teach goal setting by modeling goal setting, giving students opportunities to practice setting goals, and providing corrective feedback (Lee,

Palmer, & Wehmeyer, 2009). Teachers can also help students set realistic educational goals, which students can meet within a reasonable period of time.

Next, teachers recommend teaching students to self-monitor their own performance to determine whether they have met their goals. For example, a young woman may want to learn to apply her makeup by herself. She can judge whether she has met her goal by checking her appearance each day. She can also experience the satisfaction of choosing her own goal and acting to reach that goal. To build in opportunities to practice goal setting and self-monitoring, teachers recommend asking students at the beginning of the day to tell or list their activities planned for the day. A simple checklist can help students indicate when an activity has been completed. Students with limited communication or reading skills could use pictures to indicate activities to accomplish. By learning to set and monitor their goals, students are becoming educated about the self-determination process of acting, by choice, as the primary causal agent in an event (Wehmeyer et al., 2011).

Students also need to learn the responsibilities that go with self-determination. Being self-determined means being aware of the consequences of one's actions and taking responsibility for those consequences (Wehmeyer & Palmer, 2003). For example, students may list completing an art project or shopping for clothes as one of their activities for the day. They must also be aware of the consequences of these activities (i.e., either cleaning up after the art project or paying for clothes they choose at the mall). Students also must learn that monitoring and maintaining control of their emotions are critical components of self-determination. Students who feel they can manage their own emotional outbursts, such as anger or hurt feelings, will feel more in control of their environment (Reid, Trout, & Schwartz, 2005). Involving students in a social skills self-management program (see Chapter 6) may teach them about the benefits of self-determination.

"I teach a unit on self-determination and self-management skills. I point out to students reasons why people should exercise self-management skills in the workplace and school environment, and I teach them to monitor their own behavior."

Teacher, Cumberland County High School

"Allow students to experience the consequences of their actions. In everything they do, students must learn to be responsible for their own actions and understand why they are responsible."

Teacher, Sheffield High School

Teachers also recommend the following practices for educating students about self-determination.

- Give students the responsibility of arranging their personal daily schedule and let them manage their own time. Allow them to learn the consequences of their behavior, such as being late to class or forgetting to prepare for class. Let them experience the success of getting to their job-training sites on time and completing their job tasks on time.

- Being self-determined means knowing how to prioritize activities in one's life. Help students learn to prioritize by making lists, such as a list of things that must be done to achieve a goal (e.g., passing a driver's test) or a list of steps for preparing for an IEP meeting. Picture lists can be used with students who do not read or write.

- Managing one's behavior may be easier in some settings than in others. Just think about yourself—do you find it hard to read when the television is on or others are talking? Suggest an alternative time or place for students who are having trouble managing their behavior, such as moving to a quiet area at the public library for someone who is becoming agitated by others' talking or taking a job at a noisy industrial site for a worker who has difficulty quieting his own loud, distracting sounds.

"One of my biggest obstacles in the area of self-determination is usually the family. Independence is a scary thing for everyone, especially for parents. I've found that including the family in the very first stages of developing self-management strategies is vital."

Teacher, Hunters Lane High School

"I involve students in role-playing situations with their peers that are typical of 'real life.' I then let them decide how they will manage themselves in those situations. Role-playing with their peers helps them see what the consequences of their actions would be."

Teacher, Ridgeway High School

Educating Others About Self-Determination

Students' goals, choices, and decisions must be communicated to others who can work together to support students to act on their own choices and goals. Friends, neighbors, family members, employers, and other community leaders can also help by communicating to students the variety of choices they do have—for careers, community living arrangements, postsecondary education, recreational options, clubs, and social opportunities. Family members and others may need help themselves in realizing the capabilities that students do have. If people have been providing considerable assistance to students, such as walking a young woman to the bus stop or deciding what a young man will wear each day, then families and others likely will not be aware of what these students can do or can learn to do on their own. It may be helpful for families and others to observe students in different settings where less assistance is provided to view their existing skill repertoires—for example, when a student stops to buy a bag of chips on his own at a convenience store on the way to his college class. Educators must also be mindful of cultural differences in attitudes toward self-determination of families and others (Shogren, 2011). Some cultures place greater emphasis on independence than others, which may value family or community connectedness more.

Teachers recommend the following strategies in educating important others about self-determination.

- Interview family members either in their homes or a community setting in which they feel comfortable to learn more about their family values. Families might not feel comfortable sharing this information in the school setting.

- Collaborate with a student's family to develop a schedule of leisure and recreational activities in which the student can choose to participate at school and in the community, such as at the YMCA, Boys and Girls Club, youth group, or a community center. If parents are more involved in their children's recreational activities, then the chances that a student can act on his leisure-time choices are increased.

- Brainstorm with guidance counselors and general education teachers about possible choices of classes for each student. Have the counselor and teachers describe the content and range of courses available, such as theater arts, journalism, or horticulture, so that the student is knowledgeable about choices. Video clips or photographs of the class and talking to class members may help as well.

- Have students visit different worksites and "shadow" employees to find out what their jobs are like. Invite guest speakers into the classroom to explain different jobs and the skills required for each.

- Have open discussions with students, parents, and representatives of community businesses about realistic expectations and requirements of potential careers, such as landscaping, carpentry, or radiology. Discuss postsecondary training required for these careers and take students to visit postsecondary education sites that teach required classes.

- Encourage students to try out for different school sports teams of their choice or for other extracurricular activities. Remind them, however, that they must accept the responsibilities that accompany their choices. For example, members of the track team must provide their own transportation to practice and meets.

- Have speakers from the community, including staff from a mental health center and drug and alcohol program, speak in class to discuss choices that students have in their lives. Have them discuss with students that they have options—to control their anger, to avoid using drugs or alcohol, to exercise to relieve stress, and to make other healthy choices.

- Use the Home Inventory Form (see Form 2.5 in Chapter 2) to survey parents' as well as students' choices. How do parents' goals for their children compare with their children's choices? Discuss areas of disagreement with them, and help them negotiate a compromise.

- Help employers provide students with options that are consistent with their choices and goals for advancement so that students feel they have opportunities for promotion.

"Support from home is extremely important in this area. Ask parents to use a checklist of a student's duties taped to the refrigerator at home. At school use picture cues or tape record sequences of events."

Teacher, Hillsboro High School

TEACHING SELF-MANAGEMENT AND SELF-DETERMINATION SKILLS

LEGISLATION

The goal of self-determination for all students is clearly embedded in IDEA 2004. The amendments state that the federal government has an ongoing obligation to support programs, projects, and activities that help students acquire skills that will empower them to lead productive and independent adult lives. The amendments also state that "an essential element of our national policy [is] ensuring equality of opportunity, full participation, independent living, and economic self-sufficiency for individuals with disabilities" (§ 601). Educational personnel are required to ensure that students have the skills and knowledge to meet "the challenging expectations that have been established for all children and [to] be prepared to lead productive and independent adult lives, to the maximum extent possible" (§ 601).

"I teach students about self-determination by using behavior management techniques that link rewards and consequences to behaviors. I use a behavioral contract when necessary. I also teach them about problem solving and provide feedback to them about their strengths and needs."

Teacher, Hillcrest High School

How do students learn to become more self-determined? How do they learn to set goals, work to achieve these goals, advocate for themselves, make decisions, and solve problems? Learning to use self-management skills, such as goal setting or self-monitoring to control, guide, and direct their own behavior, is one way to promote self-determination in students (Agran, King-Sears, Wehmeyer, & Copeland, 2003). Students can learn to use the same behavioral principles, such as prompting or rewarding themselves, that teachers use to manage the behavior of individual students or entire classes (Alberto & Troutman, 2009). For example, students can learn to remind themselves to perform a desired behavior and monitor and reward themselves for good performance. Self-management strategies include such skills as self-instruction, picture prompts, self-monitoring, and self-reinforcement (Agran et al., 2003). To a large degree, students can learn that they are the ones who can determine and direct their own lives when they use self-management strategies.

Research on Self-Management Strategies in the Classroom

RESEARCH

Hundreds of studies have focused on evaluating a variety of self-management strategies to promote academic, social, employment, and other transition-related outcomes. Several reviews suggest that self-management strategies are considered effective and feasible for a range of students, including those with intellectual disabilities (Mechling, 2007), autism (Southall & Gast, 2011), learning disabilities (Joseph & Eveleigh, 2011), and emotional/behavior disorders (e.g., Carter, Lane, Crnobori, Bruhn, & Oakes, 2011), and even students without disabilities (Briesch & Chafouleas, 2009).

Case Study 5.2 *Not Just a "Piece of Cake"*

Everyone knows that Badecoli's Italian Restaurant and Pub is where politicians and local celebrities go for a good meal. That's why Hsin Tu was so glad to have gotten a job there; besides that, they were famous for having the best "Sheer Indulgence Chocolate Cake" in town. Hsin had put together a strong résumé in high school because he had many job experiences at businesses in his community. His transition teacher had worked with him on his interviewing skills, and he had gotten his new job just 1 month ago. He was excited about working as a prep cook during four lunch shifts each week.

Hsin's teacher worked closely with him at different worksites throughout high school. Hsin's teacher was always right there to help him whenever he had questions or needed assistance. Hsin always knew what to do, when to do it, and what the consequences would be because his teacher told him. As it turned out, working at Badecoli's was a much different experience for Hsin.

Although he had received employee training at Badecoli's, his transition teacher, Ms. Carlin, had expected Hsin to be much more independent on the job. Although Hsin did fine during training, his performance slipped drastically as soon as Ms. Carlin was no longer standing next to him during each shift. Hsin really didn't know what to do without her. After all, no one had ever taught him to work on his own. Everything would go along all right until he had to make a decision for himself, such as the time he ran out of tomatoes for the salad or when the food chopper broke and he was in the middle of cooking apples. As the days went on, Hsin was running into more and more difficulty at work. It wasn't such a "piece of cake" after all. In fact, Hsin didn't even like to go to work anymore. Before long, Ms. Carlin

(continued)

Case Study 5.2   *(continued)*

> got a call from Hsin's supervisor, asking her to stop by to talk about Hsin's job performance. (See Assessing Outcomes: Teaching and Evaluating Self-Management to learn how Ms. Carlin identified self-management strategies that would work well for Hsin.)

"Reminding students of the consequences of their behavior helps them to manage their own behavior. I tell students a rule such as 'wait until you go outside after the bell to tap or make a beat' and then 'make your decision to stop your behavior or miss your computer time' if the behavior persists. They self-manage their own behavior."

Teacher, Fairley High School

Teaching Self-Management

Most people use self-management strategies in different areas of their lives—a grocery list on the refrigerator, a to-do list in a daily planner or tablet computer, a recipe for cooking dinner, or self-talk to calm down. The same strategies can be taught to students to help them decrease their dependence on others and increase their independent performance and self-determination on the job, in school, at home, and around the community (Wehmeyer, Agran, et al., 2007). With so many self-management strategies available, such as self-monitoring or goal setting, identifying which one is most appropriate for a student can be challenging. For example, should you teach a young man to self-instruct, self-monitor, or use picture prompts when he forgets to greet customers at his job in a pharmacy or raise his hand before speaking in his college class? Form 5.1 lists seven steps you can use to decide which strategy will work best in a particular case. Instructions are found in Assessing Outcomes: Teaching and Evaluating Self-Management. A blank, reproducible form can be found on the accompanying CD-ROM.

A self-management strategy should match the strengths, needs, preferences, and interests of the students using it. As with all educational programming, instruction should be individualized for each student. Students will be more likely to learn a new skill, such as self-management, if they feel they will get something out of it. For example, if a student knows he will get an *A* in his high school or college class only if he gets to class on time, then he will be more likely to use a self-management technique such as setting the alarm clock each day. In addition, be a good model of self-management for your students. By showing them ways you use self-management strategies in your own life, they can see how to do it as well as the advantages of being a self-managed person. If your classroom or office is always a mess and you are always trying to find things, then your students may do the same. Yet, if they see that you always put things in their place and consequently always know where everything is, then they are likely to learn the advantages of maintaining order at home, work, and school.

In addition, teachers recommend the following strategies.

- Teach students to use self-management strategies as you would teach them to do anything else. Use learning principles such as modeling, corrective feedback, opportunities to practice, prompting, and reinforcement. Begin to withdraw your assistance as students learn to use these self-management strategies on their own.

- Learning to self-manage often means learning new skills. Give students a lot of feedback and praise as they learn. Remember, your students may have been depending on you for a long time to act for them. Now they have to act for themselves. If you meet with resistance at first, do not give up. Students will be pleased as they grow more independent.

FORM 5.1
Teaching and Evaluating Self-Management

Student: __Hsin Tu__   Environment: __Badecoli's Italian Restaurant and Pub__

1. Identify the problem.

   Co-workers report that Hsin is leaving important ingredients off of food dishes and that he is taking too long to fill food orders.

2. Verify the problem.

   Observed Hsin during a lunch shift (1 hour) and compared his performance with that of his co-workers. He is making three times as many errors and taking three times as long to complete tasks.

3. Determine acceptability.

   Supervisor is worried about Hsin's accuracy and speed, but his primary concern is with accuracy.

4. Identify natural supports in the environment.

   The restaurant has large training pictures of each step of the food preparation process, and the pictures are the same ones that co-workers use. Also, two other employees work side by side with Hsin and could assist him.

5. Select a self-management strategy.

   Use picture prompts in the form of the training pictures.

6. Teach self-management skills.

   Teach Hsin to perform each step by following the picture prompts using modeling, prompts, corrective feedback, and reinforcement. Fade instruction by moving from verbal reminders to gestural reminders to no prompts at all.

7. Evaluate the student's performance.

   Observed Hsin several weeks later—his speed and accuracy match that of his co-workers. Both wait staff and cook staff agree that Hsin's job performance is acceptable.

Form 5.1. Teaching and Evaluating Self-Management Form for Hsin Tu. (A blank, photocopiable version of this form is included on the accompanying CD-ROM.)

- Students with disabilities communicate in different ways. You may need to use many forms of communication when teaching students to manage their own behavior. A student who does not speak or read may benefit from using picture cards to self-manage. For readers, a written list carried in their wallets or backpacks may work. Be flexible and creative. Adapt self-management strategies to your students' preferred forms of communication.

- When students are first learning to manage their own behavior, consider using a reward system in which students earn points for increasing independence. As students become better in using their self-management strategies, they can learn to deliver their own points or rewards by using self-reinforcement, such as buying a soft drink after completing an exercise routine.

ASSESSMENT

Assessing Outcomes: Teaching and Evaluating Self-Management

Teaching self-management to students sounds appealing, but how do you do it? What do you do with a student who just cannot seem to get up in the morning to get to school or a student who cannot seem to control his anger and yells at the cashier when shopping? Or what about the student who does not shave, use deodorant, or brush his teeth most of the time? With so many different challenges and students, where do you start? You will find that teaching self-management is not hard if you practice the following steps. Use Form 5.1 and the description of self-management strategies that follows to guide you.

Identify the Problem

Begin by gathering information about a student's performance in a particular setting, such as at the baseball park, on the job, or on the bus to a community college class. Do people in that setting believe that the student's performance needs to be improved in some way? Finding out whether people think there is a problem is the first step in teaching self-management. You can do this by asking them questions or by having them fill out an informal assessment. Be sure to ask a variety of people who are present, such as co-workers, employers, teachers, family members, peers, community members, and the student himself.

Hsin Tu's supervisor at Badecoli's Italian Restaurant and Pub had already received three complaints about Hsin from customers' suggestion cards when he first mentioned that Hsin was having a problem. Hsin was forgetting to include some important ingredients, such as the house dressing on salads or herb garnishes on appetizers. Besides that, three waitresses had complained about how long it was taking Hsin to get food orders to them during the lunch rush. And, just as important, Hsin himself told his supervisor that he was "getting confused" by all of the orders and didn't know which ones to start on first, especially when the restaurant was crowded.

Verify the Problem

Different people in a setting may evaluate a student's performance differently. It is important to check whether a problem identified by a person really is a problem. You can do this by observing a student's performance and then comparing it with the performance of a peer or a co-worker. If the student's performance is different from a peer who is successful in that same setting, then there may indeed be a problem. Discuss your findings with others (including the student) to decide whether the problem is serious enough to address.

Ms. Carlin decided to observe Hsin for an hour during one lunch shift. Because there were two prep cooks in addition to Hsin, Ms. Carlin compared his performance with that of his co-workers. She recorded the time it took to make each salad and how many errors each employee made (which she determined by talking to the wait staff). She discovered that Hsin was working at about one third the rate of his co-workers and that errors occurred approximately three times as often. Besides that, she noticed that every time Hsin filled a salad order, he made it in a different way.

Determine Acceptability

What should a student's behavior look like? How much should it resemble the behavior of others in the same setting? The answer will vary from setting to setting. Collaborate with supervisors, teachers, college instructors, peers, recreational staff, and others, as well as the student, to discuss what performance level is acceptable in an environment and what behaviors are practical to expect. Learn to negotiate expectations with others.

Ms. Carlin sat down with Hsin's supervisor to discuss her observations. The supervisor stated that although he hoped Hsin would learn to work faster, the most important requirement was that Hsin make the salads correctly. In the meantime, he would allow Hsin's co-workers to take responsibility for making sure all of Hsin's salad orders were completed on time.

Identify Natural Supports in the Environment

Many settings often include supports that can prompt students to begin, continue, or end an activity on their own. For example, bus schedules may be listed at a bus stop, bells may signal the beginning and end of class or a work shift, or textbooks may contain a list of questions for self-study. Students can learn to use these naturally occurring supports and reinforcers to guide their behavior as they learn to self-manage. The Job Analysis Survey (Form 3.1) in Chapter 3 can be used to help you identify supports.

Ms. Carlin used the Job Analysis Survey she had completed when placing Hsin at Badecoli's to determine what supports in the restaurant could help Hsin complete his job accurately and independently. She discovered that the restaurant had training pictures that could be hung above the salad prep area. The pictures provided a visual task analysis of the required steps used for making each type of salad.

Select a Self-Management Strategy

Three questions should be asked when deciding which self-management strategy to teach a student. First, there are several self-management strategies from which to choose, such as self-instruction, permanent (picture) prompts, self-monitoring, and self-reinforcement. Which of these strategies matches the requirements of a particular setting? For example, if a job requires an employee to move around, then picture prompts that are permanently placed in a setting may not be the best choice. Second, is the procedure acceptable by others in the setting? If the setting is very quiet, such as a library, then teaching a student to self-instruct aloud would not be a good idea. Third, which strategy does the student prefer? If students are to become responsible for their own behavior, then they should be involved in selecting how they will manage their behavior.

Ms. Carlin decided that picture prompts would help Hsin manage his own work behavior. They were already available and matched what Hsin needed to know to do his salad preparation correctly. Besides that, the pictures were the same ones other employees used during their training and, therefore, would be acceptable to his co-workers. Fortunately, Hsin thought the pictures were "cool" and he was willing to give them a try.

Teach Self-Management Skills

There are three steps to teaching self-management. First, identify the steps of the target behavior, such as shaving or using an automatic teller machine, and the self-management strategy, such as self-monitoring and self-instructing. Second, teach each step of the target behavior and self-management strategy using direct instructional techniques, such as prompting, modeling, and providing feedback. Third, start withdrawing your assistance gradually as soon as possible. For example, start standing farther away from the student or visit the setting less often to promote independent performance.

Ms. Carlin decided that the easiest way to identify the steps of making salads was to make them herself as she followed each step on the training pictures that she had placed on the wall. As she did so, she checked off each picture as she performed each step. She then taught Hsin to do the same, using modeling, prompts, corrective feedback, and reinforcement. She then began to withdraw her help so that Hsin could learn to perform the steps independently. First, Ms. Carlin gave a verbal reminder as Hsin completed each step. Gradually, she began only to point to a picture if he missed a step. Then, she placed herself farther away from Hsin. Before long, Hsin was using the pictures on his own to prompt his behavior.

Evaluate the Student's Performance

When instruction is completed, teachers should periodically observe their students to determine whether their performance has maintained. Also, remember to continue to check whether students' performance is similar to the performance of others in the same setting. Finally, check the acceptability of your students' performance by asking others in the setting. Their opinion is as important as your students' actual behavior.

Ms. Carlin occasionally watched Hsin (from a distance, of course) to determine how well he was doing at work and how his performance compared with that of his co-workers. She soon discovered that as Hsin became better at following the picture prompts, his speed and accuracy also improved. Conversations with the other prep cooks and the waitresses confirmed her observations—Hsin was making salads with the best of them. And, as it turned out, Hsin had put his own self-management program in place. If he finished all of his salads on time, then he treated himself to his favorite dessert: a piece of "Sweet Indulgence Chocolate Cake." This job really was "a piece of cake" after all.

Teaching Students to Use Self-Instruction

Self-instruction involves teaching students to use their own verbal behavior, or "self-talk," to guide their performance (Wehmeyer, Agran, et al., 2007). Put simply, self-instruction means that a student tells himself to do something and then does it. Self-instruction is an effective self-management strategy to teach if students are required to move around within a setting because students' verbal behavior is always available to them—whether going to the movies with friends, riding the bus, getting dressed for school, or interacting at work or the local YMCA.

Assessing Outcomes: Teaching and Evaluating the Use of Self-Instruction

Teaching self-instruction is easy because the steps already have been developed for you. First, identify a particular behavior that a student is not performing independently. Next, follow the steps outlined in Form 5.2, the Self-Instruction Training Sequence. (A blank, reproducible form is included on the accompanying CD-ROM.) Detailed instructions for completing each of the steps follow. You may adapt the steps to fit the behavior and your student's own strengths and needs.

Self-Instruction Training Sequence

1.   Teacher models target behavior while self-instructing aloud.

The first step in teaching self-instruction is to perform the target behavior yourself while the student is watching. For example, you may model how to load a dishwasher or how to access the Internet. As you perform the behavior, say each step of the task aloud (self-instruct) as you do it.

Mr. Wallace, the physical education teacher at Haverty High School, was trying to teach his class to dance a basic rumba step. He lined up all of the students on one side of the gym and stood in front of them with his back to them. Then he began to dance the basic rumba step over and over as the students watched. As he did so, Mr. Wallace loudly said, "Step-close-step," as he performed each of the foot movements of the pattern.

2.   Student performs target behavior while teacher instructs aloud.

Next, it is the student's turn to perform the target behavior. Continue to model how to self-instruct by saying the instructions aloud as the student performs each step. Provide prompts, corrective

Self-Instruction Training Sequence

Directions: Describe the behaviors to be performed for each of these steps:

1. Teacher models target behavior while self-instructing aloud.

   Perform the basic rumba steps several times saying, "Step-close-step."

2. Student performs target behavior while teacher instructs aloud.

   Ask students to perform the basic rumba step. While watching them, call out step instructions (step-close-step). Provide corrective feedback, give repeated opportunities for students to practice, and praise students who perform the steps correctly.

3. Student performs target behavior while self-instructing aloud.

   Students will perform the basic rumba steps without instructions from the teacher. Students should self-instruct aloud (step-close-step). Continue to provide feedback to students who need assistance.

4. If appropriate, teach the student to whisper or "think" the self-instructions.

   Teacher models how to dance the rumba without self-instructing "out loud." Next, students perform the dance steps on their own, without self-instruction.

Self-Instruction Statements

Directions: Describe what the student will say (or do) for each of these statements:

1. Identifying the problem: Someone is walking over here to ask me to dance, but I'm nervous that I'll forget the correct steps.

2. Stating the possible responses to the problem: As I dance, I'll "think" the steps to myself. "Step-close-step."

3. Evaluating the response: Wow! I only stepped on her feet twice.

4. Self-reinforcing: I danced much better than last time! I'll reward myself with something from the snack table.

Form 5.2. Self-Instruction Training Sequence for Mr. Wallace's class. (A blank, photocopiable version of this form is included on the accompanying CD-ROM.)

feedback, reinforcement, and, of course, opportunities to practice as the student learns to perform the behavior independently.

Next, Mr. Wallace turned around so that he could watch the students as they danced the basic rumba step. As they moved their feet in time to the music, he continued to instruct them aloud by saying, "Step-close-step." He also corrected the students if they missed any of their steps, had them practice their steps over and over, and praised them for learning the basic step so quickly.

3. Student performs target behavior while self-instructing aloud.

Finally, it is time to turn all of the responsibility over to the student. This time the student performs the target behavior and self-instructs independently. You still may have to guide the student or provide corrective feedback, but you should discontinue your assistance as soon as possible.

Mr. Wallace now wanted the students to dance without his help. This time as they performed the basic rumba step, they self-instructed aloud, saying, "Step-close-step." Mr. Wallace was there to help a few who still had difficulty, but soon all of the students in the class were performing the step on their own to the beat of the music and their self-instructions.

4. If appropriate, teach the student to whisper or "think" the self-instructions.

Although effective in guiding your students' behavior, talking aloud to themselves may not be acceptable in some settings because it draws too much attention to the student. If appropriate, instruct the student to whisper or to say the instructions in his head.

It might be all right for the students to say their dance steps out loud while they are learning them in class, but Mr. Wallace knew that would not be "cool" on the dance floor or at the prom. He decided to model dancing the rumba without self-instructions and reminded the students that talking out loud to themselves might be a big "turn-off" for their dates.

Self-Instruction Statements

The statements students are taught to say as they self-instruct may be as simple as those used by Mr. Wallace to teach his students to do the rumba ("step-close-step"). Or they may follow more of a problem-solving format, which prompts students to identify and respond to a problem (Agran et al., 2010). Students then evaluate their responses and reinforce themselves for doing a good job (or tell themselves to try another solution if theirs did not work). The statements can be either complex or simple, as shown next.

1. *Identifying the problem:* "Here comes my boss. I always want to yell at her when I see her, but I don't want to get fired," or, "Not plugged in."

2. *Stating a possible response to the problem:* "Guess I'll try to smile and say 'Hi,'" or, "Got to plug in."

3. *Evaluating the response:* "Hey, that was pretty easy. She even smiled back," or, "That wasn't really a smile. I'll try better next time," or, "Fixed it."

4. *Self-reinforcing:* "It's a good idea to be nice. Then she's nicer to me," or, "Good."

"I teach self-management by encouraging students to voice their activities for the day every morning. This helps them to learn their responsibilities and what they plan to do each day."

Teacher, Glencliff High School

Teaching Students to Use Permanent Prompts

Permanent prompts are visual, auditory, or tactile cues that are used to prompt a desired behavior (Wehmeyer, Agran, et al., 2007). People often use some type of permanent prompt to remind them to do something, such as writing a to-do list, setting an alarm on a wristwatch or smart phone, or posting a daily or weekly schedule. In learning to use permanent prompts, students are taught to respond in a specific way when they see or hear the cue. Eventually, they will not need to have a teacher, parent, or someone else prompt them to do something.

Most school, work, and community settings already have many naturally occurring prompts for guiding behavior (Hagner et al., 1995). Traffic lights indicate when to stop or go, clocks tell you what time to go to class, and telephones ring when you should answer them. Students, however, may need to be taught to respond appropriately to these naturally occurring prompts. Or they may need additional permanent prompts to help them respond independently. Teach students to look for features of an environment that they can use to prompt their behavior. For example, a student who has difficulty remembering when medicine should be taken can be given a series of cues to remember, such as when a certain television program comes on.

Sometimes naturally occurring prompts must be adapted to better cue a student's behavior. For example, a telephone may need to "ring" by flashing a light to signal an incoming call for a student with a hearing impairment, or exit signs in a building may need to be lowered for students using wheelchairs to see them. Also, the way you adapt prompts must be socially acceptable—some students would not want to be seen carrying a picture schedule into their auto tech or art history class or the local community center.

"Place empty cans of cleaning items in the areas needing to be cleaned; therefore, the student can remember the items needed in each area. This will help students learn on their own which items to use for cleaning and where to use them."

Teacher, Ripley High School

ASSESSMENT

Assessing Outcomes: Teaching and Evaluating the Use of Picture Prompts

One way to use permanent prompts is to combine pictures with a task analysis of the steps needed to complete a job (Copeland & Hughes, 2000). For example, you could analyze each step for cleaning a bathroom in a motel or at home using Form 5.3. Then take a photograph or draw a picture of each step of the job. Post the pictures on the wall, in a book, or on a board. Give the student a marker to check off each step as he completes it. If you laminate the pictures, then they can be reused. The filled-in version of Form 5.3 provides one example of a series of picture prompts that could be used for cleaning a bathroom. Notice at the bottom of the form that a student can evaluate how many steps toward his personal goal he completed. A blank, reproducible form is included on the accompanying CD-ROM.

Teachers also report they have taught students to use picture prompts as self-management strategies in the following ways.

- Teach students to use a personal picture schedule at the beginning of the school year and in community settings to increase students' autonomy and self-determination.

- Teach a young man to wash his hands by color coding each step of hand washing with a color-coded picture chart.

Task: Cleaning a bathroom

1. Clean toilet ☑

2. Clean bathtub ☑

3. Clean sink ☑

4. Clean mirrors ☑

5. Empty trash ☑

6. Refill soap ☑

7. Refill toilet paper ☑

8. Sweep floor ☐

9. Mop floor ☐

Goal:	Steps completed:	Did I meet my goal?
7	1 2 3 4 5 6 ⑦ 8 9	☺ ☹

Form 5.3. Picture Prompt: Cleaning a bathroom. (A blank, photocopiable version of this form is included on the accompanying CD-ROM.)

- Teach students to follow their morning routines by using checklists or picture schedules.

- Teach students to match their picture card schedules with a posted main schedule so that they can make the transition independently from one activity to the next.

- Use premarked envelopes with specified dollar amounts for students to use to budget their paychecks for monthly expenses.

- Require students to display their personal schedules on their cell phone or tablet computer so they can get to their daily appointments or take their medication on time.

ASSESSMENT

Assessing Outcomes: Teaching and Evaluating the Use of Picture Schedules

Permanent prompts can be used to teach students to follow daily schedules. For students who do not tell time, use pictures of clocks with the hands set at, or showing digital faces of, the times of the day's activities either on paper or a tablet computer. Students simply need to look at the picture clocks and match the times with those on a wall clock or their wristwatch. The picture schedule then tells them in words or in pictures what to do at the specified time. They can mark off on their schedules or touch the screen of their tablet computer when they initiate each activity to monitor their own behavior. Students with complex communication challenges can also use their picture schedules to communicate their activities to others, such as the driver of an accessible van or their roommates. Forms 5.4 and 5.5 show picture schedules. Blank, reproducible forms are included on the accompanying CD-ROM.

FORM 5.4
Today's Schedule (with Analog Clock)

Student: __Robert Scott__   Day(s): __Thursdays__

Time	What should I do?	Time	What should I do?
🕐	Meet bus on corner	🕐	Clock-out from work
🕐	Arrive at work	🕐	Meet bus in front of store
🕐	Take a break	🕐	Start softball practice
🕐	Return from break	🕐	End softball practice
🕐	Leave for lunch	🕐	Meet Randy for dinner
🕐	Return from lunch	🕐	

Form 5.4. Today's schedule (with analog clock) for Robert Scott. (A blank, photocopiable version of this form is included on the accompanying CD-ROM.)

FORM 5.5
Today's Schedule (with Digital Clock)

Student: __Javier Alcarez__   Day(s): __Fridays__

Time	What should I do?	Time	What should I do?
7:20	Meet Mike to walk to school	1:40	Computer lab class
7:40	FCA club meeting (Room 212)	3:30	Pick up and deposit paycheck
8:10	American literature class	5:30	Elias picks me up from home
9:47	Consumer math class	6:00	Potluck dinner at church
11:24	Lunch with People First club	7:00	Choir practice
12:03	Industrial arts class	8:30	Dessert with friends at EZ's

Form 5.5.   Today's schedule (with digital clock) for Javier Alcarez. (A blank, photocopiable version of this form is included on the accompanying CD-ROM.)

Teaching Students to Use Self-Monitoring and Self-Reinforcement

A necessary part of self-determination is that students are aware of the consequences of their actions and the effect that their behavior has on the tasks before them and the people around them (Walker et al., 2011). For example, if a worker on quality control at an auto plant is negligent on the job, then the effect may be that faulty parts are installed in newly produced cars and the worker is fired. Or if a student continues to talk about the same topic until it becomes tiresome, then people may start avoiding the student in the school cafeteria or community recreation site. Unless students monitor their own behavior, they may perform behaviors that have unintended consequences that undermine their best interests. With practice, students can learn to evaluate, change, and reinforce their own behavior.

ASSESSMENT

Assessing Outcomes: Using Checklists to Self-Monitor and Self-Reinforce Behavior

Learning how to evaluate your own behavior takes skill and practice. Many people are so used to having others evaluate them, such as college instructors, employers, school principals, or personal exercise trainers, that they have never learned to look at and evaluate themselves. When first learning to evaluate one's behavior, a checklist that lists steps in an activity, jobs to be completed, or reminders to use appropriate social skills with peers may be helpful. The Daily Checklist in Form 5.6 shows a checklist used for completing a morning routine. The form can be adapted for nonreaders and others on the basis of their individual needs. A blank, reproducible form is included on the accompanying CD-ROM.

There are three steps when teaching students to monitor their behavior with a checklist. First, teach the student to look at the first item on the checklist. The items can be listed as words, such as on the checklist for getting ready in the morning, or as pictures or even tactile objects. Second, teach the student to look at (observe) himself as he performs the behavior indicated in the item. Third, show the student how to check off (or touch the screen of a tablet computer) whether the behavior was performed. At the end of the day or the activity, the student can tally how many of the total behaviors were completed and reward himself if his behavior was acceptable to others and to himself.

You can adapt the checklist for students to rate the quality of their performance, in addition to whether the behavior was performed. Students can also learn to evaluate their videotaped

FORM 5.6
Daily Checklist

Student: __Stacey Dean__ Week: __January 20–24__

Activity: __Morning routines__

What do I need to do?	Monday	Tuesday	Wednesday	Thursday	Friday
Make my bed	X	X	X	✓	X
Brush my teeth	✓	X	X	X	X
Take a bath/shower	✓	✓	X	✓	✓
Put on clean clothes	✓	✓	X	✓	✓
Put on deodorant	X	X	✓	X	X
Comb hair	✓	✓	✓	✓	✓
Put on my makeup	✓	✓	✓	✓	✓
Eat breakfast	✓	X	X	✓	X
Make my lunch	✓	✓	✓	✓	✓
Feed the dog and cat	X	✓	X	X	X
Total completed:	7	6	4	7	5

✓ = I did this!!!   X = I did not do this

Form 5.6.   Daily Checklist for Stacey Dean. (A blank, photocopiable version of this form is included on the accompanying CD-ROM.)

performance of expected behaviors. For example, video self-modeling has been used to teach students with disabilities to improve their social-communication, functional, and behavior skills (Bellini & Akullian, 2007). As always, use research-based learning principles, such as prompting, corrective feedback, opportunities for practice, and reinforcement when teaching a new behavior. Then withdraw your assistance as the student learns the new task.

You can adapt the following teacher-recommended strategies for teaching students to use checklists.

- Teach students who are usually untidy to use a self-monitoring chart to track their progress in keeping their desks at school or work areas on the job clean.

- Teach a student to use a self-monitoring chart to record his outbursts of anger when he goes to the gym to work out.

- Teach students to use self-monitoring charts to complete routine jobs at home or school. Students learn to evaluate their own work and reward themselves for a job well done.

- Teach students to use map applications on their cell phones or tablet computers to find their way around town and the locations of resources, such as a coffee shop, movie theater, or bookstore.

"We teach a step-by-step process for the completion of a task. Audiovisual materials such as picture cards are used in accordance with the situation. Repetition is also extremely important to my students—'one time only' is quickly forgotten."

Teacher, Raleigh Egypt High School

ASSESSMENT

Assessing Outcomes: Using Charts to Self-Monitor and Self-Reinforce Behavior

Form 5.7, the Self-Recording Chart, can be used to teach students to monitor their own behavior, such as greeting teachers and classmates or completing homework assignments. A blank, reproducible form is included on the accompanying CD-ROM. An advantage to charts such as this is that students can observe and record more than one behavior at a time. In the filled-in example, a sales associate, Jefferson Lopez, is monitoring four of his behaviors—working hard, keeping the children's section clean, greeting customers, and selling items. These behaviors can be personal goals that a student has chosen to work on. Notice that Jefferson has stated a goal for each of the behaviors for his morning shift. For example, he has chosen as a goal to greet 20 customers from 9:00 A.M. to 10:30 A.M. After observing and recording the number of customers he greeted in 15-minute intervals, Jefferson counts the total number greeted. He records on his chart that he met his goal and chooses 28 customers as his next goal.

Meeting their goal on a self-recording chart can be rewarding in itself for your students. Just filling in the chart and knowing that they met their goals can be enough to keep them continuing to perform the desired behavior, even without praise, recognition, or assistance from others. If self-recording is not enough to maintain your students' behavior, however, then they can try reinforcing themselves for meeting their goals with a desired reward, such as dining at their favorite restaurant at the end of the week.

Students can be taught to use self-recording charts to monitor and record their behaviors much in the same way that they learn to use checklists, through the application of evidence-based learning

FORM 5.7

Self-Recording Chart

Name: Jefferson Lopez   Date: October 24

Activity: Working as sales associate on floor of G.L. Brownstein Clothing Store

Time	Behaviors			
	Am I working hard?	Am I keeping the children's section clean?	How many customers have I greeted?	How many items have I sold?
9:00 A.M.	Y	Y	3	1
9:15 A.M.	Y	Y	2	—
9:30 A.M.	N	N	1	—
9:45 A.M.	Y	N	6	4
10:00 A.M.	Y	Y	3	1
10:15 A.M.	Y	N	8	5
10:30 A.M.	Y	Y	2	2
My total is	6	4	25	13
My goal is	7	3	20	15
Was goal met?	Yes (No)	(Yes) No	(Yes) No	Yes (No)
My goal for next time is. . .	7	5	28	15

Jefferson Lopez
Student's signature

Mr. Henderson
Teacher's signature

Form 5.7. Self-Recording Chart for Jefferson Lopez. (A blank, photocopiable version of this form is included on the accompanying CD-ROM.)

principles such as modeling and corrective feedback. Of course, your assistance should be withdrawn as students acquire self-monitoring skills.

Be sure to keep a self-recording chart attractive, easy to use, and easy to carry around. Use words, pictures, or symbols to match the strengths, needs, and preferences of your students. Involve your students as much as possible in constructing their charts; they are more likely to use them if they have had some choice in the behaviors and goals included. Remember that any paper chart can be reproduced in graphic form on a tablet computer, laptop computer, or cell phone.

"Give a student a 'checkoff' system to complete a job or task. For example, when a student completes a task, she drops a chip into a jar. When all the chips are in the jar, that signals that the job is complete."

Teacher, LaVergne High School

ASSESSING OPPORTUNITIES FOR SELF-DETERMINATION AND CHOICE MAKING

Learning any new skill takes opportunities for practice. This adage is particularly true for students with disabilities and with respect to behaviors they likely have had limited opportunity to exercise, such as making their own choices or decisions.

Observing Students' Opportunities for Self-Determination

It is critical to identify opportunities students have in their everyday lives in and out of school to exercise self-determination skills, such as choice making or problem solving. Research shows that they may have surprisingly little opportunity to set goals or make choices and decisions, especially regarding their own lifestyles (Washington et al., in press). Observing students over a period of time and in different settings is one way to gain information about students' opportunities to exercise self-determination skills independently.

When trying to identify a student's opportunities to exercise self-determination, it is important to focus on the student's actions, what is going on around the student, and how others react to the student. You may observe that many opportunities for self-advocacy, goal setting, or choice making occur throughout the day, such as choosing to walk or to ride the bus to work. Nevertheless, the student may not have access to these opportunities because an action or decision has already been made by someone else. Sometimes it is necessary to rely on the reports of others because a teacher cannot be present to observe a student's opportunities at all times. Encourage teachers, peers, family members, service providers, and others with whom the student comes in contact to observe a student's self-determination opportunities throughout the day, such as choices of social partners or opportunities to speak up.

Self-determination can also be included as an objective in a student's IEP (Wehmeyer, Palmer, Soukup, Garner, & Lawrence, 2007). Examples of objectives addressing self-determination are: "Given a snack machine at school, a student goes independently at the appropriate times and makes his own selection," or "Given an array of materials with several items missing to complete a task, a student independently problem-solves a solution in order to complete the task." Observing the student's behavior when confronted with such situations will indicate at least two pieces of information: 1) whether an opportunity for a self-determination action occurred and 2) whether the student gained access to the opportunity.

"Observe students during their social interactions. Listen as students discuss opportunities for choice in their daily lives. Provide examples for making choices, and discuss why certain choices should or should not be made."

Teacher, South Side High School

LEGISLATION IDEA 2004 states that all students receiving special education services must have a statement of their transition services needed to reach their postschool goals, beginning no later than the first IEP to be in effect when a student is 16, and updated annually thereafter. These services must be based on each individual student's needs, taking into account the student's strengths, preferences, and interests. Teachers must learn to observe and identify their students' individual preferences, interests, and choices to meet the IDEA 2004 mandate.

Additional teacher-recommended strategies for observing students' opportunities for self-determination include the following.

- Observe a student making everyday choices, such as whether to attend an optional school assembly or an afternoon play. Or observe a student selecting menu items that are within his budget when ordering lunch at a restaurant.

- Observe students' participation in school clubs, service organizations, and social activities. Do they take an active role in their participation? Do they volunteer when given the chance to hold an office in a club, or do they prefer to take more of a position on the sidelines?

- Observe students' participation in recreational options available in the school gym, the local YMCA, the Boys and Girls Club, or around the neighborhood. Do they speak up for themselves to express a preference to skateboard, swim, or play basketball? Or do they generally let someone else decide the activity in which they will participate?

- Observe a student and his peers as they make choices about their activities, such as which movie to go to or which assignment to begin first. Who makes the decisions, and what role does the student with a disability play in the decision-making process?

- Observe opportunities for goal setting, self-advocating, or self-evaluating that are available for students during lunch, pep rallies, parties, and clubs or while shopping, traveling, or working. Note whether students act independently or let someone else direct their actions during these times.

"To observe students' choices, I watch how much involvement they have during extracurricular activities such as homecoming events. I encourage them to work on different jobs with their classmates, and I see which jobs they choose and with whom they choose to work."

Teacher, McEwen High School

Observing Students' Opportunities for Choice Making

The extent to which students have opportunities to make choices is a critical aspect of self-determination. Historically, individuals with disabilities—particularly intellectual disabilities or autism—have had little opportunity for making choices or decisions in their daily lives (Carter, Owens, Trainor, et al., 2009; Wiltz, 2007). Not surprisingly, lack of opportunities to choose hinders the development of choice making and other self-determination skills (Wehmeyer & Garner, 2003). People with disabilities, in particular, need repeated opportunities to practice in order to acquire new skills, including choice making. Students are more likely to feel empowered to exercise other self-determined actions, such as advocating for themselves, when opportunities for them to make choices and decisions independently are increased and they act on these opportunities (Wehmeyer et al., 2011).

In contrast, most people have the opportunity to make many choices in their own lives. For example, they usually choose when to get up in the morning, what to wear, what to eat for breakfast, and whether to check their e-mail or listen to the radio as they eat. They usually have choices throughout the day at work, and, after work, they may decide whether they want to stay home and watch television, work out at the gym, or spend time with friends. In fact, people have so many choices that they may tend to take them for granted. Educators and others may not realize how few choices some students have or the limitations of their choice-making skills. Therefore, it is important that teachers and others take data on students' opportunities for choice making, whether students act on these opportunities, and whether their opportunities and choice-making skills change over time.

"To learn about students' recreational and leisure choices, I expose students to several recreational activities over a period of months and observe their performance. I do this across employment training sites too. For students who can't tell me their preferences, I note differences in their behavior as signs of preference."

Teacher, McGavock High School

Teachers have identified several strategies they have used for assessing students' opportunities to choose.

- There are many ways to collect data on students' choices. One way is to observe the choices that students make in role-play situations, such as ordering a meal or choosing a date for the prom.

- Students' choices can be recorded on checklists. You can also "set up" choice-making opportunities, such as alternative ways to complete a class assignment or whom to sit next to at a restaurant.

- Opportunities for choice in students' curricula can be identified by checking their class schedules and looking for diversity across curricular areas. Record the variety of courses in which they have been enrolled over time, such as drama or calculus, and ask students how well these represent their own choices.

- Journal writing is a good way to learn about students' choices. Have students keep journals in which they write about choices they have or have not made and their reactions to these experiences. Discuss these experiences with students on a regular basis (e.g., when a student wanted to ask a friend to go to the mall, but did not).

- Survey students and teachers about choices available in students' daily activities, such as alternative assignments available in their classes and choices of partners with whom to work.

Self-Determination Assessment Tools

RESEARCH

Several assessment tools exist for evaluating the self-determination skills and opportunities available to youth with disabilities. For example, the *AIR Self-Determination Scale* (Wolman, Campeau, DuBois, Mithaug, & Stolarski, 1994) is a 30-item tool that provides information about students' ability to perform various self-determined behaviors, their perceptions of the efficacy of those behaviors, and their knowledge about those behaviors. In addition, items enable teams to assess the opportunities available for students to engage in self-determined behavior at school or at home. Because teacher, parent, and youth versions of the scale exist, information from each of these sources can be compared and used to launch discussion among team members. The *Self-Determination Assessment*

Battery (Field, Hoffman, & Sawilowsky, 2004) includes both observational checklists and written assessments. Like the previous scale, it can be used to explore the perspectives of youth, their teachers, and their parents regarding knowledge, behaviors, and affect associated with self-determination. *The Arc's Self-Determination Scale* (Wehmeyer & Kelchner, 1995) is a self-report scale in which youth assess their own strengths and needs related to self-determination. The 72 items address the areas of psychological empowerment, autonomy, self-regulation, and self-realization. As previously noted, informal approaches such as interviews, checklists, person-centered planning meetings, observations, and situational assessments are all ways of assessing students' strengths and needs related to self-determination and independence.

ASSESSMENT

Assessing Outcomes: Observing Opportunities to Choose

How do you observe students' opportunities for choosing and the choices they make in their daily lives? Form 5.8 can be used to gather important information about the opportunities for choice that exist in an environment and whether a student makes a choice when given the opportunity. A blank, reproducible form is included on the accompanying CD-ROM. You can also observe whether the student made a choice independently or needed support.

Notice that the form allows you to observe opportunities and choices across all important settings in which a student spends time, such as at home, at work, in school, or around the community. If you are not in a setting to directly observe the student, then have someone else (or the student) record information on the form. Notice that you can also observe the student in these settings for an entire week using the form. Take a look in the next case study at two opportunities for choice that Rafael had on Tuesday during the week of December 6, which were recorded in the sample Choice-Making Opportunities form.

Case Study 5.3 *Making Choices*

Opportunity 1

Rafael got on the city bus with his sister Beulah. There were two seats available—one by itself and one next to someone whom Rafael knew from school. Rafael, who boarded the bus first, sat down next to his schoolmate. Beulah, who was recording observations on a form for Rafael's teacher, wrote down that Rafael had an opportunity to choose a bus seat and that he had chosen to sit next to someone he knew. The form also allowed Beulah to indicate whether Rafael had made his choice independently (which he did) or whether he needed assistance. This was important information because one of Rafael's IEP goals was to increase his independent choice-making skills, and another goal was to increase his social interaction with his peers. Of course, Beulah was careful to record the information discreetly; she didn't want Rafael to appear different from anyone else on the bus.

Opportunity 2

When they got off the bus downtown, Rafael and Beulah stopped first to get an ice cream cone. Rafael got in line first. When he reached the counter, the server asked, "May I take your order?" Rafael said nothing. After a while, the server asked Beulah, "What does he want?" Beulah asked Rafael to point to his choice of ice cream displayed in containers in the freezer under the counter. After looking around for a while, Rafael pointed to the container of chocolate chip ice cream. The server filled a cone with ice cream and handed it to Rafael, who eagerly began licking it.

After she had placed her own order, Beulah quickly jotted down on her observation form that Rafael had had an opportunity to choose but had needed a verbal prompt from her to make a choice.

Choice-Making Opportunities

Student: __Rafael Laguzamo__   Date: __December 6__

	Location	School	Work	Community	Home	What opportunities for choice were there?	What choice was made (including no choice)?	Was assistance provided? How?
		Check one						
Monday	Bedroom				✓	Rafael had to decide what to wear to school.	Rafael chose his favorite summer outfit.	Father helped him choose from his winter clothes.
	Science class	✓				Teacher asked students to choose partners for chemistry lab.	None	Teacher made choice for Rafael—paired him up with Jon.
	Cafeteria	✓				Rafael had to decide what he wanted to eat.	Rafael went into the pizza line.	None—Rafael always goes into the pizza line.
Tuesday	Drama class	✓				Students were asked to get in groups for an exercise.	Rafael quickly chose to be with Seth and Ali.	None—chose independently
	Auditorium	✓				Students can sign up for extracurricular clubs and activities.	Rafael signed up for every single club (all 32).	Students at booths showed him where to sign.
	City bus			✓		Only two seats were empty on the bus.	Rafael chose to sit next to a friend from school.	None—chose independently
	Ice cream parlor			✓		Employee asked, "May I take your order?"	Rafael was quiet at first but chose chocolate chip.	Sister had to provide him with a verbal prompt.
Wednesday	Coffee shop		✓			Rafael was given a choice of when to take his break.	Rafael chose to take it with a co-worker.	None—chose independently
	Guidance office	✓				Students can select courses for next semester.	None	Counselor chose classes for him.
	Science class	✓				Teacher asked students to pick a topic for an upcoming project.	None	Teacher assigned him to work with partner on "plants."

(page 1 of 2)

Form 5.8. Choice-Making Opportunities for Rafael Laguzamo. (A blank, photocopiable version of this form is included on the accompanying CD-ROM.)

	Location	Check one				What opportunities for choice were there?	What choice was made (including no choice)?	Was assistance provided? How?
		School	Work	Community	Home			
Thursday	Homeroom	✓				Students were given a chance to vote for "Most likely to...."	Rafael made his selections.	Peer had to read choices and show Rafael pictures.
	Special education classroom	✓				Teacher asked Rafael which job he would like to try next.	Rafael chose the Taco Cocina.	Teacher showed Rafael pictures of potential worksites.
	School lobby	✓				Rafael missed the bus and had to decide how to get home.	Rafael asked a friend for a ride.	Teacher helped him think through his options.
Friday	Taco Cocina		✓			Manager asked Rafael what shifts he would like to work.	Rafael chose Monday, Friday, and Saturday.	Teacher helped him look through a calendar.
	Taco Cocina		✓			Manager offered Rafael a free lunch.	Rafael chose the chalupa combination.	Teacher showed Rafael a picture menu.
	Video store			✓		Father said Rafael could pick out one movie for himself.	Rafael picked *Star Wars*.	None—chose independently
Weekend	Living room				✓	Rafael could decide how he wanted to spend the day.	He chose to watch television for a while.	None—chose independently
	Mall			✓		Rafael could decide which stores he wanted to go in.	He chose a record store, hobby shop, and gadget store	None—chose independently
	Mall			✓		Clerk asked if Rafael would like to listen to a music album.	Rafael chose a country album.	Rafael was quiet at first, friend pointed to some choices.
	Bedroom				✓	Mom asked if Rafael wanted to join them for church.	Rafael was extremely tired and decided not to go this time.	None—chose independently
	Living room				✓	Rafael could decide how he wanted to spend the afternoon.	Rafael decided to call a friend.	Mom prompted him to find something to do.

(page 2 of 2)

"Quietly observing a student and carefully collecting data can provide a good picture of the number of choices a student has or does not have over a period of time."

Transition teacher, Nashville Public Schools

It is important to identify not only how many choices a student has but also how important those choices are to a student. For example, if a student can make choices only about types of snacks to eat but not about his free time or future plans, then you would probably consider his opportunities to choose to be quite restricted.

"When I first get to know a student, I record, as much as possible, how the student reacts to choice making—how long it takes to come to a decision, how many prompts must be given, what influences the decisions, and so forth."

Teacher, Hunters Lane High School

Choices that students consistently make over time likely indicate their preferences, such as whom they choose to sit next to in class or what they choose to do with their free time. Teachers have recommended the following choice-making and preference assessment strategies.

- The Home Inventory Form (Form 2.5 in Chapter 2) is a good source of information about a student's preferences, choices, and interests. In completing the form, students, their parents, and important others provide information about the student's likes and dislikes at home, at work, and in the community. By listing activities in which they frequently engage, such as dancing or playing racquetball, students tell us much about their own preferences and choices.

- Assess students' preferences through role-playing activities. Give them choices in role-play situations that sample a variety of options, such as leisure activities or career options. Compare these findings with preferences they indicate when filling out an interest inventory or questionnaire. Discuss with each student your findings as well as the skills needed in their chosen options.

- It is important to maintain frequent communication with students regarding their choices and preferences. You may not always agree with them, such as their choice of music, clothes, or hairstyles, but you need to allow them to express their preferences.

- Pictures are helpful in assessing some students' choices and preferences. After a student has been to several worksites, help him make a connection between each site and a picture. Then use the pictures when asking the student where he would like to work.

- Have students sample a variety of jobs while in high school, such as clerical, industrial, and service jobs. The student's performance on these tasks should speak for itself as far as showing the student's preferences.

- Give students a choice of community-based training sites and options for different job choices at the sites. Allow them to experience each job for at least 2 weeks so that they can begin to learn about their preferences. Then help them make a choice of their preferred job and arrange for them to work there for at least 12–18 weeks.

COLLABORATING WITH FAMILIES, PEERS, AND OTHERS

Self-determination is as much about changing the behavior of others as it is about changing students' behavior. Educators, family members, community members, and others must let students learn to make their own decisions and choices, learn from their own successes and mistakes, and try new experiences when the opportunity comes along. Individuals who are important in students' lives must learn how to support students in making and acting on their own decisions, rather than making those decisions for them. By collaborating with others, teachers can help promote opportunities for self-determination in students' daily lives and ensure that self-determination skills are used by a student in different environments.

It is critical to talk with family members, co-workers, community members, general education teachers, school staff, and others to identify ways in which they can support a student's self-determination skills, such as letting them choose a preferred way of doing a task or decide which bus route to take home from the job. Students' peers should also be included in discussions about self-determination. Peers can provide examples of self-determination in their own lives, such as saying "no" to peer pressure or telling a date that his or her behavior is inappropriate. Peers can also model appropriate use of self-determination skills for students.

In addition, peers can help teach self-determination skills, such as goal setting (Hughes et al., 2004). Many times a student will be more likely to take a suggestion from a peer than from an adult. For example, a peer may suggest to a young woman that she would look much prettier if she would brush her hair and keep it pulled back away from her face, and the peer may remind her to practice her grooming each day. If a teacher were to make such a suggestion, then the student might feel angry or hurt. When her peer does so, however, she may pay attention and start taking responsibility for her own appearance. Parents can also assign specific tasks at home so that students can learn responsibility. Students can learn to monitor their behavior on their tasks at home and keep a record of their performance in a folder that they take to school. Remember to have parents check the students' work, too, to see whether they agree with the students' self-report.

LEGISLATION

An intent of IDEA 2004 is to increase students' participation in the mainstream of everyday life as active participants who are living independently and enjoying economic self-sufficiency. To do so, students must be self-determining. The amendments call for educators and others to raise their expectations of students and empower students to lead productive, independent adult lives. By doing so, teachers raise these students' expectations of themselves in their everyday lives. Educators are being consistent with the legislative mandate when they incorporate self-determination goals and objectives into students' daily living.

"Give students time for leisure activities in the community so they have opportunities for choices. Observe the choices they make when given freedom to choose during leisure time."

Teacher, Lebanon High School

Incorporating Self-Determination into Daily Living

All teachers hope their students will use the skills they learn in high school in their everyday lives, both before and after graduation. The generalization of skills to new settings, activities, and people is an important outcome of any educational program. Self-determination and self-management can help students do just that. Teaching students to take greater responsibility for their own behavior will help them use their skills independently in places where teachers or other service providers are not there to provide support.

Self-determination skills are important for every student to be successful on the job, in the classroom, and around the community. Everyone can benefit from learning to set goals for themselves, identify the steps needed to reach those goals, determine whether they are on-track, and adjust their behavior accordingly. Teaching students "generic" self-management strategies, such as making lists, can go a long way toward promoting self-determination in their daily lives. Students can easily adapt such strategies and use them at school or work or in other settings. For example, by learning how to make a list, students can plan meals at home, shop within their budgets at the mall, establish timelines for class assignments, or prioritize job tasks at work.

If your (and your students') goal is to have students use self-determination and self-management skills at school and work, in their homes, and in the community, then you need to teach these skills in those settings. Remember, students are more likely to use a skill (even self-management) if they learn it where you (and they) expect them to use it. Becoming self-determined often means learning new skills to decrease dependence on others. By enrolling in home economics or family life classes, for example, students may learn housekeeping and cooking skills that will allow them to live more independently in the community.

The following are examples of how teachers have promoted self-determination in students' everyday lives.

- Using a checklist, students have learned to write their own checks and balance their monthly bank statements online and on paper copies.

- A young man with diabetes has learned which foods he should or should not eat. He is allowed to select his own foods in the lunchroom, in restaurants, and when he cooks meals.

- By using a written task analysis of her job requirements, a young woman is able to work independently on the job for the first time in the food-service department of a hospital.

- Providing photographs of clean hotel rooms has helped housekeeping staff keep their jobs. They match the appearance of the rooms they are cleaning to the photographs to determine whether they have completed each of their job tasks.

- Picture cards can help students find items by themselves in the store. If they cannot count money, then they can use the "next dollar up" method to pay for the items by themselves (Cihak & Grim, 2008).

- Using a picture schedule, a young man matches the clock faces (analog or digital) on the schedule to his wristwatch. He has now learned to deliver papers on time to offices at his worksite.

- Students have learned to plan their own community-based instruction activities. They choose an activity, call to make arrangements, plan the agenda, and determine the cost of the activity.

- Students who need help putting on a uniform correctly for work have learned to match their appearance in the mirror with a picture of themselves with their uniforms on correctly.

"Choice-making opportunities exist all day long. People who work with individuals with disabilities are too accustomed to making choices for these individuals. They simply need to stop talking, stop using their hands, and stand back."

Transition teacher, Metropolitan Nashville Public Schools

Providing Opportunities for Self-Determination

Being self-determined means students are able to set their own goals in life and act toward achieving these goals. It means students are able to make choices about "big things," such as whether to go to college or get married or which career to pursue. It also means making choices and decisions about the "little everyday things" that make up life, such as whether to take a sandwich to work or buy lunch, what to wear to a meeting, or how to spend Saturday night. Self-determination is meaningless unless students have the chance to exercise their skills and rights every day—in their daily lives and their plans for the future.

Communicating their needs and wants is a big part of self-determination for students. How else can students advocate for themselves and let people know their personal decisions and choices? Picture cards, manual signing, or communication devices help some students communicate their ideas to others and speak up for themselves. Teachers recommend the following strategies for incorporating opportunities for self-determination into students' everyday lives.

- Self-determination and self-management skills should not be taught in isolation. The point of teaching these skills is to allow students to have more control in all aspects of their daily lives. It is important to assist fellow teachers in incorporating units on self-determination into the general curriculum and extracurricular activities. For example, independent living skills could be embedded into a math or an English class (Collins, Hager, & Galloway, 2011).

- A home-living apartment affiliated with a high school transition program can be an ideal way for students to try out their self-determination skills in a safe environment. Students can spend several nights per week at the apartment with supervision as part of their high school curriculum before graduating and living more on their own.

- Identify skills in which students need to gain more independence and incorporate these into daily activities to provide opportunities for students to practice self-determination and self-management skills in their daily lives.

RESOURCES

Agran, M., King-Sears, M., Wehmeyer, M.L., & Copeland, S.R. (2003). *Student-directed learning.* Baltimore, MD: Paul H. Brookes Publishing Co.

This practice-oriented book includes strategies for equipping students to use a wide range of student-directed self-monitoring, self-instruction, self-evaluation, and problem-solving strategies.

Thoma, C.A., & Wehman, P. (Eds.). (2010). *Getting the most out of IEPs: An educator's guide to the student-directed approach.* Baltimore, MD: Paul H. Brookes Publishing Co.

This resource focuses on teaching youth the skills and knowledge needed to participate fully and meaningfully in educational and transition planning processes.

Wehmeyer, M.L., Agran, M., Hughes, C., Martin, J.E., Mithaug, D.E., & Palmer, S.B. (2007). *Promoting self-determination in students with developmental disabilities.* New York, NY: Guilford Press.

This book addresses research-based and recommended practices for teaching skills to students with intellectual disabilities, autism, and other developmental disabilities that enhance self-determination.

Wehmeyer, M.L., & Field, S.I. (2007). *Self-determination: Instructional and assessment strategies.* Thousand Oaks, CA: Corwin Press.

This resource explores strategies for promoting self-determination within standards-based reforms and access to the general curriculum mandates.

Weir, K., Cooney, M., Walter, M., Moss, C., & Carter, E.W. (2011). *Fostering self-determination among children with developmental disabilities: Ideas from parents for parents.* Madison, WI: University of Wisconsin–Madison, Waisman Center, Natural Supports Project.

This free, downloadable guide includes an array of practical strategies families can use to foster self-determination beyond the school day.

WEB RESOURCES

A Life for Me, http://www.alife4me.com/

This unique cyber-community provides a forum for youth to learn about self-determination and self-advocacy.

A National Gateway to Self-Determination, http://www.aucd.org/ngsd

The National Gateway to Self-Determination is a web-based clearinghouse on resources, training, and information related to promoting self-determination.

Self-Advocacy Online, http://www.selfadvocacyonline.org

Self-Advocacy Online in an educational and networking web site for those involved in making change for people with disabilities. It includes a searchable database of self-advocacy groups.

Youthhood Community, http://www.youthhood.org

Youthhood is a web-based tool and curricular resource aimed at helping youth and young adults with disabilities plan for life after high school.

CHAPTER 6

Promoting Social Participation and Teaching Social Skills

In this chapter, you will learn how to

- Assess students' opportunities for social interaction
- Increase students' social participation in inclusive settings
- Assess and promote peer involvement and support
- Teach social interaction skills

OVERVIEW

There are few activities in people's lives that do not involve interactions with others. It is commonplace to converse with clerks, tellers, or other customers when shopping at a store, standing in line for a movie, or depositing money at the bank. Applying for a job, working out at the gym, dining out, and ordering with a credit card over the telephone all involve interacting with others. Students interact with each other and teachers or college instructors at school. Interactions occur at work with supervisors, co-workers, the secretarial pool, and customers. And, of course, there are family members, friends, and loved ones. People often feel peaceful and satisfied with life when social interactions with others are going well. Stress, tension, and unhappiness can prevail when interactions with others are not going well.

Part of having satisfying social interactions with others is the social skills people bring into a situation. If students are perceived as lacking social skills, then they may be less accepted by their peers at school and in the community or given less responsibility (Farmer et al., 2011). They also may find it harder to get and keep a job, become involved in clubs or organizations, make friends with their neighbors, or experience the other benefits of youth and adulthood. Limited social skills is a factor frequently associated with job loss among employees with disabilities (Carter & Wehby, 2003; Chadsey & Beyer, 2001). Because so much importance is placed on social skills, not meeting social expectations within a particular setting may lead to isolation and feelings of loneliness. For example, if a clerk in a hardware store continually talks about her personal problems at break, then her co-workers may try to avoid sitting near her. Students are more likely to be accepted by their peers and others within a social context—leading to possible long-term friendships—when they perform expected social skills, such as greeting others or starting a conversation about a topic of common interest.

Sometimes, students with disabilities have had little opportunity to interact with their peers either in or outside of school (Wagner et al., 2004). Teachers can collaborate with fellow educators, students' peers, worksite supervisors, recreational staff, and others to increase opportunities for social interaction, such as suggesting that a student ride home from an evening college class with a classmate. Or teachers may modify a class or curriculum to promote social interactions, such as having students work in small cooperative learning groups (Roseth, Johnson, & Johnson, 2008). Simply interacting with general education peers or community members can promote students' social skill repertoires (Carter & Hughes, 2007). As students begin to increase their involvement with their peers, however, they may need support to fit in socially, such as when they participate in general education classes and activities or are on the job or in the community. Peer buddies or co-workers can be a great source of support in helping students know what behavior is "cool," such as sharing a snack at break, and what is not, such as criticizing a peer's choice of clothes in front of others (Hughes et al., 2001). Teachers can also teach social interaction skills directly through activities such as role playing, problem solving, and peer involvement (Cook et al., 2008).

This chapter comprises four groups of strategies that teachers may use for promoting social interaction among students. Strategies are grouped by purpose—assessing students' social interaction opportunities, increasing students' social participation, assessing and promoting peer involvement and support, and teaching social interaction skills.

"I provide as many social interaction opportunities as possible in daily activities. I achieve this through inclusion in general education classes, mingling in the hallways, learning to walk appropriately in the hall with other students, and including general education students into the classroom. I also encourage families to provide opportunities for interaction as well."

Teacher, Pearl-Cohn High School

Case Study 6.1 *The Student Nobody Knows*

Olmos High School is like many schools: full of activity and life. On any given school day, visitors will notice students eating lunch together in the courtyard, congregating in the parking lot, and lining up around the snack machines. On the practice fields, football players talk on the sidelines, band members take breaks from the heat together, and JROTC officers talk about their plans after graduation. Inside the building, students are gathered in groups around lockers, laughing together and hoping the late bell will never ring. The students at Olmos are friends and enjoy the time they spend together—if only there weren't classes, homework, and tests to get in the way.

Hank had been a student at Olmos for almost 2 years. Still, most of the other members of his sophomore class had never met him. Of the few students who did know Hank, most agreed that he could be a pretty uncomfortable person to hang around. Maybe it was because Hank hardly ever started conversations with anyone. When he did, it was usually about the same thing or something embarrassing or really weird. Or maybe it was Hank's habit of walking up and hugging you, smelling your hair, and saying something such as, "Tomorrow's a half day," over and over. Hanging out with Hank was just not that much fun.

Hank spent most of his school day in general education classes. Most of his interactions, however, occurred with his teachers or paraprofessional. He rarely talked to any of his classmates and never saw them outside of school. Hank never had the chance to join any after-school extracurricular activities because he always took the school bus home right after school. That was too bad because as the bus left the school grounds, Hank always looked longingly at the other students out on the field doing warm-ups, running track, or playing baseball. He would have loved to be out there too—hanging out with "the guys" and making friends. But, the truth was, he really didn't know how to hang out with the guys—he never had the chance.

Hank's family was getting concerned that he probably never would learn how to socialize with others and make friends unless he had a chance to interact with some of his peers and join in their activities. They believed that if Hank could just interact more with general education students in classes and extracurricular activities, he could learn from them what was appropriate when interacting with others. But how could they make this happen? Hank didn't even know a single general education student's name.

"Inclusion in general education classes such as PE, health, home economics, or academics provides opportunities for social interaction skills and friendships to develop. We have many general education students who have become good friends of our students through inclusive programs."

Teacher, Maryville High School

ASSESSING STUDENTS' OPPORTUNITIES FOR SOCIAL INTERACTION

Finding out about opportunities for interaction is a first step in increasing students' social participation in school, the community, and everyday life. It may be that opportunities exist but students are just not gaining access to them. Or it may be that students spend considerable time in separate settings only with peers with disabilities, or interactions in inclusive settings are restricted to paraprofessionals or other support staff (Carter, Sisco, Brown, Brickham, & Al-Khabbaz, 2008). A student's limited social skills repertoire may simply relate to a lack of opportunity to learn or exercise these skills. The following section describes a strategy for assessing your students' opportunities for social interaction.

ASSESSMENT

Assessing Outcomes: Assessing Opportunities for Social Interaction

How much are your students interacting with their general education peers and participating in general education activities? Sometimes it is hard to know, especially when you are busy doing so many other things. Form 6.1, the Social Interaction Observation Form, can be used to keep track of a student's opportunities for social interactions occurring over a week's time. A blank, reproducible form is included on the accompanying CD-ROM. To complete the form, simply jot down every time you notice the student interacting with a peer during a class or school activity, a co-worker at work, or a neighbor or community member during everyday activities. Try to estimate how long the interaction occurred, and use the code on the form to indicate the length of the interaction. Also, note the name of the peer with whom the student was interacting. If you are not around the student throughout the day, then ask others who are in contact with the student—such as a general education teacher, a classmate, or a job coach—to help you. Remember to include opportunities to interact that occur but the student does not access, such as when a peer waves in the hallway but the student simply walks by without an acknowledgement.

FORM 6.1

Social Interaction Observation Form

Student: Sharon Kay   Week of: October 15–19

	Activity/class						
	In the courtyard before school	1st period class	2nd period class	Lunch	3rd period class (math)	Opryland Hotel worksite	Volunteering at the community center
Monday	Marco—A Stephanie—B	Industrial arts Jessica—C	Student council Mica—C Shirley—C Amanda—B	Erik—C	Briana—C Liz—B Janice—C	Caleb—A	Scott—C Robert—C Marjie—B
Tuesday	Travis—A	Physical education	Library aide	Erik—C	Liz—B Emily—A	Michael—A	Scott—C Gerald—B
Wednesday	Leslie—B	Industrial arts Toni—C	Student council Mica—C Terry—B Pat—C	Erik—C	Gretchen—C Janice—A	Casey—B	Scott—C Robert—B Phyllis—C
Thursday		Physical education	Library aide	Erik—C	Briana—C	Jennifer—A	Scott—C Volunteer—B Gerald—C
Friday	Klassing—B	Industrial arts Jessica—B Toni—C	Student council Mica—C Terry—C Amanda—C	Erik—C	Briana—B Janice—C	Leah—B	Scott—B Marjie—C Robert—C

Record each interaction with a general education peer by listing the name of the peer and the estimated length of the interaction. (*Key:* A = less than 1 minute; B = 1–5 minutes; C = more than 5 minutes)

Form 6.1.   Social Interaction Observation Form for Sharon Kay. (A blank, photocopiable version of this form is included on the accompanying CD-ROM.)

By the end of the week, you will have a good idea of the amount of time the student spends interacting, with whom, and during which activities. You may find that a student has many social interactions with a variety of peers throughout the day during different classes and extracurricular activities. Some ways teachers report that students interact include the following.

- A student who uses a wheelchair joins in a game of basketball with co-workers after work.

- A person walking through a parking lot helps a student get out of the way of an oncoming car.

- A student signs and interacts with her co-workers. The co-workers also have learned to sign to communicate with the student.

- A student with a visual impairment participates in an exercise class at the local gym with the help of other members in the class.

- A student with a physical disability who uses a cane is the football manager for the school team.

- A student with a visual impairment participates in racing and swimming events with her co-worker at a company picnic.

- A student with a speech impairment shares ideas and participates in decision making during a discussion in a world history class.

- A student with an intellectual disability tries out for the track team and is chosen to join.

- A student using a wheelchair dances with her friends at the school prom.

- A young man with a speech impairment sings a solo at church, backed up by the choir.

- A student's peers make sure that she is on the school bus, help her change buses if the bus is late or broken down, and sit and talk with her as they ride the bus to and from school.

- A student is a member of a school academic club and attends the club's out-of-town functions with a peer helper.

Or you may find that a student has few social interactions even though she attends general education classes and activities that provide opportunities to interact with peers, such as cooperative learning or club activities. In that case, you may want to use some of the strategies that follow for increasing students' social participation and teaching social skills. Research shows that simply because students are in proximity to general education peers does not ensure they are interacting with each other (Carter, Hughes, Guth, & Copeland, 2005; Hughes, Rodi, et al., 1999).

"My students interact daily during PE, lunch, and classes with their general education peers. We work on socialization skills continuously during the school day. This area generally is a problem with my students, so we constantly work on it."

Teacher, Hillsboro High School

INCREASING STUDENTS' SOCIAL PARTICIPATION IN INCLUSIVE SETTINGS

Opportunities abound in school and community settings for students to increase their interactions with classmates, co-workers, and friends. Look for activities in which students can become involved that will allow them to participate socially with others.

General Education Classes

Many benefits result from including all students in general education courses. Students receiving special education services benefit from participating in career and college readiness classes by increasing their academic and career preparation skills, as well as from having peers with whom they can learn and practice social skills (Jackson, Ryndak, & Wehmeyer, 2008/2009). General education students benefit by having the opportunity to interact with students with diverse abilities. Research shows that general education students often report feeling better about themselves and having more understanding of others when they have the chance to interact often with their peers in special education (Copeland et al., 2004).

Curriculum content is just one aspect of what is taught in general education classrooms. Students are also expected to learn to interact cooperatively with their peers. In academic classes such as economics or history, there are opportunities for social interaction through cooperative learning groups, class debates, and group projects. And students are learning skills that will help prepare them for college by participating in these activities.

In any school, you can see students walking to class together, helping each other with homework, and working on class projects together. Social relationships and social interactions are what high school is all about for students. Make use of the natural support of peers when involving students in classes. You will find that many students are eager to provide their support when asked (Hughes & Carter, 2008). Teachers share the following strategies for increasing the support of peers.

- Assign general education "buddies" to assist students whenever possible in completing assignments or participating in class discussions. Let students have free time to interact with each other at the end of class when their work is done or before the bell rings at the beginning of class.

- Going to a class for the first time can be frightening for anyone. Pair students with peers in their classes to ease the transition. Having a buddy can go a long way toward making a student feel welcome in a classroom of strangers.

- Career readiness courses, such as commercial art, automotive technology, culinary arts, and child care, often provide frequent opportunities for social interaction, such as when students work together on a car in the auto body shop or when they are preparing a meal for a group of visiting principals. Find peers within these classes to encourage interaction among classmates and help new students become full members of the class.

"Within the school environment, provide as many social opportunities as possible. Do 'PR' work with general education teachers and principals on behalf of your students. Get students involved in regular activities. Don't isolate them from the rest of the student body. Make your students visible—acceptance will eventually follow."

Teacher, Whites Creek High School

"Help students start clubs and volunteer organizations that encourage the involvement of all students, such as Unified Sports or a Red Cross volunteer club. Have PE class members help students participate in team sports or small-group activities, such as leading a warm-up session."

Teacher, Southside High School

Extracurricular Activities

Being a true member of a school community involves more than simply attending classes each day. It means playing on an athletic team, joining a club, attending a school play or concert, voting in school elections, or decorating for a homecoming dance. It also means greeting friends in the hall, sitting together at lunch, or hanging out together by the lockers before the first bell rings. By participating in extracurricular and nonacademic activities, not only do students find increased opportunities for interacting with their peers, but they also experience the benefits of being part of a community. They are also learning social skills that will benefit them after high school, such as getting along with a roommate in a college dorm. In addition, students with severe disabilities and limited verbal skills learn new social skills, such as greeting peers and conversational turntaking, by participating in recreational activities at school (Hughes et al., 2004). Teacher-recommended strategies for increasing social participation in extracurricular activities include the following.

- Lunchrooms are often the social center of a high school. Encourage students to eat lunch with their general education peers. Establish a lunch bunch program in which students from different classes eat lunch together and get to know each other's friends.

- Students congregate in hallways, around lockers, and in courtyards between classes to greet friends, share a quick conversation, or discuss weekend plans. Encourage your students to be outside the classroom before school and between classes to join and interact with their peers.

- Some students may not have transportation to or from after-school events, such as a tennis tournament, or may need help finding the Anime club meeting room. Recruit peers who are already participating in an event to help students get to and from the activity.

- Going to the school library or attending a basketball game for the first time can be confusing for any student. Have a general education peer help a student check out a book, pay for a ticket to a game, or read the scoreboard in the gym. It will make these activities more fun for both partners.

- Invite general education students to a meeting of the school's chapter of People First or other self-advocacy group. They can become involved as volunteers, interact with People First members, and learn about the self-advocacy process.

- Have a general education peer meet a student in her homeroom and go together to a pep rally, school assembly, school club, or the lunchroom. Students will think it is more fun going with someone else.

- Brainstorm the variety of ways students can participate in extracurricular activities. Students can sort through photographs as a school yearbook staff person, be in charge of equipment as a soccer team member, signal the crowd to start a cheer as a cheerleader, or help choose songs to sing as a choir member.

- Provide opportunities for different groups to interact socially. Have a picnic, dance, or party during which different school clubs, such as photography or knitting, can get together and meet each other's members.

"One of my students has difficulty remembering things. He was given one position to play on the football team, so the number of plays he has to learn is shortened. He was able to learn these plays and has become a key player on the team. At school, he receives many compliments on his performance in the games."

Teacher, McEwen High School

Work and in the Community

Students spend the majority of their day outside their school classrooms—working or recreating in their communities with friends, going to the library or a college class, or spending time at home with their families. It makes sense, then, that students need opportunities to increase their social participation and develop their social interaction skills across all of these contexts. When students practice their skills outside the school setting, they increase the likelihood that they will maintain these skills and that they will develop satisfying and supportive relationships. Teachers have a host of suggestions for increasing students' social participation outside school.

- The skills needed for asking for help at a store differ from those needed for striking up a conversation after church. Because social expectations vary from one place to another, students should have opportunities to interact with others in as many different community locations as possible.

- To improve students' job interview skills, arrange for them to interview with several different store managers. Evaluate their interviewing skills by creating a short checklist that the employer can complete.

- Eating lunch at restaurants around the community can provide students with opportunities to practice many social interaction skills, such as ordering, thanking and tipping the server, and conversing socially with peers.

- Create opportunities for out-of-school interactions. Help students work together to plan a party or picnic for school clubs in which they are members. Fundraising activities also can get them actively involved in the community.

- Encourage students to go on field trips with their general education classes, such as when an English class goes to a Shakespeare play or a music history class attends a concert. In addition to being educational, these community outings provide an opportunity for students to interact with each other in a variety of situations.

- A job is not just a place to work. Observe how employees at a worksite interact with each other, such as participating in a walking club at noon, chatting as they deliver mail to different offices, or celebrating a co-worker's birthday at break. Support students in getting involved in these activities and becoming a part of the social life of a workplace.

- Helping others is a great way to interact. Serving a meal at a homeless shelter, fixing up a halfway house, and building a wheelchair ramp are opportunities for students to interact with others and to contribute to the community.

- Some of the best opportunities for interaction occur when you put your daily schedule temporarily on hold and just take time to enjoy the moment with your students. It might be the first warm day of spring when students can go outside to a park without their jackets. Give your students a chance just to relax and spend time in a leisurely way with their peers.

"A student who is nonverbal spends a lot of time with a peer helper. For example, they eat lunch together, attend school club meetings together, and interact over the weekend, such as going to ball games or movies."

Teacher, LaVergne High School

"I arrange for each student to view a movie with a general education peer. This gives them a chance to purchase concession items, interact with a friend, and practice acceptable behavior in a social setting."

Teacher, Maplewood High School

ASSESSING AND PROMOTING PEER INVOLVEMENT AND SUPPORT

A great motivator for young people to go to school or work is to spend time with their peers— whether on the school campus, on the job, or in the community. There are many ways to increase students' involvement with peers, whether they are fellow students, co-workers, book club or gym members, or friends in the neighborhood. The story in Case Study 6.2 shows one teacher's strategy for increasing peer involvement at school.

Case Study 6.2 *Teachers Becoming Involved*

The beginning of the school year for many of the teachers sitting in staff orientation meetings at Lee High School meant having to listen to one long speech after another. Some quietly checked messages on their cell phones while others doodled on the day's handouts. Mr. Kort, however, had other ideas in mind. As a special education teacher, he was a jack-of-all-trades—community-based instruction teacher, job-training coordinator, and classroom teacher. Recognizing the importance of having general education students involved in his programs, he was already searching the auditorium for faculty who might assist him in promoting student involvement. In the back was Ms. Greiner, the student council sponsor. By the door was Coach Nichols, head of the athletic program. Two rows ahead was Mr. Luna, the school secretary, who knew all of the students.

Of course, Mr. Kort knew that the best way to increase general education students' involvement with his students was to increase his own involvement in school activities. The more that students knew him, the more willing they would be to spend time with his students. That's one of the reasons he had volunteered to be a faculty sponsor for the Beta Club and the Spanish Club. He also helped as a student advisor during fall registration. That was a good time to get students signed up as "peer buddies" in his class. He even tutored some students he didn't have in a class. Sure, it took some extra time, but Mr. Kort realized that the long-term benefits would make it worth it.

Why would a teacher work so hard to increase general education peer involvement? Mr. Kort would tell you that the answer lies in the Lee High School's mission statement to "develop citizens who participate in productive partnerships with staff, peers, parents, and community members to serve the long-term best interests of students and the community." Mr. Kort knew that all students benefit from involvement in relationships with their peers and that all students have something to learn from the differences and similarities found in others.

"General education students are involved with my students in many ways. They work with my students to complete assignments in class, train for Unified Sports, rehearse for dance presentations for a school assembly, and help in styling their hair in cosmetology class."

Teacher, Austin-East High School

"Clubs such as the debate club provide excellent opportunities for the development of social interaction skills. In classes, student leadership can be rotated so that students have the chance to lead part of the class. Peer tutoring uses the concept of 'every person knows less in some areas than you do and more in other areas than you do.' You can develop short questionnaires that allow pairing of students with unlike areas of knowledge in content areas, such as cosmetology or auto mechanics."

Teacher, Fairley High School

ASSESSMENT

Assessing Outcomes: Assessing Peer Involvement and Support

It is impossible for students to become socially involved with their peers if they do not have the opportunity to be together. After filling out the Social Interaction Observation Form (Form 6.1), you may have found that a student has very little social interaction with her peers. It may be that she has had little opportunity to do so. By examining a student's daily schedule, you can determine what opportunities for social interaction are actually available throughout the day. You can also evaluate the quality of interactions that do occur. Finally, you can identify what supports are available to and needed by the student to increase her opportunities for interaction and peer involvement. These supports could include the following.

- Personal supports such as peer buddies, interpreters, or notetakers

- Scheduling adaptations such as changing or rearranging classes

- Instructional methods such as cooperative groupings, class projects, or lab partners

- Environmental supports such as moving the location of a desk, creating a study area, or providing a communication device

Form 6.2, Social Opportunities Chart, can help you identify the frequency and quality of opportunities for social interaction that occur throughout the day for a student. (A blank, reproducible form is included on the accompanying CD-ROM.) First, fill in the time and setting in which you or a colleague is observing a student. Next, rate the frequency and quality of opportunities for interaction that occur during the time period. Then, record the supports that exist in the setting and additional supports that are needed to increase a student's opportunities for social interaction and peer involvement. Repeat throughout the day, having colleagues in different settings, such as the community or job site, provide information they have observed.

The following additional methods are used by teachers to evaluate opportunities for social interaction.

- Make a list of school activities in which general education students are typically involved, such as pep rallies, club days, homecoming events, and field trips. Next, compare your students' involvement in school activities with those on your list (Swedeen et al., 2010). You may discover that your students are more (or less) involved than you think.

- When observing students' social interactions in the community, interview parents, teachers, and the students themselves to determine which community locations they currently visit and in which locations they plan to be involved in the future.

- Interview peers, employers, co-workers, general education teachers, family members, and the student herself to obtain their perception of a student's social interactions. Their views may be very different from yours.

Social Opportunities Chart

Student: __Maricella Longmont__   Date: __January 19__

Activity/class	Time	Opportunities for social interaction	Quality of social interaction	Supports needed	Supports available
Before school	7:50 A.M. to 8:10 A.M.	1 None 2 3 Few 4 (5) Many	(1) Not good 2 3 So-so 4 5 Great	Assistance getting to the courtyard; help getting over curb	Peers could walk with her from the bus. Officer in courtyard could help lift.
Drama/theater	8:10 A.M. to 9:10 A.M.	1 None 2 3 Few 4 (5) Many	1 Not good 2 (3) So-so 4 5 Great	Help getting onto the stage where most of the class rehearses	Woodworking class could build a portable ramp. Peers/teacher could set up ramp daily.
Civics/government	9:10 A.M. to 10:05 A.M.	1 None 2 3 Few (4) 5 Many	1 Not good 2 (3) So-so 4 5 Great	Someone to change overlay on communication device; help learning to use device	Teacher could train peers to work with Maricella. Teach her to ask/sign for assistance.
Morning break	10:05 A.M. to10:20 A.M.	1 None 2 3 Few 4 (5) Many	1 Not good 2 3 So-so (4) 5 Great	Assistance getting from class to hallway/break room	Peer buddy and educational assistant are willing to help.
Consumer math	10:20 A.M. to 11:15 A.M.	1 None (2) 3 Few 4 5 Many	1 Not good 2 (3) So-so 4 5 Great	Closer proximity to her peers; activities that allow for interaction	Teacher is willing to plan small-group projects. Room could be rearranged.
Lunch	11:15 A.M. to 12:00 P.M.	1 None 2 3 Few 4 (5) Many	1 Not good 2 3 So-so 4 (5) Great	None	Maricella eats lunch with a close group of friends.
Community-based vocational instruction	12:00 P.M. to 3:20 P.M.	(1) None 2 3 Few 4 5 Many	(1) Not good 2 3 So-so 4 5 Great	Help completing job tasks; reminders to use device to greet customers	Adjust work routine to match a co-worker's routine. Set up picture prompts as reminders.
Extracurricular club (Monday, Tuesday, and Thursday)	3:20 P.M. to 4:00 P.M.	1 None 2 3 Few (4) 5 Many	1 Not good 2 3 So-so (4) 5 Great	Accessible ride to and from service projects	One club member's parents have an accessible van.

Form 6.2. Social Opportunities Chart for Maricella Longmont. (A blank, photocopiable version of this form is included on the accompanying CD-ROM.)

Q: What are some things you do with your peer buddies?

A: Katie comes to my house, and I go bowling with Jenni. They came to my birthday party at my house. We had a barbecue. We listen to the radio and just talk. We go to the mall, restaurants, and other places. We go play video games. We tell jokes and eat lunch together. We talk "boy talk" with David. We lift weights, go to work, and play games. My peer buddy's friend and I went to the prom. We went there in a limousine, and I got her a corsage. It was cool!

Q: Why do you like to spend time with your peer buddies?

A: Because they are my best friends. He is a good friend—a good pal. Because she introduces me to her friends, and now I have a lot of friends. Because it's fun! We go hear country music down-town. We talk with them. I like him. He's fun and makes me laugh. They're great! We have friendships.

Students, Metropolitan Nashville High Schools

Promoting Peer Involvement and Support in School Activities

Peers are definitely the experts when it comes to social interaction in high school. Peers are the ones who determine what fashions are "in," what sayings are "cool," and what hairstyles or clothes are definitely "out." They are also the best models of how teenagers act. By involving general education peers in school activities with your students, you can help ensure your students are interacting socially in ways that are acceptable to and expected and practiced by others in that setting. You can also learn to promote support provided by peers to increase students' social participation. Teachers share many ideas for promoting peer involvement at school.

- Students may have fears about getting involved in new classes and unfamiliar activities such as intramural tennis or French Club. Encourage general education peers to support them and ease their transition.

- Inform general education peers about the many ways they can get involved with your students, such as walking with a student to class, hanging out in the halls, sitting next to each other at a pep rally, or working together in a study hall.

- General education peers can invite students to eat lunch with them and include them in conversation with their friends. That way, everyone benefits by making new friends.

- Pair a verbal student with one who uses signing. Together, they can complete a class project and make a presentation to the class.

"One of my students was afraid to join the basketball team and stay after school for practice. A general education peer encouraged her by going with her to practice. She now suits up for each game."

Teacher, Greenville High School

"Every educational experience can be presented in such a way that appropriate social interactions are encouraged. Students can talk and physically participate together in groups. Adopting a philosophy that values and encourages positive social interaction is important for all teachers."

Teacher, Treadwell High School

Promoting Involvement of Peer Buddies and Co-workers

Like most youth, teenagers with disabilities tend to spend time with peers with whom they are most familiar—a finding that argues for increasing general education peer involvement opportunities (Carter et al., 2005). Peer buddy programs are one effective way of getting high school students together. Whether through a volunteer program or a credit course, peer buddies provide their partners with social support, assistance, and, ultimately, friendship. On the job, co-workers have been found to provide this support also (Brooke, Revell, & Wehman, 2009). Setting up a peer buddy program does not have to be difficult. Seven steps for starting a program in your school, which have been implemented in many schools (Hughes & Carter, 2008), are in Form 4.3 of Chapter 4.

In addition, teachers report involving peers and co-workers using the following strategies.

- Involve peer buddies in as many activities throughout the school day as possible, including trips to community sites, pep rallies, lunch, after-school events, and school assemblies.

- Ask peers in a general education class to keep track of the social interactions of a student who is nonverbal. They may have a different perspective than you do.

- Peer buddy and co-worker relationships can extend beyond the school day or workday, such as when a peer buddy invites a partner to attend a soccer game or when co-workers stop at a local restaurant on their way home from work.

- Roles can change in a peer-tutoring relationship. Sometimes each is a teacher and, at other times, a learner, depending on the participants' strengths and needs. The same can be true on a jobsite when employees mentor each other on work- or social-related issues.

- Peer buddies do not have to be the top academic students in your school. Sometimes students who are struggling find their niche as a peer buddy and begin to develop their own talents while they interact with their special education peers.

- Notice which co-workers tend to "buddy up" with or work near a student. Try to promote these relationships without "getting in the way"—sometimes the presence of a teacher or job coach can inhibit these interactions even if you do not mean to.

"This year I have a student in my class who has severe autism. When Kim first came into my room, she appeared to have no interest in others and only initiated interactions when she wanted to eat or go to the restroom. Then Kim developed a friendship with her peer buddy, Corie. Now she watches the door for Corie every day. When they are together, Kim makes eye contact with her buddy frequently, laughs often, and even initiates conversation. We never saw her do these behaviors before. Kim also has increased her vocal repertoire from 4 words to 11 words. We have been truly amazed with the difference peer buddies have made in the lives of our students."

Teacher, McGavock High School

LEGISLATION　IDEA 2004 reaffirms the importance of educating all students together. The amendments state that students with diverse abilities should, to the maximum extent appropriate, be educated with their general education peers and gain access to the general education curriculum and activities. IDEA 2004 also calls for providing the supports needed to promote access to general education. Having peer buddies is an evidence-based strategy for supporting students in general education settings (Carter & Hughes, in press). In addition to assisting students with class routines and assignments, peer buddies can encourage interaction between their partners with disabilities and other members of a class.

"My students need to be taught appropriate social skills from day one. A teacher needs to provide opportunities for practice—in general education, everyday school activities, and community outings. I have found role playing and having frank discussions about different situations helpful."

Teacher, Whites Creek High School

TEACHING SOCIAL INTERACTION SKILLS

Research shows that people's social behavior influences the degree to which they are viewed positively and accepted by others in a setting (Siperstein, Norins, et al., 2007). Most people learn expected social skills through their interactions and relationships with others. Some students, however, have had limited opportunity to interact with peers in inclusive settings. Others may be hindered in learning expected social skills because of speech-language impairments or intellectual disabilities. Luckily, there are many evidence-based practices available to teach social interaction skills, such as direct instruction, role playing, problem solving, and peer-delivered instruction (Carter, Sisco, et al., 2010).

Using Direct Instruction Strategies

Direct instruction for teaching social interaction skills involves modeling expected behavior, providing students opportunities to practice, giving students corrective feedback and praise for correct performance, and gradually withdrawing assistance as students acquire skills. Direct instruction is an evidence-based practice effective in teaching a variety of new behaviors (Bellini, Peters, Benner, & Hopf, 2007; Kavale & Mostert, 2004). When teaching social skills using direct instruction, it is advisable to teach in the settings in which students are ultimately expected to perform the behavior. Teachers recommend using the following direct instruction strategies.

- When eating out, model socially appropriate behaviors for students, such as using the correct piece of silverware and taking small bites of food.

- Sometimes students don't know what behavior is expected in public. Have discussions with students on appropriate behaviors for different situations, such as when inviting a friend to the movies, accepting criticism from a supervisor or college instructor, or asking for clarification of an assignment in class.

- Use direct instruction techniques to teach appropriate greetings, just as you would with any other skill. Model appropriate behavior, use prompting and corrective feedback, reinforce correct performance, and decrease your assistance as students become more proficient.

- Embed opportunities to practice social skills throughout the day—during academic classes, career preparation, and working or recreating in the community. Social skills are best taught in the context in which they will be used.

- Teach students to replace inappropriate behaviors with more appropriate alternatives. For example, students should learn to shake hands rather than hug a stranger and say, "I love you."

- Provide opportunities for students to interact with people of different backgrounds and cultures. They will learn different methods of greeting and interacting.

- Make sure that a student who uses a hearing or visual aid knows how to use it properly when interacting socially with others. Otherwise, the aid may hinder rather than help the student interact.

- Teach students to be aware of others' behavior and to watch those around them for cues on what's expected.

- Eat out as often as possible. Eating out at restaurants, shopping at the mall, ordering pizza over the telephone, and attending social functions all provide opportunities for practicing social skills by interacting with others.

- Work in the school office with a peer buddy or participate in student council with a peer because it can help students learn new social skills, such as providing information or speaking in front of groups.

- Encourage students to enroll in career and college readiness classes. Many of these classes, such as keyboarding, health sciences, and automotive trades, instruct students on how to interact appropriately on the job or at college.

"Provide class time even in academic classes for students to engage in activities that promote the development of conversation and social skills. For example, work in cooperative groups, have peers tutor each other, and assign a buddy to assist a student when necessary."

Teacher, Hillcrest High School

"We have students call and set up appointments with local employers or personnel managers who interview the students in mock job interviews. They evaluate the students' performance and provide opportunities to practice for an actual job interview. Often, the employers end up hiring the students who have participated in the mock interviews."

Teacher, Huntington High School

ASSESSMENT

Assessing Outcomes: Assessing Students' Social Skills

It is important to assess the social skills that a student already performs when beginning a program to teach social interaction skills. Skills that rarely occur, such as initiating conversation with peers, can become targets for teaching social skills. There are several published social skills programs for adolescents that you can use to evaluate your students' social skills. (See the resources section at the end of the chapter.) These programs often contain checklists you can use to observe and assess a student's social behavior in different situations, such as in school or in the community. You can also create your own checklist of social skills that focuses on only the skills that are critical within a particular setting. For example, see the Employee Social Skills Checklist (Form 2.4 in Chapter 2). Information can be gathered either by directly observing the student or by interviewing others who have observed the student. Chapter 2 addresses other informal, teacher-devised forms to use to assess students' social skills. For example, if you want to tally the occurrence of appropriate behaviors, such as greeting customers or classmates, then you can use the Event Recording Datasheet (Form 2.1). Or if you are observing how long a behavior occurs, such as engaging in conversation, then you can use the Interval Recording Datasheet (Form 2.2). Remember to adapt forms as needed for the particular behavior or social context you are targeting.

You can also use the Home Inventory Form in Chapter 2 (Form 2.5) to gather information from parents and other family members to determine which of a student's social skills are viewed as a challenge or limitation at home and outside school. Similar information can be obtained from employers or peers. You can then focus on these skills in your daily instructional programming and evaluation.

It is important to know what the "norm" is for performing social skills when evaluating a student's social skills. Assessing Outcomes: Conducting Comparative Observations in Chapter 2 provides directions for conducting comparative observations to establish a norm for a particular behavior. This is done by comparing a student's performance with that of peers or co-workers who are considered proficient within a particular environment. You then have a standard by which to evaluate a student's social skills as well as an instructional goal for educational programming (Hughes, Rodi, et al., 1999; Hughes et al., 2000). For example, by conducting comparative observations, you may determine that high school students usually talk more about their peers than about the weather; people usually initiate conversation at a rate of three times per minute; and co-workers at a particular worksite usually tease and joke with each other when on break (Hughes et al., 2011). You can then compare a student's behavior with these standards and teach skills that are expected in a particular social setting, such as when ordering a soft drink at a college snack bar.

Social behaviors that have been the focus of teachers' assessments include the following:

- How a student greets and introduces a guest speaker in class

- Whether an employee says, "Thank you," and, "Yes, sir," or "Yes, ma'am," to her supervisor

- Whether a student's choice of clothing is similar to high school peers' choices

- Whether a student says, "Excuse me," before asking a co-worker a question

- Whether a student shakes hands when greeting a newcomer rather than hugging the person

- Whether a student gets to know other co-workers during breaks at work

- If a student addresses the school principal by name rather than by yelling, "Hey, principal!"

- The extent to which others accept the student as a reflection of a student's social skills

- Whether a student's social behavior is similar to her peers' behavior at the recreation center, in student council, or at a dance

- How often an employee offers to help a customer locate an item at the grocery store

- The extent to which a student is attentive during a school assembly or an after-school play

- How often a student greets peers and co-workers appropriately

- Whether a student shakes hands, has eye contact, and introduces herself without hesitation in a new situation

- Whether a student provides help to a co-worker when asked, rather than giggling and running away

- Whether a student tells a supervisor about a mistake she has made rather than crying

- Whether a student who has had anger-management counseling handles herself appropriately in a potentially explosive situation

- The number of peers with whom a student interacts and gets along with in her general education classes

"You can't force students to interact with each other. First, you need to build acceptance of yourself and your program. Then, inclusion of your students will follow in time. Host parties and meetings in your classroom, or serve as a coach for sports teams. Having the teacher be a part of the overall school helps general education students accept and realize that it is 'cool' to sit and talk with students with disabilities."

Transition teacher, Metropolitan Nashville Public Schools

Using Role-Playing and Problem-Solving Strategies

One very effective means of teaching students social interaction skills is providing them with frequent opportunities to practice those skills. Teachers can help students learn to perform expected social behaviors across a range of social situations by role-playing common social scenarios or problem-solving solutions to typical social encounters (White, Keonig, & Scahill, 2007). For example, Presley and Hughes (2000) used role play to teach students with behavior disorders to control their anger and respond appropriately to social problem scenarios. Teachers also suggest using the following strategies to teach appropriate social skills.

- Using acceptable social skills during an interview can mean the difference between getting a job and being passed over for another applicant. If scheduling problems make it difficult to interview with business managers off campus, then try having students rehearse their skills in mock interviews with a school administrator on campus. Principals and school counselors are experienced in interviewing and can provide valuable feedback about a student's social skills.

- Although teaching social skills in the actual settings in which they will be used is usually the best context for learning, role-playing social behaviors at school can provide students with additional practice and preparation for future interactions. For example, a student could role-play and get feedback from her peers on how to ask her mother to let her choose her own clothes.

- Students can be very creative when brainstorming which behaviors are appropriate in a particular situation. Hold small-group discussions with peers in which students problem-solve which social behaviors would be acceptable during a certain interaction, such as when telling a clerk that you have not received the correct change.

- IDEA 2004 emphasizes the need for teachers to be good role models for their students. During the school day, teachers are one of the most visible models of appropriate social skills that students will see. For example, if you treat others kindly and with respect, then your students are more likely to do so, too.

- Role playing can be helpful in encouraging students who are hesitant or shy to participate in groups. Peers can provide a nonthreatening atmosphere in which students can practice new social skills, such as speaking up in class or asking a friend for his or her telephone number.

- Have students role-play interviewing each other. Then follow up these sessions by having students interview guest speakers in class.

"I like being a Best Buddy because I see the joy that I can bring into someone's life and that makes me feel good and wanted. Being a Best Buddy is a reciprocal relationship—it's a 50/50 deal. As much as my buddy gets from me, I get back from him. He means as much to me as I do to him. It's a special relationship—it's a real friendship. We both like spending time together. It's not work; it's rewarding!"

Best Buddy, Vanderbilt University Chapter

Using Peer-Delivered Social Skills Programs

Research shows that having a general education buddy who provides support and encouragement can positively affect a student's social participation both in class and in other school-related social activities (e.g., Carter & Hughes, 2005). When peer buddies support students by advocating, befriending, and modeling appropriate classroom behavior, peer acceptance of individual differences increases (Copeland et al., 2004). General education peers can also learn to teach students to solve work-related problems, sequence their tasks, and increase their independent performance (e.g., Hughes et al., 2011). Most important, peers are effective teachers of social interaction skills (see Assessing Outcomes: Peers as Teachers of Social Skills).

"The best way to have students learn social skills is through peer-tutoring programs and integration into general education settings. Teach peer tutors to interact and teach social interaction to students. I encourage peers to tell students when they are acting or talking inappropriately. I tell peers, 'If you would allow another friend to act or say that, then allow the students. If you wouldn't, then don't allow them to get away with it.'"

Teacher, Karns High School

Teachers also share many peer-involvement strategies they have used in teaching social skills to students.

- Peer buddies provide many opportunities for students to practice social skills. Take time to have students just socialize with their peer buddies—talking casually, playing cards, or looking at magazines. Students' social skills will eventually improve.

- Peers are not "shy" about providing feedback to students. If students are acting inappropriately—such as mumbling, talking too loudly, or repeating themselves continuously, or if they forget to shut the bathroom door when using the toilet—then their peers are likely to let them know. Peers are often more effective in changing these behaviors than teachers.

- Special education students can serve as peer buddies as well. Students can tutor younger children in general education classes. Cross-age tutoring helps both the tutor and tutee improve their communication, social, and academic skills.

- Students with learning disabilities or emotional/behavioral disabilities also may have much to offer to students with intellectual disabilities—and benefit greatly from the experience themselves.

"I encourage as much socialization as possible with general education peers. I include peers in the classroom as tutors and as someone to help my students in initiating interactions. Sometimes these interactions develop into friendships but not in all cases. It's tough to get sincere friendships that really last."

Teacher, Hunters Lane High School

ASSESSMENT

Assessing Outcomes: Peers as Teachers of Social Skills

With a little training and coaching, peers can be effective teachers of social skills to students with even very limited verbal skills. In the Metropolitan Nashville Peer Buddy Program, peers have learned to teach students to use "communication books" to increase their conversational initiations. Peer buddies teach students to turn pages in the book, which serves to prompt their initiations with a variety of peers. Because the students have varying abilities to speak, some can verbalize their conversational initiations aloud, whereas others show written questions to peers to start conversations. The peer buddies have been successful in teaching all their partners to increase their conversational interactions—with peers who are both familiar and unfamiliar to them (Hughes et al., 2000).

FORM 6.3

Peer Buddy Social Skills Teaching Checklist

Student: __Pamela Vidal__   Time start: __9:30 a.m.__

Date: __November 21__   Time stop: __9:50 a.m.__

Observer: __Joan Downs__   Number of minutes: __20 minutes__

Peer buddy: __Delores Walls__   Location: __Cafeteria__

Rationale

☑ 1. Peer buddy explains that he or she wants to help the student learn to talk to his or her friends at school.

☑ 2. Peer buddy explains that he or she is going to teach the student a way to talk.

Training Sequence

☑ 3. Peer buddy models using the book.

☑ 4. Peer buddy goes through all of the pictures in the book.

☑ 5. Peer buddy looks at each picture and asks the question.

☑ 6. Peer buddy instructs the student while the student uses the book to ask questions.

☐ 7. Student uses the book to ask questions.

☑ 8. Peer buddy provides a lot of verbal praise for using the book.

☑ 9. Peer buddy corrects student if student misses a step.

☑ 10. Peer buddy prompts student to use the book.

Reminder

☐ 11. Peer buddy reminds the student to use the book when he or she wants to talk to somebody.

☑ 12. Peer buddy reminds the student to start talking and do all of the talking when he or she talks to his or her next friend.

Comments

Delores did a fantastic job of explaining how to use the communication book. She modeled use of the book well but should give more verbal praise to her partner. Delores also missed several great opportunities to remind her partner to use the book at the lunch table.

Form 6.3. Peer Buddy Social Skills Teaching Checklist for Pamela Vidal. (A blank, photocopiable version of this form is included on the accompanying CD-ROM.)

Form 6.3, the Peer Buddy Social Skills Teaching Checklist, can be used as a guide for peer buddies to create a script. As the peer buddy and partner perform each step on the script, simply mark it off on the checklist. Then, follow up by observing the students with peers who did not provide social skills training. Do they continue to prompt themselves to talk by using their communication

FORM 6.4
Peer Perception Questionnaire

Student: **Janelle Ibute**   Date: **November 21**

Partner: **Mica Ackridge**   Location: **Cafeteria**

Instructions: Please circle the number that best represents the way you feel about the interaction you just experienced with your partner.

	Never	Rarely	Sometimes	Usually	Always
Did you feel that your partner interacted with you appropriately?	1	2	3	④	5
Did you enjoy this interaction?	1	2	3	④	5
Would you like to have this kind of interaction again?	1	2	3	4	⑤
Do you think that your partner enjoyed this interaction?	1	2	3	4	⑤
Do you have similar interactions when you are with your friends?	1	2	3	④	5
Comments					
It took a little time to get used to, but I enjoyed talking with Janelle! I'd like to hang out with her again.					

Form 6.4. Peer Perception Questionnaire for Janelle Ibute (completed by Mica Ackridge). (A blank, photocopiable version of this form is included on the accompanying CD-ROM.)

books? Are they having more conversations and interacting with their peers more often? If so, then there is a good chance that the peer-delivered social skills training is working. You can also ask peers with whom the students interact to see how they enjoy the conversations by asking them to fill out Form 6.4, the Peer Perception Questionnaire. Blank, reproducible versions of both forms are included on the accompanying CD-ROM.

"My second semester as a peer buddy I spent mostly with Kim in Ms. Dye's room. And that girl–whew! She was a handful. When I first got into the classroom, she would just sit there and either sleep all day or cry about something or kind of just wander around with her eyes and look and not do anything. After my first semester, I noticed how she wouldn't deal with anybody. She was just always by herself. So I would go over there and tickle her and, all of a sudden, she just livened up! It was like someone had to just talk to her one time and she burst out with life. When I first started talking to her, she really didn't have many words that she could say. Mostly she just said "milk" if she wanted milk, or if she had to go to the bathroom, she would tell us. That was about it. Then I got to talking to her and toward the end of the year, she developed more language and everything. We played games such as hand-slap games and tickled each other. The bean bag chair was the best because she just loved that thing. Kim would just lay on it and wallow all over the floor and just laugh. It was so cool! Well, that's Kim! She's cool now."

Peer buddy, McGavock High School

RESOURCES

Baker, J. (2003). *Social skills training for children and adolescents with Asperger syndrome and social-related communications problems.* Overland Park, KS: Autism Asperger Publishing Company.

This book addresses how to teach a wide range of social-communication skills that can enhance the interactions and social connections of individuals with autism and other disabilities.

Elliott, S.N., & Gresham, F.M. (2009). *Social Skills Improvement System intervention guide.* Upper Saddle River, NJ: Pearson.

This intervention guide is written to help teachers design and implement social skill intervention strategies for students.

Giler, J.Z. (2011). *Socially ADDept: Teaching social skills to children with ADHD, LD, and Asperger's* (Rev. ed.). Austin, TX: PRO-ED.

This resource is aimed at equipping practitioners and family members to teach the hidden rules of social behavior to children with a variety of disabilities.

Goldstein, A. (1999). *The PREPARE curriculum: Teaching prosocial competencies.* Champaign, IL: Research Press.

This curriculum includes 10 interventions aimed at reducing aggression, reducing stress, and reducing prejudice.

Jackson, D.A., Jackson, N.F., & Bennett, M.L. (1998). *Teaching social competence to youth and adults with developmental disabilities: A comprehensive program.* Austin, TX: PRO-ED.

This social skills training program addresses numerous social skills for secondary students and adults with intellectual and developmental disabilities.

Walker, H.M., Todis, B., Holmes, D., & Horton, G. (1988). *The Walker Social Skills Curriculum.* Austin, TX: PRO-ED.

This curricular program contains instructional scripts for 30 social skills identified by secondary practitioners and youth as critical to social competence.

CHAPTER 7

Promoting Functional Skills and Access to the General Curriculum

In this chapter, you will learn how to

- Identify individualized learning goals within the general education curriculum

- Support students' learning in inclusive classrooms

- Teach functional skills across the school day and in the community

- Provide instruction that prepares students for postsecondary education

OVERVIEW

Although many youth are apt to mention friendships, extracurricular clubs, and lunch as what they look forward to most about going to school, students spend the majority of their school day in a constellation of courses and classwork—delivered both on and off the secondary school campus—designed to provide them with the knowledge, skills, and attitudes they need now and into adulthood. The academic and functional skills students learn through their coursework should provide them with a strong foundation they can carry into their future careers, colleges, and community activities, so it is important that teachers make the most of the instructional opportunities existing in their schools and communities.

Increasingly, the general education curriculum is advocated as the preferred context within which to teach students with and without disabilities those skills that will prepare them for adulthood. Academic, elective, and related arts classes are often the locations that first come to mind when teachers think about the general curriculum. More students with disabilities are now enrolled in general education classrooms (McLeskey, Landers, Williamson, & Hoppey, in press), highlighting the importance of providing carefully designed instruction and supports that enable students to learn rigorous academic content. But the general education curriculum is also much broader than just the academic courses students take (Ryndak & Billingsley, 2004). Meaningful learning opportunities exist across a wide range of activities offered through schools, including extracurricular clubs, sports teams, student government, performing arts programs, service-learning projects, and many other school-sponsored activities (Swedeen et al., 2010). Moreover, the postsecondary campus has emerged as a new setting for learning that transition teams are encouraged to consider for young adults with significant disabilities who are still eligible for special education services (Grigal, Hart, & Migliore, 2011). Taken together, this broad range of settings can provide students with rich opportunities to gain skills and increase learning opportunities that provide a well-rounded transition experience.

This chapter focuses on planning and delivering instruction that enables students to learn academic and functional skills that will help them achieve their individualized transition goals and live an enjoyable life in their communities. This chapter includes four groups of strategies transition teachers can use to teach students with disabilities the academic and functional skills that will expand their opportunities both during and after high school. These strategies are clustered in the following sections: identifying students' individualized learning goals within a standards-based framework, supporting learning in inclusive general education classrooms, teaching everyday functional skills within and beyond the school campus, and preparing students for successful postsecondary education pathways.

LEGISLATION

IDEA 2004 emphasizes the importance of supporting students with disabilities within the same spectrum of learning experiences available to other students at a school. The opening section of this law reads: "Almost 30 years of research and experience has demonstrated that the education of children with disabilities can be made more effective by having high expectations for such children and *ensuring their access to the general education curriculum in the regular classroom, to the maximum extent possible,* [emphasis added] in order to (i) meet developmental goals and, to the maximum extent possible, the challenging expectations that have been established for all children; and (ii) be prepared to lead productive and independent adult lives, to the maximum extent possible" (§ 601). In other words, IDEA 2004 challenges schools to provide students with disabilities opportunities to learn and benefit from the broad range of courses, clubs, and other experiences already considered to be important for students attending the same school.

Case Study 7.1 *Learning Opportunities for Randy*

Randy was convinced he wanted to somehow work with computers after high school. He loved tinkering with his own desktop computer at home, having taken it apart and rebuilt it more times than he could count. Randy had also become the informal "go-to" person for computer technical support in his neighborhood. Hardly a week went by when one of his neighbors didn't ask him to stop by to install a new program, fix a frozen screen, or recover a deleted file. He loved to learn and he enjoyed having opportunities to share his skills with others.

When it came time for his annual IEP meeting, Randy's teachers and parents wanted to make sure he left high school well prepared to pursue his dream career of becoming a software designer. Everyone agreed that postsecondary education would be a necessary pathway to this line of work, but as they reflected on his current ninth-grade class schedule, they realized that Randy's coursework was unlikely to prepare him for entry into college. As a student with autism, most of Randy's coursework took place in self-contained or resource classrooms along with other students who shared his same disability. Randy was not gaining access to rigorous mathematics instruction that would teach him the skills needed to enter college and prepare for his career. Moreover, he was not enrolled in any of the high school's numerous technical course offerings, and he had few opportunities to connect with other students at Reagan High School who shared his passion for computing.

Members of the IEP team began to brainstorm how they might better provide instructional opportunities that would equip Randy with the knowledge, skills, and connections he would need to pursue postsecondary training in this area. They also thought creatively about all the places in their school and community already offering youth opportunities to explore and deepen their interests related to computing and technical careers. Determining where to provide instruction was just one part of the planning process. They also needed to determine how best to design and deliver instruction to maximize Randy's learning. After all, graduation was just 3 short years away.

INDIVIDUALIZING GOALS WITHIN THE GENERAL CURRICULUM

One distinguishing feature of special education services has always been the personalized nature of students' educational and transition programs. Educational teams—including the student—work together to develop IEP plans and goals that reflect the unique strengths, interests, preferences, and needs of each student. Thus, what may be most important for one student with a disability to learn may look somewhat different from what is emphasized for another student. At the same time, planning teams must also consider how students with disabilities will participate and make progress within the general curriculum. IDEA 2004 and NCLB call for greater alignment between the state and local standards students with and without disabilities are each expected to meet. Indeed, schools are held accountable for whether all students—including those with disabilities—meet these achievement standards.

The dual emphasis on individualized goals and aligning instruction with state and local standards can sometimes introduce a sense of tension when carrying out transition planning. Should achievement standards for all students take precedence over individual goals? Can IEP goals focus on functional skills that are not included within state achievement standards in the areas of reading and language arts, mathematics, and science? Fortunately, several strategies exist for developing standards-based IEPs for students with disabilities that still allow for thoughtful individualization (Cushing, Clark, Carter, & Kennedy, 2005; Downing, 2010; Lynch & Adams, 2008).

ASSESSMENT

Assessing Outcomes: Identifying Individualized Instructional Goals

Browder and Spooner (2011) described one promising and practical approach for crafting IEP goals and instructional plans that align with the general curriculum. Their step-by-step process for developing standards-based IEPs is summarized next.

Step 1: Start with Student-Centered Planning

Gather team members and others—including the student—who know a student well to discuss his strengths, interests, and preferences. Rather than fitting a student into a predetermined transition program, a student-centered approach focuses on designing instructional programs around a student's individual preferences, needs, and goals for his future. Identifying students' interests and preferences may require some creativity and perhaps additional time if students have complex communication challenges (see Chapter 5), but it is no less important to do. Students should contribute to the greatest extent possible to the discussions at the planning meeting (Arndt, Konrad, & Test, 2006).

Step 2: Consider Grade-Level Standards

Transition teams should also identify the relevant state standards associated with a student's grade level when crafting his educational plan. For example, standards and alternate performance indicators in the areas of language arts, science, social studies, mathematics, or other areas may be considered for a particular student. Conversations with general educators and checking your state's education web sites will be informative in identifying the most important standards. Using these prioritized standards, make a list of skills the student will need to learn this content.

Step 3: Identify Functional Skills Students Will Need Now and in the Future

State standards need not be the only source of instructional direction. Planning teams should also consider other functional skills students will need to be successful now and in the future settings in which they expect to participate, such as going to college, being active in their community, or moving into a new supported living situation. An ecological inventory can be used to identify important settings in a student's life, the activities occurring within those settings, and the skills needed to meaningfully participate in each (Downing, 2010). Given the breadth of settings transition-age youth will likely encounter, it is especially important to collaborate with others when identifying the most relevant functional skills to teach.

Step 4: Describe Current Performance Levels

Once state standards and functional skills have been prioritized, attention turns to identifying a student's present level of performance in both academic and functional skill areas. In other words, to what extent is a student already able to perform those skills identified as important to his current and future success? Answering this question well usually involves drawing on a range of informal and formal assessment information (see Chapter 2). For example, reviews of students' academic records, prior evaluations, and conversations with general educators can provide insights into their academic performance across content areas. Similarly, situational assessments, direct observations, and interviews with others can offer valuable perspective on the functional and other life skills a student already possesses (or still needs to master).

Step 5: Develop Annual Goals for Core and Other Content Areas

The planning team is now ready to craft annual IEP goals with input from the student. Annual goals should be written to address each of the core content areas identified on the IEP. Annual goals can also address other areas of importance to a particular student, however, including skills related to communication, self-determination, health, social relationships, transportation, or assistive technology. Students should be encouraged to contribute their own ideas for annual goals. After all, it is their future they are planning.

Step 6: Write Short-Term Objectives

Short-term objectives for students with significant disabilities should be written incrementally to move them toward accomplishment of their annual goals. Breaking down larger goals into smaller pieces helps when designing and sequencing instructional efforts, as well as assists teams in gauging progress toward these long-term goals.

Step 7: Determine How Students Will Gain Access to the General Curriculum

Once short- and long-term goals are identified for a student, identify where in the school or community he can best learn these skills. Some skills—particularly those related to core academic domains—are directly addressed in particular courses already offered in your school. Other skills—such as those related to communication, self-determination, or individual therapies—could be taught in classrooms as well as other school and community locations. Take care to identify the instructional settings that are most likely to support both initial learning and long-term maintenance of new academic and functional skills.

Step 8: Plan Specially Designed Instruction

The individual supports a student will need to successfully participate in key learning experiences should also be determined. Although some students with disabilities may need only limited support to participate fully in a science, civics, or culinary arts class, other students may need more extensive accommodations or modifications. For example, a student may benefit from accessing assistive technology in class activities requiring writing, peer tutoring to master a challenging math unit, or audio recordings of lectures from his English class. Teachers have drawn on a wide variety of accommodations and modifications to support the individualized learning needs of their students.

- Teaching students to use mnemonic strategies

- Providing audio-recorded, highlighted, or large-print textbooks and materials

- Presenting material in smaller, more discrete steps

- Using supplemental aids, such as vocabulary or multiplication cards

- Designing small-group instruction

- Helping students use an assignment notebook

- Designing guided notes that include the most salient information

- Providing instructions in multiple ways

- Shortening assignments, tests, or other learning activities

- Teaching self-management strategies

- Giving additional time to complete assignments or tests

- Arranging classroom seating to reduce distractions

- Providing assistance with notetaking from a teacher, peer, or someone else

- Allowing use of a word processor, spell checker, or calculator

- Establishing peer support arrangements

- Providing repeated reviews or drills

- Providing tutoring or one-to-one assistance

- Assisting students with organizational and planning strategies

- Offering breaks as needed

Planning specially designed instruction to promote access to the general education curriculum should be a collaborative endeavor. Work with general educators, paraprofessionals, related services providers, and other school staff to identify the most promising instructional and support strategies to promote student learning. Although limited shared planning time is a real barrier in most schools, it is essential that instructional planning be informed by sharing expertise, experience, and ideas.

Step 9: Select Appropriate State Assessments

The most appropriate statewide assessment should then be selected for the student. Assessment options typically include the 1) general statewide assessment, 2) general statewide assessment with modifications, and 3) alternate assessment based on alternate (or modified) achievement standards. The choice of assessment should be based on how a particular student gains access to the general curriculum rather than on his disability. In other words, a student's educational needs, not other factors, should guide the selection of the most appropriate state assessment.

Step 10: Develop a System for Monitoring Student Progress

Finally, determine which data-based approaches will be used to determine the extent to which the student is making progress toward short-term objectives and annual goals as well as any classroom-specific expectations. A number of different approaches to data collection are described in Chapter 2. In addition to evaluating permanent products or conducting direct observations, curriculum-based measurement approaches can be helpful in gauging how well a student is learning the academic content being taught in the classroom (Deno, 2003). Portfolio assessments can be used for students with more significant disabilities to collect information about their activities, accomplishments, and achievements in particular (or across) curricular areas (Kleinert & Kearns, 2010).

LEGISLATION IDEA 2004 emphasizes the involvement of all students in general education coursework and other inclusive learning opportunities on a school's campus. Specifically, it requires annual goals that enable a student to be involved in and progress in the general curriculum and to participate in extracurricular and other nonacademic activities. As teachers identify areas in which students are experiencing challenges, they should look for ways of incorporating skill instruction into the existing curriculum. This allows students to learn skills by watching their peers and to practice those same skills in the actual settings in which they are expected to be used.

As emphasized throughout this planning process, the information you gathered from observing students, conducting assessments, reviewing established standards, and collaborating with others should guide the selection of new skills to be taught to students and the locations in which instruction should be provided. Moreover, teams should prioritize these skills on the basis of input from family members, students, IEP team members, and others who know the student well. The following additional strategies have been recommended by teachers.

- You can begin to target those skills that need strengthening by examining the data you collected when observing and assessing the student in school, work, home, and community settings. These data will also serve as a performance standard by which you can evaluate the success of instruction.

- Enroll students in courses that address their areas of need. For example, vocational courses at the high school and community college levels can teach students valuable career development skills. General education English and math classes can teach academic, communication, and self-management skills. Community education courses in recreation and leisure activities can help students develop hobbies and social skills that lead to increased competence and new friendships.

- A variety of teaching techniques can be used to teach new skills to students, such as prompts and positive reinforcement. Selecting a teaching method should be based on the student's needs, the skill being taught, and the acceptability of the technique within a particular setting. For example, although most-to-least prompting may be effective in some situations, the acceptability of this strategy in some community settings may be too intrusive for some students.

- Numerous print and Internet resources are now available that describe state-of-the-art teaching techniques. Ask administrators and other colleagues about resources and techniques that may be especially effective. In addition, explore professional development and other learning opportunities that will deepen your own instructional skills.

"Students choose courses they are interested in. Even if they cannot do all that is required in that class, partial participation with assistance is always an option."

Teacher, Maryville High School

"During their IEP meetings, all students choose at least one general education class to enroll in. We allow students to choose the order of activities they do in their classrooms. We try to encourage them to choose friends. We observe a student's day and brainstorm ways and times to increase opportunities for choices."

Teacher, Rutledge High School

"All students should be responsible for striving to do the best they can no matter what their abilities or disabilities are. This is a philosophy that should be included in an educational curriculum. Student input and student self-evaluation should be incorporated into each student's high school program."

Teacher, Treadwell High School

PROVIDING INSTRUCTION IN THE CLASSROOM

Students with disabilities are spending more of their school day in inclusive classrooms where teachers are charged with promoting students' access to the general curriculum (U.S. Department of Education, 2009). It is important to identify effective instructional and support strategies within these classrooms that enable students with disabilities to participate in meaningful learning opportunities alongside their peers without disabilities (Ryndak, Moore, Orlando, & Delano, 2008/2009). Doing this well, however, can be a challenging task. Fortunately, much has been learned since the 1990s about the most promising approaches for supporting inclusive education.

Planning for Participation

Careful planning is a key ingredient of effective teaching. Determining how each student will participate in daily class activities and what he most needs to learn should be considered in advance and revisited regularly throughout the semester. A number of different tools and approaches are available to guide your planning team in answering important questions (see Assessing Outcomes: Planning for Participation and Instruction). For example, Downing (2010) suggested the following series of questions to consider when determining how best to support the learning of students with disabilities in general education classrooms.

- What is the class learning and what grade-level standard(s) does it relate to?

- What skill(s) is the student with a disability to learn and how does it relate to grade-level standards?

- What materials will be needed to highlight the critical skill to be learned?

- How will the adapted material be presented to the student? How will you get the student's attention? How will the adapted materials be used?

- What prompts will be used to teach the target skill(s) and in what order will they be delivered?

- How will the student's behavior be reinforced?

- How will mistakes or errors be corrected?

- How will the student be taught during different instructional arrangements in the room (e.g., large groups, small groups, pairs of students, independent work)?

- In what other ways will the student interact with classmates that may be unrelated to the target skill?

- How will data be collected on acquisition of the targeted skill(s)?

- How will skills be maintained and generalized to other settings and situations?

Of course, the answers to questions will be somewhat different for each student. At the same time, reflecting on these questions should lead you to identify ways in which you might more closely align the learning outcomes of students with disabilities to those of their classmates without disabilities.

"We teach decision making by providing options for assignments (with equal content and on the same level). We use computer software that provides a variety of experiences all with the same educational objective. We incorporate decision making, goal setting, logical consequences, time management, and esteem-building skills into the academic curriculum."

Teacher, Treadwell High School

"I give students opportunities to try new activities. Often, this involves encouraging students to take courses in music, art, typing, computers, or other areas that the student has never been exposed to."

Teacher, South Side High School

ASSESSMENT

Assessing Outcomes: Planning for Participation and Instruction

Many different approaches can be drawn on to outline the instruction and supports students with disabilities will need to participate meaningfully within inclusive classroom activities (e.g., Cushing et al., 2005; Giangreco, Cloninger, & Iverson, 2011; Jorgensen, McSheehan, & Sonnenmeier, 2010). Regardless of the approach you take, it is important to craft a written support plan at the start of the semester and revisit it as often as needed. For example, Form 7.1 is a completed Classroom Support Plan for Samuel Becker. Together, the classroom teacher and Samuel's special education teacher outlined the expectations for all students in the class across activities that were likely to take place during the semester, such as large- and small-group instruction, independent work, homework, and other class-specific expectations. Next, they considered the adaptations and supports Samuel would need to participate in and learn from each of these activities. Finally, because a peer support arrangement was set up for Samuel, the teachers noted several ways in which peers could support Samuel within these activities.

LEGISLATION

IDEA 2004 emphasizes the importance of making accommodations for students to promote their inclusion in general education classes and other activities. According to the amendments, students' IEPs must include a statement of the program modifications or supports that will be provided to ensure that they will be involved and progress in the general education curriculum, participate in extracurricular and other nonacademic activities, and be educated and participate with general education students. In addition, an explanation must be provided of the extent, if any, to which a student will *not* participate with students without disabilities in the general education curriculum and activities.

Classroom Support Plan

Class: American history   Student: Samuel Becker

Teacher: Ms. Alameda   Peers: Adrian and Thomas

Typical activities and routines	Expectations for all students	Needed adaptations and supports	Roles of peers in providing support
Whole-class instruction	During lectures, students listen, answer questions, and take notes; during group discussion, students are expected to relate class topics to current events.	Samuel will receive guided notes prepared by the teacher; he will sit in the first two rows to minimize distractions.	Peers will help Samuel complete his notes, share their notes, and ask clarifying questions; peers will help Samuel research current events on the Internet.
Small-group instruction	During cooperative groups, students read case examples and answer application questions; students also work in teams to prepare for weekly debates addressing historical issues.	Samuel will be part of the same group as Adrian and Thomas.	Peers will paraphrase aspects of the readings for Samuel, make connections to his experiences, and prompt him to contribute to group discussion; peers will help Samuel prepare for upcoming debates.
Independent work	Students use their textbook and other readings to answer worksheet questions.	Adapted worksheet questions will require short answers instead of essays; some worksheets will be reduced in length as needed.	When finished with their work, peers will help Samuel record his answers and check his work for accuracy.
Homework and assignments	Students typically read one chapter of the textbook per week and turn in two homework assignments.	Samuel will have access to an electronic textbook on which he can listen to the readings.	Samuel will have access to a peer tutor during his fifth-period study hall when he needs additional assistance.
Needed materials	Textbook, notebook, weekly planner	None needed	Peers will help Samuel keep his assignments and class materials organized.
Other expectations	Students are expected to arrive to class on time, bring all of their needed materials, and participate actively in class activities.	None needed	Samuel walks with his peers to and from class.

Form 7.1.   Classroom Support Plan for Samuel Becker. (From Janney, R., & Snell, M.E. [2004]. *Modifying schoolwork* [p. 64]. Baltimore, MD: Paul H. Brookes Publishing Co.; adapted by permission; and from *SNELL, MARTHA E.; BROWN, FREDDA, INSTRUCTION OF STUDENTS WITH SEVERE DISABILITIES, 7th Edition,* © 2011. Reprinted by permission of Pearson Education, Inc., Upper Saddle River, New Jersey.)

Teaching Academic and Related Skills

Good instruction is important to provide to every student in a classroom. It is also essential that effective teaching strategies be used to promote skill acquisition, maintenance, and generalization for students with disabilities, especially those with more complex disabilities. For example, some students may take a bit longer to learn a particular concept, need complex learning tasks broken down in smaller steps, or benefit from having a skill taught multiple ways. Thus, teachers should have a strong understanding of a broad range of research-based teaching practices to meet the individualized needs of their students (Council for Exceptional Children, 2009). For example, students with intellectual disabilities attending general education classes have learned to use embedded prompts in texts to identify content relevant to class assignments and self-monitor their completion of assigned tasks (Copeland, Hughes, Agran, Wehmeyer, & Fowler, 2002). The following instructional strategies have been recommended by teachers to support students in inclusive classrooms.

- Students often learn best through hands-on activities. Whenever possible, assign small-group and project-based assignments that encourage students' active learning. Students will often need some initial guidance on how to work well together.

- Provide students with frequent "opportunities to respond." Not only does this provide students more chances for active engagement, but it also increases the amount of reinforcement they will receive.

- Strategies such as constant and progressive time delay, most-to-least or least-to-most prompting, and other direct instruction strategies have strong evidence of effectiveness at teaching a wide range of skills. Apply these strategies in ways that align well with the learning styles of your students.

- Modeling can be an especially powerful teaching tool. When students see new skills demonstrated by others, they may learn these skills more rapidly. Look for ways to involve students with disabilities in working alongside their classmates because peers can be especially effective models of important skills.

- Teach students to manage their own performance. Even students with limited verbal skills can learn to respond to naturally occurring cues, such as a late bell at school, to prompt being in their seat and beginning work on time.

- Give students choices on scheduling required activities. Some students prefer tackling challenging tasks first, whereas others prefer to ease into harder assignments. Letting students choose the order in which required tasks are performed respects students' individuality, strengths, and needs.

- Traditional grading systems may be difficult to apply when students have more extensive support needs. Identify grading approaches that meaningfully capture the progress students with disabilities are making on common course content and individualized educational goals (see Assessing Outcomes: Modified Grading for Students with Significant Disabilities).

"General education teachers can incorporate vocational objectives into their English or math curriculum. Copies of the academic objectives (scope and sequence) should be available to special education teachers so that they can assist in teaching math and language skills to better prepare students for success."

Teacher, Treadwell High School

"By developing a task analysis of activities we are teaching, we are able to determine what steps of a routine are learned, what still needs to be taught, and when progress is being made."

Transition teacher, Nashville Public Schools

ASSESSMENT

Assessing Outcomes: Modified Grading for Students with Significant Disabilities

Grading a student should be a collaborative process between special and general education teachers. Talk with general educators about whether and how to modify current grading policies to best capture the progress of individual students. Form 7.2 is a modified grading system that can be adapted for use with students with significant disabilities enrolled in general education classrooms. Change the form as needed to reflect those skills specified in your student's IEP. A blank, reproducible form is included on the accompanying CD-ROM.

Supporting Social Participation

Inclusive classrooms can offer rich learning opportunities, not just in terms of academic content but also socially. Simply attending a general education class (or any other setting), however, does not guarantee students will "fit in" socially with their peers or learn targeted social and communication skills. Sometimes a classroom setting must be altered or changes must be made in a curriculum to accommodate a student. For example, students in keyboarding class often work alone on their assignments using individual computers. Teachers also may not emphasize social interaction opportunities in order to maintain a formal atmosphere. It may be that a naturally occurring break time, such as at the beginning or end of class, could be used as an acceptable time for students to socialize with each other, similar to what co-workers do on their breaks at work. There may be projects that students could work on in groups or students could rotate the assigned person to supervise the work of others. These simple modifications can promote appropriate social interactions and are consistent with accommodating students' individual needs. The following teacher-recommended strategies can be used to foster social-related learning opportunities in inclusive classrooms.

- Some classes support only infrequent social interaction among students. If increasing social interaction is an important educational goal for a student, then help the student schedule classes that are of interest to him and allow opportunities to build social competence.

- Survey the daily settings in which students participate to identify changes that will increase their opportunities for social interaction. These changes are often fairly simple, such as pulling desks together during a class assignment, coordinating co-workers' breaks so that they occur at the same time, or encouraging a student to join a community fitness center instead of exercising at home alone.

- In classes, rotate student leadership throughout the school year. By providing students with opportunities to direct a portion of the class, such as moderating a discussion or making a class presentation, students gain confidence in their social abilities and learn valuable leadership skills.

"When the teacher allows student leadership in the classroom paired with responsibility for tasks, competence is developed. Role playing allows students to see themselves as others see them."

Teacher, Fairley High School

FORM 7.2

Modified Grading System for Students in General Education Classrooms

Student: ___Shonda Amendelian___

General education teacher: ___Ms. Levy___

Grading period (circle one): 1 ② 3 4 5 6

Course title: ___Government___

Suggested modifications: ___Shonda benefits when class instructions and assignments are written out and kept in her sight. She gets along well with her peers and works especially well with a partner who can provide her with support.___

Directions: Each time you grade the class members on assigned work or tests, you may choose to grade this student on the above modified criteria, if appropriate. Please return this sheet to me at the end of the grading period. Thank you!

Objectives	8/11	8/14	8/19	8/21	8/25	8/27	9/1	9/4	9/8	9/10	9/16	Average
Is on time	P	I	P	I	I	I	P	I	I	I	I	97
Has materials	P	P	P	I	I	P	I	I	I	I	P	95
Sits in assigned seat	S	P	I	I	I	I	I	I	I	I	I	97
Follows directions	U	U	S	P	P	S	P	I	P	I	I	87
Asks for help appropriately	P	P	P	I	I	I	I	P	I	P	I	95
Interacts with peers appropriately	I	P	I	I	I	I	I	I	I	I	I	99
Follows classroom rules	U	S	U	S	U	P	S	P	P	S	P	81
Completes tasks as instructed	S	S	S	S	P	S	S	P	S	P	P	84
Has positive attitude	I	I	I	I	I	I	I	I	I	I	I	100
Completes modified assignments	P	P	P	S	P	S	P	P	P	S	P	87

(Date)

Suggested codes:

I = 100: Meets objective independently
P = 90: Needs a prompt to meet objective
S = 80: Requires several prompts to meet objective
U = 70: Unable to meet objective

Scoring: You may assign either a letter grade or a numerical grade.

Signed: ___Andrea Jones___
  Special education teacher

Form 7.2. Modified Grading System for Students in General Education Classrooms for Shonda Amendelian. (A blank, photocopiable version of this form is included on the accompanying CD-ROM.)

"Through observations of students during daily activities, I develop one-to-one relationships with the students in order to discuss appropriate and inappropriate behavior and activities. Through role playing and 'rap' sessions, I let the student see what skills are needed to become a better citizen who will be accepted by the community."

Teacher, Raleigh Egypt High School

PROVIDING INSTRUCTION OUTSIDE THE CLASSROOM AND IN THE COMMUNITY

Not all teaching and learning has to happen within the four walls of a traditional classroom for both students with and without disabilities (Halle & Dymond, 2008/2009). Schools and communities naturally provide numerous learning opportunities that take place away from rows of desks and chairs. Planning teams should carefully consider the many opportunities available to learn and apply functional skills within extracurricular clubs, cafeterias, community settings, and other contexts in which students spend their school day (Carter, Swedeen, Moss, & Pesko, 2010). In addition to providing engaging learning environments, these activities and settings can help students develop a host of academic, social, leisure, and other functional skills that foster lifelong enjoyment.

Unfortunately, many students with disabilities miss out on these learning opportunities. According to the NLTS–2, more than one third of youth with disabilities had not participated in an organized group at school or in the community during the past year (Wagner, Cadwallader, & Marder, 2003). This involvement may be especially limited for students with more significant disabilities (Kleinert, Miracle, & Sheppard-Jones, 2007; Simeonsson et al., 2001). Thus, it is especially important that IEP teams are intentional about planning for and working on students' educational and transition goals within and outside the classroom walls. In addition, school staff should work to identify and remove any barriers to students' participation in extracurricular and other school-sponsored activities, such as attitudinal, programmatic, and support-related barriers. Administrators can be instrumental in these efforts by communicating to the student body, staff, and families that extracurricular involvement is an important component of comprehensive transition education for all students. See Hughes and Carter (2008) for a description of schoolwide strategies for promoting a climate of acceptance for students of diverse abilities and cultural backgrounds.

Case Study 7.2 *Another Success*

Autumn was quickly giving way to winter, and Carlos was gradually feeling at home at Washington High. Carlos kept himself quite busy, juggling his time among classes, job training, and responsibilities at home. Mr. Kleeb was also proud of the success that Carlos was finding and continued to search for ways to help him demonstrate the many strengths he possessed. As a result, Carlos was quite happy in his new school community.

Mr. Kleeb knew, however, that the amount of acceptance and involvement Carlos had in school, work, and community settings would be influenced by how competent he appeared in those settings. Using informal assessment methods would help to determine which of Carlos's skills might need additional supports and instruction. With the help of a translator, Mr. Kleeb adapted a home inventory for Carlos and his father to complete in Spanish, their primary language. Carlos and his father together decided that Carlos would benefit from instruction in daily living skills such as budgeting, doing laundry,

(continued)

Case Study 7.2   *(continued)*

and cleaning the house and through greater involvement in community activities. Mr. Kleeb was grateful for their input and decided to talk with other team members to get their input.

Mr. Kleeb spoke with several general education teachers and discovered that each expressed similar concerns regarding Carlos's social involvement in their classes. Although Carlos had made some friends at work, he appeared to be uncomfortable when interacting with his same-age peers. A conversation with a paraprofessional confirmed that social skills instruction would be an important goal. Mr. Kleeb decided to interview Carlos's peer, who frequently worked with him in cooperative learning groups. The peer suggested that Carlos might fit in better if he learned to participate in some recreation and leisure activities that were popular in the area, such as snowmobiling and ice hockey. At the same time, his peers could learn some of the activities that Carlos enjoyed, such as soccer.

Conversations with those individuals who were involved in Carlos's education provided a multitude of suggestions. Mr. Kleeb gathered the team together to prioritize educational goals and determine who should carry out instruction and how. Presenting the results of his observations, assessments, and conversations, Mr. Kleeb helped others see which new skills would need to be taught and encouraged others to identify ways of incorporating these new skills into daily activities. In doing so, each team member was helping Carlos become more competent and better accepted.

LEGISLATION

IDEA 2004 requires planning teams to consider the supplemental aids, services, and supports students with disabilities will need to "participate in extracurricular and other nonacademic activities" at their school (§ 300.320[a][4][ii]). Although such activities can provide rich opportunities to learn and apply academic and life skills, planning teams often focus too narrowly on involvement in formal coursework to the neglect of other instructional opportunities that exist throughout every middle and high school (Powers et al., 2005). Think beyond the classroom as you consider a student's goals for the upcoming school year.

Providing Instruction Outside of the Classroom

Simply learning how to perform a new skill does not mean that a student will use the skill consistently in all of the settings in which it is required. Teachers should provide students with frequent opportunities to practice skills to assist them in becoming more fluent. Also, students should have the opportunity to practice a new skill across a variety of classroom settings, tasks, and people. Students who are provided with such learning opportunities are much more likely to generalize those newly learned skills to other contexts. The following teacher-recommended instructional strategies can be drawn on when teaching students outside of the classroom.

- Talk with students' supervisors, parents, and community leaders to determine which skills that are critical in other settings should be reinforced by practice in the classroom.

- Practice makes perfect. Giving students frequent opportunities to practice new skills throughout the day and in different settings will ensure that those skills are mastered more quickly and performed when needed.

- Find ways of increasing students' involvement in extracurricular and community activities. The more students are able to participate in such activities, the more opportunities they will have to practice important skills.

- Incorporate student preferences and interests into skill instruction. Discuss interests with students who are verbal, or use trial-and-error experiences with new activities with students who are nonverbal.

- Remember, a new skill must be reinforced in order for it to be maintained. For example, if you are teaching a student to use a vending machine, then it is critical that the student completes the whole activity and gets the reinforcement (e.g., candy bar, can of soda). People do not continue putting money in vending machines unless they get something for it.

- As you design a task analysis of a job, consider modifying steps that will allow the student to learn and maintain a new skill more easily. Avoid making learning a new task harder than it needs to be. For example, color-coding automotive tools can help a student select the appropriate one for a job.

- Teach skills that are functional within the student's settings. Generic skills, such as sorting, are not likely to be maintained unless they are functional, useful, and reinforced within the everyday settings in which a student participates. For example, if a student is taught to order from a table at a sit-down restaurant but orders only take-out from a drive-thru, then ordering from a table is not likely to be maintained.

"If I observe a weakness that a student might have, we will repeat and practice that task on the job. Also, if needed, I will set up the same (or similar) tasks at school for them to practice and work on."

Teacher, Pearl-Cohn High School

ASSESSMENT

Assessing Outcomes: Functional Skill Training

Hygiene skills, such as dressing and grooming, are critical to helping students meet expectations for personal appearance within virtually any setting. Make sure when you teach these skills that they are consistent with those expected in a particular setting. For example, students should follow the dress code in their workplace or in the gym where they work out. It is also critical to have parents reinforce appropriate hygiene skills at home. The following is an example of how to teach Joe Wethers one important self-care skill: grooming. Form 7.3 is a completed Data Collection System for this skill. A blank, reproducible form is included on the accompanying CD-ROM.

1. Identify the target behavior (e.g., Grooming and hygiene skills: Joe will shave his face before coming to school).

2. Determine the student's current level of functioning (e.g., Joe is able and knows how to shave. He just seems to forget to do so on a regular basis).

3. Develop a plan for teaching the skill(s) (e.g., Picture prompts and verbal reinforcement will be used in teaching the skill).

4. Monitor the student's progress in meeting the goal, and modify the plan as necessary (e.g., Collect continuous data to make instructional decisions/changes when necessary).

Collaborating with Others to Provide Instruction

Most students have an increasing number of opportunities to be involved in different school, work, and community settings throughout high school. For example, many service clubs host school-sponsored food drives, neighborhood cleanups, or other community projects. Many students hold part-time jobs while they go to school; some play in bands or sing in a choir; and others pursue hobbies, such as working on cars, climbing the wall at a local recreation center, or taking dance lessons. As students increase their involvement in these diverse settings, it becomes particularly important for teachers to collaborate with parents, peers, fellow teachers, co-workers at students' worksites, and community members when providing skill instruction. By working together, those involved in students' lives can ensure support for and access to meaningful learning opportunities. Teachers recommend the following strategies for collaborating in this way.

FORM 7.3

Data Collection System

Student: __Joe Wethers_____   Date: __October_____   Observer: __Ms. Lauderdale_____

Behavior: __Joe will shave his face before coming to school._____

Date	Yes or no	Comments
10/2	N	Joe said he didn't have razors. I took him to store to purchase more.
10/3	N	Joe said he forgot. I gave him verbal reminders just before he left.
10/4	Y	Great job!
10/5	—	Absent today
10/6	N	Joe said he forgot again! I gave him a picture card to remind him.
10/9	Y	Looked good! Joe was proud!
10/10	Y	Great job!
10/11	N	Joe said he ran out of time before his ride came.
10/12	Y	Great job!
10/13	Y	Great job!

Y = __Shaved before school_____   N = __Did not shave before school_____

Form 7.3. Data Collection System for teaching grooming to Joe Wethers. (A blank, photocopiable version of this form is included on the accompanying CD-ROM.)

- Not every discussion about instructional support has to take place within an IEP meeting. Conversations in the faculty lounge, before or after school, or at departmental and faculty meetings can provide a time when teachers can speak with one another about how best to provide instruction, accommodations, and/or modifications for a student.

- Talk with family members about the types of skills they would like to see taught within and beyond the classroom. By working together, you can identify ways in which those skills can be consistently promoted both at school and at home.

- Brainstorm with peers ways they can assist in supporting the learning of classmates with significant disabilities in classes, clubs, or other school activities. Peers can be quite effective at modeling for and/or teaching one another important skills.

"Discuss choices with students, and have them self-monitor their choices. Monitor students' participation in extracurricular activities through observation and discussion. Have peer tutors attend class and record students' choices of friends, tasks, and so forth."

Teacher, Karns High School

"I talk to students' general education teachers. I ask them to tell me problems that they see with the students. Then I incorporate teaching solutions or ways to deal with these problems into instruction."

Teacher, McEwen High School

LEGISLATION

IDEA 2004 states that the federal government has an ongoing obligation to support programs that enable students to acquire the skills that will empower them to lead productive and independent adult lives. In addition, teachers are required to assist students in developing the competence needed for participation in school and postschool settings, such as postsecondary education, vocational training, employment environments, independent living, and community activities. As a result, transition services must include "instruction, related services, community experiences, the development of employment and other postschool adult living objectives, and, when appropriate, acquisition of daily living skills and functional vocational evaluation" (§ 602).

PREPARING FOR POSTSECONDARY EDUCATION

Postsecondary education is the pathway to an increasing number of careers in the United States (Carnevale & Desrochers, 2003). For youth and young adults with disabilities who aspire to certain occupations—such as those in health care, education, or social service sectors—going to college can provide the preparation students need to enter and be successful in their chosen profession, but the benefits of a college experience are much broader than simply career preparation. Students can explore areas of personal interest, develop relationships with peers from all across the country (and around the world), gain independence skills, encounter new ideas and perspectives, and have fun. Indeed, college can be an important part of a well-rounded transition experience for many students.

Preparing for postsecondary education must begin long before the first day after graduation. Students must acquire academic knowledge and skills throughout their schooling in order to gain admission into college and take on new classes successfully (see strategies in this chapter). Students will also benefit from learning independence and self-determination skills to help them make the transition to settings in which the guidance of teachers and family members is less readily available (see Chapter 5). Social skills can also influence the extent to which students will develop the friendships and supports they will need to enjoy college life (see Chapter 6). Because many students work part time to help them pay for college, the employment skills students possess can affect their ability to persist in school (see Chapter 8). It is clear that waiting until senior year to begin thinking about college simply means waiting too late. Transition teachers can play a vital role in helping students navigate this process early in and throughout students' secondary school years.

RESEARCH

Since the 1990s, increasing numbers of students with disabilities are entering college or gaining access to some other type of postsecondary education in the early years after leaving high school. In fact, pursuing some type of postsecondary education was a goal on the transition plans of more than 4 out of 5 youth with disabilities (Cameto et al., 2004). During the 8 years after leaving high school, approximately 60% of young adults with disabilities had eventually continued on into a community college; vocational, business, or technical school; or 4-year college or university (Newman, Wagner, Cameto, Knokey, & Shaver, 2010). Although students with hearing impairments, visual impairments, speech-language impairments, and learning disabilities enrolled at the highest rates, increasing numbers of college programs are opening their doors to students with intellectual disabilities (Grigal et al., 2011). In fact, as of 2011, there were more than 150 postsecondary program options for students with intellectual disabilities and numerous programs in the early stages of launching.

Case Study 7.3 *The Acceptance Letter*

Simone Barclay couldn't believe the letter had finally arrived. Her peers at school had given her all sorts of advice about what to expect on this day. A thick envelope means you got in, one friend said. Getting a letter too late in the spring means you didn't, said another. Simone ran into the house and sat in the living room surrounded by her father and four sisters. Full of both excitement and trepidation, Simone carefully slipped open the envelope and peeked inside. She would be a freshman at Elmbrook College in the fall!

When Simone was younger, no one really expected her to consider college. After all, none of the students with intellectual disabilities in her district had pursued this path after high school. Instead, most students stayed on the high school campus until age 22 when they were no longer eligible for special education services. But Simone's perspective began to change early in her high school career. Enrolled primarily in inclusive general education classes, Simone heard many of her friends without disabilities talking about the colleges and universities they dreamed of attending. Why shouldn't she also go to college?

Although Mr. Barclay had not attended college himself, he was very supportive of Simone's dream for her future. Similarly, several special education teachers at the school had heard about the growing number of postsecondary education programs for students with intellectual disabilities and wondered whether such a program would work in their local community. Together with other members of the IEP team, they began planning the ways in which they could support Simone in learning the skills she would need to get into and find success on the college campus.

At about the same time, Elmbrook College was launching a new joint initiative with the local school district aimed at increasing the presence of students with intellectual disabilities on the campus. The school had a strong commitment to diversity and inclusivity, and they felt their students with and without disabilities would have a richer experience if they had opportunities to learn alongside and get to know one another. Students with intellectual disabilities would take one or two classes each semester (usually as an audit or for noncredit), work in an on-campus job, and live in one of the dorms. Although Simone was excited about taking classes related to her interest in art and working in the ceramics studio, she most looked forward to attending football games, hanging out with new friends at the student center, and having some newfound independence from her sisters. A new adventure awaited Simone in the fall. She had much to do to prepare.

Preparing Students for Postsecondary Education

Making the transition from high school to college is a big change for any student. A world of choices and challenges suddenly opens that never existed before. For students living on a campus in a dorm, there is no parent there to wake them up for class. Students can choose to sleep late or set an alarm in order to wake up on time for class. Many class projects and assignments are due several weeks or more in the future, requiring students to budget their time to avoid having to scramble at the last minute to hand in their work by the due date. Weekends offer many options for free time, such as hanging out in the student recreation center, going to a movie, or playing cards late into the night. It can be easy to get wrapped up in activities and suddenly realize that it is already Sunday night and tomorrow's readings for class lay untouched in a pile of books, CDs, and candy wrappers. With thoughtful preparation while still in high school, however, students can learn skills to promote their success as they make the transition to college. The following teacher-recommended strategies are offered for providing instruction that will prepare students for college or other postsecondary learning opportunities.

- Most students will need considerable help learning about and navigating the college search and admissions process. Find out where this information is already taught within the school or community. Discuss with teachers or program sponsors how students with disabilities might gain access to the instruction already being provided in these settings.

- College programs usually offer students a level of independence and self-direction that they have not previously experienced. Some students may struggle if they have not learned certain self-determination and self-management skills. Provide students with early opportunities to learn these skills.

- A variety of campus resources and supports are usually available to assist college students with disabilities. Unlike in high school, where teachers usually offer these supports, college students will need to seek out needed assistance on their own as well as self-disclose their disabilities. Teach students how to do this effectively.

- Going to college can be very costly. Paying for tuition, fees, books, supplies, room and board, insurance, and occasional recreational activities can be expensive and limit college access for substantial numbers of people with disabilities living in poverty. Teach students and their families how to apply for campus, state, and federal aid programs; scholarships; and other potential financial awards.

- Effective use of technology can be critical to the success of students on campus. Teach students to use everyday and specialized technologies that can promote their participation and learning within campus activities.

Collaborating with Others

Like all other areas of transition education, preparing youth with disabilities for postsecondary pathways can be enhanced when multiple people work together. Youth, their families, high school teachers, guidance counselors, college staff, adult agencies, and any number of other stakeholders have access to unique information, resources, and connections to contribute to this process. Finding efficient ways of sharing these assets can enable more young people with disabilities to realize their dream of going to college. Teachers recommend the following collaboration strategies for promoting postsecondary preparation.

- The experiences and expectations of families related to postsecondary education can influence students' interest in and preparation for college. Talk early and often with parents about their support for postsecondary education, the ways in which they are helping their child make the transition to college, and the support they need from the school and others to do so well.

- Most high school guidance counselors have numerous resources to help students undertake the search process, select appropriate programs, and complete their applications. For example, they may host a college fair day, help arrange campus visits, compile college brochures, or offer test preparation resources. Collaborate with these partners to ensure that students with disabilities are encouraged and supported to gain access to these same resources.

- Connect youth and their families to their state vocational rehabilitation office. In some cases, these programs can provide services or financial support that enable young adults with disabilities to pursue postsecondary training that leads to a meaningful career.

- The lack of accessible and reliable transportation can be a real barrier to college for many young people with significant disabilities. Explore public transportation options, carpooling, ride share programs, and on-campus living as potential avenues for addressing this challenge.

As graduation rates for students with disabilities steadily improve, providing effective transition services to promote successful postschool education or employment is a key measure of accountability for schools charged with meeting the needs of students with disabilities. Indicator 14 requires schools to track the "percent[age] of youth who had IEPs, are no longer in secondary school and who have been competitively employed, *enrolled in some type of postsecondary school, or both,* [emphasis added] within one year of leaving high school" (20 U.S.C. 1416[a][3][B]). Thus, the postsecondary outcomes of young adults with disabilities can provide valuable insights into the quality and impact of transition education programs provided while students are still in secondary school.

RESOURCES

CAST: Center for Applied Special Technology, http://www.cast.org

> CAST is an educational research and development organization working to expand learning opportunities for all individuals through universal design for learning.

HEATH Resource Center, http://www.heath.gwu.edu/

> The HEATH Resource Center is a web-based clearinghouse on postsecondary education for individuals with disabilities that serves as an information exchange of educational resources, support services, and opportunities. The center gathers, develops, and disseminates information in the form of resource papers, fact sheets, web site directories, newsletters, and resource materials.

The IRIS Center, http://www.iris.peabody.vanderbilt.edu

> The IRIS Center offers free, online interactive resources that translate research about the education of students with disabilities into practice. Their materials cover a wide variety of evidence-based topics, including behavior, response to intervention, learning strategies, and progress monitoring.

National Alternate Assessment Center, http://www.naacpartners.org

> The National Alternative Assessment Center focuses on 1) bringing together and building on high-quality, technically sound alternate assessments, 2) demonstrating high-quality design through their selected partner states, 3) administering all types of alternate assessments, and 4) providing technical assistances through high-quality dissemination practices.

National Center on Educational Outcomes, http://www.cehd.umn.edu/nceo/

> The National Center on Educational Outcomes provides national leadership in designing and building educational assessments and accountability systems that appropriately monitor educational results for all students, including students with disabilities and English language learners.

National Center on Universal Design for Learning, http://www.udlcenter.org

> The National Center on Universal Design for Learning (UDL) supports the effective implementation of UDL by connecting stakeholders in the field and providing resources and information about UDL, advocacy, implementation, research, and resources.

Think College: College Options for People with Intellectual Disabilities, http://www.think college.net

> Think College focuses on research, training, technical assistance, and dissemination in postsecondary education for people with intellectual and developmental disabilities.

CHAPTER 8

Teaching Employment Skills and Promoting Career Development

In this chapter, you will learn how to

- Assess students' career-related instructional needs
- Help students gain access to meaningful career development experiences
- Teach skills that promote employment success
- Collaborate with others to support employment

OVERVIEW

Most adults can speak first-hand to the ways in which work contributes to their quality of life, satisfaction, and well-being. Obviously, jobs provide income that can open up new opportunities and raise standards of living. But work offers other benefits as well by creating opportunities to develop new friendships and supportive relationships with others, providing a chance to make valued contributions, and encouraging deeper involvement in community life. Thus, making sure young people graduate from high school with the skills, attitudes, and experiences that will prepare them for a meaningful career throughout adulthood is an important emphasis of public education. In fact, IDEA 2004 states that one purpose of special education is to ensure that "all children with disabilities have available to them a free and appropriate public education that emphasizes special education and related services designed to meet their unique needs and *prepare them for further education, employment, and independent living*" [emphasis added] (§ 1400).

Holding a part-time job after school or on the weekends, participating in a school-sponsored internship, or connecting to a summer job are all ways of gaining valuable early work experiences. In fact, this is a fairly typical experience in the United States, with almost 90% of youth reporting having worked at some point during high school (Zimmer-Gembeck & Mortimer, 2006). Yet, finding and keeping a good job can be a difficult task for many youth and young adults with disabilities. Many youth with disabilities lack the experiences, skills (both work related and social related), and attitudes that enable them to locate, keep, and enjoy a good-paying job that aligns with their interests and builds on their strengths. Thus, the efforts teachers devote to designing high-quality instruction and providing hands-on work experiences that prepare youth for the world of work are an important element of effective transition programming.

This chapter comprises four groups of strategies teachers can use to prepare youth with disabilities for meaningful careers after high school. Strategies are grouped by purpose: assessing students' career-related needs and interests, expanding students' career development opportunities, teaching employment and related skills, and collaborating with others to support successful work experiences.

Case Study 8.1 *Dressed for Success*

Selena was sure she wanted to own her own clothing store when she left high school. She loved keeping up with the latest styles and her friends always joked that Selena was one of Central High School's "best dressed" students. The local retail store at which she and her friends regularly shopped was always busy and so this career choice also seemed like a great way to make a lot of money. Selena also knew that running a store would mean steep discounts on the newest fashions. Although her parents encouraged her to go to college after high school, Selena was firmly set on opening her own clothing store. Nothing could stop her.

Ms. Dykstra listened carefully as Selena shared these dreams at her IEP meeting. As a transition coordinator at the school, Ms. Dykstra was pleased that Selena had such a clear idea about the kind of career path she wanted to pursue. It was not uncommon for other students on her caseload to simply shrug their shoulders when asked about their work-related goals. At the same time, Ms. Dykstra had some very real concerns. Despite being a senior, Selena had never actually held a paid job. Because Selena had also never worked in a clothing store, Ms. Dykstra wondered whether she fully understood what it was like to work in—let alone manage or run—a retail store. After all, shopping at a store was quite a different thing than working there. Moreover, Ms. Dykstra knew relatively little about the extent to which Selena possessed the range of skills she would need to find success working in such a setting. For example, in reviewing Selena's coursework and grades, Ms. Dykstra saw that Selena had long struggled in the core academic areas of math and reading. She also observed that Selena sometimes experienced some challenges working collaboratively with classmates and getting along with certain teachers in the past. Would these difficulties limit her opportunities in the workplace? Could Selena really ever own or manage her own clothing store? How could Ms. Dykstra find out the answers to these questions?

RESEARCH

Early Work Experiences for Young People with Disabilities

Numerous studies have documented the benefits that come to youth with disabilities through involvement in early work experiences while still in high school (Benz, Lindstrom, & Yovanoff, 2000; Vondracek & Porfeli, 2003). For example, a part-time job can provide a real-life setting for learning different functional and social skills, inform students' career planning for the future, broaden their social networks, and help them become more self-determined. When those middle and high school work experiences are successful, they can also raise the career-related expectations of youth with disabilities and their parents, as well as the employers and community members who have the opportunity to get to know them. It is not surprising, therefore, that having paid work experience during high school is considered one of the most important predictors of whether a student with disabilities will find gainful employment in the years after leaving high school (Baer et al., 2003; Carter, Austin, & Trainor, in press; Fabian, 2007; Shandra & Hogan, 2008).

Yet, many students with disabilities miss out on these important learning opportunities. According to the NLTS-2, only 36% of youth with intellectual disabilities, 15% of youth with autism, 53% of youth with emotional disturbance, and 60% of youth with learning disabilities held a paid job at any time during the year prior to being surveyed (Wagner et al., 2003). Graduating from high school without these early work experiences may contribute to later unemployment, underemployment, and lowered expectations into adulthood. Up to 8 years after leaving high school, only 38% of young adults with intellectual disabilities, 37% of young adults with autism, 50% of young adults with emotional disturbance, and 67% of young adults with learning disabilities were reported to be currently employed (Newman et al., 2011). As a result, it is strongly advocated that students with disabilities be connected to paid work experiences prior to leaving high school (Rusch et al., 2009).

ASSESSING CAREER-RELATED INSTRUCTIONAL NEEDS

Identifying individualized employment needs is an initial step in preparing students for their future careers. Each of your students will likely have received different levels of preparation for successful employment experiences. Some students may not yet possess the skills needed to search effectively for available job openings, complete required application materials, and interview successfully for a position. Other students may not have learned the importance of dressing appropriately for the job, calling in when sick or running late, or requesting days off in advance from a supervisor. Still others may benefit from learning essential social-related job skills, such as speaking appropriately to supervisors and co-workers, accepting constructive criticism, or responding appropriately to joking. Consequently, it is important to carefully reflect on which skills and behaviors are most essential to address first as part of your instruction.

One starting point involves identifying those skills valued most highly by employers. For example, you might talk with local businesses about the specific qualities they are looking for in new employees, interview a student's immediate supervisor about the skills needed to successfully perform job responsibilities, or observe at a new jobsite to learn which skills are most often utilized by employees. Although there are generic skills that are relevant across multiple employment sectors, work-related expectations can also vary widely from one employer to the next. Thus, it is important to determine which demands are specific to the types of jobs students are interested in pursuing or currently hold.

Attention can then turn toward determining whether your students are able to perform these identified skills in the ways that are likely to meet the expectations of employers. Some students may not yet have acquired particular skills. Other students may perform expected skills to some degree but will benefit from additional instruction aimed at increasing their fluency or maintenance of those skills. Remember that a constellation of diverse skills are often needed to support a successful work experience. Not only will students need to be able to perform specific work-related tasks, but they will also benefit from learning 1) skills that will enhance their relationships with co-workers and customers, 2) related skills that can promote acceptance (e.g., grooming and hygiene skills), and 3) mobility skills that enable them to get to and from the job on time. The following strategies can be used by teachers to identify their students' individualized instructional needs.

- It can be difficult to determine which skills students will need to learn when they have not yet had their first work experience. Situational assessments (see Chapter 3) and job sampling can provide students with opportunities to try out new jobs while providing you with opportunities to assess their instructional needs.

- Draw on previously developed lists of entry-level skills typically valued by employers. Such lists can be obtained by talking with vocational teachers at your school, reviewing published curricula and assessment tools, or visiting the Department of Labor's web site (see the resources section at the end of the chapter). If you are unsure about which of these listed skills are most important for your students, then ask their supervisors to review your lists to help you prioritize skills.

- When students are already involved in a school-sponsored job, internships, or short-term job placement, observing students at the jobsite is one of the most direct ways to evaluate their instructional and support needs. Be as unobtrusive as possible when conducting these observations. The data collection tools described in Chapter 2 can be drawn on to carry out these observations.

- As students accrue multiple job experiences throughout middle and high school, data often are collected on the skills students have learned (and still need to learn). Review evaluation records associated with these prior job experiences to identify any key needs that have persisted across time.

- Ask supervisors and co-workers about the specific skills they identify as needing strengthening. As individuals who are intimately familiar with the task- and social-related expectations of the job, they have an important vantage point from which to recommend additional instruction.

- Social and behavioral challenges exhibited at school may also present similar difficulties in the workplace or community. Consider whether instruction and support will also need to be directed toward addressing these challenges in the workplace.

"I stress the importance of and have many discussions with students about responsibility, good manners, positive attitudes, and work performance."

Teacher, Pearl-Cohn High School

ASSESSMENT

Assessing Outcomes: Identifying Job-Related Instructional Needs

Pinpointing those job-related skills that are most important to teach begins by assessing the degree to which students are able to perform those skills considered important to success on the job. Form 8.1 compiles a list of 40 skills in 4 areas often considered to contribute to success (Bullis & Davis, 1996; Carter & Wehby, 2003; Chadsey & Beyer, 2001). A blank, reproducible version of this form is included on the accompanying CD-ROM. *Work-production–related behaviors* include those nonsocial behaviors that contribute to employee productivity. *Task-related social behaviors* include interactive behaviors directly related to the performance of job tasks. *Non–task-related social behaviors* are not directly related to task performance, but performance of these behaviors may contribute to increased social integration and acceptance. *General work behaviors* refers to generic behaviors that have relevance across a wide variety of entry-level employment positions. For each of the skills, the rater(s) indicates the extent to which the student currently performs the behavior. If the rater has not yet had an opportunity to observe the student perform a skill, then the *unsure* option can be checked. The bottom of the form includes additional space to elaborate on any of the ratings.

It can be particularly helpful to solicit the perspectives of multiple people who are familiar with workplace standards and the students' on-the-job performance when evaluating students in each of

Job-Related Skills Assessment

Student employee: __Spencer Blackner__   Worksite: __Anderson Design Company__   Date: __May 19__

Name of person completing the form: __Jonathan Smith__   Role: ☑ Supervisor   ☐ Job coach   ☐ Student

	Very poorly	Somewhat poorly	Somewhat well	Very well	Unsure
Work-production–related behaviors					
Carrying out instructions that need immediate attention	☐	☐	☐	☑	☐
Completing quality work	☐	☐	☑	☐	☐
Working well without the close supervision of others	☐	☐	☑	☐	☐
Solving routine work-related problems without help	☐	☐	☑	☐	☐
Working well under pressure	☐	☐	☐	☑	☐
Working at the speed expected by the supervisor	☐	☐	☑	☐	☐
Working at a job continuously without getting distracted	☐	☐	☑	☐	☐
Performing job responsibilities without having to be asked	☐	☐	☑	☐	☐
Task-related social behaviors					
Working together with others as a member of a team	☐	☑	☐	☐	☐
Accepting help from co-workers	☑	☐	☐	☐	☐
Asking a supervisor for assistance or help when needed	☐	☑	☐	☐	☐
Speaking appropriately to a supervisor	☐	☐	☑	☐	☐
Offering to help co-workers or customers	☑	☐	☐	☐	☐
Asking for an explanation when instructions are unclear	☐	☑	☐	☐	☐
Referring questions to others when unsure of the answer	☐	☑	☐	☐	☐
Asking a co-worker for assistance or help when needed	☑	☐	☐	☐	☐
Following directions given by a co-worker or supervisor	☑	☐	☐	☐	☐
Finding necessary information prior to starting a job task	☐	☐	☑	☐	☐

(page 1 of 2)

	Very poorly	Somewhat poorly	Somewhat well	Very well	Unsure
Accepting constructive criticism without getting angry or upset	☐	☑	☐	☐	☐
Talking about job frustrations with a supervisor	☐	☑	☐	☐	☐
Non–task-related social behaviors					
Refraining from swearing or using objectionable language	☐	☐	☐	☑	☐
Making friends with co-workers	☑	☐	☐	☐	☐
Listening to the other person when involved in a conversation	☐	☑	☐	☐	☐
Speaking in an appropriate tone of voice	☐	☐	☑	☐	☐
Using polite language (e.g., thank you, please, excuse me)	☐	☐	☑	☐	☐
Responding appropriately to joking or teasing	☑	☐	☐	☐	☐
Disagreeing with co-workers without arguing or yelling	☐	☑	☐	☐	☐
Refraining from interrupting others at inappropriate times	☐	☐	☑	☐	☐
Avoiding complaining too much	☐	☐	☑	☐	☐
Offering compliments to others	☑	☐	☐	☐	☐
Discussing personal problems only in appropriate situations	☐	☐	☐	☐	☑
Starting conversations with co-workers about nonwork topics	☑	☐	☐	☐	☐
General work behaviors					
Maintaining good personal hygiene	☐	☐	☐	☑	☐
Requesting days off of work from the supervisor	☐	☐	☑	☐	☐
Returning from break or lunch on time	☐	☐	☐	☑	☐
Arriving to work on time	☐	☐	☐	☑	☐
Taking responsibility for own actions at work	☐	☐	☑	☐	☐
Calling in to work when sick or running late	☐	☐	☐	☑	☐
Dressing appropriately for the job	☐	☐	☐	☑	☐
Accepting unexpected schedule changes	☐	☐	☐	☐	☑
Comments					

Spencer is a hard worker who always completes tasks at a high level of quality. However, he has a difficult time getting along with co-workers and customers. He definitely prefers tasks in which he can work alone.

these areas. For example, supervisors can let you know whether a student's work performance meets their own expectations. Job coaches and transition teachers often are able to complete more extended observations of the students and may be working directly with students on learning specific tasks. And students themselves can also provide valuable insights into how well they feel they are doing in each of these areas. Targeted discussions about the sources of any discrepancies may be warranted whenever substantial differences in ratings exist across these raters.

Case Study 8.2 *Kenneth Learns to Laugh*

Rube Alweis, Kenneth's job coach, was concerned. Kenneth was one of his best workers, he liked Kenneth immensely, and he didn't want Kenneth to lose his job. In retrospect, maybe Kenneth's manager and co-workers hadn't been well prepared for accepting someone with Kenneth's differences into the workplace. Rube decided he had a job to do.

First, Rube arranged a meeting with the hotel manager and Kenneth's co-workers. During the meeting, Rube discussed the purpose of Kenneth's employment-training program and explained that it gave students such as Kenneth a chance to learn work and social skills needed for successful long-term employment. Trying out different jobs gave transition students the opportunity to see which jobs they liked best and which jobs were a good match with their particular skills, interests, and preferences.

Rube also mentioned that many students like Kenneth hadn't had much opportunity to work or interact with others in an employment situation, and, consequently, they hadn't learned what social interaction behaviors were typically expected in a workplace. Rube gave the hotel manager and Kenneth's co-workers the opportunity to voice their expectations of a hotel employee. They all agreed that they liked someone who smiled and said, "Good afternoon," in the halls; joked at break; and would make eye contact, wave, or smile when they worked together in the same area. Rube explained that if they modeled this same behavior with Kenneth, he would be more likely to meet their expectations. Rube also reminded them that Kenneth was one of the best laundry workers at the hotel, as evidenced by his work record, and that it would be advantageous to the hotel to keep him employed.

In closing the meeting, Rube reminded everyone that they could talk to him about any concerns they have about Kenneth. If any problems came up, Rube would be glad to meet with them to come up with a solution. Rube thanked everyone for supporting the employment-training program and for attending the meeting. He was glad he remembered to joke around with everyone and maintain a sense of humor during the meeting. Rube knew it was important to establish a rapport with the employees at Kenneth's worksite if he wanted Kenneth to be accepted.

Finally, Rube reminded himself to redouble his efforts to model an attitude of acceptance around Kenneth and around everyone at the worksite. By doing so, others would learn how easy it is to interact with people whose behavior might be a little different. So, when he passed Kenneth in the hall as he left the meeting, Rube yelled out, "Hey, Buddy!" put his "dukes" up, and pretended to go in for a shot with his fist at Kenneth's nose. Kenneth responded with a big grin and a "high-five." His co-workers looked in amazement—they had never even seen Kenneth smile! Before long, however, they, too, were taking "jabs" in the air at Kenneth in the break room and when passing him in the halls. Hearing Kenneth chuckle just made their day.

CONNECTING STUDENTS TO EARLY CAREER DEVELOPMENT EXPERIENCES

Some of your students may already be involved in off-campus work experiences, such as a summer internship, part-time job, or school-sponsored vocational training. Others, however, may not yet be connected to the types of early work experiences that can set them on a course toward a meaningful career after high school or college. Indeed, these early work experiences seem to be most elusive for students with intellectual disabilities, autism, and emotional/behavioral disabilities (Carter, Austin, & Trainor, 2011; Carter, Trainor, Cakiroglu, Swedeen, & Owens, 2010). Connecting students with work experiences in the community that align with their learning needs, interests, and future career goals is an important aspect of providing employment-related instruction. After all, instruction tends to be most effective when provided in the actual settings in which students will be expected to use those skills.

"To assess students' job preferences, I go on the job with them. I am there with the students all day during a typical day at each of their jobsites. I observe their behavior and talk to those who are in each environment to determine their job preferences."

Teacher, Cleveland High School

Identifying Students' Career Interests and Goals

Exploring students' career-related interests, prior experiences, instructional needs, and long-term goals is one starting point for identifying strong job matches and meaningful learning contexts for students. Students may be more motivated to learn new skills when they see the relevance of those learning opportunities to their personal plans for the future. A variety of approaches for identifying students' interests are addressed throughout Chapters 2 and 6. In addition, the following teacher-recommended strategies can be helpful in identifying the career interests and goals of your students.

- Many youth—particularly younger students—may not yet have thought deeply about the career path they would like to pursue. This is especially true for students with significant disabilities, for whom expectations for community employment often are low and conversations about future careers all too infrequent. Career exploration activities can expose these students to a range of possible career paths and help them begin to think about the kinds of jobs they would like (or definitely not like) to have.

- Ask parents and other family members to share with you what they have learned about a student's work-related interests and aspirations for adulthood. Quite often, they have already had many conversations about what the student would like to do when she grows up and they bring unique perspectives about the types of jobs that would suit her particularly well.

- One of the best and most direct ways to find out which types of jobs would be motivating to your students is simply to ask them. Even when students share unexpected or seemingly unrealistic career aspirations (e.g., professional basketball player, rock star), these conversations can help you pinpoint the types of job responsibilities that most interest them.

- Have frequent conversations with your students during class about the different occupational paths available to them. Numerous print and computer-based career awareness resources are available from educational publishers or online. The Bureau of Labor Statistics' *Occupational Outlook Handbook* can be especially helpful for students to explore (see the resources section at the end of the chapter).

- Invite local employers—individually or as part of a panel of presenters—to speak to your classes about the work that their business or organization does, the expectations they hold for their employees, their recommendations for how students can begin to prepare for such a job, and the employment outlook in this industry sector. In addition, arrange for your students to periodically visit local businesses and organizations to expose them to new career possibilities they had not yet considered.

- A variety of career interest assessments can be drawn on to increase students' awareness of career possibilities as well as the responsibilities, salaries, and hiring prospects associated with each of these career paths.

"Assess job preferences by providing as many types of job training as possible. Keep records of previous jobs, and take pictures and videos so the student can remember the site. Stay at one site long enough so the student can get to know it. Keep a logbook of students' feelings and comments, and discuss these with the student."

Itinerant transition teacher, Metropolitan Nashville Public Schools

"Making career choices takes time! If you start at age 14, your vocational training will allow your students enough time to sample a variety of jobs, including summer jobs. This is important to helping them choose a career area."

Teacher, Halls High School

ASSESSMENT

Assessing Outcomes: Identifying and Connecting Youth to Relevant Work Experiences

Students should play a prominent role in making decisions about their own lives (Test et al., 2004), including decisions about where they will work during and after high school. Students are usually in the best position to provide information about their personal interests and goals. So, it is important to have conversations with them—and others who know them well—about their short- and long-term employment interests and goals. Form 8.2 is a Student Job Planning Tool that can be used to help identify these interests and track progress toward identifying a good job match while still enrolled in school. A blank, reproducible version of this form is included on the accompanying CD-ROM.

The first section lists who contributed to the planning process. Students—including youth with complex communication challenges—should always have a prominent voice in the planning process. In addition, involving family members, school staff, community members, and others who know the student well ensures that a breadth of perspectives are drawn on to inform the planning process. After determining who should be part of the planning process, attention can turn to identifying the student's "big-picture" or long-term goals related to their future career. Guiding questions for these conversations—directed first to the student—might include the following: What are you really good at? What do you like to do? What kind of careers most interest and excite you? Next, the team identifies more immediate employment-related goals (i.e., ones that can be accomplished during high school) to move the student toward her long-term goals. Carefully anchoring experiences during high school to these long-term goals can help career development opportunities build on one another. The following discussion prompts can serve as a catalyst for answering this question well.

- What types of jobs have you had in the past? Are you working right now? Did you work this past school year or summer?

- What types of work experiences now could help you meet your goals for after high school?

- What would be your top three places to work this school year or summer?

- What other kinds of jobs sound interesting to you? What do you like to do in your spare time?

- What types of jobs or work responsibilities would you definitely not want to do?

Student Job Planning Tool

Student: __Madison Whitt__   Date: __February 19__

1. Who was part of this meeting/conversation?

__Madison Whitt__	__Student__	(student must be present)
__Dr. Lyons__	__Guidance counselor__	(role/relation to student)
__Gregg Whitt__	__Father__	(role/relation to student)
__Nancy Geitner__	__Special education teacher__	(role/relation to student)

2. What are some of the student's long-term, "big picture" career goals for life after high school?

Madison would like to work for a professional organization—such as a law firm or nonprofit—that does environmental work.

3. What are the student's short-term goals in the areas of employment and future careers?

- Madison would like to work a few hours per week with a small business to learn basic office skills.
- She is also interested in volunteering with a local environmental group to learn about community organizing work.
- Finally, she would like to strengthen her knowledge of environmental issues.

4. List each short-term employment goal and answer each question.

Work-related goals	What are some possible places in our community to do this?	Who do we already know—or need to seek out—who might help the student connect to these experiences?	What supports or resources are needed to make this happen?	Who will take responsibility for following up on this possibility?
Get a part-time job in an office environment	Two large office parks are located close to Madison's neighborhood.	Mr. Whitt knows someone who is a member of the local small business network.	Madison will need help completing applications and preparing for interviews.	Mr. Whitt will contact the business network. Madison will complete job applications with help from Ms. Geitner.
Volunteer with a local environmental group	Smith County Conservation Society, County Fish and Wildlife Service, Friends of the Parks Society	Madison has two friends who are volunteering twice per month. Dr. Lyons knows someone at the local Community Foundation who compiles volunteer opportunities.	Madison may need help learning to use the local transportation system, as well as encouragement to try a new activity on her own.	Madison will talk with her friends about their experiences volunteering with the Conservation Society. Dr. Lyons will get Madison contact information for the Community Foundation.

(page 1 of 2)

Form 8.2. Student Job Planning Tool for Madison Whitt. (Adapted from Carter, E.W., Swedeen, B., & Trainor, A.A. [2009]. The other three months: Connecting transition-age youth with disabilities to meaningful summer experiences. *Teaching Exceptional Children, 41*[6], 18–26. Copyright © 2009 by the Council for Exceptional Children, Inc. www.cec.sped.org. All rights reserved.) (A blank, photocopiable version of this form is included on the accompanying CD-ROM.)

FORM 8.2. *(continued)*

Work-related goals	What are some possible places in our community to do this?	Who do we already know—or need to seek out—who might help the student connect to these experiences?	What supports or resources are needed to make this happen?	Who will take responsibility for following up on this possibility?
Learn more about environmental issues	The high school has an Environmental Club that meets biweekly and several science classes on the topic.	Ms. Geitner knows the Environmental Club sponsor, and she has connections with the local adult education program director.	None	Ms. Geitner will introduce Madison to Mr. Abel, the club sponsor.
Research nearby colleges that offer an environmental studies major	Eastwood Community College, Drury State University, Oneida College	Dr. Lyons has numerous college guides in his offices and has several contacts at local colleges.	Madison will need help researching colleges and completing any application materials.	Dr. Lyons will invite Madison to an upcoming college fair. Mr. Whitt will help Madison request college applications and assist her with preparing financial aid applications.

(page 2 of 2)

- What is important to you in an after-school or summer job?

- What is available in our community that might be a good fit with your interests?

Once a student's employment interests and short-term goals are identified, attention should turn toward identifying job opportunities that align well with these aspirations. For each work-related goal, the team should identify 1) possible places in the community to gain this experience, 2) people who could help the student connect to these experiences, 3) supports and/or resources needed to make this idea for a relevant work experience a reality, and 4) who will take responsibility for following up on this possibility (see question prompts embedded on the form). Consider the following questions when exploring which supports, resources, and connections a student might need to realize her short-term employment goals.

- Are there skills the student should learn to better prepare her to find and keep this job?

- Will the student need ongoing support on the job? If so, who might provide that support?

- Will the student need someone to check in on her periodically?

- Are there transportation issues, scheduling issues, family concerns, or other issues that need to be considered?

- What roles will the student play connecting to this career development experience?

- What roles will family members, teachers, community members, or others play?

"Assist students in planning and choosing appropriate courses to enroll in during high school according to their interests. If job sampling has been done, students should have a good idea where their interests and abilities lie. Enlist help from the school guidance counselor and the vocational rehabilitation counselor. Give students options and allow them to make their own choices."

Teacher, Whites Creek High School

"I try to help students have realistic career and personal goals. For example, it may be difficult for some students with physical limitations to play football. I try to let them know that they have other options, such as being manager of the football team or participating in other ways. By getting out and trying different options, students learn more about what they can do."

Teacher, Henry County High School

Identifying Career Development Opportunities for Youth

Although hands-on work experiences are increasingly recommended as meaningful contexts for teaching employment-related skills, other avenues exist through which students also might gain valuable career development experiences. For example, most middle and high schools offer a range of opportunities related to career assessment, planning, exploration, instruction, and connecting that are designed to enhance the employability and preparation of youth with and without disabilities (Carter, Trainor, et al., 2010; Guy, Sitlington, Larsen, & Frank, 2009). Sometimes these activities are formal and take place over the course of an entire semester or school year; other activities are more informal and short term. Talk with other teachers, counselors, and administrators at your school to compile a list of available career development opportunities before launching new programs or initiatives specifically for students with disabilities (Swedeen et al., 2010). For example, the following activities are ones that might already be offered in or through your school.

- Career interest or aptitude assessments conducted for students
- Job-shadowing programs
- Interviewing or practicing résumé writing
- Speakers brought in from local businesses and organizations
- Career exploration courses
- Job fairs or career days
- Tours of local businesses or industries
- College fairs or college days
- Tours of local colleges or technical schools
- Career or job counseling
- Apprenticeship programs
- Paid or unpaid internships
- Tech-prep programs
- Career or job resource center

- Written career plans for students
- Cooperative education programs
- School-based enterprises or businesses
- Job placement services for students
- Mentorship programs with employers

"Have various speakers from the community come to class or take the students to them. Have them speak about their jobs, the education and training they had to have, and the chances for advancement on their jobs."

Teacher, McEwen High School

"Expose students to career opportunities that would stimulate their interests and are within their skill levels. For example, we take trips to area vocational schools to see the programs offered, skills needed for different careers, financial obligations, salary possibilities, and job placement success in different fields."

Teacher, Whitehaven High School

Finding paid jobs in the community for students with disabilities—particularly during difficult economic times—can sometimes be a challenge. Teachers often report having limited time to focus on job development efforts or limited prior training on how to build these community connections effectively (Trainor, Carter, Owens, & Swedeen, 2008). Yet, the efforts school staff make to develop productive and lasting relationships with local businesses can help ensure students are able to find employment experiences that align with their interests and future goals. Investing time learning about the needs of local businesses can provide insights into what employers are looking for in youth employees.

LEGISLATION

ADA 2008 states that "employers with 15 or more employees may not discriminate against qualified individuals with disabilities" (29 CFR 1630.4) and requires businesses to provide qualified individuals with disabilities equal opportunities to benefit from the full range of employment-related opportunities available to individuals who do not have a disability. In addition, the law prohibits employers from discriminating in the areas of recruitment, hiring, training, pay, promotions, social activities, and other benefits related to employment. The law also places restrictions on the types of questions that can be asked about someone's disability prior to a job offer being made. Finally, the law requires employers to make "reasonable accommodations" for otherwise qualified individuals with disabilities.

Assessing Students' Choices and Preferences

Students who have had few prior work experiences are not likely to know what their choices and preferences are in this area. Moreover, they may not know how realistic their choices are unless they can act on and experience the consequences of these decisions. Of course, you can often determine the choices and preferences of some students by simply asking them. When students communicate in nontraditional ways, however, such as by gesturing or using an augmentative and alternative communication system, explore alternative ways to assess their

FORM 8.3

Student Job History Form

Student: Amanda Jocz

		Dates: 8/10 to 12/10	Dates: 1/11 to 5/11	Dates: 8/11 to 12/11
Basic information	Worksite	Community Blood Bank	Heimer, Lief, & Ali Law Offices	Varner's Family Restaurant
	General job types or positions experienced	Receptionist, front desk, courier	Janitor, copy person	Wait staff, bus staff, cashier
	Job tasks experienced	Answering telephones, filing, customer service, deliveries	Mopping, painting, photocopying, filing	Washing dishes, food prep, cashier, customer service
	Location and transportation	1 ②3 N/A	1 ②3 N/A	①2 3 N/A
Task characteristics	Job task requirements	1 ②3 N/A	1 2 ③ N/A	①2 3 N/A
	General mobility	①2 3 N/A	1 ②3 N/A	1 ②3 N/A
	Gross motor demands	①2 3 N/A	1 ②3 N/A	①2 3 N/A
	Fine motor demands	1 ②3 N/A	1 2 ③ N/A	①2 3 N/A
	Length of work tasks	1 ②3 N/A	1 2 ③ N/A	①2 3 N/A
	Variability of daily job tasks	①2 3 N/A	1 2 ③ N/A	1 ②3 N/A
	Problem-solving requirements	①2 3 N/A	1 ②3 N/A	1 ②3 N/A
	Production rate	①2 3 N/A	1 2 ③ N/A	①2 3 N/A
	Work product quality	1 ②3 N/A	1 2 ③ N/A	①2 3 N/A
	Continuous working requirements	①2 3 N/A	1 2 ③ N/A	①2 3 N/A
Task-related characteristics	Co-worker presence	①2 3 N/A	1 2 3 Ⓝ/Ⓐ	①2 3 N/A
	Nontask social contacts	1 2 ③ N/A	1 2 ③ N/A	①2 3 N/A
	Social atmosphere of worksite	1 ②3 N/A	1 2 ③ N/A	①2 3 N/A
	Interaction with customers	1 2 ③ N/A	1 2 ③ N/A	①2 3 N/A
	Supervisory contact	1 2 ③ N/A	1 2 ③ N/A	①2 3 N/A
Environmental characteristics	Distraction level	1 ②3 N/A	1 ②3 N/A	1 ②3 N/A
	Comfort factors	1 ②3 N/A	1 ②3 N/A	1 ②3 N/A
	Equipment/tool use	①2 3 N/A	1 ②3 N/A	①2 3 N/A
Natural supports	Environmental support	①2 3 N/A	1 ②3 N/A	①2 3 N/A
	Supervisor/co-worker support	1 ②3 N/A	1 2 ③ N/A	①2 3 N/A

Key: 1 = excellent job match; 2 = fair job match; 3 = poor job match; N/A = not applicable.

Form 8.3. Student Job History Form for Amanda Jocz. (From Renzaglia, A., & Hutchins, M. [1995]. *A model for longitudinal vocational programming for students with moderate and severe disabilities.* Grant funded by the U.S. Department of Education, Office of Special Education and Rehabilitation Services; adapted by permission.) (A blank, photocopiable version of this form is included on the accompanying CD-ROM.)

choices and preferences in this area. It is all the more important to observe these students carefully to determine what choices they are trying to communicate. The following strategies for assessing students' preferences and choices have been recommended by teachers.

- Allow students to experience different job situations so they can determine their employment preferences. Observe their behavior at different worksites using Form 8.3, the Student Job History. (A blank, reproducible form is included on the accompanying CD-ROM.) Differences in performance across jobs may provide a potential indication of their job preferences. Discuss students' performance and interests with them. The form can easily be adapted for other settings, such as a recreational program or college campus setting.

- Track students' work experiences throughout high school by monitoring their progress using the Student Job History Form. Make sure their job preferences are addressed in their worksites and their job histories reflect professional growth throughout their high school years.

- Give students frequent options throughout the day, such as choosing the topic of a class project or which employer to interview with at a job fair. Allow them to choose which options are most acceptable to them. Interview students to identify their preferences for jobs, general education classes, extracurricular clubs, or leisure time activities.

- Provide job sampling on and off the high school campus. Complete work experience résumés with notes regarding students' preferences for different worksites.

"Evaluate a student's opportunities for choice making across different environments and daily activities. This is very important because many of our students have had limited opportunities to make choices."

Teacher, Cumberland High School

Case Study 8.3 *If Angelo Had Tried Job Sampling*

Angelo Rust entered Walt Whitman High School as a freshman at age 15. He had no work experience when he walked into the office of Ms. Gustafson, the high school vocational counselor, early in September. Ms. Gustafson explained to Angelo that besides taking his regular academic courses, he could enroll in Whitman's Job Experience Program. The Job Experience Program would give Angelo the chance during his high school years to try out, or sample, different kinds of jobs. Counselors in the program would help Angelo find jobs, and they would make sure that he had the opportunity to try out a variety of work experiences so that he could begin to figure out which career areas most interested him. By targeting a particular area, Angelo could determine the skills that he needed and whether he could get them through his high school classes or if he needed postsecondary training or education. The counselors would also keep a record of his job experiences to help him identify his career preferences and to begin to develop a résumé for potential employers.

The Job Experience Program sounded like a good idea to Angelo. He could use some part-time work while he went to school, and he really did need some help to find a job. Also, he wasn't sure what kind of jobs were available and what he really wanted to do when he finished school. He did know that he liked being with little kids such as his nieces. He didn't know, however, whether there even was a job where he could work with little kids all day. Maybe he could find out in the job program.

During the next few years, Angelo discovered that Ms. Gustafson was right. He did get to try out new jobs when he wasn't in school. Some he liked, such as the child care program, and some he didn't like at all, such as the auto body shop. Each time he sampled a new job, his career counselor would

(continued)

complete his Student Job History Form. By the time he entered his senior year, his job history was getting quite long. Besides the child care center and the auto body shop, he already had had jobs in an office, a landscaping business, and an advertising company. When Angelo and his counselor, his parents, and his employers discussed Angelo's job history, they all agreed: The job he liked best and in which he performed best was working as an aide at the child care center. Because of this interest, Angelo enrolled in the child care classes at school. His instructor, Ms. Chickie, was thrilled with his exceptional performance in class and was overjoyed that a male was interested in going into preschool teaching. Male teachers were desperately needed in preschool, but Angelo was the first young man to enroll in her child care classes during the 8 years she had taught at Walt Whitman High School.

Angelo was grateful for the job sampling he had had in Whitman's Job Experience Program. He had learned which career he wanted in life by having the chance to try different jobs. By comparing his jobs and how he performed on them, Angelo learned that child care was the best job match for him. Now he had some real career plans. When he finished high school, Angelo planned to go to college, where he could complete his certification program as a preschool teacher.

TEACHING EMPLOYMENT AND RELATED SKILLS

As in any other area of transition, students with disabilities will benefit from carefully planned instruction to learn the skills, attitudes, and behaviors critical to success in the workplace. Natural opportunities exist in most middle and high schools to learn many of these skills through the vocational classes, school-sponsored work experiences, on-campus jobs, and off-campus internships already sponsored by the school. Helping students with disabilities gain access to these existing career development opportunities can foster inclusive learning experiences and diminish the need for launching new programs (Swedeen et al., 2010). At the same time, many students with disabilities will benefit from receiving more intensive or ongoing skill instruction related to finding, maintaining, and enjoying their jobs.

Teaching Job Search Skills

Most adolescents—with and without disabilities—will profit from learning effective strategies related to finding available job openings, completing job applications, interviewing well, and negotiating a job offer. The following teacher-recommended approaches can be used to help students develop these important job search skills.

- Create a task analysis of the job search process from start to finish. Walk students through each step of the process over the course of a semester or instructional unit, providing numerous examples and hands-on practice experiences.

- Invite local business representatives to visit your class to talk about the job search process from the "employer perspective." Your students will learn how these employers prefer to be approached and the skills and qualities they look for in potential employees. In addition, allow time for students to ask their own questions about the job search process.

- Show students how to gain access to local resources to assist them in their personal job search. For example, many communities have one-stop career centers, local employment offices, web-based job banks, or other resources that can be drawn on by students. Knowing whom to turn to for help is an important skill for students given the time-limited nature of transition services.

- Students can be effective at teaching one another the strategies they have learned from their own job searches. Starting a "job club" can provide a place for students to discuss their own experiences in the job market and assist one another in problem-solving challenges they encounter.

- Numerous career development curricula are available for students with and without disabilities. Talk with vocational teachers and guidance counselors at your school to identify the most promising resources. Many of these resources may already be sitting on a bookshelf in your school.

Teaching On-the-Job Skills

Effective instruction for teaching employment-related skills often involves modeling expected behaviors, providing frequent practice opportunities, giving corrective feedback or praise for correct performance, and gradually fading assistance as students learn new skills (see Chapters 5–7). Although such direct instruction can certainly be provided by job coaches and special educators in the workplace, co-workers and supervisors often represent more natural instructors. Quite often, they are the best experts on the performance levels and social expectations that will promote success on the job. Whenever appropriate, involve them in supporting students in the workplace. Teachers suggest using the following on-the-job instructional strategies.

- Develop a task analysis that clearly lists each step of the activities students are expected to complete (see Form 2.3). This list can be used to guide instruction, collect performance data, and evaluate students' progress.

- Some students will not be able to meet all of the expectations of the job in the same way as other co-workers. Discuss with a supervisor whether modifications can be made to the selected tasks or alternative performance strategies can be implemented.

- Initially, students may benefit from having you close by as they work toward mastering new skills in the workplace. It is important to gradually fade your proximity as these skills are learned, however, so that students can practice these skills when direct support is not always available.

- As students gain experience on the job, teach students to use self-management strategies that can help promote independent performance and generalized use of their new skills.

"If a student was working as a courtesy clerk at a grocery store, I would talk with her co-workers. Most cashiers started out as courtesy clerks and would be able to monitor the student's progress the most."

Teacher, Central High School

"Any worker will be more productive if given the opportunity to be a part of the decision-making process. I realize that for many of my students this would require more support than for others. This is an area where a good working knowledge of the individual is needed."

Teacher, Cleveland High School

"Observe a student who is going to work and how she is dressed. Help her decide whether her choice of dress is suitable for her particular job position."

Teacher, Beech High School

"I think student independence is very important. Students are not always going to have the close supervision of a teacher or job coach. It is important for students to be able to make their own decisions and to know how to go about making appropriate choices."

Teacher, Pearl-Cohn High School

ASSESSMENT

Assessing Outcomes: Job Sampling

Job sampling is a process for providing students with a variety of employment experiences throughout their middle and high school years. Job sampling means having the opportunity to work at a variety of worksites over a period of time, either as a temporary trainee or as a paid employee. Each worksite opportunity may last a few months or longer, giving the student the chance to find out what the job is really like. Job sampling also provides students with opportunities to explore different careers they may wish to pursue as they make the transition to adulthood.

Students can begin to identify their preferred employment options by sampling different jobs reflecting a variety of task, social, and setting characteristics. From middle school to the time they leave high school, students may sample as many as 5–10 different job opportunities. Teachers should keep careful records of students' job experiences, their performance on the job, and their preferred job types. Three forms included in this book can help teachers keep records of these experiences—the Job Analysis Survey (Form 3.1), the Work Performance Evaluation form (Form 3.2), and the Student Job History Form (Form 8.3).

The Job Analysis Survey is used to identify important task, social, environmental, and support characteristics at a worksite. A Job Analysis Survey should be completed for every worksite in which a student participates during job sampling. By doing so, you can identify important factors that may relate to a student's success on a particular job and why she may prefer one job to another. A student's performance on the job is evaluated using the Work Performance Evaluation form. This form allows you to evaluate the student's performance in relation to relevant factors at the worksite and to evaluate the support that is available to the student or that may be needed.

The final form to complete is a Student Job History Form. The Student Job History Form draws together the information compiled on the Job Analysis Survey and Work Performance Evaluation, which are filled out for each job experience. Be sure to complete the Student Job History Form while a student is working at each new worksite. If you wait until a student leaves, then you may forget what her performance was like. By comparing a student's performance on different jobs, you can identify the best "job match"—that job in which the characteristics of the job best match the student's skills, interests, and preferences.

Compare a student's performance on different jobs to identify her job preference. After completing a Student Job History Form, you should have a good idea of which type of job a student prefers. Next, discuss your findings with the student and her parents, employers, and others to determine whether they agree. When a good "job match" is identified, the student's job-training experiences can focus on the identified career area, whether in the areas of technology, journalism, forestry, or medical arts. Continue to keep a record of the student's job experiences on the Student Job History Form because it can also be used to help develop a résumé for a student to use when applying for new jobs.

Teaching Related Skills

There is much more to success and satisfaction on the job than simply performing assigned work-related tasks well. A job also provides a context within which students can develop new friendships, connect to recreational and leisure opportunities outside of work, and feel part of a workplace community. In addition to learning how to do their job well, students will also benefit from instruction that enhances their connections to others and fosters a sense of belonging and contribution. Developing these related skills—often called collateral skills—can help make the difference between students having a job they tolerate and a job they really love. Consider the following teacher-suggested strategies for teaching collateral skills to students.

- Many youth and young adults with disabilities experience difficulties traveling around their community independently (Kessler Foundation and National Organization on Disability, 2010). Lack of mobility can limit the opportunities they have to be involved in social-related activities that may take place beyond their work shift. Teaching students to gain access to local transportation options, arrange for a ride, walk safely to nearby activities, or problem-solve their transportation challenges can assist them to be involved in these activities.

- Some students may benefit from strengthening communication skills that help them maintain friendship connections with their co-workers on those days when they are not working. For example, some students may need help learning how to make telephone calls, send text messages, e-mail others, access social media (e.g., Facebook), or connect using other widely used modes of communication.

- Most jobs include regular opportunities for employees to get to know their co-workers, whether while working on shared tasks or during lunch or other breaks. Teaching students social-related skills that build personal connections, such as initiating a conversation, asking about shared interests, greeting others, or sharing advice, can be an important way to help students "fit in" and feel part of the workplace. Chapter 6 includes numerous strategies for teaching these social-related skills.

- Co-workers sometimes form sports teams, go bowling after work, get together for a company picnic, or participate together in community service activities. Students may miss out on important workplace connections when they lack the skills needed to participate in these activities.

Case Study 8.4   *A Member of the Team*

The arrival of spring signals the long-awaited beginning of softball season in the town of San Angelo. A visitor to the small community might wonder why so much fuss is made over just another game. Local businesses gather their employees together Tuesday and Friday nights to "slug it out" as company pride is either forged or broken on the softball diamond. Families and friends gather in the stands to cheer on Ed's Automotive, Cumberland Manufacturing, or any of the other company teams that have assembled that evening.

Despite the numerous spectators and athletes gathered around the fields this evening, Kelly Parlatour is focused on one player in particular, Scott Meijer. Kelly has been Scott's special education teacher throughout high school and remembers very clearly the first time he mentioned that he wanted to join the team. At the beginning of the past school year, Scott had not been involved in many community activities and had few relationships outside his immediate family. His mother was deceased, his father worked evenings, and his two brothers no longer lived at home. Yet, as Scott described his hopes after

(continued)

Case Study 8.4   *(continued)*

graduation, it became clear that he desired close friendships and involvement in the community. Later that month, the IEP team met to help Scott plan his future.

Mr. Meijer talked with a family friend about getting Scott a job at Jacobson Electronics as a cashier. The vocational rehabilitation counselor arranged for Scott to be trained by another employee, although the counselor provided assistance when necessary. When Mr. Meijer expressed concern over Scott's getting to and from work, Kelly helped Scott find a co-worker who would be willing to drive him in exchange for splitting the cost of the gas. Scott loved his job immensely and developed some fantastic relationships with the people with whom he worked. It wasn't surprising, then, when Scott was asked to be the catcher for the company softball team.

Scott began preparing for the season early. He rode with a friend to the batting cages three times per week. At practice, a couple of the team's star players paired with Scott to teach him some basic fielding skills. Scott was able to get to know his co-workers outside the store when they went out for dinner after practice. On this particular evening as Kelly watched, Scott stood next to home plate, waving his bat in the air, eager to hit one "out of the park." Kelly's smile showed how proud she was of Scott and how grateful she was to all of the people who supported Scott in his goal to be "a member of the team."

COLLABORATING WITH OTHERS

Equipping youth with disabilities well for the world of work often requires the involvement of multiple people and partners. Certainly, some students already have formulated clear career goals, know how to find résumé-building experiences that will prepare and launch them for this career, and are finding success within a part-time job or internship experience they really enjoy. For many other students with disabilities, however, the support, instruction, and connections they receive from their family, teachers, friends, and other community members will be critical in helping them prepare for a meaningful career (Trainor et al., 2011).

Collaborating with Parents and Other Family Members

Parents and other family members can be powerful allies in supporting early work experiences for their children with disabilities. But they also may need information, resources, and/or guidance from schools to support their children in this area. Investing time equipping parents to advocate with and on behalf of their children in the area of employment is time well spent. After all, these family members will be an enduring presence and source of support in these students' lives long after public school services and supports have ceased. The following ideas are offered by teachers for engaging families in supporting the career development of youth with disabilities.

- Lack of accessible transportation is often a real barrier to involvement in work and community activities for youth and young adults with disabilities (Abeson, 2005). This is particularly true for students with more extensive support needs. By working closely with parents throughout the planning process, it may be possible to identify ways in which parents or other family members can assist in meeting some of a student's work-related transportation needs.

- Parent expectations can make a real difference in whether students with disabilities are successful in finding paid employment, both during and after high school (Carter, Austin, & Trainor, 2011). Parents may be more likely to encourage their children to pursue school-sponsored or community-based work experiences when teachers discuss the value of supporting early work experiences, inform them about the job-related school and community services available to their children, and address any concerns they hold about these experiences.

- Some parents may be hesitant to support early work experiences out of concern that their child's financial benefits may be negatively affected. Provide parents with accurate and understandable information about the ways in which newly earned income might affect financial and other supports the family receives. Numerous incentives to work exist for youth and young adults with disabilities. Information about these incentives can be found at the U.S. Department of Labor's Office of Disability Employment Policy's web site (see the resources section at the end of the chapter).

- Recognize that one out of every four children with disabilities lives in a family with earnings below the poverty level (Fujiura & Yamaki, 2000; Parish, Rose, & Andrews, 2010). Thus, not every family will have the resources available to partner with schools and support their child's career development in similar ways. Ask parents about how the school might best assist them in supporting their child's transition experiences.

- Encourage parents to identify household chores for their children in order to foster greater responsibility and teach important work-related skills. Such attitudes and skills will also serve students well in the workplace.

- Parents and other family members will also learn about a student's work experiences through everyday conversations at home or when stopping by during, before, or after a shift. Ask these individuals to share with you their personal insights into how the job is going, whether their family member is enjoying the work, and/or any services or supports that might be helpful.

"I talk with parents to see what the student's chores are at home. In planning with parents, additional chores can be given, and even enhanced, with in-school jobs."

Teacher, LaVergne High School

Collaborating with Supervisors and Co-Workers

Developing working partnerships with supervisors and co-workers can be important to supporting students' success on the job. Although you can certainly learn much about the workplace through observations and site visits, employers are intimately familiar with the expectations, responsibilities, and relationships that characterize a particular workplace, and co-workers usually have a strong sense of the factors that can contribute to a sense of belonging among the team. As suggested by teachers, ongoing and open communication with these individuals can be especially helpful when determining how best to support your students' involvement in the workplace:

- Before employment training begins for a student, openly discuss with employers and co-workers the expectations they have for each other on the job. It can be hard for a new employee to "fit in" at a new worksite unless she knows exactly what is expected. For example, if the policy at a downtown office is that employees go directly to the administrative assistant rather than to a co-worker when they run out of supplies, then that expectation should be made clear to everyone on the job.

- Ask co-workers and others about the strengths they see exhibited by your students on the job. They may be able to share unique perspectives on what is going especially well, strengths you may not otherwise have had the opportunity to see.

- Checking in regularly with a student's supervisor can help make sure small challenges are adequately addressed long before they become major concerns. Remember, however, that employers are usually quite busy with other responsibilities. Agree on strategies for sharing evaluation information that will work well for the supervisor.

Collaborating with Local Employer Networks

Existing formal networks of employers in small and large communities can be drawn on to support schools in finding local employment opportunities for youth with and without disabilities. For example, local chambers of commerce—associations of businesses and other organizations whose purpose is to promote the economic interests of the local community—represent a potential natural partner for high schools. These networks have a presence in nearly every small and large community and are comprised of representatives from a broad range of industry sectors and community organizations. In fact, there are more than 8,000 chambers in the United States. Teachers can approach these employer networks to ask about whether they would be willing to partner with the high school in any of the following ways.

- Co-sponsoring a job fair for youth with disabilities
- Hosting a "job shadowing" day or a career exploration event for youth with disabilities
- Creating a directory of employers with jobs or internships available for youth with disabilities
- Providing feedback to teachers on their career development and related programs
- Offering mock-interviewing or résumé-writing practice for youth with disabilities
- Including information about the school's vocational programs on their web site, in their newsletters, and through other dissemination avenues
- Helping match youth with disabilities to job openings in the community
- Inviting guest speakers from the high school to talk about the employment needs of youth with disabilities at one of their regular meetings

Even if a representative of a chamber of commerce cannot directly help the high school by contributing their own time and resources, they may instead be able to assist transition teachers in connecting to employers in their network who may be willing to offer support in one or more of the following ways.

- Offering "job shadow" experiences to youth with disabilities
- Providing paid or unpaid work experiences for youth with disabilities
- Speaking to other employers in the community about their own positive experiences hiring youth with disabilities
- Visiting schools to talk with youth about what businesses are looking for in new employees
- Helping develop on-the-job training programs to support youth

At the same time, a local employers network—and the individual businesses and organizations that are members of such networks—may also benefit from receiving input and guidance from schools to build their own capacity to better support youth with disabilities in the workplace. Consider offering to speak at an upcoming chamber breakfast, meeting, or event to talk about any of the following topics.

- The benefits of hiring youth with disabilities
- Tax incentives available when hiring people with disabilities

- Ways to recruit youth with disabilities as employees

- Supports provided by schools to employers who elect to hire youth with disabilities

Although not every network will be able or willing to support a school's career development efforts, Carter, Trainor, Cakiroglu, and colleagues (2009) found that many chambers of commerce and employer networks considered these supports to be relatively feasible to offer to their local high schools. They may not often be asked to partner in these specific ways, however. When approaching these groups, remember that many may be unfamiliar with the needs of youth with disabilities. Thus, it may be helpful to provide these employer networks with information, resources, and guidance that expands their awareness of the capabilities of youth with disabilities and increases their knowledge of the availability of supports for these youth.

Collaborating with Other Community Members

Because career development experiences typically exist both on and off of the school campus, it can be helpful to develop partnerships with other members of the community to expand meaningful employment opportunities for youth with disabilities. For example, city leaders may already be—or could become—strong advocates for expanding work opportunities throughout the community. Local organizations and civic groups often know where service and volunteer opportunities are in their city. Public and private transportation providers can be essential allies when mobility issues present barriers to students getting to and from work during the summer months or outside of the school day. Numerous employment and disability support agencies may be willing to offer guidance and resources for developing successful partnerships with employers. Meeting with these various community members individually— or as part of a communitywide conversation—to explore ways of working together can help ensure that school staff are not bearing sole responsibility for the employment preparation of youth in your community (Trainor, Carter, Swedeen, & Pickett, in press).

Collaborating with Youth

The importance of actively involving students and their families in all aspects of the transition process has been emphasized throughout this book and across the transition field. This involvement is no less important when it comes to the area of career preparation. In addition to sharing their interests and preferences related to employment, youth can also provide input into the skills they feel more or less confident performing, the supports they would need to be more successful on the job, and the lessons they are learning about their career paths. Engaging students in reflecting on and talking about these issues can also help foster their self-determination development. The following teacher-identified strategies can be used to more fully involve youth and their families in all aspects of the career preparation process.

- After students have had a chance to "learn the ropes" at their new job, ask them to share their perspectives on their satisfaction with their current job (see Assessing Outcomes: Evaluating Students' Job Satisfaction). This process of self-evaluating can help them pinpoint which aspects of a job are most important, as well as decide what career options would best suit their preferences.

- Regularly talk with your students about their experiences in the workplace. This is especially important when students are working independently (or without regular on-the-job support) or are involved in after-school and summer jobs. Ask them: What is going really well? What do they wish was different? What supports do they need to be successful and feel more a part of the workplace? Are there other jobs they would like to pursue instead?

"Involving students in their IEP teams and meetings is critical. They have the right to have input into their programs. The total outcome of their education will be improved because they will have made their own choices—with help from their family and teachers."

Teacher, Volunteer High School

"We want to be seen as leading the way to a better future for all people with disabilities. We want to be seen as people who advocate for transportation, housing, jobs, education, health care, and other issues. We want to be seen as active, productive, and contributing citizens in the community."

Southern Collaborative of Self-Advocates, People First of Tennessee, Georgia, and Alabama

ASSESSMENT

Assessing Outcomes: Evaluating Students' Job Satisfaction

Success on the job can be influenced by how satisfied students are with various aspects of their work. After all, students who enjoy their jobs may be more likely to keep their jobs, and vice versa. Once students have had an opportunity to accrue some experience in the workplace, talk with them about how satisfied they are with different aspects of their current work. Form 8.4 is a brief tool you can use to gauge your students' satisfaction with different aspects of their job. A blank, reproducible version of this form is included on the accompanying CD-ROM. Although the student should initially fill this form out herself, the answers she provides can lead to some productive discussions with teachers about communicating needs with supervisors, exploring new job possibilities, and/or working well even amidst less desirable aspects of a job.

Case Study 8.5 *Expanding Employment Options in Cherry Hill*

The transition team at Cherry Hill High School was "gung ho" about connecting students with disabilities at their school to a progression of early work and career development experiences before they graduated. Several of these staff had recently attended sessions on supported and customized employment at a national conference. And the transition team had also begun to notice that students who held paid jobs or internships during high school seemed to have a much easier time talking about their career interests and goals for the future during transition planning meetings. Despite their great enthusiasm, the task of finding career development experiences and work placements for the more than 200 students with disabilities at their large, urban high school seemed daunting. As special educators, their days were already quite full with instructional responsibilities and few of them had any training in job development. How could they draw on the support of others in their community to meet the career-related needs of their students?

The teachers determined that successfully expanding youth employment opportunities in the city of Cherry Hill was going to require engaging a much broader segment of the community. Their high school could simply not go it alone. Mr. Brock, one of the vocational teachers, approached the local chamber of commerce to ask if they could introduce his fellow teachers and himself to local employers who were hiring in areas of interest to their students. He wrote a small article for the chamber's monthly newsletter—which reached more than 1,200 local employers—describing the high school's school-to-work program and inviting interested businesses to contact him for more information. Mr. Brock also spoke at the fall chamber breakfast about the benefits of hiring youth with disabilities and the supports the school could offer to employers who were willing to make this investment.

(continued)

FORM 8.4

Job Satisfaction Form for Youth Employees

Student: __Evan Rogers__   Worksite: __Blevner's Flower Mart__

Start date: __September 12__   Survey date: __December 7__

Job responsibilities: __Organizing the stock room, assisting customers, unpacking shipments__

	Rate your satisfaction with each of the following aspects of your current job.				
	Not at all	A little	Some-what	Very	Extremely
Pay	☐	☐	☑	☐	☐
Hours of work	☐	☐	☐	☑	☐
Work environment	☐	☐	☑	☐	☐
Variety in work responsibilities	☐	☐	☑	☐	☐
Opportunities to use your skills	☐	☐	☑	☐	☐
Recognition for good work	☐	☐	☐	☐	☑
Freedom to make decisions	☐	☐	☐	☑	☐
Amount of responsibility	☐	☐	☐	☑	☐
Attention paid to your suggestions	☐	☐	☐	☑	☐
Relationship to co-workers	☐	☐	☐	☐	☑
Relationship to your supervisor	☐	☐	☐	☐	☑
Relationship to customers	☐	☐	☐	☐	☑
Opportunities for advancement	☑	☐	☐	☐	☐
Other: __Distance from home__	☐	☐	☐	☐	☑
Other: _____	☐	☐	☐	☐	☐
Overall job satisfaction	☐	☐	☐	☑	☐

What changes could be made to make this job better?

Working in the cooler for long stretches gets cold. I need a better jacket to use on delivery days.

What parts of this job do you want to stay the same?

I love getting to see and meet so many different customers who live in my neighborhood. It is great working close to home.

Comments:

I'd like to keep the job for the rest of the summer, but I definitely want to try something new next fall.

Form 8.4. Job Satisfaction Form for Youth Employees for Evan Rogers. (*Source:* Carter & Wehby, 2003.) (A blank, photocopiable version of this form is included on the accompanying CD-ROM.)

Case Study 8.5   *(continued)*

> Ms. Oakes, a special education teacher, invited a number of large and small employers—along with several local colleges, training programs, and municipal government leaders—to come to a career and college fair to be held at the high school. Although the event was open to all students in the high school, the team made especially sure that students with disabilities and their families were encouraged and supported to attend. In advance of the event, the vocational and special education teachers worked with students to prepare their résumés, practice interview questions, and talk about the various career options that would be represented at the fair.
>
> The team also recognized that employment opportunities for youth with disabilities were still fairly limited in Cherry Hill. Many employers were simply unaware of the youth with disabilities in their community, or they were somewhat reluctant to hire these students. Many parents had never considered community-based jobs to be a real possibility for their children. And although the community had numerous formal and informal supports that could be drawn on to support youth employment, these assets were not being accessed much by the school. So, the team hosted a community-wide conversation one winter evening to explore ways in which the Cherry Hill community might work better together to raise expectations and expand opportunities for youth employment locally. Over coffee and desserts, youth, family members, employers, employment and adult agency staff, school staff, and other community members met to discuss the following question: What can we do as a community to expand meaningful work opportunities for youth with disabilities in Cherry Hill? Around small tables, people discussed their own ideas for making change in this area. Ms. Greggs—an assistant principal—then facilitated a time of whole-group discussion to share the best ideas that people had heard. The strategies that were shared (and the personal connections people made) that evening provided a launching point for several new initiatives aimed at making the Cherry Hill community more inclusive for its citizens with disabilities.

RESOURCES

CareerOneStop, http://www.careeronestop.org

> Sponsored by the U.S. Department of Labor, this web site includes an array of tools to help job seekers, students, employers, and career professionals.

Employment and Disability Institute, http://www.ilr.cornell.edu/edi/c-employment.cfm

> The Employment and Disability Institute conducts research focused on inclusive workplaces, effective employment, and disability policy.

Institute for Community Inclusion, http://www.communityinclusion.org

> The Institute for Community Inclusion carries out research, education, and dissemination on a range of issues, including employing people with disabilities, making the transition from school to adult life, and promoting technology that aids participation in community and work activities.

National Center on Secondary Education and Transition, http://www.ncset.org

> The National Center on Secondary Education and Transition coordinates national resources, offers technical assistance, and disseminates information related to secondary education and transition for youth with disabilities in order to create opportunities for youth to achieve successful futures.

National Collaborative on Workforce and Disability for Youth, http://www.ncwd-youth.info

> The National Collaborative on Workforce and Disability for Youth assists state and local workforce development systems to better serve all youth, including youth with disabilities and other disconnected youth. They disseminate numerous resources related to career development.

National Youth Employment Coalition, http://www.nyec.org

> The National Youth Employment Coalition is a national membership network that improves the effectiveness of organizations seeking to help all youth become productive citizens.

Occupational Outlook Handbook, http://www.bls.gov/oco/home.htm

> This online handbook describes the training and education needs, earnings, job prospects, and working conditions of hundreds of different types of jobs.

U.S. Department of Labor, Office of Disability Employment Policy, http://www.dol.gov/odep/

> The mission of the Office of Disability Employment Policy is to provide national leadership by developing and influencing disability employment-related policies and practices affecting an increase in the employment of people with disabilities.

References

Abeson, A. (2005). Living life in the community: The role of transportation in inclusion. *Impact, 18*(3), 2–3, 35.

Agran, M. (1997). *Student directed learning: Teaching self-determination skills.* Pacific Grove, CA: Brooks/Cole Publishing Co.

Agran, M., & Hughes, C. (2008). Asking student input: Students' opinions regarding their individualized education program involvement. *Career Development for Exceptional Individuals, 31*, 69–76. doi: 10.1177/0885728808317657

Agran, M., King-Sears, M.E., Wehmeyer, M.L., & Copeland, S.R. (2003). *Student-directed learning.* Baltimore, MD: Paul H. Brookes Publishing Co.

Agran, M., Wehmeyer, M., Cavin, M., & Palmer, S. (2010). Promoting active engagement in the general education classroom and access to the general education curriculum for students with cognitive disabilities. *Education and Training in Autism and Developmental Disabilities, 45*, 163–174.

Alberto, P., & Troutman, A.C. (2009). *Applied behavior analysis for teachers* (8th ed.). Upper Saddle River, NJ: Merrill.

Allen, W.T. (2000). *Read my lips: It's choice.* St. Paul, MN: Governor's Council on Developmental Disabilities, Department of Administration.

Americans with Disabilities Act (ADA) of 1990, PL 101-336, 42 U.SC. §§ 12101 *et seq.*

Americans with Disabilities Amendments Act (ADA) of 2008, PL 110-325, 42 U.S.C. §§ 12101 *et seq.*

Arndt, S.A., Konrad, M., & Test, D.W. (2006). Effects of the self-directed IEP on student participation in planning meetings. *Remedial and Special Education, 27*, 194–207. doi: 10.1177/07419325060270040101

Baer, R.M., Flexer, R.W., Beck, S., Amstutz, N., Hoffman, L., Brothers, J., et al. (2003). A collaborative follow-up study in transition service utilization and post-school outcomes. *Career Development for Exceptional Individuals, 26*, 7–26. doi: 10.1177/088572880302600102

Bellini, S., & Akullian, J. (2007). A meta-analysis of video modeling and video self-modeling interventions for children and adolescents with autism spectrum disorders. *Exceptional Children, 73*, 264–287.

Bellini, S., Peters, J.K., Benner, L., & Hopf, A. (2007). A meta-analysis of school-based social skills interventions for children with autism spectrum disorders. *Remedial and Special Education, 28*, 153–162. doi: 10.1177/07419325070280030401

Benz, M.R., Lindstrom, L., & Yovanoff, P. (2000). Improving graduation and employment outcomes of students with disabilities: Predictive factors and student perspectives. *Exceptional Children, 66*, 509–529.

Bond, R., & Castagnera, E. (2006). Peer supports and inclusive education: An underutilized resource. *Theory Into Practice, 45*, 224–229. doi: 10.1207/s15430421tip4503_4

Briesch, A.M., & Chafouleas, S.M. (2009). Review and analysis of literature on self-management interventions to promote appropriate classroom behaviors (1988–2008). *School Psychology Quarterly, 24*, 106–118. doi: 10.1037/a0016159

Brigance, A. (2011). *Brigance Transition Skills Inventory.* North Billerica, MA: Curriculum Associates.

Brooke, V.A., Revell, G., & Wehman, P. (2009). Quality indicators for competitive employment outcomes: What special education teachers need to know in transition planning. *Teaching Exceptional Children, 41*(4), 58–66.

Browder, D.M., & Spooner, F. (2011). *Teaching students with moderate and severe disabilities.* New York, NY: Guilford Press.

Bullis, B., & Davis, C. (1996). Further examination of job-related social skills measures for adolescents and young adults with emotional and behavioral disorders. *Behavioral Disorders, 21*, 160–171.

Cameto, R., Levine, P., & Wagner, M. (2004). *Transition planning for students with disabilities. A special topic report of findings from the National Longitudinal Transition Study–2.* Menlo Park, CA: SRI International.

Carnevale, A.P., & Desrochers, D.M. (2003). *Standards for what? The economic roots of K–16 reform.* Princeton, NJ: Educational Testing Service.

Carter, E.W. (2011). Supporting peer relationships. In M.E. Snell & F. Brown (Eds.), *Instruction of students with severe disabilities* (7th ed.). Upper Saddle River, NJ: Merrill.

Carter, E.W., Austin, D., & Trainor, A.A. (2011). Factors associated with the early work experiences of adolescents with severe disabilities. *Intellectual and Developmental Disabilities, 49*, 233–247. doi: 10.1352/1934-9556-49.4.233

Carter, E.W., Austin, D., & Trainor, A.A. (in press). Predictors of postschool employment outcomes for young adults with severe disabilities. *Journal of Disability Policy Studies.* doi: 10.1177/1044207311414680

Carter, E.W., Cushing, L.S., & Kennedy, C.H. (2009). *Peer support strategies for improving all students' social lives and learning.* Baltimore, MD: Paul H. Brookes Publishing Co.

Carter, E.W., & Hughes, C. (2005). Increasing social interaction among adolescents with intellectual disabilities and their general education peers: Effective interventions. *Research and Practice for Persons with Severe Disabilities, 30*, 179–193. doi: 10.2511/rpsd.30.4.179

Carter, E.W., & Hughes, C. (2006). Including high school students with severe disabilities in general education classes: Perspectives of general and special educators, paraprofessionals, and administrators. *Research and Practice for Persons with Severe Disabilities, 31,* 174–185.

Carter, E.W., & Hughes, C. (2007). Social interaction interventions: Promoting socially supportive environments and teaching new skills. In S.L. Odom, R.H. Horner, M. Snell, & J. Blacher (Eds.), *Handbook on developmental disabilities* (pp. 310–329). New York, NY: Guilford Press.

Carter, E.W., & Hughes, C. (in press). Promoting social competence and supportive relationships. In P. Wehman (Ed.), *Life beyond the classroom* (5th ed., pp. 249–268). Baltimore, MD: Paul H. Brookes Publishing Co.

Carter, E.W., Hughes, C., Guth, C., & Copeland, S.R. (2005). Factors influencing social interaction among high school students with intellectual disabilities and their general education peers. *American Journal on Mental Retardation, 110,* 366–377. doi: 10.1352/0895-8017(2005)110[366:FISIAH]2.0.CO;2

Carter, E.W., Lane, K.L., Crnobori, M., Bruhn, A.L., & Oakes, W.P. (2011). Self-determination interventions for students with and at risk for emotional and behavioral disorders: Mapping the knowledge base. *Behavioral Disorders, 36,* 100–116.

Carter, E.W., Moss, C.K., Hoffman, A., Chung, Y., & Sisco, L.G. (2011). Efficacy and social validity of peer support arrangements for adolescents with disabilities. *Exceptional Children, 78,* 107–125.

Carter, E.W., Owens, L., Trainor, A.A., Sun, Y., & Swedeen, B. (2009). Self-determination skills and opportunities of adolescents with severe intellectual and developmental disabilities. *American Journal on Intellectual and Developmental Disabilities, 114,* 179–192. doi: 10.1352/1944-7558-114.3.179

Carter, E.W., Sisco, L.G., Brown, L., Brickham, D., & Al-Khabbaz, Z.A. (2008). Peer interactions and academic engagement of youth with developmental disabilities in inclusive middle and high school classrooms. *American Journal on Mental Retardation, 113,* 479–494. doi: 10.1352/2008.113:479-494

Carter, E.W., Sisco, L.G., Chung, Y., & Stanton-Chapman, T. (2010). Peer interactions of students with intellectual disabilities and/or autism: A map of the intervention literature. *Research and Practice for Persons with Severe Disabilities, 35,* 63–79.

Carter, E.W., Swedeen, B., Moss, C.K., & Pesko, M.J. (2010). "What are you doing after school?" Promoting extracurricular involvement for transition-age youth with disabilities. *Intervention in School and Clinic, 45,* 275–283. doi: 10.1177/1053451209359077

Carter, E.W., Swedeen, B., & Trainor, A.A. (2009). The other three months: Connecting transition-age youth with disabilities to meaningful summer experiences. *Teaching Exceptional Children, 41*(6), 18–26.

Carter, E.W., Trainor, A.A., Cakiroglu, O., Cole, O., Swedeen, B., Ditchman, N., & Owens, L. (2009). Exploring school-business partnerships to expand career development and early work experiences for youth with disabilities. *Career Development for Exceptional Individuals, 32,* 145–159. doi: 10.1177/0885728809344590

Carter, E.W., Trainor, A.A., Cakiroglu, O., Swedeen, B., & Owens, L. (2010). Availability of and access to career development activities for transition-age youth with disabilities. *Career Development for Exceptional Individuals, 33,* 13–24. doi: 10.1177/0885728809344332

Carter, E.W., Trainor, A.A., Sun, Y., & Owens, L. (2009). Assessing the transition-related strengths and needs of adolescents with high-incidence disabilities. *Exceptional Children, 76,* 74–94.

Carter, E.W., & Wehby, J.H. (2003). Job performance of transition-age youth with emotional and behavioral disorders. *Exceptional Children, 69,* 449–465.

Certo, N.J., Luecking, R.G., Murphy, S., Brown, L., Courey, S., & Belanger, D. (2008). Seamless transition and long-term support for individuals with severe intellectual disabilities. *Research and Practice for Persons with Severe Disabilities, 33,* 85–95.

Certo, N.J., Mautz, D., Pumpian, I., Sax, C., Smalley, K., Wade, H.,…Batterman, N. (2003). A review and discussion of a model for seamless transition to adulthood. *Education and Training in Developmental Disabilities, 38,* 3–17.

Chadsey, J., & Beyer, S. (2001). Social relationships in the workplace. *Mental Retardation and Developmental Disabilities Research Reviews, 7*(2), 128–133. doi: 10.1002/mrdd.1018

Cihak, D.F., & Grim, J. (2008). Teaching students with autism spectrum disorder and moderate intellectual disabilities to use counting-on strategies to enhance independent purchasing skills. *Research in Autism Spectrum Disorders, 2,* 716–727. doi: 10.1016/j.rasd.2008.02.006

Cimera, R.E. (2007). Utilizing natural supports to lower the cost of supported employment. *Research and Practice for Persons with Severe Disabilities, 32,* 184–189.

Clark, G.M. (2007). *Assessment for transition planning.* Austin, TX: PRO-ED.

Clark, G.M., & Patton, J.R. (2006). *Transition Planning Inventory–Updated Version: Administration and resource guide.* Austin, TX: PRO-ED.

Cobb, R.B., & Alwell, M. (2009). Transition planning/coordinating interventions for youth with disabilities: A systematic review. *Career Development for Exceptional Individuals, 32,* 70–81. doi: 10.1177/0885728809336655

Collins, B.C., Hager, K.L., & Galloway, C.C. (2011). Addition of functional content during core content instruction with students with moderate disabilities. *Education and Training in Autism and Developmental Disabilities, 46,* 22–39.

Cook, C.R., Gresham, F.M., Kern, L., Barreras, R.B., Thornton, S., & Crews, S.D. (2008). Social skills training for secondary students with emotional and/or behavioral disorders: A review and analysis of the meta-analytic literature. *Journal of Emotional and Behavioral Disorders, 16,* 131–144. doi: 10.1177/1063426608314541

Copeland, S., & Hughes, C. (2000). Acquisition of a picture prompt strategy to increase independent performance. *Education and Training in Mental Retardation and Developmental Disabilities, 35,* 294–305.

Copeland, S.R., Hughes, C., Agran, M., Wehmeyer, M.L., & Fowler, S.E. (2002). An intervention package to support high school students with mental retardation in general education classrooms. *American Journal on Mental Retardation, 107,* 32–45.

Copeland, S.R., Hughes, C., Carter, E.W., Guth, C., Presley, J., Williams, C.R., & Fowler, S.E. (2004). Increasing access to general education: Perspectives of participants in a high school peer support program. *Remedial and Special Education, 26,* 342–352. doi: 10.1177/07419325040250060201

Council for Exceptional Children. (2009). *What every special educator must know: Ethics, standards, and guidelines* (6th ed.). Arlington, VA: Author.

Cushing, L.S., Clark, N.M., Carter, E.W., & Kennedy, C.H. (2005). Access to the general education curriculum for students with severe disabilities: What it means and how to accomplish it. *Teaching Exceptional Children, 38*(2), 6–13.

Cushing, L.S., & Kennedy, C.H. (1997). Academic effects on students without disabilities who serve as peer supports for students with disabilities in general education classrooms. *Journal of Applied Behavior Analysis, 30,* 139–152. doi: 10.1901/jaba.1997.30-139

Deno, S.L. (2003). Developments in curriculum-based measurement. *Journal of Special Education, 37,* 184–192. doi: 10.1177/00224669030370030801

Downing, J.E. (2010). *Academic instruction for students with moderate and severe intellectual disabilities in inclusive classrooms.* Thousand Oaks, CA: Corwin Press.

Dymond, S.K., Renzaglia, A., & Slagor, M.T. (2011). Trends in the use of service learning with students with disabilities. *Remedial and Special Education, 32,* 219–229. doi: 10.1177/0741932510362173

Elementary and Secondary Education Act of 1965, PL 89-10, 20 U.S.C. §§ 241 *et seq.*

Fabian, E.S. (2007). Urban youth with disabilities: Factors affecting transition employment. *Rehabilitation Counseling Bulletin, 50,* 130–138. doi: 10.1177/00343552070500030101

Farmer, T.W., Leung, M., Weiss, M.P., Irvin, M.T., Meece, J.L., & Hutchins, B.C. (2011). Social network placement of rural secondary students with disabilities: Affiliations and centrality. *Exceptional Children, 78,* 24–38.

Field, S., & Hoffman, A. (2003). Preparing youth to exercise self-determination: Quality indicators of school environments that promote the acquisition of knowledge, skills, and beliefs related to self-determination. *Journal of Disability Policy Studies, 13,* 114–119. doi: 10.1177/10442073020130020701

Field, S., & Hoffman, A. (2007). Self-determination in secondary transition assessment. *Assessment for Effective Intervention, 32,* 181–190. doi: 10.1177/15345084070320030601

Field, S., Hoffman, A., & Sawilowsky, S. (2004). *Self-determination assessment battery.* Detroit, MI: Wayne State University Press.

Fowler, C.H., Walker, A.R., & Rowe, D. (2010). *Age-appropriate transition assessment guide* (2nd ed.). Charlotte, NC: University of North Carolina at Charlotte, National Secondary Transition Technical Assistance Center.

Fujiura, G.T., & Yamaki, K. (2000). Trends in demography of childhood disability and poverty. *Exceptional Children, 66,* 187–199.

Giangreco, M.F., Cloninger, C.J., & Iverson, V.S. (2011). *Choosing outcomes and accommodations for children (COACH): A guide to educational planning for students with disabilities* (3rd ed.). Baltimore, MD: Paul H. Brookes Publishing Co.

Griffin, C., Hammis, D., & Geary, T. (2007). *The job developer's handbook: Practical tactics for customized employment.* Baltimore, MD: Paul H. Brookes Publishing Co.

Griffin, M.M. (2011). Promoting IEP participation: Effects of interventions, considerations for CLD students. *Career Development for Exceptional Individuals, 34,* 153–164. doi: 10.1177/0885728811410561

Grigal, M., & Hart, D. (2010). *Think college! Postsecondary education options for students with intellectual disabilities.* Baltimore, MD: Paul H. Brookes Publishing Co.

Grigal M., Hart, D., & Migliore, A. (2011). Comparing the transition planning, postsecondary education, and employment outcomes of students with intellectual and other disabilities. *Career Development for Exceptional Individuals, 34,* 4–17. doi: 10.1177/0885728811399091

Guy, B.A., Sitlington, P.L., Larsen, M.D., & Frank, A.R. (2009). What are high schools offering as preparation for employment? *Career Development for Exceptional Individuals, 32,* 30–41. doi: 10.1177/0885728808318625

Hagner, D., Butterworth, J., & Keith, G. (1995). Strategies and barriers in facilitating natural supports for employment of adults with severe disabilities. *Journal of The Association for Persons with Severe Handicaps, 20,* 110–120.

Halle, J.W., & Dymond, S.K. (2008/2009). Inclusive education: A necessary prerequisite to accessing the general curriculum? *Research and Practice for Persons with Severe Disabilities, 33*(4), 196–198.

Halpern, A.S. (1985). Transition: A look at the foundations. *Exceptional Children, 51,* 479–502.

Halpern, A.S., Herr, C.M., Doren, B., & Wolf, N.K. (2000). *Next S.T.E.P.: Student transition and educational planning* (2nd ed.). Austin, TX: PRO-ED.

Hughes, C. (2001). Transition to adulthood: Supporting young adults to access social, employment, and civic pursuits. *Mental Retardation and Developmental Disabilities Research Reviews, 7,* 84–90. doi: 10.1002/mrdd.1012

Hughes, C., & Avoke, S.K. (2010). The elephant in the room: Poverty, disability, and employment. *Research and Practice for Persons with Severe Disabilities, 35,* 5–14.

Hughes, C., & Carter, E.W. (2000). *The transition handbook: Strategies high school teachers use that work!* Baltimore, MD: Paul H. Brookes Publishing Co.

Hughes, C., & Carter, E.W. (2002). Informal assessment procedures. In C.L. Sax & C.A. Thoma (Eds.), *Transition assessment: Wise practices for quality lives* (pp. 51–69). Baltimore: Paul H. Brookes Publishing Co.

Hughes, C., & Carter, E.W. (2008). *Peer buddy programs for successful secondary school inclusion.* Baltimore, MD: Paul H. Brookes Publishing Co.

Hughes, C., Copeland, S.R., Guth, C., Rung, L.L., Hwang, B., Kleeb, G., & Strong, M. (2001). General education students' perspectives on their involvement in a high school peer buddy program. *Education and Training in Mental Retardation and Developmental Disabilities, 36,* 343–356.

Hughes, C., Fowler, S.E., Copeland, S.R., Agran, M., Wehmeyer, M.L., & Church-Pupke, P.P. (2004). Supporting high school students to engage in recreational activities with peers. *Behavior Modification, 28,* 3–27.

Hughes, C., Golas, M., Cosgriff, J., Brigham, N., Edwards, C., & Cashen, K. (2011). Effects of a social skills intervention among high school students with intellectual disabilities and autism and their general education peers. *Research and Practice for Persons with Severe Disabilities, 36,* 46–61.

Hughes, C., Guth, C., Hall, S., Presley, J., Dye, M., & Byers, C. (1999). Inclusion on the high school level: The Metropolitan Nashville Peer Buddy Program. *Teaching Exceptional Children, 31*(5), 32–37.

Hughes, C., Hwang, B., Kim, J., Killian, D.J., Harmer, M.L., & Alcantera, P. (1997). A preliminary validation of strategies that support the transition from school to adult life. *Career Development for Exceptional Individuals, 20,* 1–14. doi: 10.1177/088572889702000101

Hughes, C., & Kim, J. (1998). Supporting the transition from school to adult life. In F.R. Rusch & J.G. Chadsey (Eds.), *Beyond high school: Transition from school to work* (pp. 367–382). Belmont, CA: Wadsworth.

Hughes, C., Kim, J., Hwang, B., Killian, D.J., Fischer, G.M., Brock, M.L., ... Houser, B. (1997). Practitioner-validated secondary transition support strategies. *Education and Training in Mental Retardation and Developmental Disabilities, 32,* 201–212.

Hughes, C., Rodi, M.S., Lorden, S.W., Pitkin, S.E., Derer, K.R., Hwang, B., & Cai, X. (1999). Social interactions of high school students with mental retardation and their general education peers. *American Journal on Mental Retardation, 104,* 533–544.

Hughes, C., Rung, L.L., Wehmeyer, M.L., Agran, J., Copeland, S.R., & Hwang, B. (2000). Self-prompted communication book use to increase social interaction among high school students. *Journal of The Association for Persons with Severe Handicaps, 25,* 153–166.

Hunt, P., & McDonnell, J. (2007). Inclusive education. In S.L. Odom, R.H. Horner, M.E. Snell, & J. Blacher (Eds.), *Handbook of developmental disabilities* (pp. 269–291). New York, NY: Guilford Press.

Individuals with Disabilities Education Act Amendments (IDEA) of 1997, PL 105-17, 20 U.S.C. §§ 1400 *et seq.*

Individuals with Disabilities Education Act (IDEA) of 1990, PL 101-476, 20 U.S.C. §§ 1400 *et seq.*

Individuals with Disabilities Education Improvement Act (IDEA) of 2004, PL 108-446, 20 U.S.C. §§ 1400 *et seq.*

Jackson, L.B., Ryndak, D.L., & Wehmeyer, M.L. (2008/2009). The dynamic relationship between context, curriculum, and student learning: A case for inclusive education as a research-based practice. *Research and Practice for Persons with Severe Disabilities, 34,* 175–195.

Janney, R., & Snell, M.E. (2004). *Modifying schoolwork* (2nd ed.). Baltimore, MD: Paul H. Brookes Publishing Co.

Job Accommodation Network. (2011). *Workplace accommodations: Low cost, high impact.* Morgantown, WV: Author.

Jorgensen, C.M. (1992). Natural supports in inclusive schools: Curricular and teaching strategies. In J. Nisbet (Ed.), *Natural supports in school, at work, and in the community for people with severe disabilities* (pp. 179–215). Baltimore, MD: Paul H. Brookes Publishing Co.

Jorgensen, C.M., McSheehan, M., & Sonnenmeier, R.M. (2010). *The Beyond Access Model: Promoting membership, participation, and learning for students with disabilities in the general education classroom.* Baltimore, MD: Paul H. Brookes Publishing Co.

Joseph, L.M., & Eveleigh, E.L. (2011). A review of the effects of self-monitoring on reading performance of students with disabilities. *Journal of Special Education, 45,* 43–53. doi: 10.1177/0022466909349145

Kavale, K.A., & Mostert, M.P. (2004). Social skills interventions for individuals with learning disabilities. *Learning Disability Quarterly, 31*–43.

Kessler Foundation and National Organization on Disability. (2010). *2010 survey of Americans with disabilities.* Washington, DC: Author.

Klein, A. (2011, September 6). Congress returns to face ESEA, education funding issues. *Education Week, 31*(3). Retrieved from http://www.edweek.org/ew/articles/2011/09/06/03congress.h31.html?tkn=YRWFQnm0voL0I3McS%2FBg8KLs4rVL5ckz4gF9&cmp=clp-sb-cec

Kleinert, H.L., & Kearns, J.F. (2010). *Alternate assessment for students with significant cognitive disabilities: An educator's guide.* Baltimore, MD: Paul H. Brookes Publishing Co.

Kleinert, H.L., Miracle, S., & Sheppard-Jones, K. (2007). Including students with moderate and severe intellectual disabilities in school extracurricular and community recreation activities. *Intellectual and Developmental Disabilities, 45,* 46–55. doi: 10.1352/1934-9556(2007)45[46: ISWMAS]2.0.CO;2

Kochhar-Bryant, C.A. (2007). The summary of performance as transition "passport" to employment and independent living. *Assessment for Effective Intervention, 32,* 160–170. doi: 10.1177/15345084070320030401

Kochhar-Bryant, C.A., & Izzo, M.V. (2006). Access to post-high school services: Transition assessment and the summary of performance. *Career Development for Exceptional Individuals, 29,* 70–89. doi: 10.1177/08857288060290020601

Lakin, K.C., & Stancliffe, R.J. (2007). Residential supports for persons with intellectual and developmental disabilities. *Mental Retardation and Developmental Disabilities Research Reviews, 13,* 151–159. doi: 10.1002/mrdd.20148

Lambert, N., Nihira, K., & Leland, H. (1993). *AAMR Adaptive Behavior Scale-School* (2nd ed.). Austin, TX: PRO-ED.

Lee, S.H., Palmer, S., & Wehmeyer, M.L. (2009). Goal-setting and self-monitoring support for access to the general education curriculum. *Intervention in School and Clinic, 44,* 139–145. doi: 10.1177/1053451208326053

Luecking, R.G. (2008). Emerging employer views of people with disabilities and the future of job development. *Journal of Vocational Rehabilitation, 29,* 3–13.

Luecking, R.G. (2009). *The way to work: How to facilitate work experiences for youth in transition.* Baltimore, MD: Paul H. Brookes Publishing Co.

Lynch, S., & Adams, P. (2008). Developing standards-based individualized education program objectives for students for student with significant needs. *Teaching Exceptional Children, 40*(3), 36–39.

Martin, J.E., Marshall, L., Maxson, L.L., & Jerman, P. (1993). *Self-directed IEP.* Longmont, CO: Sopris West Educational Services.

Martin, J.E., Van Dycke, J.L., Christensen, W.R., Greene, B.A., Gardner, J.E., & Lovett, D.L. (2006). Increasing student participation in IEP meetings: Establishing the self-directed IEP as an evidence-based practice. *Exceptional Children, 72,* 299–316.

Mazzotti, V.L., Rowe, D.A., Kelley, K.R., Test, D.W., Fowler, C.H., Kohler, P.D., & Kortering, L.J. (2009). Linking transition assessment and postsecondary goals: Key elements in the secondary transition planning process. *Teaching Exceptional Children, 42*(2), 44–51.

McLeskey, J., Landers, E., Williamson, P., & Hoppey, D. (in press). Are we moving toward educating students with disabilities in less restrictive settings? *Journal of Special Education.* doi: 10.1177/0022466910376670

Mechling, L.G. (2007). Assistive technology as a self-management tool for prompting students with intellectual disabilities to initiate and complete daily tasks: A literature review. *Education and Training in Developmental Disabilities, 42,* 252–269.

Metzel, D.S., Boeltzig, H., Butterworth, J., Sulewski, J.S., & Gilmore, D.S. (2007). Achieving community membership through community rehabilitation provider services: Are we there yet? *Intellectual and Developmental Disabilities, 45,* 149–160. doi: 10.1352/1934-9556(2007)45[149:ACMTCR]2.0.CO;2

Migliore, A., & Butterworth, J. (2008). *Postsecondary education and employment outcomes for youth with intellectual disabilities.* Boston, MA: Institute for Community Inclusion. Retrieved from http://www.statedata.info/datanotes/datanote.php?article_id=267

National Center for Education Statistics. (2006). *Characteristics of the 100 largest public elementary and secondary school districts in the United States: 2003-04 statistical analysis report.* Washington, DC: U.S. Department of Education. Retrieved from http://nces.ed.gov/pubs2006/2006329.pdf

National Center for Education Statistics. (2007). *Status and trends in the education of racial and ethnic minorities.* Washington, DC: U.S. Department of Education. Retrieved from http://nces.ed.gov/pubs2007/minoritytrends/tables/table_7_2.asp?referrer=report

National Center for Education Statistics. (2010). *Status and trends in the education of racial and ethnic minorities.* Washington, DC: U.S. Department of Education. Retrieved from http://nces.ed.gov/pubs2010/2010015/tables/table_24_1.asp

Newman, L., Wagner, M., Cameto, R., & Knokey, A.M. (2009). *The post-high school outcomes of youth with disabilities up to 4 years after high school: A report of findings from the National Longitudinal Transition Study–2 (NLTS–2).* Menlo Park, CA: SRI International. Retrieved from http://www.nlts2.org/reports/2009_04/nlts2_report_2009_04_complete.pdf

Newman, L., Wagner, M., Cameto, R., Knokey, A.M., & Shaver, D. (2010). *Comparisons across time of the outcomes of youth with disabilities up to 4 years after high school.* Menlo Park, CA: SRI International.

Newman, L., Wagner, M., Knokey, A.M., Marder, C., Nagle, K., Shaver, D., & Wei, X. (2011). *The post-high school outcomes of young adults with disabilities up to 8 years after high school.* Menlo Park, CA: SRI International.

Nirje, B. (1972). The right to self-determination. In W. Wolfensberger (Ed.), *Normalization: The principle of normalization* (pp. 176–200). Toronto, Ontario, Canada: National Institute on Mental Retardation.

Nisbet, J., & Hagner, D. (Eds.). (2000). *Part of the community: Strategies for including everyone.* Baltimore, MD: Paul H. Brookes Publishing Co.

No Child Left Behind Act of 2001, PL 107-110, 115 Stat. 1425, 20 U.S.C. §§ 6301 *et seq.*

Olmstead v. L.C. (1999). 527 U.S. 581, 119 S.Ct. 2176.

Parish, S.L., Rose, R.A., & Andrews, M.E. (2010). TANF's impact on low-income mothers raising children with disabilities. *Exceptional Children, 76,* 234–253.

Povenmire-Kirk, T.C., Lindstrom, L., & Bullis, M. (2010). De escuela a la vida adulta/From school to adult life: Transition needs for Latino youth with disabilities and their families. *Career Development for Exceptional Individuals, 33,* 41–51. doi: 10.1177/0885728809359004

Powers, K.M., Gil-Kashiwabara, E., Geenan, S.J., Powers, L., Balandran, J., & Palmer, C. (2005). Mandates and effective transition planning practices reflected in IEPs. *Career Development for Exceptional Individuals, 28,* 47–59. doi: 10.1177/08857288050280010701

Powers, L.E., Ellison, R., Matuszewski, J., & Turner, A. (2004). *TAKE CHARGE for the future.* Portland, OR: Portland State University Regional Resource Center.

Presley, J.A., & Hughes, C. (2000). Peers as teachers of anger management to high school students with behavioral disorders. *Behavioral Disorders, 25,* 114–130.

Rehabilitation Act Amendments of 1992, PL 102-569, 29 U.S.C. §§ 701 *et seq.*

Rehabilitation Act of 1973, PL 93-112, U.S.C. §§ 701 *et seq.*

Reid, R., Trout, A.L., & Schwartz, M. (2005). Self-regulation interventions for children with attention deficit/hyperactivity disorder. *Exceptional Children, 71,* 361–377.

Renzaglia, A., & Hutchins, M. (2005). *A model for longitudinal vocational programming for students with moderate and severe disabilities.* Washington, DC: U.S. Department of Education, Office of Special Education and Rehabilitation Services.

Richter, S.M., & Mazzotti, V.L. (2011). A comprehensive review of the literature on summary of performance. *Career Development for Exceptional Individuals, 34,* 176–186. doi: 10.1177/0885728811399089

Roseth, C.J., Johnson, D.W., & Johnson, R.T. (2008). Promoting early adolescents' achievement and peer relationships: The effects of cooperative, competitive, and individualistic goal structures. *Psychological Bulletin, 134,* 223–246. doi: 10.1037/0033-2909.134.2.223

Rubin, K.H., Bukowski, W.M., & Laursen, B. (Eds.). (2009). *Handbook of peer interactions, relationships, and groups.* New York, NY: Guilford Press.

Rusch, F.R. (2008). *Beyond high school: Preparing adolescents for tomorrow's challenges* (2nd ed.). Upper Saddle River, NJ: Pearson Prentice Hall.

Rusch, F.R., Hughes, C., Agran, M., Martin, J.E., & Johnson, J.R. (2009). Toward self-directed learning, post-high school placement, and coordinated support: Constructing new transition bridges to adult life. *Career Development for Exceptional Individuals, 32,* 53–59. doi: 10.1177/0885728809332628

Ryndak, D., & Billingsley, F. (2004). Access to the general education curriculum. In C.H. Kennedy & E. Horn

(Eds.), *Including students with severe disabilities* (pp. 55–56). Boston, MA: Allyn & Bacon.

Ryndak, D.L., Moore, M.A., Orlando, A.M., & Delano, M. (2008/2009). Access to the general curriculum: The mandate and role of context in research-based practice for students with extensive support needs. *Research and Practice for Persons with Severe Disabilities, 33/34,* 199–213. doi:10.2511/rpsd.33.4.199

Sanford, C., Newman, L., Wagner, M., Cameto, R., Knokey, A., & Shaver, D. (2011). *The post-high school outcomes of young adults with disabilities up to 6 years after high school.* Menlo Park, CA: SRI International.

Schalock, R.L., & Keith, K.D. (1993). *The Quality of Life Questionnaire.* Worthington, OH: IDS Publishing.

School-to-Work Opportunities Act of 1994, PL 103-239, 20 U.S.C. §§ 6101 *et seq.*

Shandra, C.L., & Hogan, D.P. (2008). School-to-work program participation and the post-high school employment of young adults with disabilities. *Journal of Vocational Rehabilitation, 29,* 117–130.

Shogren, K.A. (2011). Culture and self-determination: A synthesis of the literature and directions for future research and practice. *Career Development for Exceptional Individuals, 34,* 115–127. doi: 10.1177/0885728811398271

Shukla, S., Kennedy, C.H., & Cushing, L.S. (1999). Intermediate school students with severe disabilities: Supporting their social participation in general education classrooms. *Journal of Positive Behavior Interventions, 1,* 130–140. doi: 10.1177/109830079900100301

Simeonsson, R.J., Carlson, D., Huntington, G.S., McMillen, J.S., & Brent, J.L. (2001). Students with disabilities: A national survey of participation in school activities. *Disability and Rehabilitation, 23,* 49–63. doi: 10.1080/096382801750058134

Siperstein, G.N., Norins, J., & Mohler, A. (2007). Social acceptance and attitude change: Fifty years of research. In J.W. Jacobson, J.A. Mulick, & J. Rojahn (Eds.), *Handbook of intellectual and developmental disabilities* (pp. 133–154). New York, NY: Springer.

Siperstein, G.N., Parker, R.C., Bardon, J.N., & Widaman, K.F. (2007). A national study of youth attitudes toward the inclusion of students with intellectual disabilities. *Exceptional Children, 73,* 435–455.

Sitlington, P.L., & Clark, G.M. (2007). The transition assessment process and IDEIA 2004. *Assessment for Effective Intervention, 32,* 133–142. doi: 10.1177/15345084070320030201

Sitlington, P.L., Neubert, D.A., & Clark, G.M. (2009). *Transition education and services for students with disabilities* (5th ed.). Upper Saddle River, NJ: Prentice Hall.

Southall, C.M., & Gast, D.L. (2011). Self-management procedures: A comparison across the autism spectrum. *Education and Training in Autism and Developmental Disabilities, 46,* 155–171.

Stodden, R.A., & Roberts, K.D. (2008). Transition legislation and policy: Past and present. In F.R. Rusch (Ed.), *Beyond high school: Preparing adolescents for tomorrow's challenges* (2nd ed., pp. 24–53). Upper Saddle River, NJ: Pearson.

Stokes, T.F., & Baer, D.M. (1977). An implicit technology of generalization. *Journal of Applied Behavior Analysis, 10,* 349–367. doi: 10.1901/jaba.1977.10-349

Suitts, S.T. (2010). *A new diverse majority: Students of color in the South's public schools.* Atlanta, GA: Southern Education Foundation. Retrieved from http://www.southern education.org

Swedeen, B., Carter, E.W., & Molfenter, N. (2010). Getting everyone involved: Identifying transition opportunities for youth with severe disabilities. *Teaching Exceptional Children, 43*(2), 38–49.

Test, D.W., Mason, C., Hughes, C., Konrad, M., Neale, M., & Wood, W.M. (2004). Student involvement in individualized education program meetings. *Exceptional Children, 70,* 391–412.

Test, D.W., Mazzotti, V.L., Mustain, A.L., Fowler, C.H., Kortering, L., & Kohler, P. (2009). Evidence-based secondary transition predictors for improving post-school outcomes for students with disabilities. *Career Development for Exceptional Individuals, 32,* 160–181. doi: 10.1177/0885728809346960

Thoma, C.A., Bartholomew, C.C., & Tamura, R. (2010). Student involvement in assessment. In C.A. Thoma & P. Wehman (Eds.), *Getting the most out of IEPs: An educator's guide to the student-directed approach* (pp. 63–78). Baltimore, MD: Paul H. Brookes Publishing Co.

Thompson, J.R., Wehmeyer, M.L., & Hughes, C. (2010). Mind the gap! Implications of a person-environment fit model of intellectual disability for students, teachers, and schools. *Exceptionality, 18,* 168–181. doi: 10.1080/09362835.2010.513919

Trainor, A.A. (2008). Using cultural and social capital to improve postsecondary outcomes and expand transition models for youth with disabilities. *Journal of Special Education, 42,* 148–162. doi: 10.1177/0022466907313346

Trainor, A.A., Carter, E.W., Owens, L., & Swedeen, B. (2008). Special educators' perceptions of summer employment and community participation opportunities for youth with disabilities. *Career Development for Exceptional Individuals, 31,* 144–153. doi: 10.1177/0885728808323717

Trainor, A.A., Carter, E.W., Swedeen, B., Owens, L., Cole, O., & Smith, S.A. (2011). Perspectives of adolescents with disabilities on summer employment and community experiences. *Journal of Special Education, 45,* 157–170. doi: 10.1177/0022466909359424

Trainor, A.A., Carter, E.W., Swedeen, B., & Pickett, K. (in press). Community conversations: An approach for expanding and connecting opportunities for employment for adolescents with disabilities. *Career Development for Exceptional Individuals.* doi: 10.1177/0885728811419166

U.S. Chamber of Commerce. (2005). *Fast facts on business tax credits and deductions for employment of people with disabilities.* Washington, DC: Author.

U.S. Department of Education. (2009). *28th annual report to Congress on the implementation of the Individuals with Disabilities Education Act of 2006.* Washington, DC: Author.

Vondracek, F.W., & Porfeli, E.J. (2003). The world of work and careers. In G.R. Adams & M.D. Berzonsky (Eds.), *Blackwell handbook of adolescence* (pp. 109–128). Malden, MA: Blackwell Publishing.

Wagner, M., Cadwallader, T.W., Garza, N., & Cameto, R. (2004). Social activities of youth with disabilities. *NLTS-2 Data Brief, 3*(1), 1–4.

Wagner, M., Cadwallader, T., & Marder, C. (2003). *Life outside of the classroom for youth with disabilities.* Menlo Park, CA: SRI International.

Walker, A.R., Uphold, N.M., Richter, S., & Test, D.W. (2010). Review of the literature on community-based instruction across grade levels. *Education and Training in Autism and Developmental Disabilities, 453,* 242–267.

Walker, H.M., Calkins, C., Wehmeyer, M.L., Walker, L., Bacon, A., Palmer, S.B., ... Johnson, D.R. (2011). A social-ecological approach to promote self-determination. *Exceptionality, 19,* 6–18. doi: 10.1080/09362835.2011.537220

Washington, B.H., Hughes, C., & Cosgriff, J.C. (in press). High-poverty youth: Self-determination and involvement in educational planning. *Career Development for Exceptional Individuals.* doi: 10.1177/0885728811420135

Wehmeyer, M.L., Abery, B.H., Zhang, D., Ward, K., Willis, D., Hossain, W.A., ...Walker, H.M. (2011). Personal self-determination and moderating variables that impact efforts to promote self-determination. *Exceptionality, 19,* 19–30. doi: 10.1080/09362835.2011.537225

Wehmeyer, M.L., Agran, M., Hughes, C., Martin, J.E., Mithaug, D.E., & Palmer, S.B. (2007). *Promoting self-determination in students with developmental disabilities.* New York, NY: Guilford Press.

Wehmeyer, M.L., & Garner, N.W. (2003). The impact of personal characteristics of people with intellectual and developmental disability on self-determination and autonomous functioning. *Journal of Applied Research in Intellectual Disabilities, 16,* 255–265. doi: 10.1046/j.1468-3148.2003.00161.x

Wehmeyer, M.L., & Kelchner, K. (1995). *The Arc's Self-Determination Scale.* Arlington, TX: The Arc of the United States.

Wehmeyer, M.L., Lawrence, M., Kelchner, K., Palmer, S., Garner, N., & Soukup, J. (2004). *Whose future is it anyway? A student-directed transition planning process* (2nd ed.). Lawrence, KS: Beach Center on Disability.

Wehmeyer, M.L., & Palmer, S.B. (2003). Adult outcomes for students with cognitive disabilities three years after high school: The impact of self-determination. *Education and Training in Developmental Disabilities, 38,* 131–144.

Wehmeyer, M.L., Palmer, S.B., Smith, S.J., Davies, D.K., & Stock, S. (2008). The efficacy of technology use by people with intellectual disabilities: A single-subject design meta-analysis. *Journal of Special Education Technology, 23,* 21–30.

Wehmeyer, M.L., Palmer, S.B., Soukup, J.H., Garner, N.W., & Lawrence, M. (2007). Self-determination and student transition planning knowledge and skills: Predicting involvement. *Exceptionality, 15,* 31–44. doi: 10.1080/09362830709336924

White, S.W., Keonig, K., & Scahill, L. (2007). Social skills development in children with autism spectrum disorders: A review of the intervention literature. *Journal of Autism and Developmental Disorders, 37,* 1858–1868. doi: 10.1007/s10803-006-0320-x

Will, M. (1984). *OSERS programming for the transition of youth with disabilities: Bridges from school to working life.* Washington, DC: U.S. Department of Education, Office of Special Education and Rehabilitation Services.

Wiltz, J. (2007). Self-determined roommate selection for individuals with intellectual disabilities: Barriers and new directions. *Journal of Policy and Practice in Intellectual Disabilities, 4,* 60–65. doi: 10.1111/j.1741-1130.2006.00097.x

Wolfensberger, W. (1983). Social role valorization: A proposed new term for the principle of normalization. *Mental Retardation, 21,* 234–239.

Wolman, J.M., Campeau, P.L., DuBois, P.A., Mithaug, D.E., & Stolarski, V.S. (1994). *AIR self-determination scale and user guide.* Palo Alto, CA: American Institutes for Research.

Woodcock, R.W. (2011). *Woodcock Reading Mastery Tests* (3rd ed.). Circle Pines, MN: American Guidance Service.

Zimmer-Gembeck, M.J., & Mortimer, J.T. (2006). Adolescent work, vocational development, and education, *Review of Educational Research, 76,* 537–566.

Index

Page numbers followed by *f* indicate forms; those followed by *t* indicate tables.